Computer Science Handbook

Volume I

Computer Science Handbook
Volume I

Edited by **Tom Halt**

LANRYE
INTERNATIONAL

New Jersey

Published by Clanrye International,
55 Van Reypen Street,
Jersey City, NJ 07306, USA
www.clanryeinternational.com

Computer Science Handbook: Volume I
Edited by Tom Halt

International Standard Book Number: 978-1-63240-111-3 (Hardback)

Printed in the United States of America.

Contents

Preface

Computer Science is a field that focuses on the study of the applications, principles, and technologies of computing and consequently computers. It involves the study of data and data structures and the algorithms to process these structures, computer-related topics such as artificial intelligence, numerical analysis, operations research, principles of computer architecture - hardware and software, as well as language design, structure, and translation techniques. Computer science is a field that provides a foundation of knowledge for those with career goals in a variety of computer-related and computing professions. It has various subfields that can be divided into a plethora of theoretical and practical disciplines. Computer science is also an interdisciplinary field and has strong connections to other disciplines. Many problems in business, science, health care, engineering and other arenas can be solved efficiently with computers, but finding a solution requires expertise in the field of computer science. This discipline has a wide variety of specialties. Applications of computer science include software systems, computer architecture, artificial intelligence, graphics, software engineering and computational science. This discipline draws from a common core of computer science knowledge and various specialty areas focus on particular problems. This is a field that is rapidly becoming one of fastest growing in the industry and the demand for skilled graduates is also on the rise.

I am grateful to those who put their hard work, effort and expertise into these research projects as well as those who were supportive in this endeavor.

Editor

QPSO-Based Adaptive DNA Computing Algorithm

Mehmet Karakose[1] and Ugur Cigdem[2]

[1] *Computer Engineering Department, Firat University, Elazig, Turkey*
[2] *Computer Programming Department, Gaziosmanpaşa University, Tokat, Turkey*

Correspondence should be addressed to Mehmet Karakose; mkarakose@firat.edu.tr

Academic Editors: P. Agarwal and Y. Zhang

DNA (deoxyribonucleic acid) computing that is a new computation model based on DNA molecules for information storage has been increasingly used for optimization and data analysis in recent years. However, DNA computing algorithm has some limitations in terms of convergence speed, adaptability, and effectiveness. In this paper, a new approach for improvement of DNA computing is proposed. This new approach aims to perform DNA computing algorithm with adaptive parameters towards the desired goal using quantum-behaved particle swarm optimization (QPSO). Some contributions provided by the proposed QPSO based on adaptive DNA computing algorithm are as follows: (1) parameters of population size, crossover rate, maximum number of operations, enzyme and virus mutation rate, and fitness function of DNA computing algorithm are simultaneously tuned for adaptive process, (2) adaptive algorithm is performed using QPSO algorithm for goal-driven progress, faster operation, and flexibility in data, and (3) numerical realization of DNA computing algorithm with proposed approach is implemented in system identification. Two experiments with different systems were carried out to evaluate the performance of the proposed approach with comparative results. Experimental results obtained with Matlab and FPGA demonstrate ability to provide effective optimization, considerable convergence speed, and high accuracy according to DNA computing algorithm.

1. Introduction

DNA computing is a new field of research which performs computing using the biomolecular structure of DNA molecules. The first study performed in the field of DNA computing was the solution of the problem of traveling salesmen composed of 7 cities by Adleman using real DNA molecules [1]. The application was realized by creating solution environment in the biology laboratory and using biochemical reactions. The cities and distances that make up the problem of traveling salesmen were coded using DNA series and all ways that might be solution were created using polymer chain reaction. Upon the success of the study performed a new algorithm for the solution of multivariable problems was acquired. In the continuation of this study Lipton solved satisfiability problem included in NP (nonpolynomial) problem class using DNA computing in a similar way [2]. Lipton demonstrated the application and that DNA computing can be used for the solution of the problems containing logical equations as well. After this study Lin et al. [3] performed the

design and optimization of PI (proportional integral) parameters using DNA computing. Ding and Ren used similar DNA computing algorithm with the abovementioned study for setting turbid inspecting parameters [4]. Kim and Lee applied DNA computing algorithm with a different method for setting the PID parameters [5]. In the study performed DNA molecules were used in coding and setting the PI parameters. The results of the application through computer simulation indicated that high success was acquired in this field. Wang et al. compared DNA computers and electronic computers and suggested that DNA computers were more advantageous [6]. As a result of the applications given above, DNA computing was developed rapidly and used in many scientific studies [7–15]. It has been used frequently, particularly in NP problems, coloring problems of graphics in setting the inspecting parameters, arithmetic operations, signal processing problems, and ciphering the data [16–24]. DNA computing algorithm performs computing using the natural characteristics of DNA molecules. Those characteristics include parallel operations, storing high amount of data, providing energy saving, and having significant role in computing. Those characteristics are listed quite effectively in the solution of complex and difficult problems. In order to use the DNA computing more effectively, scientists dealt with the design of total natural DNA computers composed of DNA molecules [25].

In Section 2 of this study, DNA computing algorithm is explained in detail. In Section 3 QPSO algorithm is mentioned. In Section 4 DNA computing is made applicable with QPSO algorithm; parameters that increase the effectiveness of DNA computing algorithm are found using QPSO and used for the proposed algorithm. And in the last section the acquired simulation results are given. It is understood from the simulation results that the proposed method produces better values and is more successful.

2. DNA Computing Algorithm

DNA computing is a new optimization algorithm performing computing using DNA molecules which store genetic information of the living things. While performing the computing using DNA, DNA bases that make up the ground of the DNA molecules are used. DNA bases are Adenine (A), Guanine (G), Cytosine (C), and Thymine (T) and in this study they have been converted into numerical values including A-0, G-1, C-2, and T-3 [9]. Adenine and Thymine and Guanine and Cytosine complete each other [26–28]. DNA molecules have a structure due to the double and triple hydrogen ties among those bases and in the computing process where number of hydrogen ties is used. In Particular the completion situations of DNA bases and numbers of hydrogen ties are used in the computing performed in solution environments. There are 2 hydrogen ties between Adenine and Thymine and 3 hydrogen ties between Guanine and Cytosine [27]. DNA molecules exist in the form of single serial and double spiral serial. Using the single DNA serials synthesis and reproduction of DNA molecules is realized. Double spiral DNA serials are created according to the Watson-Crick complementation rule. According to this rule Adenine and Thymine and Guanine and Cytosine combine. No emergence is possible. DNA molecules have many advantages including performing parallel operations, storing high amount of data, and using those data for many years without any corruption. These advantages are used sufficiently while performing the computing; the algorithm produces better results. In Figure 1, the general structure of the DNA molecule was shown.

Parallel computing provides a quick conclusion for operations. It is possible to complete the problems that require very big operation volumes and take a long time in the solution with DNA molecules. Some similar problems have many variables and parameters. Coding these variables and parameters and modeling the system generally require data. DNA molecules make great contributions to the solution of these problems with their capability to store data. While DNA computing is applying, the errors are made in the sequence of DNA serials to affect the result negatively. As a result of DNA computing, the values acquired with other optimization algorithm are not deemed to be final results. The studies

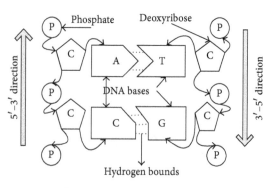

FIGURE 1: The general structure of the DNA molecule.

performed on DNA computing have been implemented in two different manners. The most commonly used method among these is the computing performed in solution environment [26–28]. The cost of performing the computing in solution environment is more because machines are needed to produce DNA serials and DNA synthesis. Furthermore solution should be prepared and solution tubes should be used. Systems named gel electrophoresis are needed for acquiring and analyzing the results [22, 23]. And another algorithm used for DNA computing is the numerical DNA computing algorithm. In this algorithm DNA serials are created in electronic computers and they are converted into numerical values for computing. Although the cost of computing performed electronically is less, the mentioned advantages of DNA molecules cannot be applied on problems completely because when the DNA molecules are used in solution environment, they only can use the abovementioned characteristics.

Numerical DNA computing algorithm is similar to the genetic algorithms; however it is different from genetic algorithms. It uses A, T, G, and C bases rather than dual number of the systems and the solution set of the problems is composed of these bases [29]. Furthermore DNA computing has two new mutation operations. These are enzyme and virus mutations and provide great advantage while computing is performed. Enzyme mutation is the operation of deletion in one or more DNA parts from any DNA serial. And virus mutation is the operation of adding one or more DNA parts to any DNA serial [9, 19, 20]. Enzyme and virus mutations provide continuous renewal of the population and prevent focusing on local optimum points, thus give the algorithm a global search capacity. In Table 1, the conversion of DNA serials into numerical data has been given.

3. QPSO Algorithm

QPSO is an algorithm having the capacity of global searching. This algorithm has been developed inspired by living things that move as masses including insects, bees and were used for the solution of many problems in the literature. In the QPSO algorithm which is a population-based algorithm, individuals act together and compose the masses. While the speed of population is used in PSO algorithm, the next position of the

TABLE 1: Coding table of DNA computing algorithm.

	DNA coding system A, G, C, T	Quartet coding system 0, 1, 2, 3	Binary coding system 00, 01, 10, 11	Decimal coding system	Minimum value of K_p and K_i	Maximum value of K_p and K_i
K_p	AGT, TAA, TTT	013, 300, 333	000111, 110000, 111111	$0*16+1*4+3*1=7$ $3*16+0*4+0*1=48$ $3*16+3*4+3*1=63$	0	63
K_i	GTT, CCA, AGC	133, 220, 012	011111, 101000, 000110	$1*1+3*1/4+3*1/16=1.9375$ $2*1+2*1/4*0*1/16=2.5$ $0*1+1*1/4+2*1/16=0.375$	0	4

population is determined by taking the average of the best results acquired by the particles that make up the population in QPSO locally. In order to update the speeds and positions of the particles in QPSO algorithm, (1), (2), and (3) are used [30].

While preparing the algorithm the best information acquired by each particle (pbest) and the best information realized by the mass (gbest = min (pbest)) variables are used. Using these two variables the movement point of the mass P value is calculated using (1). The Q1 and Q2 variables in (1) represent random numbers produced in the interval 0-1. In determining the next position of the mass QPSO algorithm uses the variable of mbest which is the best arithmetic average of mass instead of gbest. mbest value is calculated using (2). In (2) n represents the population size. After computing the mbest value for the next step of the population the x value is computed by using (3). The β variable in (3) is a value to be determined by the applier. And the u variable is another one which takes value at the interval of 0-1:

$$p = \frac{(Q1 * pbest + Q2 * gbest)}{Q1 + Q2}, \quad (1)$$

$$mbest = \frac{(\sum_{m=1}^{n} pbest_i)}{n}, \quad (2)$$

$$x(i+1) = p \pm \beta \cdot |mbest - x(i)| \cdot \ln\left(\frac{1}{u}\right). \quad (3)$$

4. QPSO-Based Adaptive DNA Computing Algorithm

In order to increase the global search capacity and effectiveness of DNA computing algorithm in problem solving, parameters should be applicable. The size of the population suitable for this algorithm (Pb), maximum operation number (N), Crossover rate (Mu), enzyme proportion (E), and virus proportion (V) affect the local and global search capacity of the algorithm positively. Making all these parameters adaptable simultaneously can sometimes give negative results. The real target aimed by adapting the parameters is to increase the diversity in the population and prevent the focusing on local optimum points. Furthermore the adaptable algorithms can easily be applied for the solution of many optimization problems. In this study it is aimed to find the optimum values of the parameters considering the conformity values acquired by the population in all iterations of the algorithm. Using the

equation depending on conformity function together with the QPSO algorithm, the parameter values are determined. The acquired values are taken as optimized parameter values when optimum solution is achieved. These parameters which are fixed at the beginning are made dynamic and increasing the effectiveness of the algorithm is aimed. In Figure 2, the steps of QPSO based on numerical DNA computing algorithm are shown.

As shown in Figure 3, the proposed approach can be modeled to find the parameters values of DNA computing algorithm using a QPSO algorithm. In the proposed model variables of K_p and K_i are coded with DNA serials at the length of 3 bases. K_p and K_i values are created randomly using A, G, C, and T bases and converted into numerical data using 0, 1, 2, and 3 values, respectively. The serials are converted into first system of 4 then system of 10 and used in numerical environment. The parameter values used for making adaptive DNA computing are explained as follows.

Population Size (Pb). Population size is one of the most significant characteristics that contribute to the solution of the problem. The size of the problem and its complex structure are taken into consideration while determining the value of those parameters. When the population size is increased, a broader solution area is created. The time of solution gets longer. Furthermore unnecessary expansion of the solution area causes big time losses and the solution time for the problem increases rapidly. For this reason optimum value should be selected in the applications. In setting of the population size, (4) is used. The f variable given in (4) is the conformity function used for the algorithm. $f(n)$ gives the conformity value of the nth element of the population, and $f(1)$ gives the conformity value of the first element of the population. Max(f) gives the maximum value of the population and min(f) gives the minimum value. These two values provide information about the distribution of the values belonging to population elements. The number 15 given in (4) is the base value and it is used for the purpose of the probability of the size of the population to be zero. It is determined with the method of trial and error:

$$Pop\_size = \frac{(\max(f) - \min(f))}{(f(n) - f(1))} + 15. \quad (4)$$

Maximum Number of Operations (N). Maximum number of operations gives the number of processes of the cycle

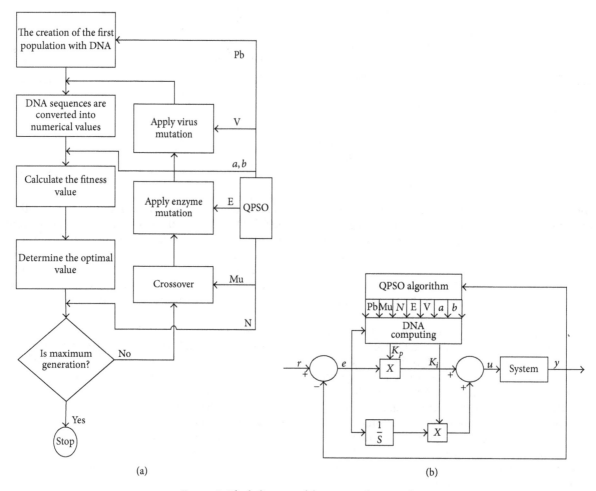

(a)   (b)

FIGURE 2: Block diagram of the proposed approach.

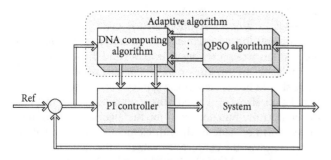

FIGURE 3: Schematic diagram of the model.

in the DNA computing algorithm. When the maximum number of operations is increased, the completing time of the cycles is extended and the number of the performed operations increases. In Particular the number of elements that composes the population and the number of the variables used in the problem are big; the completion time of the algorithm increases rapidly and this causes loss of time and economic losses. Keeping the maximum number of operations in the lowest level decreases the efficiency of the algorithm. The best values should be determined considering

all those situations. In this study, in order to find maximum number of operations, (5) has been used. The number 5 given in (5) is the base value and it is used for the purpose of the probability of the size of the maximum number of operations to be zero and it is determined with the method of trial and error:

$$\text{Maximum\_generation\_number} = \left(f\left(n \right) + f\left(1 \right) \right) * \text{Pb} + 5.$$
$$(5)$$

Crossover Rate (Mu). With Crossover, new elements are created by using the existing population elements. While determining the Crossover rate, the number and selection of the elements to be crossed are taken into account. When the Crossover rate is kept high, the number of elements to be selected increases and the change of the set that shall be created newly is provided. However it is probable that the new created elements may be values close to the parent elements. Furthermore the number of elements to be crossed being high prolongs the duration of completion of the algorithm. In this study (6) has been used for the purpose of finding the Crossover rate. When (6) is used, crossover rate in all

TABLE 2: Comparison results of DNA and adaptive DNA computing algorithms.

Algorithm	K_p	K_i	Settling time	Overshoot %
DNA-PI	30	0.1250	0.08	14
Adaptive DNA-PI	17	0.4375	0.08	~0

TABLE 3: Values of DNA and adaptive DNA computing parameters.

Parameters	DNA computing	Adaptive DNA computing
Population size	80	60
Maximum generations	20	40
Crossover rate	%100	%32
Enzyme and virus rate	%30	%12
a and b	15, 12	11.8203, 1.9700

iterations is applied at a proportion of 80%:

$$\text{Crossover\_rate} = \text{Pop\_size} * 0.8. \tag{6}$$

Enzyme (E) and Virus (V) Proportion. The most significant two parameters used in this study are enzyme and virus mutations. While enzyme mutation provides the deletion of a certain proportion of elements from the population, virus mutation provides the addition of a certain proportion of elements to the population. These two parameters are only used with DNA computing unlike others. The implementing adaptive DNA computing enzyme and virus proportions should be selected well because when the enzyme mutation is not applied in the correct time, it may lead to the loss of elements with good conformity values. One should be careful that the algorithm does not create unnecessary solution area while implementing virus mutation. Equation (7) has been used in the study performed in order to determine enzyme and virus proportions. With the change of the population size, the variation of population at a proportion of 30% is provided in ever iteration. In the selection of the equations found through the trial and error method were taken into consideration and the values acquired by running the system many times were examined in detail and the equations have been given their final forms:

$$\text{e\_v} = \text{Pop\_size} * 0.3. \tag{7}$$

The algorithmic steps of DNA computing algorithm are explained in detail as follows.

Step 1. The first population is created with DNA serials randomly.

Step 2. The serials created were firstly converted into system of four and then into decimal system as it is explained in Table 3 and converted into numerical data. The operations of coding and converting are given in Table 3 in detail. The population elements converted into numerical data are sent to the simulation environment and the error values created in the system are determined.

Step 3. The error values from the simulation are placed in the conformity function and conformity values are obtained. The population elements that minimize sum conformity values are used as the new K_p and K_i values. Equation (8) has been selected for the determination of the conformity value. This conformity function may change in accordance with the preference of the applier as it is explained above.

Step 4. The adaptive parameter values to be used for the adaptive DNA computing algorithm and cycle are found using QPSO and sent to the system. Equation (9) is used for the QPSO conformity function. In the selection of the conformity function the results found through the method of trial and error were taken into consideration and the values acquired by running the system many times were examined in detail and the equations have been given their final forms.

Step 5. The elements of the population created firstly are subjected to Crossover process and new population is created. Using Steps 2 and 3 new K_p and K_i are determined.

Step 6. The population applied enzyme and virus mutation and new population is created. Applying Steps 2, 3, and 4 new K_p and K_i values are determined.

Step 7. The best conformity values found in the above steps are compared. K_p and K_i values in the step where the conformity value is minimum are sent to the system.

Step 8. Those steps are applied till the maximum number of operations is achieved. At the end of maximum operations the most suitable K_p and K_i values are determined:

$$f\left(K_p, K_i\right) = \text{sum}\left(\text{abs}\left(e\right)\right), \tag{8}$$

$$f\text{\_qpso} = a * \text{sum}\left(e^2\right) + b * \text{max}\left(\text{yout}\right), \tag{9}$$

$$a = \text{average}\left(f\text{\_qpso}\right) * c1, \tag{10}$$

$$b = \text{average}\left(f\text{\_qpso}\right) * c2. \tag{11}$$

5. Experimental Results

A transfer function given with equation (12) that is modeling position control of a DC motor was used for the performance measurement of the proposed method. DNA computing algorithm was applied for setting the PI parameters and Matlab m-file was written. For finding the simulation results, the model given in Figure 3 was created in the Simulink environment and the results were obtained. The parameter values used for DNA computing are given in Table 3:

$$G(s) = \frac{2.2}{8.96e-6s^3 + 7.27e-3s^2 + 0.945s}. \tag{12}$$

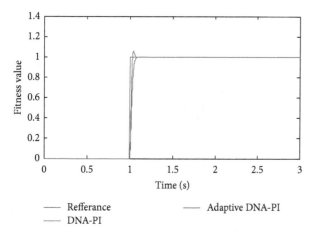

FIGURE 4: Adaptive algorithm results.

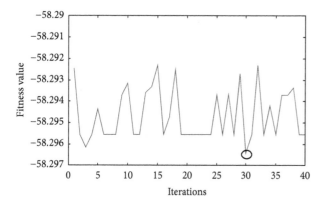

FIGURE 5: The fitness values of adaptive DNA computing algorithm.

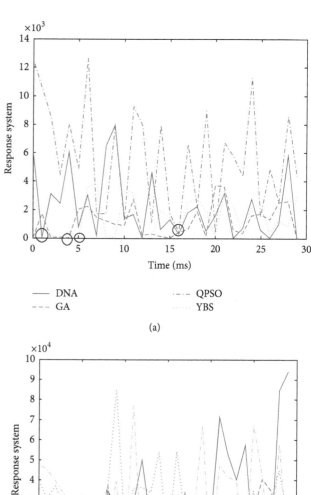

(a)

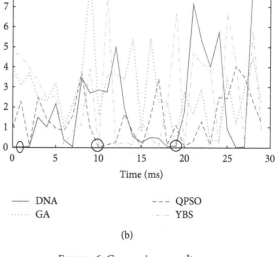

(b)

FIGURE 6: Comparison results.

In the application performed, QPSO-based DNA computing algorithm was used for the optimization of the PI parameters. Although various conformity functions were used in the optimization of the PI parameters, in this study the sum of absolute value of error was selected as the conformity function. With the use of this function which is sensitive even to the errors with minimal values it was targeted that upper excess, increase, and setting times would give better results. In the Matlab/Simulink study performed the size of the population used in the application was taken as 80, maximum number of operations as 20, and reference value as 1. For the detection of K_p and K_i values (8) has been used as the conformity function. While performing coding with DNA computing algorithm K_p and K_i values were coded with DNA basis using data of 6 bytes. Firstly 80 individuals in the population were used and each individual was represented with data of 12 bytes. The first 6 bytes of those data of 12 bytes were used for K_p and the other 6 bytes were used for K_i. In every iteration enzyme and virus mutation as much as 30% of the population was applied and the change of the individual was provided as much as population size * 0.3 and the population was renewed. In the application performed, the population elements created in the algorithms were sent to the system and determination of the PI elements has been provided. The results produced by the system as a result of running the program many times are given in Table 3 and Figure 4.

As it is given in Table 2, using the adaptive DNA computing algorithm K_p is found to be 17, K_i 0.4375, placement time 0.08 seconds, and maximum excess approximately 0%. In Figure 4, the comparison of the results found with adaptive DNA computing to DNA computing is given. The maximum excess value found with DNA computing algorithm made adaptive is approximately 0% while the maximum excess value found with DNA computing is computed as approximately 14%. Those results indicate that adaptive DNA computing gets better results.

In Table 3 DNA computing parameters made adaptive with the QPSO algorithm and DNA computing parameters are given. With the activation of the algorithm with QPSO parameter values have changed. With the QPSO algorithm population size was revised as 60, maximum number of operations as 40, Crossover rate as 32%, and enzyme and virus proportion as 12%. New values were applied by being sent to DNA computing algorithm. The values of a and b used for the conformity function were 15 and 12 when the algorithm started and with the QPSO algorithm they were acquired as 11.8203 and 1.9700 and used for the system. The performance of the proposed approach and comparison results are shown in Figures 5 and 6, respectively. As shown in these figures, the proposed approach finds faster than other algorithms.

6. Conclusions

DNA computing that the key advantage is parallelism has the natural capabilities of DNA and large information storage abilities. But this computation model has some problems for numerical implementation in real world applications. In particular, the parameters of the DNA computing algorithm are determined by trial and error in the literature. This determination method is usually very difficult, inefficient, and inflexible. A new QPSO-based adaptive DNA computing algorithm is proposed and implemented for optimization problems in this study. The seven parameters of DNA computing algorithm has been simultaneously and online tuned with QPSO for adaptive operation in the proposed approach. Experimental results obtained with computation of parameters of PI controller for system identification application consistently show that proposed approach has effective optimization, high accuracy and high convergence speed according to traditional DNA computing algorithm. In addition, general search capability of the method is not dependent on local optimum points and applicability of the proposed approach is easier, simpler, and faster than traditional DNA computing algorithm.

References

[1] L. M. Adleman, "Molecular computation of solutions to combinatorial problems," *Science*, vol. 266, no. 5187, pp. 1021–1024, 1994.

[2] R. J. Lipton, "Using DNA to solve NP-complete problems," *Science*, vol. 268, no. 5210, pp. 542–545, 1995.

[3] C.-L. Lin, H.-Y. Jan, and T.-S. Hwang, "Structure variable PID control design based on DNA coding method," in *Proceedings of the IEEE International Symposium on Industrial Electronics (IEEE-ISIE '04)*, pp. 423–428, May 2004.

[4] Y. Ding and L. Ren, "DNA genetic algorithm for design of the generalized membership-type Takagi-Sugeno fuzzy control system," in *Proceedings of the IEEE International Conference on Systems, Man and Cybernetics*, vol. 5, pp. 3862–3867, October 2000.

[5] J. J. Kim and J. J. Lee, "PID controller design using double helix structured DNA algorithms with a recovery function," *Artificial Life and Robotics*, vol. 12, no. 1-2, pp. 241–244, 2008.

[6] Y. Wang, G. Cui, and Z. Wang, "Research on DNA computer with coprocessor organizational model," in *Proceedings of the 8th International Conference on High-Performance Computing in Asia-Pacific Region (HPC Asia '05)*, vol. 6, pp. 544–549, December 2005.

[7] X. Zhang, Y. Niu, and Y. Wang, "DNA computing in microreactors: a solution to the minimum vertex cover problem," in *Proceedings of the 6th International Conference on Bio-Inspired Computing: Theories and Applications (BIC-TA '11)*, pp. 236–240, September 2011.

[8] R. Sridhar and S. Balasubramaniam, "GIS integrated DNA computing for solving travelling salesman problem," in *Proceedings of the IEEE Symposium on Computers & Informatics (ISCI '11)*, pp. 402–406, mys, March 2011.

[9] U. Çiğdem and M. Karaköse, "Using of DNA computing for tuning of parameters of PI and fuzzy controllers," in *Proceedings of the Automatic Control National Symposium*, pp. 665–670, Izmir, Turkey, 2011.

[10] F. Li, Z. Li, and J. Xu, "DNA computing model based on photo-electric detection system with magnetic beads," in *Proceedings of the 6th International Conference on Bio-Inspired Computing: Theories and Applications (BIC-TA '11)*, pp. 170–175, September 2011.

[11] Y. Huang and L. He, "DNA computing research progress and application," in *Proceedings of the 6th International Conference on Computer Science and Education (ICCSE '11)*, pp. 232–235, August 2011.

[12] J. Xu, X. Qiang, Y. Yang et al., "An unenumerative DNA computing model for vertex coloring problem," *IEEE Transactions on Nanobioscience*, vol. 10, no. 2, pp. 94–98, 2011.

[13] S. Mitra, R. Das, and Y. Hayashi, "Genetic networks and soft computing," *IEEE/ACM Transactions on Computational Biology and Bioinformatics*, vol. 8, no. 1, pp. 94–107, 2011.

[14] H. Jiao, Y. Zhong, L. Zhang, and P. Li, "Unsupervised remote sensing image classification using an artificial DNA computing," in *Proceedings of the 2011 7th International Conference on Natural Computation (ICNC '11)*, pp. 1341–1345, July 2011.

[15] Z. Yin, C. Hua, and B. Song, "Plasmid DNA computing model of 0-1 programming problem," in *Proceedings of the IEEE 5th International Conference on Bio-Inspired Computing: Theories and Applications (BIC-TA '10)*, pp. 148–151, September 2010.

[16] J. Xu, X. Qiang, K. Zhang et al., "A parallel type of DNA computing model for graph vertex coloring problem," in *Proceedings of the IEEE 5th International Conference on Bio-Inspired Computing: Theories and Applications (BIC-TA '10)*, pp. 231–235, September 2010.

[17] Y. Huang, Z. Yin, and Y. Tian, "Design of PID controller based on DNA computing," in *Proceedings of the International Conference on Artificial Intelligence and Computational Intelligence (AICI '10)*, pp. 195–198, October 2010.

[18] Z. Yin, B. Song, C. Zhen, and C. Hua, "Molecular beacon-based DNA computing model for maximum independent set problem," in *Proceedings of the International Conference on Intelligent Computation Technology and Automation (ICICTA '10)*, pp. 732–735, May 2010.

[19] C.-L. Lin, H.-Y. Jan, and T.-S. Hwang, "Structure variable PID control design based on DNA coding method," in *Proceedings of the IEEE International Symposium on Industrial Electronics*, pp. 423–428, May 2004.

[20] C.-L. Lin, H.-Y. Jan, and T.-H. Huang, "Self-organizing PID control design based on DNA computing method," in *Proceedings of the IEEE International Conference on Control Applications*, pp. 568–573, September 2004.

[21] C. V. Henkel, *Experimental DNA computing [Ph.D. thesis]*, Leiden University, 2005.

[22] Z. F. Qiu, *Advance the DNA computing [Ph.D. thesis]*, Texas A&M University, College Station, Tex, USA, 2003.

[23] M. O. Rahman, A. Hussain, E. Scavino, M. A. Hannan, and H. Basri, "Object identification using DNA computing algorithm," in *Proceedings of the IEEE Congress on Evolutionary Computation*, pp. 1–7, 2012.

[24] J. M. Chaves-González and M. A. Vega-Rodríguez, "DNA sequence design for reliable DNA computing by using a multiobjective approach," in *Proceedings of the 13th IEEE International Symposium on Computational Intelligence and Informatics*, pp. 73–79, 2012.

[25] H. Zhang and X. Liu, "A general object oriented description for DNA computing technique," in *Proceedings of the International Conference on Information Technology and Computer Science (ITCS '09)*, pp. 3–6, July 2009.

[26] H. Jiao, Y. Zhong, and L. Zhang, "Artificial DNA computing-based spectral encoding and matching algorithm for hyperspectral remote sensing data," *IEEE Transactions on Geoscience and Remote Sensing*, vol. 50, no. 10, pp. 4085–4105, 2012.

[27] W. Liu, S. Sun, and Y. Guo, "A DNA computing model of perceptron," in *Proceedings of the Pacific-Asia Conference on Circuits, Communications and System (PACCS '09)*, pp. 710–712, May 2009.

[28] Q. Zhang, X. Xue, and X. Wei, "A novel image encryption algorithm based on DNA subsequence operation," *The Scientific World Journal*, vol. 2012, Article ID 286741, 10 pages, 2012.

[29] J. Xu, X. Qiang, Y. Yang et al., "An unenumerative DNA computing model for vertex coloring problem," *IEEE Transactions on Nanobioscience*, vol. 10, no. 2, pp. 94–98, 2011.

[30] M. Xi, J. Sun, and W. Xu, "Parameter optimization of PID controller based on Quantum-Behaved Particle Swarm Optimization Algorithm," *Complex Systems and Applications-Modelling*, vol. 14, supplement 2, pp. 603–607, 2007.

2

On the Development of Speech Resources for the Mixtec Language

Santiago-Omar Caballero-Morales

Technological University of the Mixteca, Road to Acatlima K.m. 2.5, 69000 Huajuapan de León, OAX, Mexico

Correspondence should be addressed to Santiago-Omar Caballero-Morales; scaballero@mixteco.utm.mx

Academic Editors: J. M. Corchado, R. Dahyot, A. Paun, L. J. M. Rothkrantz, and R. Valencia-Garcia

The Mixtec language is one of the main native languages in Mexico. In general, due to urbanization, discrimination, and limited attempts to promote the culture, the native languages are disappearing. Most of the information available about the Mixtec language is in written form as in dictionaries which, although including examples about how to pronounce the Mixtec words, are not as reliable as listening to the correct pronunciation from a native speaker. Formal acoustic resources, as speech corpora, are almost non-existent for the Mixtec, and no speech technologies are known to have been developed for it. This paper presents the development of the following resources for the Mixtec language: (1) a speech database of traditional narratives of the Mixtec culture spoken by a native speaker (labelled at the phonetic and orthographic levels by means of spectral analysis) and (2) a native speaker-adaptive automatic speech recognition (ASR) system (trained with the speech database) integrated with a Mixtec-to-Spanish/Spanish-to-Mixtec text translator. The speech database, although small and limited to a single variant, was reliable enough to build the multiuser speech application which presented a mean recognition/translation performance up to 94.36% in experiments with non-native speakers (the target users).

1. Introduction

Research on spoken language technology has led to the development of automatic speech recognition (ASR), Text-to-Speech (TTS) synthesis, and dialogue systems. These systems are now used for different applications such as in mobile telephones for voice dialing, GPS navigation, information retrieval, dictation [1–3], translation [4, 5], and assistance for handicapped people [6, 7].

ASR technology has been used also for language learning, and examples of these can be found in [8–10] for English, [11] for Spanish and French among others, and [12] for "sign" languages. These interfaces allow the user to practice their pronunciation at home or work without the limitations of a schedule. These also have the advantage of mobility as some of them can be installed in different computer platforms or even mobile telephones for basic practicing. However, although there are applications for the most common foreign languages, there are limited (if any) applications for native or ancient languages.

In Mexico there are around 89 native languages still spoken by 6.6 millions of native speakers. Although the number of speakers may be significant (considering the total number of inhabitants in Mexico), this number is decreasing, specially in the south-central region, which includes a region known as "La Mixteca" (The Mixteca Region). This region covers parts of the states of Puebla, Guerrero, and Oaxaca as shown in Figure 1. The native inhabitants of The Mixteca are known as "The Mixtec", and their origin can be traced back to 1500 B.C. As with other native groups in Mexico, their presence has been in decline since the beginning of the Spanish colonization of the Americas.

Nowadays, the population of native speakers of the Mixtec language is further decreasing given urban migration and development, culture rejection, and limited attempts to preserve the language. This has been expressed by people living in communities in The Mixteca Region of Mexico, and this can be corroborated by national statistics that show that the number of people who spoke any native language, 6.3 millions in 2000 (7.1% of the total population), decreased

The Mixteca Region

FIGURE 1: Mixteca Region within the Mexican territory.

to 6.0 millions in 2005 (6.6% of the total population), and this amount was even higher in 1990 (7.5% of the total population) [13]. This increases the possibility of native languages being lost, as some dialects or variations had less than 10 known speakers (i.e., Ayapaneco, 4 speakers; Chinanteco of Sochiapan, 2 speakers; Mixtec of the Mazateca Region, 6 speakers [13]). In this case, historic antecedents or information about the language is not recorded, making it very difficult to recover or save some parts of the language. This may happen to other languages with more speakers. The Mixtec language, with approximately 480,000 speakers, has been reported to lose annually 200 speakers.

To preserve a language is not an easy task, because all characteristics such as grammar rules, written expression, speech articulation, and phonetics must be documented and recorded. Although there are books and dictionaries that among the word definitions include examples about how to pronounce them, this is not as complete as listening to the correct pronunciation from a native speaker. This goal is considered to be attainable by the use of modern technology such as that used for foreign language learning [10, 11] to promote the language among non-native speakers and, thus, to contribute to its preservation.

However, for the Mixtec, any of the goals of preservation, learning/teaching, or promotion of the language is very limited as the availability of native speech corpora is almost non-existent for the development of any speech application.

There are many challenges due to the wide range of variations of the Mixtec language, the limited availability of native speakers willing to participate in such projects (e.g., creating training speech corpora), and their lack of knowledge about the formal writing and phonology of the language. Because of this situation, the development of a Mixtec ASR system with large vocabulary is not achievable. Thus, the use of a speaker adaptation technique on a one-native speaker ASR system was studied.

Hence, this paper presents the development of two major resources: (1) a single native speech corpus of a variation of the Mixtec language, labelled at the phonetic and orthographic levels, and (2) two speech applications: (a) an ASR system and (b) a Mixtec-to-Spanish/Spanish-to-Mixtec speech translator. Non-native speakers were considered the target users for these applications because it is important to arouse the interest in the language of the population with more presence in Mexico, the Spanish-speaking people. This may contribute to a change in attitude towards not only the language, but also towards the culture itself, which can be more beneficial for the purposes of preservation.

The speech applications, trained with the native speech database, performed with recognition accuracies up to 94% when tested by non-native speakers, providing meaningful results about the reliability of the database for the development of basic ASR systems. At this point it is important to mention that the ASR systems recognize Mixtec vocabulary by means of speaker adaptation and that assessment of Mixtec pronunciation by the non-native speakers is not performed. Thus, the ASR systems should not be used for the task of evaluation of the validity of a non-native speaker's pronunciation. However the Mixtec speech corpus can be used to perform the research needed for that purpose.

The structure of the paper is as follows: in Section 2 the general characteristics of the Mixtec language variation used for this work are presented, while in Section 3 the building process of the native speech database with this variation are presented. Then, in Section 4 the design of the speech application systems, which includes the supervised training of the system's acoustic models, and the adaptation technique for its use by non-native users, are presented. The details of the testing methodology by the non-native users and the performance of the developed systems are then presented and analyzed in Section 5. Finally, in Section 6 the conclusions and future work are discussed.

2. The Mixtec Language

The Mixtec language, or "Tu'un Savi" (Tongue/Language of the Rain) [14], is present mainly in the states of Guerrero, Puebla, and Oaxaca. However, some variations of the language are also present in the states of Sinaloa, Jalisco, and Yucatán. With a number of speakers of approximately 480,000, this is one of the main native or indigenous languages in Mexico. The Mixtec is a tonal language [14], where the meaning of a word relies on its tone, and because of the geographic dispersion of the Mixtec population, there are differences in tones, pronunciations, and vocabularies between communities, which in some cases restricts the communication between them [15]. Because of this, each variation of the Mixtec language is identified by the name of a community, for example, Mixtec from Tezoatlán [16], Mixtec from Yosondúa [17], or Mixtec of Xochapa [18]; existing significant differences between vocabularies and their meanings: "cat" and "mouse" are, respectively, referenced as "chító" and "tiín" by the Mixtec of Silacayoapan and as "vilo" and "choto" by the Mixtec of the South East of Nochixtlán. Hence, the Mixtec cannot be considered as a single and homogeneous language, and there is still a debate about its number of variations. The National Indigenous Languages Institute (better known by its acronym INALI) in Mexico has identified 81 variations [19], while the Summer Institute of Linguistics has identified 30 variations [20].

Because of this diversity there is no conscensus about a standardized phonetic alphabet for the Mixtec. Thus, continuous revision of the Mixtec alphabet is performed by native and non-native researchers of the language. The Academy of the Mixtec Language "Ve'e Tu'un Savi" (House of the Language of the Rain) [14] identified eight vowels and 20 consonants, pointing out that in some variants only five, six, or seven vowels are used. In contrast, the Summer Institute of Linguistics (SIL) [18] identified five vowels and 22 consonants for the Mixtec of Xochapa in Guerrero. In addition to these differences in phoneme definitions, the tones are also subject to uncertainty. Although generally only

TABLE 1: Examples of Mixtec words with tones.

Word	Meaning
ñoó	Night
ñoo	Town
ñoo	Palm
yukú	Who
yuku	Mountain
yuku	Leaf

three tones are identified (high, medium, and low), other researchers have identified up to 20 tones [14]. Hence, even for the native community of researchers, continuous revisions of the phoneme alphabet are performed.

Because of this, a reduced version of the different Mixtec phoneme alphabets was established for the labelling of the speech corpus and the construction of the ASR applications. This is explained in the following section.

2.1. Phonetics. In general, the Mixtec has three characteristic tones: high, medium, and low [14, 16–18, 21–24]. In Table 1 some examples of words that change their meanings based on the tone applied to their vowels are shown, where (_) is used to identify the low tone, (′) the high tone, and the medium tone is left unmarked [14]. Although there are other tone representations, where the low tone also is represented with a horizontal line over the vowel [21], usually the high tone is represented with the diacritical (′). The tones are applied on the vowels, and for this work, the standard five vowels /a/, /e/, /i/, /o/, and /u/ were selected.

Based on the phonemes identified in [14, 18, 21–24] and by integrating the different tones in the vowels, the repertoire shown in Table 2 was defined. The Mixtec phonemes are represented in terms of the International Phonetic Alphabet (IPA) and the Spanish Mexican Phonetic Alphabet (Mexbet) [25]. For the Mixtec vowels, the low tone is represented by the diacritical (`) while the high tone is represented by (′), and the medium tone is unmarked to keep consistency.

The phonetics of the Mixtec has some differences when compared with the Mexican Spanish language. For example, from Table 2:

(i) the Mixtec phoneme /dj/ represents a phoneme equivalent to the Mexican Spanish phoneme /s/ [26], while /nd/ represents the composition of the sequence /n/+/d/ as in the Mixtec word "ndí" (light); the same applies to /ng/ which represents the sequence of /n/+/g/ as in the word "súngòo" (to settle);

(ii) the Mixtec phoneme /sh/ is pronounced as /ʃ/ in the English word "she"; in contrast, /ch/ is pronounced as /t͡ʃ/ in the word "change";

(iii) there are short pauses, uttered as a glottal closure between vowels within a word, which are represented by /'/ such as in the words "tu'un" (language) or "ndá'a" (hand); however, in other words such as "ka'avi" (to study) and "ndá'aita" (bouquet), /'/ does not represent a short pause; instead it represents the

FIGURE 2: San Juan Diquiyú, place of origin of the Mixtec variant for the speech corpus.

TABLE 2: Repertoire of Mixtec phonemes.

Description	IPA	Mixtec	Mexbet
Voiceless bilabial stop	p	p	p
Voiceless dental stop	t	t	t
Voiceless velar stop	k	k	k
Voiced bilabial stop	b	b	b
Voiced dental stop	d	d	d
Voiced velar stop	g	g	g
Voiceless palatal affricate	tʃ	ch	tS
Voiceless palatoalveolar fricative	ʃ	sh	
Voiceless labiodental fricative	f		f
Voiceless alveolar sibilant	s	s, dj	s
Voiceless velar fricative	x	j	x
Voiced palatal fricative	ʒ	y	Z
Bilabial nasal	m	m	m
Palatal nasal	ɲ	ñ	ñ
Alveolar nasal	n	n	n
Alveolar lateral	l	l	l
Alveolar trill	r	r	r
Alveolar flap	ɾ		r(
Close front unrounded vowel	i	i, í, ì	i
Close-mid front unrounded vowel	e	e, é	e
Open front unrounded vowel	a	a, á, à	a
Close-mid back rounded vowel	o	o, ó, ò	o
Close back rounded vowel	u	u, ú, ù	u
Glottal stop	ʔ	'	
Additional		nd, ng	ks
			_D, _G
			_N, _R
		sil	sil

extension of the vowel. Hence, phonetic labelling of Mixtec speech requires special attention. In the IPA, the pause is represented by the glottal stop /ʔ/;

(iv) the Mixtec phoneme /n/ is pronounced as in the Mexican Spanish word "Nada" (or as in the English word "Nothing") if it is placed before a vowel, but is mute if placed after the vowel.

For the Mexican Spanish, the inclusion of the archiphonemes /_D/, /_G/, /_N/, and /_R/ in Mexbet

was proposed to define the neutralization of the following couples of phonemes: /d/-/t/, /g/-/k/, /n/-/m/, and /ɾ/-/r/ [25]. To represent the pronunciation of the sequence of phonemes /k/ and /s/ (as in the English word "extra"), the phoneme /ks/ was added. For both alphabets (Mixtec and Mexican Spanish), the /sil/ phoneme was added to represent the silence.

3. The Mixtec Speech Corpus

The vocabulary and representative text for the speech corpus were taken from educational material designed by Professor Maximino Sánchez Ventura from the local Cultural Center of the city of Huajuapan de León (Oaxaca, México). He is a native speaker of the Mixtec variant of San Juan Diquiyú (see Figure 2) which is located at the south of Huajuapan de León, in the municipality of Tezoatlán de Segura y Luna. San Juan Diquiyú has a population of approximately 556. Because the Mixtec of San Juan Duquiyú shares similarities with other variations in Oaxaca, there was confidence about using it as the reference variation.

The educational material of Professor Maximino consisted of a collection of 15 traditional Mixtec narratives. For this work, seven were selected, where the first narratives were used for beginners and the last ones for more advanced non-native learners. In Figure 3 the process followed to obtain the speech corpus from the Mixtec narratives is shown. Each narrative was read a certain number of times (see Figure 3) by Professor Maximino, the reference native speaker. These repetitions were recorded in the Media Lab of the Technological University of the Mixteca in WAV format with a sampling rate of 44,100 Hz and one audio channel (monaural). Approximately 45 minutes of native Mixtec speech was recorded. These recordings were then transcribed at the phonetic and word levels (TIMIT standard) using the list of phonemes defined in Table 2, the assistance of Professor Maximino, and spectral analysis using the software WaveSurfer as presented in Figure 4. Note the spectral differences given by the tones between the vowels /a/ (am = /a/ medium tone) and /á/ (ah = /a/ high tone) and /i/ (im) and /í/ (ih).

In total, the Mixtec speech corpus consisted of 931 words with a vocabulary of 192 (unique) words. The frequency (number of occurrences) of the vocabulary words

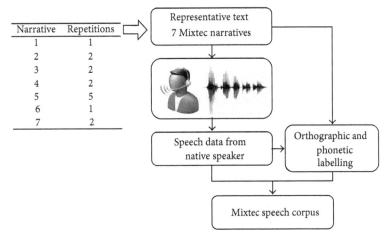

Narrative	Repetitions
1	1
2	2
3	2
4	2
5	5
6	1
7	2

FIGURE 3: Steps to obtain the Mixtec speech corpus.

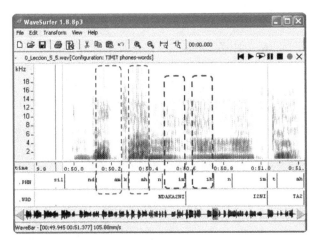

FIGURE 4: Orthographic and phonetic labelling of the Mixtec speech corpus.

is presented in Table 3. These words have the frequency of phonemes presented in Figure 5. Based on the phoneme distributions of Figure 5, it was considered that the corpus contained enough samples from each Mixtec phoneme for the supervised training of the acoustic models of an ASR system. A minimum of six was established given the experiments reported in [27] where, for disordered speech, an ASR system was able to achieve accuracies up to 100% when trained with at least six samples of a word. It is important to mention that the phonemes /g/ and /ng/ are not present in this variant; thus, these were not considered.

4. Mixtec Speech Applications

The initial application built with the Mixtec speech corpus was a speaker-adaptive ASR system. The main elements of this system, which became the baseline for more complex applications, are shown in Figure 6. In the following sections a description of the construction of each of these elements is presented.

4.1. Speaker-Adaptive ASR Baseline System. An ASR system uses a Bayesian approach to estimate the most likely word sequence $\widehat{W}$ out of all possible legal word sentences from a language model L given some acoustic input O:

$$\widehat{W} = \arg \max_{W \in L} \Pr(W \mid O). \tag{1}$$

The language model contains all the possible word output sequences for a certain application, and the acoustic input is the speech signal. By using Bayes' rule, (1) can be expressed as follows:

$$\widehat{W} = \arg \max_{W \in L} \frac{\Pr(O \mid W) \Pr(W)}{\Pr(O)}. \tag{2}$$

Although $(\Pr(O|W)\Pr(W))/(\Pr(O))$ is estimated for each possible sentence in the language, $\Pr(O)$ does not change for each sentence and thus can be ignored in (2). Hence,

$$\widehat{W} = \arg \max_{W \in L} \Pr(O \mid W) \Pr(W). \tag{3}$$

Hence, the most likely sequence of words $\widehat{W}$ given some acoustic observation O can be estimated as the product of two probabilities [28]:

(i) $\Pr(W)$, the *prior probability*, which is obtained from the *language model L*;

(ii) $\Pr(O \mid W)$, the *observation likelihood*, which is obtained from the *acoustic model*.

$\Pr(W)$ is usually estimated/modelled by using N-gram grammars, and $\Pr(O \mid W)$ by using Hidden Markov Models (HMMs) [29] or artificial neural networks (ANN).

In this work the modules of the software HTK [30] were used to build the elements of the Mixtec baseline ASR system which include the N-grams and the acoustic models. The details are presented in the following sections.

4.1.1. Acoustic Models (Pr(O | W)). Hidden Markov Models (HMMs) [28–30] were used for the acoustic modelling of

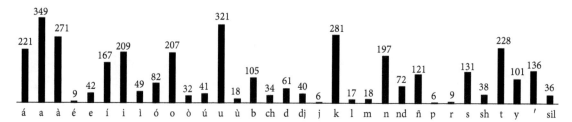

FIGURE 5: Frequency distribution of phonemes in the Mixtec speech corpus.

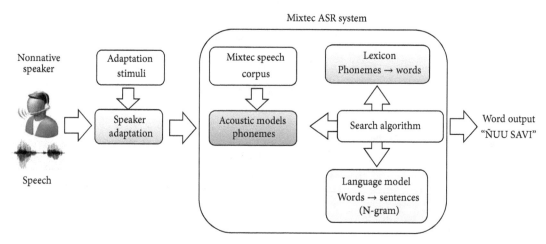

FIGURE 6: Elements of the speaker-adaptive Mixtec ASR system.

each phoneme in the Mixtec speech corpus. In general terms, an HMM consists of the following parameters which are presented in Figure 7:

(i) a set of states $Q = \{q_0, q_1, \ldots, q_N\}$, where q_0 and q_N are non-emitting states (not associated with observations). Each state has associated a probability function which models the emission of certain acoustic observations (see $B = \{b_j(\mathbf{o}_t)\}$ later);

(ii) a transition probability matrix $A = \{a_{01}, a_{02}, \ldots, a_{NN}\}$, where each a_{ij} represents the transition probability from state i to state j and $\sum_{j=1}^{N} a_{ij} = 1$ for all i;

(iii) a set of observation likelihoods (emission probabilities) $B = \{b_j(\mathbf{o}_t)\}$, where each term represents the probability of an acoustic observation vector $\mathbf{o}_t$ being generated from a state j. In practice, $b_j(\mathbf{o}_t)$ is modelled as a weighted sum of Gaussian probability density functions (a Gaussian mixture):

$$b_j(\mathbf{o}_t) = \sum_{k=1}^{K} C_{jk} N\left(\mathbf{o}_t, \boldsymbol{\mu}_{jk}, \boldsymbol{\Sigma}_{jk}\right), \qquad (4)$$

where K denotes the number of mixture components, C_{jk} is the weight for the k-th mixture component satisfying $\sum_{k=1}^{K} C_{jk} = 1$, and $N(\mathbf{o}_t, \boldsymbol{\mu}_{jk}, \boldsymbol{\Sigma}_{jk})$ denotes a single Gaussian density function with mean vector $\boldsymbol{\mu}_{jk}$ and covariance matrix $\boldsymbol{\Sigma}_{jk}$ for state j.

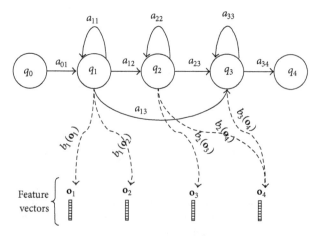

FIGURE 7: Three-state left-to-right topology of a phoneme HMM.

The topology of an HMM reflects the structure of the process that is modelled, and the left-to-right topology presented in Figure 7 is commonly used to model subword units (phonemes) which can be concatenated to form words [30]. This topology was used for all the phoneme HMMs of the baseline ASR system, and 10 Gaussian mixture components were considered for each state.

The training speech corpus (set of acoustic observations) was coded into MFCC feature vectors with the HTK module *HCopy*. The front end used 12 MFCCs plus energy, delta, and acceleration coefficients [30].

TABLE 3: Frequency of the vocabulary in the Mixtec speech corpus.

No.	Word	Freq.
1	ÀNE'ECHOOS	1
2	ÁN	2
3	ÁTOKÓ	2
4	CHÁ	8
5	CHÁNÍ	1
6	CHÁNÍTÀ	1
7	CHI	11
8	DIKIYÚ	2
9	DJÀVÌ	2
10	DJAÁ	5
11	DJAMA	6
12	DJE'E	2
13	DJEETÀ	1
14	DJÍ'Í	2
15	DJÍO	4
16	DJIÁ	2
17	I	2
18	Í'A	1
19	ÍDJONA	1
20	ÍN	10
21	ÍNI	5
22	ÍÑÒ	2
23	IIN	4
24	INÍXOO	7
25	KÀKÀ	2
26	KÁ'A	2
27	KÁ'ANO	4
28	KÁ'AVI	26
29	KÁN'AN	4
30	KÁNDOI	1
31	KAMA	2
32	KÌVÌ	4
		129
33	KIÁ	2
34	KIDJÍ	1
35	KO'OAN	2
36	KÒ'O	4
37	KÒÒÍÚN	17
38	KOÍÑO	1
39	KOKUMI	2
40	KOÑO	1
41	KOÓ	4
42	KOTO	1
43	KOÚN'UN	5
44	KOÚNI	2
45	KOÚSA	2
46	KOÚVI	2
47	KÙÌÀ	3
48	KÙTAKU	1
49	KUÀ'À	19
50	KUÀ'ÀKÁ	1

TABLE 3: Continued.

No.	Word	Freq.
51	KUÁ'A	2
52	KUÁCHÍ	5
53	KUALÍ	3
54	KUI'Í	3
55	KUÍ	4
56	KUÍI	2
57	KUKU	2
58	KUTÁ'AVI	6
59	KUTÓ	1
60	KUÚ	2
61	LAA	5
62	LÓ'O	5
63	LULI	2
64	ME'Í	1
		113
65	MIÍ	7
66	NA	32
67	NÀ	10
68	NÀVE'E	2
69	NÁ	4
70	NÁ'ANO	2
71	NANÍ	3
72	NAVA'ATI	2
73	NDÁ'A	4
74	NDA'Á	4
75	NDÁ'AITA	1
76	NDÁKAA	2
77	NDÁNDEI	1
78	NDAKÁNI	1
79	NDAKONÓ	2
80	NDATO	5
81	NDEEYÉ	2
82	NDÌÍNI	2
83	NDÌKUA	2
84	NDÌTIVI	1
85	NDÍ	5
86	NDICHÍ	4
87	NDIDJAÁ	4
88	NDIDJI	4
89	NDIKÁNDÍ	17
90	NDISÁN'AN	1
91	NDOVA'A	3
92	NDÙ'Ú	1
93	NDUTÁ	3
94	NDUTATÍ	2
95	NDUTÍ	5
96	NE'EKÁ	1
		139

TABLE 3: Continued.

TABLE 3: Continued.

No.	Word	Freq.	No.	Word	Freq.
97	NÌXÌKÀ	1	147	TA	19
98	NÌYA′A	2	148	TA′Á	2
99	NÌYAN′AN	1	149	TÀ	40
100	NÍ	9	150	TÀKUIÍ	7
101	NÍKÉE	4	151	TÀKUIÍAN	1
102	NIKÀ′A	1	152	TÀYUU	2
103	ÑA	34	153	TÁ	26
104	ÑA′Á	22	154	TÁN′AN	4
105	ÑÀ	2	155	TÁNDÀ′À	9
106	ÑÓCHÍ	4	156	TÁTÁ	5
107	ÑÓO	8	157	TAA	2
108	ÑUU	43	158	TAAN	1
109	ÑUUYIVI	4	159	TATA	2
110	NÒO	4	160	TI′A	1
111	NÒYÁ′AVI	4			207
112	NOO	2	161	TIDJO	4
113	NOÓ	3	162	TÓO	2
114	OON	2	163	TÓOKA	1
115	PÁ′A	3	164	TOÓN	1
116	PERU	3	165	TÚKU	2
117	RACHÉE	3	166	ÙXÌ	7
118	RO′O	3	167	UN′UN	17
119	SA′A	2	168	VA′A	18
120	SÀ′À	5	169	VE′E	4
121	SÀDJANÁNI	1	170	VE′ECHÓON	1
122	SÀDJANDÁKU	7	171	VIKO	5
123	SÀKAA	2	172	XÌ′Ì	1
124	SÀKEE	2	173	XÍ′Í	8
125	SÀKONI	8	174	XÍKÁ	1
126	SÀKOÓ	2	175	XÍTI	1
127	SÀKOON	2	176	XOO	2
128	SÀKUÁ	2	177	YÁVI	3
		195	178	YATI	2
129	SÀKUU	17	179	YÍÍ	2
130	SÀNANÍ	3	180	YITO	8
131	SÀNDAKÀÀ	5	181	YÒO	1
132	SÀNDITA	7	182	YÓ	12
133	SÀNDÚ	1	183	YÓ′O	5
134	SÀNDUKÚ	2	184	YOO	1
135	SÀSA′A	2	185	YOÓ	4
136	SÀSÀÀ	6	186	YU′Ú	2
137	SÀTÁVA	1	187	YÙ′Ù	2
138	SÀTAÁ	2	188	YÙKÙ	1
139	SÀVÌ	17	189	YÚKU	1
140	SÀXI′Í	2	190	YUKUTOÓN	25
141	SÀXITO	2	191	YUTA	2
142	SÀYOO	11	192	YUTÁ	2
143	SÁXI	1			148
144	SAÁ	2			
145	SANDOI	3			
146	SATA	2			

Then, the supervised training of the HMMs with the speech corpus (labelled at the phonetic level) was performed with the Baum-Welch and Viterbi algorithms by using the following HTK modules [30].

(i) *HInit* was used for the individual initialization of the phoneme HMMs. In this case, the initial HMM parameters are estimated by iteratively computing Viterbi alignments between the coded training speech corpus and the associated phonetic labels.

(ii) *HRest* was used to refine the initialized parameters obtained with *HInit*. Re-estimation of the parameters of the individual HMMs is performed with the Baum-Welch algorithm and the labelled training corpus.

(iii) *HERest* was used to further refine the HMMs initialized with *HInit/HRest* with a process called *embedded training*. In contrast to individual HMM training as performed by *HInit/HRest*, embedded training consists in re-estimating the parameters of all HMMs in parallel with the Baum-Welch algorithm.

4.1.2. Lexicon. The lexicon, or phonetic dictionary, was made at the same time as the phonetic labelling of the speech corpus. The phoneme sequences that formed each word in the vocabulary were defined by spectral and perceptual analysis as commented in Sections 2 and 3.

4.1.3. Language Model L(Pr(W)). Word-bigram language models (2-grams) were estimated from the word transcriptions of the corpus. This was suitable given the size of the training corpus (see Table 3). The following HTK modules were used for this purpose.

(i) *HLStats* was used to compute label statistics for the purpose of generating a language model. These statistics are estimated from the word transcriptions of the speech corpus and consist in, for example, the probabilities of occurrence of each single word in the corpus (unigram probabilities; see Table 3). If configured to estimate bigram probabilities, it provides the associated probabilities of occurrence for the different pairs of words found in the word transcriptions. For unseen pairs of words, *backed-off* bigram probabilities can be estimated from the unigram probabilities.

(ii) *HBuild* was used to build a word network with the statistics estimated with *HLStats*. This module generated the statistical language model for the baseline ASR system.

An important parameter to control the influence of the language model in the recognition process is the *scale grammar factor*. This factor is defined as the amount by which the language model probability is scaled before being added to each token as it transits from the end of one word to the start of the next [30]. As this factor increases, the recognizer relies more on the language model instead of the acoustic signal to predict what the speaker said (e.g., the language model restrictions have more importance). The module *HVite* (see Section 4.1.4) allows the adjustment of the scale grammar factor during the recognition process, and for this work a value of 10 was used.

4.1.4. Search Algorithm. Speech recognition was performed with the Viterbi algorithm implemented with the module *HVite* of HTK [30]. This module takes as input the coded speech to be recognized and integrates the elements described in Sections 4.1.1, 4.1.2, and 4.1.3 for the estimation of $\widehat{W}$ (see (3)). Internally, the features of the input speech are compared with the learned patterns of the phoneme HMMs. The sequence of HMMs that describe the speech signal with a maximum likelihood is restricted to form valid words with the integration of the lexicon. Then these words are restricted with the information of the language model to form valid sequences or sentences which are the main output of the recognition process ($\widehat{W}$).

4.1.5. Speaker Adaptation. Note that the Mixtec ASR baseline system only will show good performance when tested by the native speaker used to build the training speech corpus. For its use by non-native speakers (the target users) this is a disadvantage. Non-native speakers were considered the target users because it is important to arouse the interest in the language of the population with more presence in Mexico, the Spanish-speaking people. This may contribute to a change in attitude towards not only the language, but also towards the culture itself, which can be more beneficial for the purposes of preservation.

Commercial ASR systems are trained with thousands or millions of speech samples from different speakers, which leads to speaker-independent (SI) systems. When a new user wants to use such system, it is common to ask the user to read some words or narratives (adaptation stimuli) to provide speech samples that will be used by the system to adapt the SI acoustic models to the patterns of the user's voice. SI ASR systems are robust enough to get benefits by the implementation of adaptation techniques such as MAP or MLLR [28, 30].

For this work there are challenges given by the wide range of variations in tones and pronunciations and the limited availability of native speakers to obtain training speech corpora. Because of this situation, the development of a Mixtec SI ASR system is not achievable. Thus, the use of a speaker adaptation technique on this one-native speaker ASR system was studied.

Maximum likelihood linear regression (MLLR) [30, 31] was the adaptation technique used for the native ASR baseline system in order to make it usable for non-native speakers. A selection of words from the Mixtec speech corpus was defined to allow the user to provide enough speech samples from the phonemes listed in Table 2 and Figure 5. These words are shown in Table 4 and have the frequency distribution of phonemes shown in Figure 8, which has a correlation coefficient of 0.6543 with the distribution of the speech corpus (Figure 5). Hence it was considered that the adaptation samples were representative of the speech corpus.

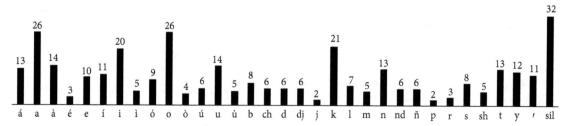

FIGURE 8: Frequency distribution of phonemes in the Mixtec adaptation stimuli.

FIGURE 9: Integration of the baseline Mixtec ASR for other speech applications.

TABLE 4: Adaptation stimuli words.

ÑUU DIKIYÚ VA'A KÁNDOI
YÓ NDAKONÓ XOO NOO ÑA
KUTÓ KUTÁ'AVI KOÚVI NDEEYÉ
YÓ'O TIDJO CHI KÒ'O PERU RO'O
KOÚNI ÁTOKÓ KÒÒÍÚN LULI
SÀSÀÀ KUALÍ NÒYA'AVI ÑÓO
YÓ'O DJAMA LULI LÓ'O RACHÉE
KOKUMI DJÀVÌ SÀYOO SÀTÁVA
TÀKUIÍ SÀNDÚ DJEETÀ SÀYOO
ÍDJONA YUTÁ YATI TÀYUU
DJAÁ NÌXÌKÀ YÙKÙ SÁXI
ÙXÌ LAA NDATO CHÁNÍ
KÙTAKU ÀNE'ECHOOS XÍKÁ VE'E
ÑÓCHÍ CHÁ NÍKÉE KAMA
ÍÑÒ ÑA'Á MIÍ VA'A PÁ'A DJAMA
NDIDJI NDÙ'Ú NDÌÍNI SÀNDITA

MLLR is based on the assumption that a set of linear transformations can be used to reduce the mismatch between an initial acoustic model set and the adaptation data. In this case, these transformations were applied to the mean and variance parameters of the Gaussian mixtures of the Mixtec baseline HMMs, being performed in two steps with the module *HERest* of the HTK software.

(i) Global adaptation: a global base class was used to specify the set of HMM components that share the same transformation. A first execution of *HERest* was performed to generate a global transformation that was applied to every Gaussian component of the baseline HMMs.

(ii) Dynamic adaptation: in the second execution of *HERest*, the global transformation was used as an input transformation to adapt the model set, producing better frame/state alignments which were then used to estimate a set of more specific transformations by using a regression class tree. For this work, the regression class tree had 32 terminal nodes [30] and was constructed with the module *HHEd*. The regression class tree is important to cluster together components that are close in acoustic space, so they can be transformed in similar way. Thus, the transformations obtained with the second execution of *HERest* were more specific to certain groupings of Gaussian components and were estimated according to the "amount" and "type" of adaptation data that was available (see Table 4). Because each Gaussian component of an HMM belongs to one particular base class, the tying of each transformation across a number of mixture components can be used to adapt distributions for which there were no observations at all. With this process all models can be adapted, and the adaptation process is dynamically refined when more adaptation data becomes available [30].

4.2. Mixtec-to-Spanish/Spanish-to-Mixtec Speech Translators.
The baseline Mixtec ASR was integrated into two translation systems as shown in Figure 9. The baseline Mexican Spanish ASR system was also built with a native speaker, following the phonetic definitions of the Master in Hispanic Linguistics Javier Octavio Cuétara [25] (see Mexbet in Table 2). The details of this system, with the same elements as the Mixtec ASR system, are freely available in [32] and thus will not be reviewed in this paper. Instead, the details of the translation systems will be explained.

Speech translation is a difficult area of research as there are systematic, idiosyncratic, and lexical differences (translation divergences) between source and target languages [28]. Hence, direct translation (word by word) can lead to unsatisfactory results. For this work, the approach of statistical machine translation (MT) with weighted finite state transducers (WFSTs) was used [28, 33, 34]. In the Statistical MT, translation is performed from a source language S to a target language T where the best translated sentence into the target language $\widehat{T}$ is the one whose probability $\Pr(T \mid S)$ is the highest. Based on the noisy channel model and the Bayes' rule [28], $\widehat{T}$ can be estimated as

$$
\begin{aligned}
\widehat{T} &= \arg\max_{T} \Pr(T \mid S) = \arg\max_{T} \frac{\Pr(S \mid T)\Pr(T)}{\Pr(S)} \\
&= \arg\max_{T} \Pr(S \mid T)\Pr(T).
\end{aligned}
\tag{5}
$$

From (5), $\Pr(S \mid T)$ is termed the *translation model* and $\Pr(T)$ the *language model* of the target language. For the Mixtec (X) to Spanish (P) translator $S \rightarrow X$ and $T \rightarrow P$, and (5) becomes

$$
\begin{aligned}
\widehat{P} &= \arg\max_{P} \Pr(P \mid X) = \arg\max_{P} \frac{\Pr(X \mid P)\Pr(P)}{\Pr(X)} \\
&= \arg\max_{P} \Pr(X \mid P)\Pr(P).
\end{aligned}
\tag{6}
$$

The following transducers were defined to compute the elements of (6):

(i) X, the sequence of words of the incoming sentence in Mixtec (for the Spanish-to-Mixtec translator, the incoming sequence is P);

(ii) TM_{XP}, the translation model, which maps the sequences of words from X to the most representative words in P, which depends on $\Pr(X \mid P)$ (for the Spanish-to-Mixtec translator, the model is TM_{PX});

(iii) P, the language model $\Pr(P)$, which is estimated from the word-bigram language model of the Spanish translations of the Mixtec narratives. For the Spanish-to-Mixtec translator, the language model $\Pr(X)$ consists of the one estimated from the Mixtec speech corpus as presented in Section 4.1.

Thus, the Mixtec-to-Spanish process of estimating the most probable sequence of words $\widehat{P}$ given X can be expressed as

$$
\widehat{P} = \tau^{*}\left(X \circ \text{TM}_{XP} \circ P\right).
\tag{7}
$$

In contrast, the Spanish-to-Mixtec process of estimating $\widehat{X}$ given P can be expressed as

$$
\widehat{X} = \tau^{*}\left(P \circ \text{TM}_{PX} \circ X\right).
\tag{8}
$$

In (7) and (8), τ^{*} denotes the operation of finding the most likely path through a transducer and $\circ$ denotes composition of transducers [34]. It is important to observe that the translation systems were restricted by the stored vocabulary of the Mixtec speech corpus. Thus, the language model of the baseline Spanish Mexican ASR system consisted of the Spanish translation of the Mixtec narratives. The translation from Mixtec to Spanish was assisted by Professor Maximino for the modelling of $\Pr(X \mid P)$ and $\Pr(P \mid X)$. The probabilities of the translation models were estimated by counting single and multiple word alignments between Mixtec and Spanish words following the *phrase alignment* approach described in [28]. The probabilities of the word bigram language models were also estimated by counting.

In Figures 10 and 11 some graphic examples of the translation model are shown. In Figure 10, "ña'á" means "woman" and if followed by "djí'í" (with a probability of 0.0625) then means "wife". In this case, one ("ña'á") and two ("ña'á djí'í") words in the source language are aligned to a single word in the target language ("woman", "wife"). Thus, some words combine their meanings to form concepts that relates to them. For example, "ùxì" means "ten"; however if it is followed by "ín", which means "one", then the meaning becomes "eleven". The same applies to "school" which is translated from "ve'e" ("house") and "ká'avi" ("to study") (e.g., house to study). Something similar happens to verb tenses as presented in Figure 11. A fragment of the real translation model transducer for the Mixtec-to-Spanish translator is shown in Figure 12 (for visibility purposes the probabilities were removed).

The definitions of the transducers for the Spanish-to-Mixtec translator were performed following the same methodology for the Mixtec-to-Spanish translator. Thus, they will not be discussed in this section. Finally, the implementation tool for the transducers was the FSM Library [34, 35] from AT&T, and for computational convenience, all probabilities were converted into logarithmic probabilities.

4.3. Graphical User Interfaces. In Figure 13 the main window of the speech interface for the applications of the Mixtec and Spanish ASR systems is shown. The programming platform was MATLAB 2008 using the GUIDE toolbox. There are two main panels: "Adaptación de Usuario" (Speaker Adaptation) and "Reconocedor y Traductor de Voz" (Speech Recognizer and Translator).

The first panel has two buttons, where each one leads to a module to perform adaptation of the associated baseline ASR system for its use by a new non-native speaker. Thus, the button "Para Mixteco" (For Mixtec) opens the window shown in Figure 14, and the button "Para Español" (For Spanish) opens the window shown in Figure 15.

The adaptation modules work as follows: in both Figures 14 and 15, there are two fields, "Escribe Nombre de Usuario", (Write Name of the User) and "Selecciona Usuario" (Select User), which are set to register a new user to start the adaptation process. When the user writes his/her name in the field "Escribe Nombre de Usuario" the interface updates the list of the pop-up menu "Selecciona Usuario" and creates the directories to store the MLLR transformations. If the user is already registered, an informative message is shown. Once this task is finished the user can proceed to record

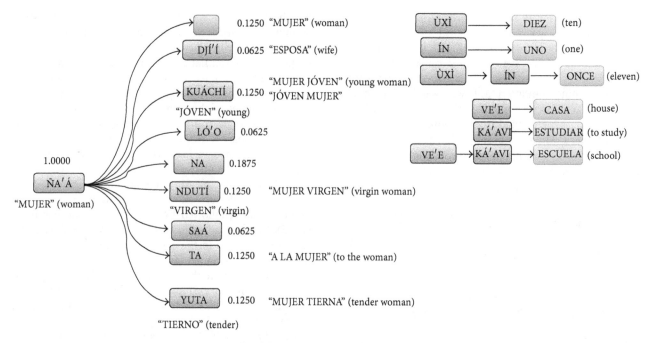

FIGURE 10: Example of the Mixtec-to-Spanish translation model (TM_{XP}).

FIGURE 11: Example of verb tenses in the Mixtec-to-Spanish translation model (TM_{XP}).

the adaptation data, which is shown on each of the buttons located under these fields. For both Mixtec and Spanish, the stimuli consist of 16 sentences. Note that in Figure 14 the adaptation sentences defined in Table 4 are shown.

As the interfaces are considered for non-native speakers of the Mixtec language, the stimuli buttons of Figure 14 are accompanied by a button labelled "Escuchar" (Listen). The user by pressing that button can listen to the native pronunciation of the associated stimuli sentence as support to practice the pronunciation before recording the adaptation speech. The speech is recorded, by pressing the stimuli button, where one click starts the recording and another finishes it. After all sentences are recorded the user just needs to press "Realiza Adaptación" (Perform Adaptation) to perform MLLR adaptation of the HMMs of the baseline ASR. The adapted models and transformations are stored (or updated) into the personal directories of the user. After the adaptation process some information about the performance of the (now) speaker-adaptive system is shown. Under "Precisión del Reconocedor Base" (Accuracy of the Baseline Recognizer) the performance of the unadapted baseline is shown, while the performance of the adapted baseline is shown under "Precisión del Reconocedor Adaptado" (Accuracy of the Adapted Recognizer). The metric of performance for the ASR

systems is the percentage of word recognition accuracy, Acc, which is computed as

$$\text{Acc} = \frac{N - D - S - I}{N} \times 100. \tag{9}$$

In (9), D, S, and I are deletion, substitution, and insertion errors in the recognized speech (text output of the ASR system). N is the number of words in the correct ASR's output [30]. As presented in Figure 14, the unadapted ASR system achieved an accuracy of 44.62% on the adaptation stimuli, and 93.85% after the system was adapted with the spoken stimuli for the non-native speaker Omar.

The second panel of the main window has also two buttons, "Mixteco-Español" (Mixtec-Spanish) and "Español-Mixteco" (Spanish-Mixtec), where each one leads to the associated translator, which are shown in Figures 16 and 17. By pressing the "Mixteco-Español" the window shown in Figure 16 is loaded, which enables Mixtec speech recognition, translation to Mexican Spanish, and text-to-speech synthesis. Initially the user must select his/her name in the pop-up menu "Selecciona Usuario" (Select User). When doing this, the MLLR transformations and directories for that user are loaded. Then, by pressing "Traducción de Voz" (Speech Translation) the interface starts to record the speech of the

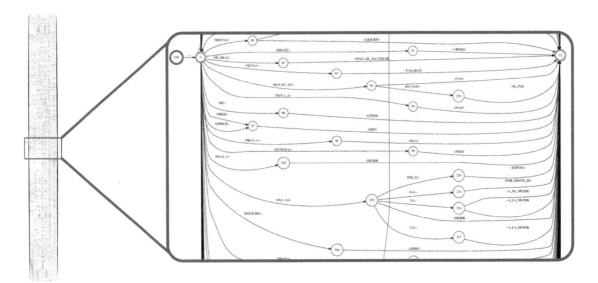

FIGURE 12: Fragment of the TM$_{XP}$ transducer.

FIGURE 13: Main window of the speech interface with the Mixtec ASR system.

user which has non-native Mixtec pronunciation. When the user finishes, he/she just needs to press again the button "Traducción de Voz". This starts the recognition process, which displays under the button the recognized Mixtec words (in this case, "ñuu yukutoón"). Then, internally, the interface converts this string (X) into a format suitable for its composition with the TM$_{XP}$ and P transducers and manages the FSM Library to perform this task and provide the most likely translation $\widehat{P}$ which is also displayed (in this case, "el pueblo de Tilantongo" = "the town of Tilantongo"). $\widehat{P}$ is then given to a speech synthesizer which "reads" these words. For this purpose the Windows XP Speech Application Programming Interface (SAPI) ver 5.0 and the Spanish voice Isabel from ScanSoft were used.

In addition to this function, the user can get access to all the Mixtec narratives by pressing the buttons "1–7" located at the bottom of the window under "Lecciones de Mixteco" (Mixtec Lessons). In Figure 16 the lesson or narrative "3" was selected. There, each button plays a sentence of the narrative which is spoken by the native speaker, and next to them the associated Spanish translation is shown. The same lessons can be accessed from the Spanish-to-Mixtec translator shown in Figure 17. Finally, the user also can access a Mixtec-to-Spanish dictionary by pressing the button "Diccionario Mixteco Español" which lists all Mixtec words in the speech corpus and their equivalents in Spanish.

5. Performance of the Speech Applications Built with the Speech Corpus

Initially the Mixtec ASR system was tested with the training speech corpus to analyze its performance for classification of known data. For the recognition task a scale grammar factor of 10 was used as mentioned in Section 4.1.3. A word recognition accuracy (9) of 97.85% ($N = 931, D = 0, S = 10, I = 10$) was obtained, which is considered high and normal considering that ASR is performed on the training data [30]. This word output was then transcribed at the phonetic level to analyze the performance of phoneme recognition. For this task, the original phonetic labels of the corpus were compared with the phonetic transcription of the word output. In Figure 18 the phoneme confusion matrix obtained from this comparison is presented. Observe that, because no words were deleted in the word output, there are no deleted phonemes in the transcription, and thus, the entries in the column "Del" (Deletions) are zero. In contrast, there are entries in the row "Ins" (Insertions) because in the word

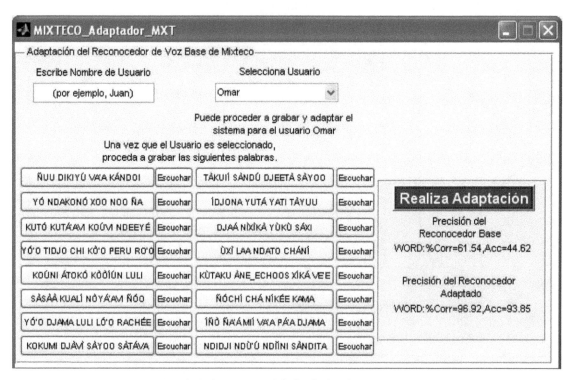

FIGURE 14: Speaker adaptation module for the baseline Mixtec ASR system.

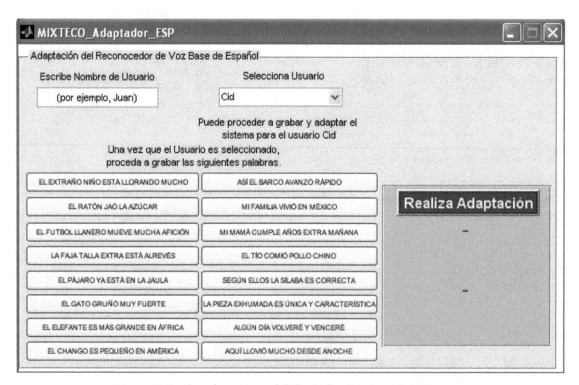

FIGURE 15: Speaker adaptation module for the baseline Spanish ASR system.

output there were inserted words ($I = 10$). Substitution of phonemes (misclassification) is almost non-existent because $S = 10$ and $N = 931$ in the word output. In general, the phoneme recognition accuracy was of 99.10% ($N = 3655$, $D = 0$, $S = 22$, $I = 11$) which is considered important to

demonstrate that the modelling of the Mixtec phonemes by the baseline ASR was performed satisfactorily.

Now the tests of the ASR applications on the speech of different users are discussed. Ten non-native speakers, five males (M) and five females (F), were recruited to test

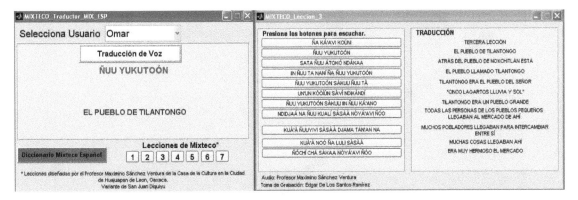

Figure 16: Mixtec-to-Spanish speech translator.

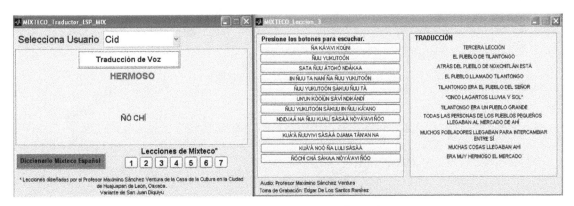

Figure 17: Spanish-to-Mixtec speech translator.

the performance of the ASR applications. Prior to using the speech interfaces for adaptation and recognition/translation, all speakers received three hours of informative sessions which were distributed over three days. In these sessions, information about the pronunciation of the Mixtec words from the 7 narratives, including the audios from the native speaker, was reviewed.

After the informative sessions, the speakers used the adaptation interfaces (see Figures 14 and 15) to perform registration and MLLR adaptation. Then, they proceeded to use the recognition/translation interfaces (see Figures 16 and 17). In total, five test sessions were performed, which consisted in the speakers reading three narratives or lessons with different levels of difficulty: 1 (easy level), 3 (medium level), and 6 (hard level). The test narratives in Mixtec were separated into 49 sentences with a total of 202 words, while the narratives in Spanish were separated into 48 sentences with a total of 210 words. The metric of performance of the speech recognizers was the word recognition accuracy (see (9)). The results are presented in Figures 19 and 20 for both recognition systems.

For the speaker adaptive Mixtec ASR, mean recognition accuracies are within the range of 88.81%–93.07% for the female speakers and within 90.79%–95.64% for the male speakers, achieving a total of 90.79%–94.36%. The mean variability in performance, measured by the standard deviation, across the test sessions is slightly higher for the male speakers than for the female speakers (1.86 > 1.58). On the other hand,

for the Mexican Spanish ASR system the mean accuracies are higher, being within the range of 92.19%–94.29% for the female speakers, and 94.10%–96.00% for the male speakers. Consistently, although very slightly, the variability across sessions is higher for the male speakers (0.96 > 0.90). Nevertheless both performances are comparable to human transcription (96%–98%) and commercial ASR for non-native/indigenous speech with vocabularies <1000 words (80%–96%) [36].

Note that performance variability is significantly higher for the Mixtec system (1.44 > 0.84), which may be due to the system being used by non-native speakers (who are natives of the other system). However the performance observed in the Mixtec system is very similar across all test sessions to the Spanish Mexican system, and both correlate to each other with a coefficient of 0.682.

For a metric to measure the quality of a translation, there are many techniques as the translation word error rate (TWER) and the character error rate (CER) [33]. For this work, TWER was used for the assessment of the translations. TWER is defined as the minimum number of word substitution, deletion, and insertion operations required to convert the target sentence provided by the translation system into the reference translation, divided by the number of words of the reference translation. For the Mixtec-to-Spanish and Spanish-to-Mixtec translators, the reference translations are shown next to each lesson (see Figures 16 and 17). Hence, while identifying the deletion, substitution, and deletion

Recognized phonemes (ASR output)

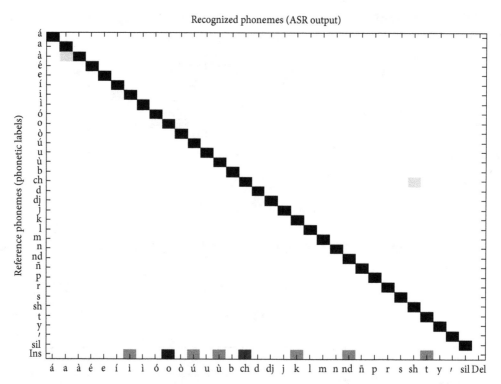

FIGURE 18: Phoneme confusion matrix of the baseline Mixtec ASR system on the training speech corpus.

Test speakers	Gender	Mean accuracy					Standard deviation
		TS1	TS2	TS3	TS4	TS5	
5	F	88.81	90.50	91.19	93.07	91.78	1.58
5	M	92.77	92.67	90.79	95.64	91.49	1.86
Total average		90.79	91.58	90.99	94.36	91.63	1.44

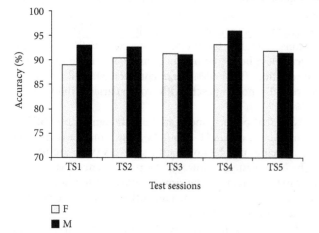

FIGURE 19: Accuracy of the speaker-adaptive Mixtec ASR system.

Test speakers	Gender	Mean accuracy					Standard deviation
		TS1	TS2	TS3	TS4	TS5	
5	F	92.19	92.48	93.90	93.43	94.29	0.90
5	M	94.10	94.10	94.29	96.00	95.81	0.96
Total average		93.14	93.29	94.10	94.71	95.05	0.84

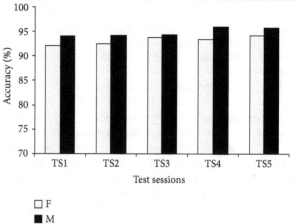

FIGURE 20: Accuracy of the speaker-adaptive Mexican Spanish ASR system.

errors in the recognition tasks (to measure the accuracy), the same kind of errors was identified to assess the TWER. In Tables 5 and 6 the mean TWERs of the Mixtec-to-Spanish and Spanish-to-Mixtec translators are presented. The TWERs are slightly higher for the Mixtec translations, although in general these are less than 20%, which is within the ranges reported by other computer-assisted translation systems [33].

Both results correlate to each other with a coefficient of 0.57379.

The results in Table 5 were compared with those presented in Figure 19. It was assumed that high recognition accuracy was needed to get good translation levels (low

TABLE 5: TWER of the Mixtec-to-Spanish translator.

Source: Mixtec		Target: Mexican Spanish					
Test speakers	Gender	Mean TWER					Standard deviation
		TS1	TS2	TS3	TS4	TS5	
5	F	19.90	18.86	18.67	18.38	19.33	0.60
5	M	18.29	18.95	17.81	17.05	17.24	0.78
	Total average	19.10	18.90	18.24	17.71	18.29	0.56

TABLE 6: TWER of the Spanish-to-Mixtec translator.

Source: Mexican Spanish		Target: Mixtec					
Test speakers	Gender	Mean TWER					Standard deviation
		TS1	TS2	TS3	TS4	TS5	
5	F	20.59	19.80	18.61	20.40	19.01	0.86
5	M	18.81	19.50	18.91	18.22	19.31	0.50
	Total average	19.70	19.65	18.76	19.31	19.16	0.39

TWERs), although this is also dependent on the translation model. The results in Table 5 correlate to the recognition accuracies presented in Figure 19 with a coefficient of −0.62237, indicating a significant inverse relationship. The same was obtained when the results in Table 6 were compared with those in Figure 20, obtaining a correlation coefficient of −0.72027. Thus there is a significant relationship between low TWER and high ASR accuracy.

6. Conclusions and Future Work

In this paper the development of a Mixtec speech corpus and two speech applications (built with this resource) was presented. The development of speech corpora is very challenging for the Mixtec language given the high diversity of tones, alphabets, and vocabulary, which vary among regions. Also because of the almost non-existent formal knowledge of the native speakers about the grammar, syntax, and writing rules of their Mixtec language variation. Hence, although there are many people who speak the language, they do not know how to write it or read it, and this restricts greatly the development of speech corpora and also other means to preserve the language.

Hence, only native professional linguists could be suitable to develop the resource. However the availability of people with this background, or with formal knowledge, is not broad, which makes it very difficult to develop large speech corpora. The problem had to be delimited, and thus, it was considered to focus on a single variant and one native speaker with knowledge to ensure accurate phonetic and orthographic labelling of native speech samples for purposes of developing speech applications.

The steps followed to develop the single-speaker corpus were presented in Sections 2 and 3, and in order to test its usefulness as a resource for the development of ASR systems, two applications were developed: a speaker-adaptive Mixtec ASR system and a Mixtec-to-Spanish/Spanish-to-Mixtec translator. These were presented in Section 4, and

the results presented in Section 5 give confidence about the attainable use of the corpus for other applications as language learning interfaces.

With recognition accuracies up to 94% across different test sessions with ten non-native speakers, the developed applications can be used for basic learning activities. For formal language learning tasks, the approach must be different in order to assess the pronunciation of a non-native speaker, and it would be essential to have native speech data from female speakers. On the other hand, the translation between Spanish and Mixtec showed TWERs around 20%, which are within ranges of well-documented computer-assisted translation performance. The translation field is as difficult as the recognition field, and for the Mixtec language much more work is needed to develop robust performance for larger vocabularies and different variations. However, the advances presented in this paper can be used as starting point for future researchers in Mixtec or other under resourced languages.

Among the ongoing and future work, the following can be mentioned:

(i) to develop techniques to increase the performance of the native speaker-adaptive (SA) ASR system (when acoustic resources are limited for supervised training);

(ii) to increase the training speech corpus: add more vocabulary words and increase the complexity to the narratives, recruit more native speakers (both genders) in order to develop a native SI ASR system, and test the system with more users with different levels of expertise in the Mixtec language (preferably native speakers);

(iii) to improve the GUI to increase usability: incorporate learning methodologies to extend the use of the ASR system for users that do not have previous knowledge of the language (with no informative sessions) and integrate a measure of performance for the level of knowledge or practicing that the user gets by using the speech application;

(iv) to extend the modelling of the grammar rules of the translation and language models to reduce TWER in the translation systems;

(v) to develop a TTS synthesizer for the Mixtec variant of San Juan Diquiyú.

Acknowledgments

The author wishes to thank Professor Maximino Sánchez Ventura from the local Cultural Center of the city of Huajuapan de León in Oaxaca, Mexico, and Professor Gabriel Caballero from the Technological University of the Mixteca, for their support for the development of this work. This work was partially funded by the Mexican Ministry of Public Education (Secretaria de Educación Pública (SEP)) under the Teacher Improvement Program (Programa de Mejoramiento del Profesorado (PROMEP)), Project UTMIX-PTC-019.

References

[1] IBM, "Embedded ViaVoice," 2012, http://www-01.ibm.com/software/pervasive/embedded_viavoice/.

[2] Nuance, "Dragon Speech Recognition Software," 2012, http://www.nuance.com/dragon/index.htm.

[3] Philips, "SpeechExec Pro Transcribe," 2012, http://www.dictation.philips.com/products-solutions/product/speechexec_transcription_software/.

[4] Carnegie Mellon University: The Interactive Systems Laboratories. JANUS Speech Translation System, 2012, http://www.is.cs.cmu.edu/mie/janus.html.

[5] W. Wahlster, "Mobile speech-to-speech translation of spontaneous dialogs: an overview of the final Verbmobil system," in Verbmobil: Foundations of Speech-to-Speech Translation, W. Wahlster, Ed., Springer, Berlin, Germany, 2000.

[6] M. Parker, S. Cunningham, P. Enderby, M. Hawley, and P. Green, "Automatic speech recognition and training for severely dysarthric users of assistive technology: the STARDUST project," Clinical Linguistics and Phonetics, vol. 20, no. 2-3, pp. 149–156, 2006.

[7] M. Hawley, S. Cunningham, F. Cardinaux et al., "Challenges in developing a voice input voice output communication aid for people with severe dysarthria," in Proceedings of European Conference for the Advancement of Assistive Technology in Europe, 2007.

[8] J. Dalby and D. Kewley-Port, "Explicit pronunciation training using automatic speech recognition technology," Computer-Assisted Language Instruction Consortium, vol. 16, no. 3, 1999.

[9] English Computerized Learning Inc, "Pronunciation Power Speech Test," 2012, http://www.englishlearning.com/products/pronunciation-power-speech-test/.

[10] Lesson Nine GmbH, "Babbel," 2012, http://es.babbel.com/#Reconocimiento-de-voz.

[11] Rosetta Stone, "Rosetta Stone Version 4 TOTALe," 2012, http://www.rosettastone.com/.

[12] S. Cox, M. Lincoln, J. Tryggvason et al., "The development and evaluation of a speech-to-sign translation system to assist transactions," International Journal of Human-Computer Interaction, vol. 16, no. 2, pp. 141–161, 2003.

[13] Instituto Nacional de Estadística y Geografía (INEGI), "Hablantes de Lengua Indígena en México," 2012, http://cuentame.inegi.org.mx/poblacion/lindigena.aspx?tema=P.

[14] Academia de la Lengua Mixteca, Bases para la Escritura de tu'un savi, Colección Diálogos, Pueblos Originarios de Oaxaca, México, 2007.

[15] D. Mindek, Mixtecos: Pueblos Indígenas del México Contemporáneo, Comisión Nacional para el Desarrollo de los Pueblos Indígenas, 2003.

[16] J. Ferguson de Williams, Gramática Popular del Mixteco del Municipio de Tezoatlán, San Andrés Yutatío, Oaxaca, Instituto Lingüístico de Verano, 2007.

[17] K. Beaty de Farris, P. García, R. García, J. Ojeda, A. García, and A. Santiago, Diccionario Básico del Mixteco de Yosondúa, Oaxaca, Instituto Lingüístico de Verano, 2004.

[18] S. Stark, A. Johnson, and B. González de Guzmán, Diccionario Básico del Mixteco de Xochapa, Guerrero, Instituto Lingüístico de Verano, 2003.

[19] Instituto Nacional de Lenguas Indígenas, Catálogo de las Lenguas Indígenas Nacionales: Variantes Lingüísticas de México con sus autodenominaciones y referencias geoestadísticas, 2008, http://www.inali.gob.mx/pdf/CLIN_completo.pdf.

[20] Instituto Lingüístico de Verano en México, Familia Mixteca, 2012, http://www-01.sil.org/mexico/mixteca/00e-mixteca.htm.

[21] R. M. Alexander, Mixteco de Atatlahuca, Instituto Lingüístico de Verano, 1980.

[22] L. Anderson and R. Alejandro, Vocabulario de los Verbos de Movimiento y de Carga: Mixteco de Alacatlatzala, Guerrero, Instituto Lingüístico de Verano, 1999, http://www.sil.org/americas/mexico/mixteca/alacatlatzala/P001-Vocab-MIM.pdf.

[23] A. García and R. Miguel, Nadakua'a Ndo Tee Ndo Tu'un Ndo: Aprendamos a Escribir Nuestro Idioma, Instituto Lingüístico de Verano, 1998.

[24] M. Morales and J. North, Ná Cahví Tuhun Ndáhv Ta Ná Cahyí Ña: Vamos a Leer y Escribir en Mixteco (Mixteco de Silacayoapan, Oaxaca), Instituto Lingüístico de Verano, 2000.

[25] J. Cuétara, Fonética de la Ciudad de México: Aportaciones desde las Tecnologías del Habla [MSc. Dissertation], National Autonomous University of México (UNAM), 2004.

[26] L. A. Pineda, L. Villaseñor, J. Cuétara et al., "The Corpus DIMEx100: transcription and evaluation," Language Resources and Evaluation, vol. 44, no. 4, pp. 347–370, 2010.

[27] P. Green, M. Hawley, P. Enderby et al., "STARDUST speech training and recognition for dysarthric users of assistive technology," in Proceedings of Association for the Advancement of Assistive Technology in Europe (AAATE '03), 2003.

[28] D. Jurafsky and J. H. Martin, Speech and Language Processing, Pearson: Prentice Hall, Upper Saddle River, NJ, USA, 2009.

[29] L. R. Rabiner, "Tutorial on hidden Markov models and selected applications in speech recognition," Proceedings of the IEEE, vol. 77, no. 2, pp. 257–286, 1989.

[30] S. Young and P. Woodland, The HTK Book (For HTK Version 3.4), Cambridge University Engineering Department, Cambridge, UK, 2006.

[31] C. J. Leggetter and P. C. Woodland, "Maximum likelihood linear regression for speaker adaptation of continuous density hidden Markov models," Computer Speech and Language, vol. 9, no. 2, pp. 171–185, 1995.

[32] G. Bonilla-Enríquez and S. O. Caballero-Morales, "Communication interface for mexican spanish dysarthric speakers," Acta Universitaria, vol. 22, no. NE-1, pp. 98–105, 2012.

[33] J. Civera, E. Cubel, A. Lagarda et al., "Computer assisted translation using finite state transducers," *Procesamiento del Lenguaje Natural*, vol. 35, pp. 357–363, 2005.

[34] M. Mohri, F. Pereira, and M. Riley, "Weighted finite-state transducers in speech recognition," *Computer Speech and Language*, vol. 16, no. 1, pp. 69–88, 2002.

[35] M. Mohri, *Weighted Finite-State Transducer Software Library— Lecture*, 2007, http://www.cs.nyu.edu/~mohri/asr07/lecture_2 .pdf.

[36] National Institute of Standards and Technology (NIST), *The History of Automatic Speech Recognition Evaluations at NIST*, 2009, http://www.itl.nist.gov/iad/mig/publications/ASRhistory/index.html.

3

Compositional Mining of Multiple Object API Protocols through State Abstraction

Ziying Dai,[1] Xiaoguang Mao,[1] Yan Lei,[1] Yuhua Qi,[1] Rui Wang,[1] and Bin Gu[2]

[1] *School of Computer, National University of Defense Technology, Changsha 410073, China*
[2] *Beijing Institute of Control Engineering, Beijing 100190, China*

Correspondence should be addressed to Xiaoguang Mao; xgmao@nudt.edu.cn

Academic Editors: S. H. Rubin, S. Saini, Y. Takama, and Y. Zhu

API protocols specify correct sequences of method invocations. Despite their usefulness, API protocols are often unavailable in practice because writing them is cumbersome and error prone. Multiple object API protocols are more expressive than single object API protocols. However, the huge number of objects of typical object-oriented programs poses a major challenge to the automatic mining of multiple object API protocols: besides maintaining scalability, it is important to capture various object interactions. Current approaches utilize various heuristics to focus on small sets of methods. In this paper, we present a general, scalable, multiple object API protocols mining approach that can capture all object interactions. Our approach uses abstract field values to label object states during the mining process. We first mine single object typestates as finite state automata whose transitions are annotated with states of interacting objects before and after the execution of the corresponding method and then construct multiple object API protocols by composing these annotated single object typestates. We implement our approach for Java and evaluate it through a series of experiments.

1. Introduction

In object-oriented programs, programmers write code by invoking various application programming interfaces (APIs). In general, not all method invocation sequences are legal. There are constraints on the temporal order of invocations of related methods. For example, programmers should not *write* into a file after it has been *closed*. *API protocols* specify which API method call sequences are allowed. API protocols are very useful in many software engineering activities. They can aid the generation of test cases [1]. Program verification tools can use API protocols as input to prove the absence of protocol violations [2, 3], and program analysis tools can use them to find certain errors [4–7]. In addition, formal specifications including temporal API specifications can support the understanding of correct software behavior [8], which is central to software maintenance.

As writing API protocols is cumbersome and requires expert knowledge of corresponding APIs, they are often missing, incomplete, or out of date despite their usefulness. To address this problem, researchers have developed specification mining techniques to mine API protocols from API

client programs [9–17]. Many existing approaches focus on API protocols of single objects [14–16]. However, an object is not isolated; they interact by invoking each other's methods. Single object protocols are too restrictive because some API protocols can only be expressed by specifying multiple interacting objects. For instance, we must consider a collection and its iterator together to specify one of their safety properties that the contents of the collection should not be modified while its iterator is being used. Experiments in previous work [6] show that 41% of the detected issues can be only found with multiple object protocols.

According to the *information hiding* principle of object-oriented software engineering, states of an object should only be accessed and modified through the methods defined in this object's interface. Since objects interact by invoking each other's methods, the receiver object of a method invocation typically interacts with the method's parameter objects and return object if any. Moreover, objects can transitively affect other objects' behavior. As methods typically receive parameters as input and produce a return, object interactions are common. There are possible hundreds of millions of objects during the execution of realistic programs. For dynamic analysis approaches, the input trace data is usually very large (e.g., more than 240 million runtime events [10] and more than 98 million runtime events [11]). These objects compose a large and complex *interaction net*, which poses a major challenge to the mining of multiple object API protocols. On the one hand, we should consider all object interactions to mine precise and complete specifications. On the other hand, large sets of interacting objects lead to very high computational overhead that compromises the usefulness of the specification mining approach.

Typestates [18] are intended for capturing API protocols. The observation behind typestates is that whether an operation is available on an object depends not only on the type of the object but also its internal states. Researchers develop several typestate systems for object-oriented programs [19, 20]. State abstraction techniques to mine typestates based on explicit object states [14, 15] have been proven effective to mine useful API protocols of single objects. The main idea of these techniques is to use abstract values of object fields (or returns of the *observer* methods) to label states during the mining process. In this paper, we apply the idea of state abstraction to mine API protocols of multiple interacting objects. Our insight is that by labelled object states, we can conveniently identify the order of method invocations from different objects. We give a clear definition of *object interactions* based on the type definitions of objects, and it can capture all interacting objects. Based on this definition, our miner first mines single object typestates as finite state machines (FSMs) whose states are labelled by abstract field values and whose transitions are labelled with explicit states of interacting objects before and after the execution of the corresponding methods. Second, our miner extracts the typestates of the declared types (maybe concrete super types of the runtime types of objects or even abstract types) of parameters and returns of methods from the typestates of their implementing subtypes. Then, our miner products typestate FSMs of interacting objects without violations of the interacting constraints annotated with transitions of single object typestates. At last, state labels are discarded, and we get multiple object API protocols. The most important feature of our miner is that each object is mined separately without considering methods of other objects, which guarantees the scalability of our approach. The naive product of the typestate FSMs of different objects cannot capture the constraints of object interactions because the product allows arbitrary interleavings of method invocations from different objects.

Previous work on mining multiple object API protocols employs various approaches to cope with this challenge [10, 11, 13, 17, 21, 22]. In order to reduce the complexity of the analysis of object interactions, they utilize various heuristics to focus on small sets of related objects and methods and then mine subtraces of these related events by commonly used specification inference techniques. Pradel and Gross [10] present the method-centric approach that runtime events issued during a method's execution are assumed to be related to each other. Nguyen et al. [22] also confines interacting objects to the source code of a single method. Lee et al. [11] propose the event specification approach that methods involved in a unit test run are assumed to be interacting

with each other. Yang et al. [17] and Nguyen et al. [21] utilize the predefined small specification templates such as the alternating pattern over event pairs to mine simple patterns dynamically and statically, respectively. Gabel and Su [13] first mine small patterns based on the predefined simple templates and then use inference rules to compose them to construct complex properties. These approaches are shown to be able to mine useful protocols. However, because the potential interactions with an object are determined by the type definition (e.g., signatures of methods) of the object, there may be some unpreferred object interactions that are filtered out. These approaches exchange some object interactions for the scalability. In contrast, our approach can capture all object interactions that manifest during runtime and scalably mine arbitrarily complex multiple object API protocols by composing the typestates of single objects.

The rest of this paper is organized as follows. Section 2 introduces the background of object-oriented typestate systems and discusses their drawbacks when they are used to formalize API protocols. Section 3 discusses our approach to mining multiple object API protocols by composing typestates of single objects. Section 4 describes our implementation for Java and presents the experimental evaluation of our approach. Section 5 discusses related work, and Section 6 concludes.

2. Background: Object-Oriented Typestates

The formalism of multiple object API protocols mined in this paper is inspired by the object specifications of several existing object-oriented typestate systems [19, 20]. Because typestates reflect how state changes of objects can affect valid method invocations, a typestate is an abstraction over concrete object states and can be characterized by the values of all fields of an object. Typestates are mapped onto the fields of the implementing class by defining a predicate for each typestate, called a *state invariant*, which can be any boolean combination of state tests, state comparisons, integer comparisons, boolean constants and fields. The substitutability of subtypes for super types is preserved by the *state refinement* that a subtype can define a set of substates as special cases of an existing state. The specification of a method can be changed through the *method refinement*. A method can be respecified more precisely in a subtype based on the refined substates. The main role of typestates is to specify methods. Equation (1) gives a simplified method specification language for typestates of object-oriented programs:

$$M := C \mid M \land M,$$
$$C := V \longrightarrow V, \qquad (1)$$
$$V := (s_1, \ldots, s_n).$$

A method is specified with an intersection of cases, which means that all these cases hold. A *case* represents a state transition which is denoted as $A \longrightarrow B$ to express that a method requires a source state A and produces a destination state B. The source state is a vector consisting of the states of the receiver of the method and its arguments (in their order in the signature). The destination state has one more state for the method's return object if any. Nondeterminism of state transitions can be expressed using the intersections of different cases. For example, $A \rightarrow B \wedge A \rightarrow C$ represents that starting at state A, executions of a method can transition to state B or state C. The state invariant is evaluated to test whether an object is in a particular state. Either statically checked [19] or dynamically checked [20], state invariants of typestates are evaluated for every method invocation: source state violations are flagged as precondition violations, and destination state violations are flagged as postcondition violations. Source states and destination states are actually treated as preconditions and postconditions of corresponding methods, respectively.

These typestate systems have been proven useful for modeling protocols in object-oriented programs [19, 20]. However, there are mainly two drawbacks of them to specify API protocols. First, it is not trivial to derive state invariants as this requires expert knowledge of underlying classes. If there is any, semantic information of APIs is mainly within informal documents and needs to be manually extracted. Second, because typestates are tagged with state invariants which rely on values of fields of corresponding classes, these typestate systems cannot specify abstract types, such as interfaces and abstract classes in Java. Abstract types usually represent high-level abstractions and obey many common and important properties. Specifications of abstract types are more clear, explicit, and compact than that of their implementing classes.

3. Technical Approach

This section discusses the details of our approach. In Section 3.1, we define several concepts to formalize the idea of typestates composition. In Section 3.2, we present how to mine single object typestates annotated with object interactions through state abstraction. In Section 3.3, we present the technique to extract typestates for super types from typestates of their implementing subclasses. In Section 3.4, we discuss how to compose single object typestates into API protocols of multiple interacting objects.

Figure 1 shows the typestates of interactions between BufferedInputStream and its wrapped InputStream mined by our approach. This is the running example throughout our paper. All classes presented as examples in this paper are from the standard APIs of the Java language except explicitly stated. These typestates capture the *resource-wrapping protocol* that closing the wrapping resource will implicitly close the wrapped resource, so the wrapped resource can not be used any more after its wrapping resource is closed. The *is* part of this figure is the typestates of InputStream and the *bis* part is that of BufferedInputStream. Because InputStream is an abstract class, we obtain its typestates by extracting submodels from typestates of its implementing type through a state-preserving submodel extraction algorithm. Directed dashed lines represent interactions between these two typestate models. The directed dashed line from state 1 of *is* to <init> of *bis* denotes that an InputStream object should be in its state 1 before passed

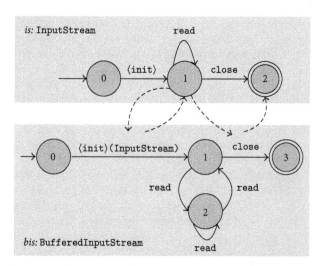

FIGURE 1: Typestates of interactions between BufferedInputStream and its wrapped InputStream mined by our approach. *is* denotes the above highlighted part of the figure, and *bis* denotes the below highlighted part of the figure.

into <init> of BufferedInputStream as the parameter. This dashed line characterizes the common usage that the <init> of BufferedInputStream follows <init> of InputStream. The directed dashed line from close of *bis* to state 2 of *is* denotes that after the execution of close of BufferedInputStream, the wrapped InputStream is in its final state 2. This dashed line specifies the safety property that the wrapped InputStream cannot be used any more after the close of its wrapping BufferedInputStream.

3.1. Approach Overview. Here we give a high-level overview of our mining approach.

Definition 1 (trace). A *trace* $T = \langle e_1, \ldots, e_n \rangle$ is a sequence of events, where an *event* $e = (s_1, m, s_2)$ is a triple, with m is the method execution, s_1 is the state of the training program just before m enters, and s_2 is the state of the training program just after m exits. For object-oriented programs, the program state is typically a set of objects each of which consists of a set of field-value pairs. We write $s.o$ as the state of o when s denotes the state of the program.

Definition 2 (interaction specification). Suppose t is a reference type (classes or interfaces in Java, excluding arrays). For every public method $t_r \ m(t_1, \ldots, t_n)$ of T, where m is the method name, t_r is the return type, and $t_1, \ldots, t_n$ are parameter types, we omit *void* and primitive types of parameters and return and only keep reference types. The *interaction specification* S_t of t is the set M of all its public methods with retained reference parameters and returns. We use P_t to denote all retained parameters and returns in S_t.

The interaction specification of a type is determined by its definition. We neither make assumptions nor employ heuristics. This is the power of our approach that it has the potential to capture all objects interacting with an object. For example,

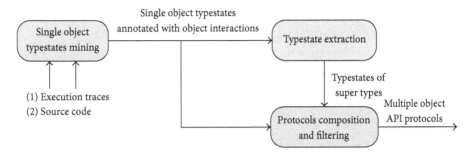

FIGURE 2: The architecture of our approach.

the interaction specification of `BufferedInputStream` is the set {`<init>` (`InputStream`), `<init>` (`InputStream`, _)} with _ as the place holder to indicate the position of each parameter. Methods that have no reference parameters and no reference return are omitted.

Definition 3 (interacting objects). During runtime, if a method is invoked, its parameters and return of reference type if any are bound to *null* or specific objects. At some point during runtime, for an object o of reference type t, its *interacting objects* (objects interacting with it) form a set O_o that includes all objects that are bound to the parameters and returns of the methods in the interaction specification of t. We define the function $b : P_t \rightarrow O_o \cup \{null\}$ to manifest the mapping between the interaction specification and the interacting objects. b involves as the program runs.

For an object, its interacting objects involve as the program runs. When a method is invoked at the first time for this object, the parameter objects and return object if any are added to O. If a method is invoked a second time, new bound objects are added to O, and old objects bound to the same parameter or return are replaced. The concept of interacting objects reflects one fact of dynamic analysis that object interactions that we can mine are limited to observed executions of underlying programs. Please note that the number of interacting objects in O for an object will not exceed the number of parameters and returns of all methods in the interaction specification of the type of this object. For example, when the method `BufferedInputStream. <Init>` enters, the interacting objects of its receiver includes only one object that is bound to its parameter `InputStream`.

Definition 4 (multiple object API protocols). *Typestates annotated with interactions* for a reference type t are a nondeterministic finite state machine (NDFSA) M with transition annotations that $M = (Q, \Sigma, \delta, \lambda, S, F)$, where Q is a finite set of states that represent abstract object states, Σ is the alphabet that consists of the methods in the interaction specification of t, δ is the transition relation that is a subset of $Q \times \Sigma \times Q$, $\lambda : \delta \rightarrow (P_t \rightarrow C)$ is the annotation function that determines the state change for each interacting object and transition in δ, where C is the set of state changes. A *state change* of one interacting object represents that the state of this object changes from one to another, which can be denoted as $s_1 \rightarrow s_2$ to express that the execution of the corresponding

method associated with this transition requires a source state s_1 and produces a destination state s_2. S is the set of start states, and F is the set of final states. *Multiple object API protocols* for a set of objects are the set of typestates annotated with interactions, among which typestates of interacting objects are composed. By *composed*, we mean that all states in the interaction annotations are mapped to corresponding states in typestates of an type.

Figure 1 presents such an example of multiple object API protocols.

Figure 2 depicts the architecture of our approach. We take two types of inputs: the first is the source code of the target APIs, that is, for the identification of interaction specifications. The second are program execution traces with recorded values of object fields. We first mine single object typestates through state abstraction. These typestates are also annotated with abstract states of interacting objects to record object interactions. We then extract the typestates for super types from typestates of their implementing subclasses. At the last step, different typestates are composed together to get the API protocols of multiple interacting objects.

3.2. Mining Single Object Typestates Annotated with Interactions. We adopt the state abstraction technique to mine single object typestates and object interactions. To produce succinct and general models, abstract field values instead of concrete ones are used to label states. We use the same state abstraction function *abs* as [15], which is as follows: values of reference fields (objects or arrays) are abstracted to *null* (=*null*) or *not null* ($\neq$ *null*), values of numerical fields are abstracted to *larger than zero* (>0), *less than zero* (<0), or *equal to zero* (=0), and values of boolean fields remain unchanged. This state abstraction approach has been proved successful in mining single object typestate models [14, 15]. Algorithm 1 presents the algorithm to mine typestates of an object with interaction annotation. We define the function $f : \delta \rightarrow (P_t \rightarrow \wp(C))$ to record all observed state changes of objects bound to a parameter or return for a transition from the beginning of the program execution to now. $\wp(C)$ denotes the power set of C. Each state change is associated with a *frequency,* that is, the number of times this state change is observed. For each event of the object o, we determine abstract states of o and all its interacting objects just before and after the invocation. We get a transition of the method that goes from the source state to the destination state of o and

---

Input: T as *trace* of events of an object o
            S as interaction specification of type t of o
            abs as the state abstract function
Output: $M = (Q, \Sigma, \delta, \lambda, S, F)$ as *typestates* for o
(1)   initialize M to be empty
(2)   **foreach** event $e = (ps_1, m, ps_2) \in T$ in the order in T **do**
(3) $s_1 = abs(ps_1.o)$
(4) $s_2 = abs(ps_2.o)$
(5)   create a transition $t = (s_1, m, s_2)$
(6) $\delta = \delta \cup t$
(7)   **foreach** interacting object o_i of o when e occurs **do**
(8) $s_i = abs(ps_1.o_i)$
(9) $s_i{'} = abs(ps_2.o_i)$
(10)   increment frequency of $s_i \rightarrow s_i{'}$ by 1
(11) $f(t)(b^{-1}(o_i)) = f(t)(b^{-1}(o_i)) \cup \{s_i \rightarrow s_i{'}\}$
(12)   **if** runtime type of o' is different from that in *IS* **then**
(13)   associate o_i to s_i and $s_i{'}$
(14)   **endif**
(15)   **endfor**
(16)   **endfor**
(17)   **foreach** $t \in \delta$ **do**
(18)   **foreach** $p \in P_t$ **do**
(19) $\lambda(t)(p) = \mathrm{MAX}(f(t)(p))$
(20)   **endfor**
(21)   **endfor**
(22)   **return** M

ALGORITHM 1: The algorithm to mine single object typestates annotated with interactions.

add it to the model M. We annotate this transition with state changes of all interacting objects of o. When the algorithm runs to the end of the trace, we determine the annotation function λ by choosing the most frequent state transition (MAX(C)) and discarding others. The typestates of a concrete class consists of the union of all states and transitions of the typestates of all its objects. The annotation function has the value of the most frequent state change for each transition and parameter or return. The approach to get typestates of a super type is discussed in Section 3.3.

A state of interacting objects within the interaction annotations is associated with a parameter or return of the method in the interaction specification. If the declared type of the parameter or return is different from the runtime type of the interacting object bound to it, we also associate this interacting object with this state. This association is requisite for later typestates composition because different implementations of a type do not necessarily have the same fields. The typestates of single objects are mined in the per object way, which is essential to make our approach scalable. The time complexity of the algorithm in Algorithm 1 is determined by the length of the trace and the complexity of the interaction specification. If the trace contains m events and the interaction specification has n parameters and returns of all its methods, the complexity of the algorithm is $O(m \times n)$.

3.3. Extracting Typestates for Super Types. Abstract types such as interfaces and abstract classes in Java and the inheritance are common in object-oriented programs. The behavior of a super type can be manifested by objects of its implementing subclasses. However, except public methods declared in the super type, its implementing subclass usually has additional public methods. These additional methods are either specific to the implementing class or belong to another super type that the class implements simultaneously. The declared types of the parameters and returns of the methods in the interaction specifications may be abstract or super types of the type of the bound interacting objects. To get the multiple object API protocols of the interaction specifications, the additional methods that do not belong to the declared types must be removed from the typestates of the interacting objects. Moreover, to enable the composition of the typestates of single objects, states in the original typestates must be preserved in the result typestates with the additional methods removed. Existing FSM transformation algorithms [23] based on the accepted languages are not applicable here. In this section, we design an algorithm to extract the typestates of a super type from the typestates of its implementing subclasses, and meanwhile the states in the original typestates are preserved.

We first formalize the problem. Assume that the typestates of a super type are $M_s = (Q_s, \Sigma_s, \delta_s, \lambda_s, S_s, F_s)$, and the typestates of one of its implementing subclass are $M = (Q, \Sigma, \delta, \lambda, S, F)$ and $\Sigma_s \subseteq \Sigma$. We define the typestate extraction function te: $\Sigma^* \rightarrow \Sigma_s^*$ as follows: (1) te(a) = a, if $a \in \Sigma_s$; (2) te(a) = ε, if $a \notin \Sigma_s$; (3) te($\omega_1\omega_2$) = te(ω_1)te(ω_2). Intuitively, the function te transforms a string into a new one that preserves only the interesting symbols in their original order. Based on te, we can formalize the typestates extraction problem as how to compute M_s from M, while $L(M_s) = \{\omega \mid \exists \omega' \in L(M), \text{ s.t. } \omega = \text{te}(\omega')\}$ and $Q_s \subseteq Q$ hold.

Input: $M = (Q, \Sigma, \delta, \lambda, S, F)$ as typestates of type t
Output: $M_s = (Q_s, \Sigma_s, \delta_s, \lambda_s, S_s, F_s)$ as typestates of super type s of t
(1)   initialize an empty FSM M_s
(2)   initialize an empty set of transitions *worker*
(3)   **foreach** $q \in S$ **do**
(4)   mark q as *visited*
(5)   **foreach** $e = (q, m, q')$ such that $m \in \Sigma_s$ **do**
(6)   add e to *worker*
(7)   **endfor**
(8)   **endfor**
(9)   **while** there is a $e = (q, m, q')$ in *worker* **do**
(10)   remove e from *worker*
(11)   **if** q' is not *visited* **then**
(12)   mark q' as *visited*
(13)   **foreach** $e' = (q', m', q'')$ such that $m' \in \Sigma_s$ **do**
(14)   add e' to *worker*
(15)   **endfor**
(16)   **endif**
(17)   **foreach** $p \in \mathrm{cl}(M, \Sigma_s, q)$ such that $p \neq q$ **do**
(18)   add (q, m, p) to M_s
(19)   **endfor**
(20)   remove duplicated transitions in M_s
(21)   return M_s
Procedure $\mathrm{cl}(M, \Sigma_s, q)$
(1)   *worker* = *result* = $\{q\}$
(2)   **while** there is a state p in *worker* **do:**
(3)   add p to *result*
(4)   remove p from *worker*
(5)   **foreach** $(p, a, r) \in \delta$ such that $a \in \Sigma - \Sigma_s$ **do:**
(6)   **if** $r \notin result$ **then:**
(7)   add r to *worker*
(8)   **endif**
(9)   **endfor**
(10)   **endwhile**
(11)   **return** *result*

ALGORITHM 2: The algorithm to extract the typestates for a super type from the typestates of its implementing subtypes.

To solve this problem, we introduce the closure function cl: $Q \rightarrow \wp(Q)$. The function cl maps a state to a set of states that are reachable from this state by following zero or more transitions with uninteresting input symbols. Formally, we define cl as follows: (1) for all $q \in Q$, $q \in \mathrm{cl}(q)$; (2) for all $p \in \mathrm{cl}(q) \wedge$ for all $a \in \Sigma - \Sigma_s$, $\delta(p, a) \in \mathrm{cl}(q)$. Now, we define the extended closure function ecl as follows:

$$\mathrm{ecl}\left(Q'\right) = \bigcup_{q \in Q'} \mathrm{cl}(q), \quad Q' \subseteq Q. \tag{2}$$

Based on cl and ecl, we formally specify $M_s = (Q_s, \Sigma_s, \delta_s, \lambda_s, S_s, F_s)$ where $Q_s \subseteq Q$, $\delta_s(q, a) = \mathrm{ecl}(\delta(q, a))$, $\lambda_s = \lambda\lceil_{\Sigma_s}$, that is, the restriction of λ to Σ_s, $S_s = \mathrm{ecl}(S)$ and $F_s = \{q \mid \mathrm{cl}(q) \cap F \neq \emptyset\}$. The most important feature of M_s is $Q_s \subseteq Q$. The algorithm to solve this problem is presented in Algorithm 2. For each transition (q, m, q') of M with $m \in \Sigma_s$, compute $\mathrm{cl}(q')$. For every state $p \in \mathrm{cl}(q')$, add a transition (q, m, p) to M_s. The worst case complexity of this algorithm is $O(m^2 \times n^2)$, where m is the number of states of the typestates and n is the number of transitions of the typestates. The complexity of this algorithm is high; however, we expect no high overhead in practice as typical typestates FSMs are small with a few tens of states and transitions.

If there are multiple implementing classes for a super type, we simply union typestates extracted from them. Such subtypestates are separate from each other, and we call them *typestates parts*. Every typestates part is tagged by the type of the implementing class where it is extracted. Simple union may produce large typestates, but we appreciate the merit that all states of different typestate parts are preserved from their implementing classes. Formally, if there are n implementing classes of a super type and the n extracted typstates parts are $M_1 = (Q_1, \Sigma, \delta_1, \lambda_1, S_1, F_1), \ldots, M_n = (Q_n, \Sigma, \delta_n, \lambda_n, S_n, F_n)$, we define the protocol of the abstract type $M = (Q, \Sigma, \delta, \lambda, S, F)$, where

$$Q = \bigcup_{i=1}^{n} Q_i, \qquad \delta = \bigcup_{i=1}^{n} \delta_i, \qquad \lambda = \bigcup_{i=1}^{n} \lambda_i,$$

$$S = \bigcup_{i=1}^{n} S_i, \qquad F = \bigcup_{i=1}^{n} F_i. \tag{3}$$

3.4. Typestates Composition and Filtering. We generate multiple object typestates by composing typestates of single objects. We perform the composition by finding the same state in corresponding typestates for every state in the interaction annotation. An algorithm to do this is presented in Algorithm 3. For a state s associated with an argument or return p in the interaction annotation of a transition, we try to identify the state s' in the typestates of the declaring type t of p that has the same field-value label as s. If t is a concrete class, s' is in the states of the typestates of this concrete class. If t is an abstract type, s' is in the states of the typestate part of the typestates of this abstract type, which is extracted from the typestates of the object associated with s'. After finding the same state for every state in interaction annotations of all typestates, we discard the labels of states and identify them by abstract names such as numbers. We assure that within typestates of a type, states with different field-value labels have different names.

Because we discard the state labels, the final multiple object typestates specify the proper order of method executions. To check the behavior of a single object, the legal method execution sequences are the strings accepted by the typestates of the type of the object without considering the interaction annotations. The ordering constraints of method executions from different objects are imposed by the interaction annotation of typestate transitions. To check multiple object typestates, for a transition with method m, all state changes in its interaction annotation must be validated. To validate a state change, for every argument p of m, the method called on p immediately before m enters must be one of the methods directly reaching the source state of p in the state change, and the method called on p immediately after m exits must be one of the methods directly leaving the destination state of p in the state change. If there is any return object of m, the method executed on it immediately after m exits must be one of the methods directly leaving its state in the state change. Method executions from different objects can be arbitrarily interleaved if there are not direct or indirect constraints from the interaction annotations between them.

During typestate composition, we apply several rules to filter out uninteresting interactions. These uninteresting interactions stem from the common knowledge of software designs and limitations of the approach to mine single-object typestates through state abstraction. The latter case will be further discussed in Section 4.3. The first rule we utilize is the *package-based filtering* that is commonly used in multiple object API protocol mining approaches [4, 10, 11]. The rule assumes that objects from different packages are not likely to obey some common API protocols. Adhering to this rule, we only compose typestates of types from the same package. The second rule we utilize is that typestates with only one state are not considered. Typical one-state typestates include typestates for immutable objects such as strings, class wrappers, and classes without fields. One-state typestats cannot specify any method invocation orders. The last rule is that a state change is discarded if (1) this change has the same source and destination state, and (2) the object corresponding to this change is neither a parameter nor the return of the method of transition associated with this change, and (3) the transition associated with this change does not go into a final state. This rule is important to filter out many uninteresting interactions based on the observation that if the destination state of a state change does not change from the source state, the corresponding two objects often do not interact with each other. The condition (3) is to preserve interactions that the cleanup of an object usually implicitly cleans up its interacting objects. For example, during the mining of the typestates in Figure 1, the last rule filters out interaction annotations of read of `BufferedInputStream` but preserves the interaction annotation of close of `BufferedInputStream`.

4. Implementation and Results

In this section, we describe the implementation and empirical evaluation of our approach. we also discuss several limitations of our current implementation.

4.1. Implementation. To obtain information required to mine typestates, We must *trace* program executions. For this purpose, we write an agent using Java Virtual Machine Tool Interface (JVMTI) [24]. JVMTI is convenient to trace programs in many aspects such as that it is easy to access the call stack and that we can attach a unique tag to every object. For both single-threaded and multithreaded applications, events are recorded in the order of their occurrence, that is, the order of events is preserved globally. In this way, object interactions with events coming from different threads can be recognized. The agent is attached to Java Virtual Machine and writes the flow of events to plain text files. To mine typestates, we need both information of method executions and information of object states. The tracing agent records three types of events: *Method Entry, Method Exit,* and *Field Modification*. A *Field Modification* event is issued when some value is assigned to a field of an object. Table 1 presents the event types and recorded information for all events handled by the agent. The largest file we analyzed is about 2.2 GB in size and contains more than 106 million runtime events.

For a *Method Entry* event of a constructor, we create a `State` object to represent the `state` of the created object. All fields of the object have default values of the Java language. When a *Field Modification* event on this object is encountered, we update the corresponding field with the new value in the `State` object. The *Field Modification* event also captures the initialization of a field at its declaration. In this way, the `State` object maintains the state of the corresponding object. The object state maintained in the `State` object is used to extract abstract field values during typestates mining.

We can configure events of what types are to be traced, for example, by providing a package name to indicate that the tracing agent will record events of all public types in this package. Because we aim to mine API protocols, only *Method Entry* and *Method Exit* events of public instance methods are traced. The interaction specifications of types and other type information are obtained using Java's reflection utilities. We need access to the bytecode of target types. However, source code is not necessary. Our tracing agent is based on JVMTI that allows a much less complex and thus less error-prone implementation of the tracer. The downside of this approach

```
Input:    state s in a state change, typestates for every concerning type
Output:   state s' with the same field-value label as s
(1)     take M = (Q, Σ, δ, λ, S, F) of t that is the type associated with s
(2)     if t is a concrete class then
(3)         foreach s_M ∈ Q do
(4)             if s_M has the same field-value label as s then
(5)                 s' = s_M
(6)                 break
(7)             endif
(8)         endfor
(9)     else
(10)        take the object o associated with s
(11)        find the typstate part M' of M extracted from o
(12)        foreach s_M ∈ Q' do
(13)            if s_M' has the same field-value label as s then
(14)                s' = s_M'
(15)                break
(16)            endif
(17)        endfor
(18)    return s'
```

ALGORITHM 3: The algorithm to find the same state in corresponding typestates for a state in the state change of interaction annotations.

TABLE 1: Types of events and corresponding information traced by the tracing agent.

Event	Traced information
Method entry	Thread name, stack depth of this method, method name and signature, types and values for all parameters
Method exit	Thread name, stack depth of this method, method name and signature, type and value for return
Field modification	Type of class of object, type of declaring class of field, object tag, field name and type, new value

is that the tracing agent incurs significant runtime overhead. However, our general approach is modular and is not bound to this tracing agent. Any traces that contain method executions with parameter and return values and states of involving objects can be fed into our typestates miner.

4.2. Empirical Evaluation. This section describes the experiments of applying our approach to several benchmarks from the literature. At first, we give the experimental setup and an overview of the benchmarks. Second, we show that object interactions are common by analyzing the interaction specifications of target APIs and present the mined typestates. Third, we evaluate the quality of mined typestates by examining whether they characterize typical APIs usages. For this aspect, we compare typestates for the same type mined from different applications. Finally, we discuss several typestate models automatically mined by our approach.

We apply our approach to mine typestates of types from three packages and their subpackages of Oracle Java JDK 6:

`java.lang`, `java.util` and `java.io`, totally 17 packages. APIs in these packages obey important properties and are widely used as experimental targets in the literature [10, 11]. Training programs in our experiments are benchmarks from the DaCapo benchmark suite 2006-10-MR2, which ensures a controlled and reproducible execution of all benchmarks [25]. We use the tracing agent to record events into a plain text file for each of these benchmarks. We limit the execution time of every program to half an hour. Although programs do not run to its end for tracing, the result traces contain large enough numbers of events for our experimental evaluation. Table 2 presents the traces used in our experiments. The elapsed execution time for two separate stages, namely, single object typestates mining (Section 3.2) and typestates extraction (Section 3.3), is also presented in Table 2. The time for typestates composition is not presented. Because we assign every state a unique number as its abstract name and record it in state changes during the process of mining single object typestates annotated with interactions, much of the work of typestates composition is saved. As our approach framework is modular, we present the algorithm for typestate composition in Algorithm 3 for potential use when other state labelling techniques or alternative implementations are used. The time used to mine typestates of single objects is roughly linear to the number of events in the input trace. The total time of the typestates mining is typically less than 10 minutes for a benchmark program. It is low considering the huge number of input events and is fast than recent work in the literature [10, 11]. Although having the complexity of $O(m \times n)$, where m is the number of states of the typestates and n is the number of transitions of the typestates, extracting typestates for super types is fast, typically in several minutes, because common single object typestates have a very small number of states and transitions.

TABLE 2: Traces used in the experiments and analysis times in minutes.

Application	No. of events	Execution time	
		Single object typestate mining	Typestate extraction
antlr	8,079,678	6.5	1.2
bloat	7,235,945	7.5	1.6
chart	9,636,350	8	1.5
eclipse	5,348,521	3	0.7
fop	8,446,844	8.4	1.2
hsqldb	10,629,268	5	1.7
jython	812,978	0.5	0.2
luindex	7,196,849	9.5	0.4
lusearch	5,324,886	10	0.7
pmd	9,279,565	9.2	1.4
xalan	6,042,106	3.5	2.7

TABLE 3: Object interactions for target APIs. The third column is the number of types with no less than 10 interaction, and the last column is the average number of interactions per type.

Package	No. of interactions	No. of types (≥10)	Average number
java.lang	390	14	9.3
java.util	443	13	6.4
java.io	105	0	1.7

TABLE 4: Results of mined typestates. The third column is the total number of interactions for the package, and the last column is the number of mined typestates models with no less than 10 interactions.

Package	No. of single object typestates	No. of interactions	No. of models (≥10)
java.lang	27	161	3
java.util	32	77	0
java.io	30	23	0

Interaction specifications specify object interactions that potentially occur during runtime. Because the interaction specification of a type is determined by the type's definition (or structure), we present the statistics of object interactions collected from interaction specifications of public types in the target packages in Table 3. An *interaction* in this table is a pair of different types $\langle t_1, t_2 \rangle$ that t_2 is the type of a specific parameter of or that of the return of a specific public method of t_1. They provide the background for evaluating multiple object typestates mining approaches. The data is obtained by analyzing the bytecode of target types with the Java reflection utilities. In accordance with the definition of the interaction specification, we only care for public types and public methods here. It can be seen that java.lang is more complex in terms of objects interactions with an average of 9.4 interactions per type. The least complex package is java.io that still has an average of 1.7 interactions per type. These indicate that common types will interact with more than one other type, and object interactions are common among APIs. In addition, there are a nontrivial number of types that potentially interact with many other types simultaneously. For example, in the package java.lang, there are 14 types that have no less than 10 interactions. Object interactions are not only common but also complex. During inspecting interaction specifications of these types, we also find that there are no simple indicators of which interaction being more likely to obey common usage protocols than others. So it is important to capture as many as possible object interactions to mine precise and complete typestates. Although the *package-based filtering* has been proved useful in practice, it is not easy to distinguish methods of the same type in terms of their protocol-obeying likeliness. The results of mined typestates are presented in Table 4. Compared with Table 3, It can be seen that there is a large part of types and interactions that are not covered by the mined typestates. However, this is due to the training programs that use only part of the target APIs. Our mining approach can capture all object interactions. we mine more object interactions from the package java.lang

because it is the most heavily used package by nearly all of the training programs. Due to the unavailability of tools and corresponding results, we cannot quantitatively evaluate the coverage of object interactions of other multiple object protocol mining approaches currently [10, 11].

To answer the question that whether our mined multiple object typestates describe typical API protocols, we have to evaluate the quality of mined typestates. To this end, we compare typestates of the same type mined from different applications. If the typestates appear in the results of at least two different applications, we can think that the typestates are not application specific but manifesting common API usage. We find that if two typestates models of the same type are mined from different applications and we do not consider interaction annotations, it is always the case that one is included in the other in that states and transitions of one typestate model is the subset of that of the other model, respectively. This is due to the fact that objects of the same type have the same abstract states under the same state abstraction function. Our miner can mine a model for each object created during the program execution. However, nearly all the benchmark programs create objects of some types that are never used by other benchmark programs. So we limit the inspected models to these ones that have to be mined from at least two benchmark programs. Because our major concern is object interactions, we choose to analyze state changes for transitions. Assume typestates M_1 of type t and Γ as the set of all typestates models of type t mined from benchmarks different from that of M_1. We consider a transition e_1 of M_1 is validated if there is one typestates model M_2 that (1) M_2 has a transition e_2 that has the same source state, destination state, and method as that of e_1, respectively, and (2) e_1 and e_2 have the same state change for each of interacting objects associated with the method of these two transitions. To measure the percentage of validated transitions of typestates, we compare the results from the benchmarks for the target packages together. The results are presented in Table 5. The results are very promising. Overall, most (84.0%) of transitions are validated. We conclude that most of mined typestates of multiple objects

TABLE 5: Quality of mined typestates.

Application	No. of transitions	No. of validated transitions	Percentage
antlr	384	329	85.7%
bloat	303	241	79.5%
chart	331	288	87.0%
eclipse	286	210	73.4%
fop	429	392	91.4%
hsqldb	408	331	81.1%
jython	335	264	78.8%
luindex	453	380	83.9%
lusearch	362	250	69.1%
pmd	402	398	99.0%
xalan	425	405	95.3%
Overall	4118	3488	84.0%

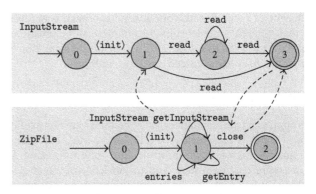

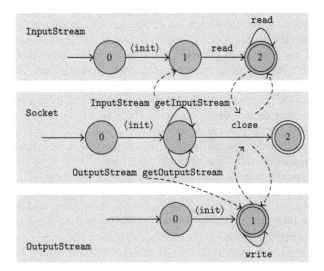

FIGURE 3: Mined typestates of `ZipFile` and `InputStream`.

FIGURE 4: Mined typestates of `Socket`, `InputStream` and `OutputStream`.

characterize common API usage instead of being incidental and application specific.

We discuss another typestates model mined by our approach. Figure 3 presents the typestates of `ZipFile` and `InputStream`. After an `ZipFile` object is constructed, several methods may be invoked, such as entries and `getEntry`. The `getInputStream` method returns an `InputStream` object. The dashed line from `getInputStream` to state 1 of `InputStream` indicates this interaction. Then, the method read is invoked to read bytes from this input stream. After finishing work, the method `close` is called to close the zip file. The dashed lines between `close` and state 3 of `InputStream` manifest that the close of the zip file also transitions the `InputStream` object to its final state. This captures the API protocol that `close` of `ZipFile` also closes the `InputStream` returned by `getInputStream`. Another interesting finding from Figure 3 is that `close` of `ZipFile` actually does not call close of `InputStream`. After inspecting the source code, we confirm this and find that `ZipFile` ensures the no usage of `InputStream` after its `close` call by a different way. The typestates of `InputStream` are extracted from objects of type `ZipFileInputStream`, that is, a private inner class of `ZipFile`.

4.3. Discussions. In this section, we discuss several characteristics of our approach, mainly its drawbacks. Our approach is based on a simple state abstraction mechanism to label states. Although it is shown to be able to mine some useful single object typestates [14, 15], we find during our experiments that this state abstraction mechanism prevents us from mining some typical multiple object typestates. To compare our approach with other researcher's work [11], we mine several typestate models from traces of the conformance tests of the Apache Harmony project [26]. One of them is the `Socket` specification presented in Figure 4. The typestates capture the property that `close` of `Socket` also closes `InputStream` returned by `getInputStream` and `OutputStream` returned by `getOutputStream`. However, there are only two states in typestates of `InputStream` and only one state in typestates

of `OutputStream` due to limitations of the used state abstraction (when counting the number of states, we do not consider the initial state, that is, the source state of a constructor). This permits read after `InputStream` is closed and write after `OutputStream` is closed which are illegal. At the same time, typestates in Figure 4 manifest a characteristic of our approach that some semantic unrelated events from different objects can be arbitrarily interleaved, which can enhance the completeness of mined typestates. For example, read of `InputStream` and write of `OutputStream` are separate from each other and can be arbitrarily interleaved because there are no direct or indirect interaction annotations between them. For approaches that take specification mining as a language learning problem from a set of input strings, it is not easy to capture this semantic unrelatedness without enough input samples.

There are approaches such as [27] that try to mine *deep* models. For the state abstraction, they do not simply map fields of reference types to *null* or *not null*, but also consider the fields of fields. However, considering unrelated fields can lead to unnecessary states that complicate the mined typestates. For example, states 1, 2, and 3 in the typestates of `InputStream` in Figure 4 are redundant to only represent the behavior of read. Because our general approach is modular in that different state labelling techniques can be integrated with it, new effective state abstraction mechanism can be employed to enhance mined typestates in future.

5. Related Work

An approach to mine single object typestates based on explicit object states is presented in [14, 15]. A typestate automaton for an object is a nondeterministic finite state automaton. Its states represent object states and are labeled with values of all fields of this object, and its transitions represent executions of methods of this object and are labeled with method names. A special state *ex* exists as the destination state of all method executions that throw an exception. For each method execution called on an object, there is a transition from the source state to the destination state. They combine all the transitions by merging states with the same field-value label to mine the typestates model of this object. The typestates automaton for a class consists of the union of all states and transitions of typestate automata of all its objects. Abstract states instead of concrete states are used in typestate automata. As states of typestate automata are usually anonymous, field-value labels of states are discarded, and states are identified by assigned abstract names. Our approach currently uses the same state abstraction function as [14, 15]. As we aim to mine normal behavior of programs, we do not consider method executions that throw exceptions and do not include a similar error state in our typestates. There are two main differences between their approach and ours. First, they cannot mine typestates of abstract types. Second, they can not mine interactions between objects; that is, they can only mine single object typestates. Dallmeier et al. [15] also present the techniques to systematically generate test cases that cover previously unobserved behavior to enrich mined single object typestates. Because the poor behavior coverage of traces is a common problem for all dynamic specification mining approaches, it is possible to adapt their test generation technique to enrich typestates of multiple objects.

Pradel and Gross [10] define the concept of *object collaborations* to capture related events based on the assumption that methods generally implement small and coherent pieces of functionality, and so the method invocations issued during a method's execution are related to each other. A collaboration is a sequence of method invocations associated with their receivers. To limit the number of events, they limit the depth of nested calls to a certain nesting level. Then, they apply several heuristics including the *package-based filtering* to filter out unrelated events. Similar object collaborations are grouped into a collaboration pattern. At last, an FSM is mined for each collaboration pattern. There are mainly two drawbacks of their approach. First, their approach can mine models for objects that are not interacting with each other when events of these objects are issued during a method's execution. Second, their approach may fail to group related events together when they exceed the scope of the execution of a method.

Lee et al. [11] present the *event specification* approach to capture related events based on the assumption that unit tests perform the behavior of tightly interacting objects, and so methods involved in a unit test likely obey some specification. An event specification is a set of methods together with a set of reference types, each of which is the type of a parameter or return of a method. Several heuristics including the *package-based filtering* are applied to further filter events involved in a unit test execution. At last, an event specification includes events that are directly or indirectly related. Two events are directly related if and only if they share at least one common receiver, method argument or method return, and related if and only if they are connected through a sequence of directly related events. Compared with their event specification, our interaction specification contains all public methods and all reference parameters and returns of these methods of a type. However, event specification does not ensure this. Their approach relies on the availability and quality of unit test cases. In addition, a unit test case may not contain complex interactions of many objects.

To maintain scalability, approaches to mine multiple object typestates based on predefined property templates can only mine models for simple property templates such as alternating templates over event pairs [4, 17] and resource usage patterns over event triples [28]. The predefined, simple property templates make learning an arbitrarily complex specification impossible. Gabel and Su [13] propose to learn simple generic patterns and compose them to construct large, complex specifications. They use two simple patterns *alternation* and *resource ownership* and two composition rules *branching* and *sequencing*. Their approach is shown to be able to capture most temporal specifications published in the literature. Our approach complements to theirs in that the interaction specifications of our approach are determined by the structure of the type, and they naturally capture all potential interactions.

Nguyen et al. [22] present a graph-based approach to mine the usage patterns of one or multiple objects from the source code. To model object usage, they present the graph-based representation called graph-based object usage model which includes action nodes of method calls, control nodes of control structure, and data flow among these nodes. They first extract object usage from the source code and then mine object usage patterns by identifying object usages with frequent appearance. Based on the observation that isomorphic graphs also contain isomorphic (sub)graphs, they mine the patterns increasingly by size (i.e., the number of nodes). Similarly to Pradel and Gross [10], their graph-based object usage models are extracted from individual methods, and the data flow analysis to determine the data dependency among nodes is intraprocedural and explicit. So their approach has the two drawbacks of Pradel and Gross [10] discussed above.

6. Conclusions

This paper presents a general multiple object typestates mining approach. We first mine single object typestates through state abstraction. These typestates are also annotated with abstract states of interacting objects to record object interactions. We then extract typestates for super types from typestates of their implementing classes. At the last step, different typestates are composed together to get typestates of multiple interacting objects. Our approach is scalable and useful in that it can mine typestates of typical API behavior with low learning complexity. However, the state abstraction mechanism used here is not very effective to mine multiple object typestates. In future, we plan to refine our approach by integrating new state labelling techniques.

Acknowledgments

This work was supported by the National Natural Science Foundation of China under Grant nos. 91118007, 90818024, and 61133001, and the National High Technology Research and Development Program of China (863 program) under Grant nos. 2011AA010 106 and 2012AA011201, and the Program for New Century Excellent Talents in University.

References

[1] R. M. Hierons, K. Bogdanov, J. P. Bowen et al., "Using formal specifications to support testing," *ACM Computing Surveys*, vol. 41, no. 2, 2009.

[2] M. Das, S. Lerner, and M. Seigle, "ESP: path-sensitive program verification in polynomial time," in *Proceedings of the ACM SIGPLAN Conference on Programming Language Design and Implementation (PLDI '02)*, pp. 57–68, June 2002.

[3] T. Ball and S. K. Rajamani, "The SLAM project: debugging system software via static analysis," in *Proceedings of the 29th ACM SIGPLAN-SIGACT Symposium on Principles of Programming Languages (POPL '02)*, pp. 1–3, January 2002.

[4] W. Weimer and G. C. Necula, "Mining temporal specifications for error detection," in *Proceedings of the 11th international conference on Tools and Algorithms for the Construction and Analysis of Systems (TACAS '05)*, pp. 461–476, 2005.

[5] D. Hovemeyer and W. Pugh, "Finding bugs is easy," in *Proceedings of the 19th Annual ACM Conference on Object-Oriented Programming, Systems, Languages, and Applications (OOPSLA '04)*, pp. 132–135, October 2004.

[6] M. Pradel, C. Jaspan, J. Aldrich, and T. R. Gross, "Statically checking API protocol conformance with mined multi-object specifications," in *Proceedings of the International Conference on Software Engineering (ICSE '12)*, pp. 925–935, 2012.

[7] M. Pradel and T. R. Gross, "Leveraging test generation and specification mining for automated bug detection without false positives," in *Proceedings of the International Conference on Software Engineering (ICSE '12)*, pp. 288–298, 2012.

[8] D. Malayeri and J. Aldrich, "Practical exception specifications," in *Advanced Topics in Exception Handling Techniques*, C. Dony, J. L.. Knudsen, Al. Romanovsky, and A. Tripathi, Eds., pp. 200–220, Springer, Berlin, Germany, 2006.

[9] G. Ammons, R. Bodik, and J. R. Larus, "Mining specifications," in *Proceedings of the 29th ACM SIGPLAN-SIGACT Symposium on Principles of Programming Languages (POPL '02)*, pp. 4–16, 2002.

[10] M. Pradel and T. R. Gross, "Automatic generation of object usage specifications from large method traces," in *Proceedings of the 24th IEEE/ACM International Conference on Automated Software Engineering (ASE '09)*, pp. 371–382, November 2009.

[11] C. Lee, F. Chen, and G. Rosu, "Mining parametric specifications," in *Proceedings of the 33rd International Conference on Software Engineering (ICSE '11)*, pp. 591–600, 2011.

[12] C. Goues and W. Weimer, "Specification mining with few false positives," in *Proceedings of the 15th International Conference on Tools and Algorithms for the Construction and Analysis of Systems: Held as Part of the Joint European Conferences on Theory and Practice of Software, ETAPS, 2009, (TACAS '09)*, pp. 292–306, 2009.

[13] M. Gabel and Z. Su, "Javert: fully automatic mining of general temporal properties from dynamic traces," in *Proceedings of the 16th ACM SIGSOFT International Symposium on the Foundations of Software Engineering (SIGSOFT '08/FSE-16)*, pp. 339–349, November 2008.

[14] V. Dallmeier, C. Lindig, A. Wasylkowski, and A. Zeller, "Mining object behavior with ADABU," in *Proceedings of the 4th International Workshop on Dynamic Analysis (WODA '06)*, pp. 17–23, May 2006.

[15] V. Dallmeier, N. Knopp, C. Mallon, G. Fraser, S. Hack, and A. Zeller, "Automatically generating test cases for specification mining," *IEEE Transactions on Software Engineering*, vol. 38, no. 2, pp. 243–257, 2012.

[16] J. Whaley, M. C. Martin, and M. S. Lam, "Automatic extraction of object-oriented component interfaces," in *Proceedings of the ACM SIGSOFT 2002 International Symposium on Software Testing and Analysis (ISSTA '02)*, pp. 218–228, July 2002.

[17] J. Yang, D. Evans, D. Bhardwaj, T. Bhat, and M. Das, "Perracotta: mining temporal API rules from imperfect traces," in *Proceedings of the 28th International Conference on Software Engineering (ICSE '06)*, pp. 282–291, May 2006.

[18] R. E. Strom and S. Yemini, "Typestate: a programming language concept for enhancing software reliability," *IEEE Transactions on Software Engineering*, vol. 12, no. 1, pp. 157–171, 1986.

[19] R. DeLine and M. Fahndrich, "Typestates for objects," in *Proceedings of the European Conference on Object-Oriented Programming (ECOOP '04)*, pp. 465–490, 2004.

[20] K. Bierhoff and J. Aldrich, "Lightweight object specification with typestates," in *Proceedings of the 10th European Software Engineering Conference Held Jointly with 13th ACM SIGSOFT International Symposium on Foundations of Software Engineering (ESEC/FSE-13)*, pp. 217–226, September 2005.

[21] A. Wasylkowski, A. Zeller, and C. Lindig, "Detecting object usage anomalies," in *Proceedings of the 6th Joint Meeting of the European Software Engineering Conference and the 14th ACM SIGSOFT Symposium on the Foundations of Software Engineering (ESEC/FSE '07)*, pp. 35–44, September 2007.

[22] T. T. Nguyen, H. A. Nguyen, N. H. Pham, J. M. Al-Kofahi, and T. N. Nguyen, "Graph-based mining of multiple object usage patterns," in *Proceedings of the 7th Joint Meeting of the European Software Engineering Conference and the ACM SIGSOFT Symposium on The Foundations of Software Engineering (ESEC/FSE '09)*, pp. 383–392, August 2009.

[23] E. Rich, *Automata, Computability, and Complexity: Theory and Applications*, Pearson Education, 2009.

[24] "Java Virtual Machine Tool Interface," http://download.oracle.com/javase/docs/technotes/guides/jvmti.

[25] S. M. Blackburn, R. Garner, C. Hoffmann et al., "The DaCapo benchmarks: java benchmarking development and analysis," in *Proceedings of the 21st Annual ACM SIGPLAN Conference on Object-Oriented Programming Systems, Languages, and Applications (OOPSLA '06)*, pp. 169–190, October 2006.

[26] "Apache Harmony," http://harmony.apache.org.

[27] V. Dallmeier, A. Zeller, and B. Meyer, "Generating fixes from object behavior anomalies," in *Proceedings of the 24th IEEE/*

ACM International Conference on Automated Software Engineering (ASE '09), pp. 550–554, November 2009.

[28] M. Gabel and Z. Su, "Symbolic mining of temporal specifications," in *Proceedings of the 30th International Conference on Software Engineering (ICSE '08)*, pp. 51–60, 2008.

4

Research on an Infectious Disease Transmission by Flocking Birds

Mingsheng Tang,[1,2] Xinjun Mao,[1] and Zahia Guessoum[2]

[1] *College of Computer, National University of Defense Technology, Changsha 410073, China*
[2] *LIP 6, Université Pierre et Marie Curie, 75006 Paris, France*

Correspondence should be addressed to Mingsheng Tang; tms110145@gmail.com

Academic Editors: P. Agarwal, S. Balochian, and Y. Zhang

The swarm intelligence is becoming a hot topic. The flocking of birds is a natural phenomenon, which is formed and organized without central or external controls for some benefits (e.g., reduction of energy consummation). However, the flocking also has some negative effects on the human, as the infectious disease H7N9 will easily be transmited from the denser flocking birds to the human. Zombie-city model has been proposed to help analyzing and modeling the flocking birds and the artificial society. This paper focuses on the H7N9 virus transmission in the flocking birds and from the flocking birds to the human. And some interesting results have been shown: (1) only some simple rules could result in an emergence such as the flocking; (2) the minimum distance between birds could affect H7N9 virus transmission in the flocking birds and even affect the virus transmissions from the flocking birds to the human.

1. Introduction

Swarm intelligence is becoming a hot research topic, which could be presented in natural, social, or artificial systems. It is often inspired by natural systems, especially biological systems. The flocking of birds is a classical phenomenon of swarm intelligence without central control [1]. How could birds fly in a flocking? Each bird only confirms the simple rules of alignment, cohesion, and separation, and then these birds could fly in a flocking. Why do birds fly in a flocking? Because it could reduce the power requirements of birds and could bring other benefits for these birds [2–4].

However, it also brings some problems, for example infectious diseases could spread quickly among the flocking birds. Moreover, these infectious diseases may be transmitted to the human such as the infectious disease H7N9 which is spreading in China [5]. This paper will study the wild flocking birds and its effect on the infectious disease spread from the viewpoint of the transmission of the infectious disease H7N9. In order to facilitate modeling the flocking and the spread of H7N9 between birds and human, this paper proposes a general model, zombie-city model, which contains five core concepts: agent, role, environment, social network, and rule. Based on this model, we could construct and analyze the artificial flocking birds and also could model the artificial society. We will study the spread of H7N9 in the flocking birds and H7N9 transmission from birds to the human.

This paper is organized as follows: Section 2 introduces the zombie-city model. Section 3 models the flocking and artificial society with the zombie city and then presents the experiments results. Section 4 summarizes the work.

2. Zombie-City Model

2.1. Meat-Model of Zombie-City Model. In the zombie-city model [6], there are mainly five concepts, including agent, environment, social networks, roles, and rules. Rules could constrain agents, environments, and social network; that is, the agents, the environment, and the social network must conform to these rules. Besides, agents have their own capabilities (e.g., movement), and agents may be infected with

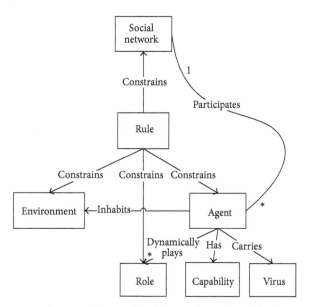

FIGURE 1: Metamodel of the zombie-city model.

viruses so that they will carry viruses to play the zombie roles. Figure 1 presents the metamodel of the zombie-city model.

(i) *Agent*. It is a proactive, automatic, and self-adaptive entity. It could interact with other agents and has some capabilities such as interaction and sensing the social relationships with other agents. And agents could dynamically play different roles to adapt to the environmental, social, or their own changes.

(ii) *Social Network*. It is made up of social relationships between agents, which construct the social structure. Meanwhile, it must conform to the rules such as scale-free network.

(iii) *Environment*. It is the space where agents inhabit, which is made up of grids. The environment also must conform to the rules.

(iv) *Rule*. It is constraining agents, social network, the environment and roles, and all of them do not act against the discipline or the norm.

(v) *Role*. It is the abstract of agents. In some emergent situations, we could define various special roles, for example, agents infected with viruses could be seen as the role of patient. Agents could dynamically play different roles according to various situations. Besides, roles should also be constrained by rules.

(vi) *Capability*. It is the ability of agents such as movement and interaction. Agents could own some natural capabilities, including self-adaptive capability though dynamically playing different roles according to various situations.

(vii) *Virus*. It is the entity that has not behavioral features and could be transmitted among agents by interactions or other ways. It could be considered as a property of agents to denote or indicate whether agents carry the virus. It is a very important concept for emergency management.

2.2. Formal Specification of the Zombie-City Model. A zombie-city model could be described by 5 tuples, as $Model ::= \langle AGENT, SN, EN, ROLE, RULE \rangle$, where

(i) $AGENT = \{a_1, a_2, \ldots, a_n\}$, for any $a_i(1 \leq i \leq n)$, where a_i is an agent and $AGENT$ is a finite set of agents.

(ii) $SN = \{l_k \mid 1 \leq k \leq (n-1)^2\}$, where l_k is a link of the social network, SN is a set of links, and social network is constructed by links between these agents.

(iii) $EN = \{g_1, g_2, \ldots, g_l\}$, where $g_i(1 \leq i \leq l)$ is a grid and EN is a finite set of grids.

(iv) $ROLE = \{b_1, b_2, \ldots, b_m\}$, for any $b_i(1 \leq i \leq m)$, where b_i is a role and $ROLE$ is a finite set of roles.

(v) $RULE = \{r_1, r_2, \ldots, r_k\}$, for any $r_i(1 \leq i \leq k)$, where r_i is a rule. $RULE$ is a finite rules set of rules. This set could be divided into four subsets: R_A, R_S, R_E, and R_R. R_A is a finite rule set for agents, R_S is a finite rule set for the social network, R_E is a finite rule set for the environment, and R_R is a finite rule set for roles.

We use CID to express the set of all the identifications, and cid is a specific one, that is, cid ∈ CID.

(i) *Agent*. For any $a \in AGENT$, $a ::= \langle cid, AT, AC, N_l, N_r \rangle$, where

   (a) *cid* is the identification of the agent;
   (b) *AT* is the attributes of the agent;
   (c) *AC* is the actions of the agent that the agent could do;
   (d) N_l is a finite set of identifications of links that the agent is participating;
   (e) N_r means a set of identifications of roles that the agent is playing.

(ii) *Role*. For any $r \in ROLE$, $r ::= \langle cid, AT, AC \rangle$, where

   (a) *cid* is the identification of the role;
   (b) *AT* is the attributes of the role;
   (c) *AC* is the actions of the role that the role could do.

(iii) *Environment*. For any $e \in EN$, $e ::= \langle cid, AT, AC \rangle$, where

   (a) *cid* is the identification of the environment;
   (b) *AT* is the attributes of the environment;
   (c) *AC* is the actions of the environment that the environment could do.

(iv) *Social Network.* For any $l \in SN, l ::= \langle cid, AT, (a_i, a_j)\rangle$

    (a) *cid* is the identification of the link;

    (b) *AT* is the attributes of the link;

    (c) $(a_i, a_j) \in 2^{AGENT \times AGENT}$ denotes a link from agent a_i to agent a_j. For an undirected graph, $(a_i, a_j) = (a_j, a_i)$, and for directed graph, $(a_i, a_j) \neq (a_j, a_i)$.

(v) *Rule.* For any $u \in R_A \bigcup R_R \bigcup R_E \bigcup R_S$, $u ::= Condition \mid Event \rightarrow (AT \mid AC)$, where

    (a) *Condition* is the internal state or attribute of the agent, role, environment, or link of the social network in the system;

    (b) *Event* is the set of events that happens in the system;

    (c) *AT* is the set of attributes of the agent, role, environment, or link of the social network in the system;

    (d) *AC* is the set of actions of the agent, role, environment, or other actions in the system.

2.3. Social Network. For an undirected graph, $a \prec_t b\,(a, b \in AGENT)$ means that agent a links with agent b at moment t, which is equal to $b \prec_t a$. $LINK(a, t)$ denotes the set of agents in which agent a connects with at moment t, that is, $LINK(a, t) = \{b \mid a \prec_t b \land b \in AGENT\}$.

For a directed graph, let $a \prec_t b\,(a, b \in AGENT)$ denote that agent a links to b, and agent a is the source of this link. $LINK^S(a, t)$ denotes the set of agents that agent a connects, and agent a is the source of these links, that is, $LINK^S(a, t) = \{b \mid a \prec_t b \land b \in AGENT\}$. Let $LINK^T(a, t)$ indicate the set of agents that links to agent a at the moment t, and agent a is the target of these links, that is, $LINK^T(a, t) = \{b \mid b \prec_t a \land b \in AGENT\}$. Therefore, the set of agents that agent a connects at moment t contains the agents that agent a links to and the agents that link to agent a, that is, $LINK(a, t) = LINK^S(a, t) \bigcup LINK^T(a, t)$.

For describing the initialization process of a static social network and the growing process of a dynamic social network, we have defined two primitives: *Create()*, *Delete()*. $SN(t)$ denotes the set of social links in an artificial society at the moment t.

    (i) *Create*(a_i, a_j). For the undirected graph, $a_i \nprec_t a_j$, that is, $a_j \notin LINK(a_i, t)$ and $a_i \notin LINK(a_j, t)$, $LINK(a_i, t+1) = LINK(a_i, t) \bigcup \{a_j\}$ and $LINK(a_j, t+1) = LINK(a_j, t) \bigcup \{a_i\}$; for the directed graph, $a_i \nprec_t a_j$, $LINK^S(a_i, t+1) = LINK^S(a_i, t) \bigcup \{a_j\}$ and $LINK^T(a_i, t+1) = LINK^T(a_i, t)$, $LINK^S(a_j, t+1) = LINK^S(a_j, t)$, and $LINK^T(a_j, t+1) = LINK^T(a_j, t) \bigcup \{a_i\}$. For both two graphs, the link $l = (a_i, a_j)$ and $SN(t+1) = SN(t) \bigcup \{l\}$.

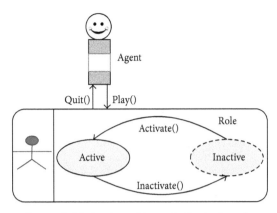

FIGURE 2: Mechanism of dynamically playing role.

    (ii) *Delete*(a_i, a_j). For the undirected graph, $a_j \in LINK(a_i, t)$ and $a_i \in LINK(a_j, t)$, $LINK(a_i, t+1) = LINK(a_i, t) \setminus \{a_j\}$ and $LINK(a_j, t+1) = LINK(a_j, t) \setminus \{a_i\}$; for the directed graph, $a_j \in LINK^S(a_i, t)$ and $a_i \in LINK^T(a_j, t)$, $LINK^S(a_i, t+1) = LINK^S(a_i, t) \setminus \{a_j\}$ and $LINK^S(a_j, t+1) = LINK^S(a_j, t)$, $LINK^T(a_i, t+1) = LINK^T(a_i, t)$ and $LINK^T(a_j, t+1) = LINK^T(a_j, t) \setminus \{a_i\}$. For both two graphs, the link $l = (a_i, a_j)$ and $SN(t+1) = SN(t) \setminus \{l\}$.

2.4. Self-Adaptive Mechanism of Agents. Agents have the capabilities of self-adaption though dynamically playing roles. Figure 2 presents the self-adaptive mechanism of dynamically playing roles. For example, if agent a is a student (i.e., agent a plays *student* role) and has been infected by an infectious disease, then agent a should adapt the change to transforming its role into *patient* role and go to a hospital. That means agent a will play the *patient* role, and the *student* role of agent a will be *inactive*. After agent a recovers, agent a will not play the *patient* role, that is, quit the *patient* role. Agent a will go back to play the *student* role, which means to *activate* the *student* role. The self-adaptive mechanism could be accurately described by formalization.

Let $a \in_t c$ denote that agent a plays c role at time t. Use $ROLE(a, t)$ to denote the set of roles that agent a plays at moment t, that is, $ROLE(a, t) = \{c \mid a \in_t c\}$. In order to describe the mechanism of dynamically playing roles, let $ROLE^A(a, t)$ indicate the set of active roles that agent a plays at moment t, and let $ROLE^I(a, t)$ denote the set of inactive roles that agent a plays at moment t. Therefore, the set of roles that agent a plays at moment t includes active roles and inactive roles, that is, $ROLE(a, t) = ROLE^A(a, t) \bigcup ROLE^I(a, t)$. In order to describe the process of dynamically playing roles, we define four primitives, including *Play()*, *Quit()*, *Activate()*, and *Inactivate()*.

    Play(c). $c \notin ROLE(a, t), ROLE^A(a, t+1) = ROLE^A(a, t) \bigcup \{c\}$, and $ROLE^I(a, t+1) = ROLE^I(a, t)$. That means that the agent will play and join the role and the role is active.

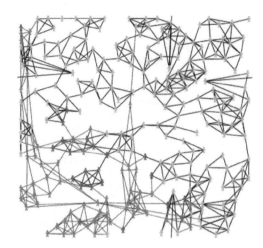

FIGURE 3: A snapshot of agents playing different roles (different colours) in the zombie-city model.

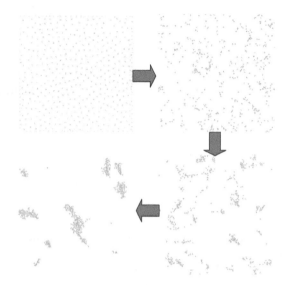

FIGURE 4: The processes of the flocking.

Quit(c). $c \in ROLE^A(a,t)$, $ROLE^A(a, t + 1) = ROLE^A(a, t) \setminus \{c\}$, and $ROLE^I(a, t + 1) = ROLE^I(a, t) \bigcup \{c\}$. That means that the agent will not play the role and the role will quit from the set of roles that the agent plays.

Activate(c). $c \in ROLE^I(a,t)$, $ROLE^I(a, t + 1) = ROLE^I(a, t) \setminus \{c\}$, and $ROLE^A(a, t + 1) = ROLE^A(a, t) \bigcup \{c\}$. That means that the agent will make the role active and behaviors of the agent will be affected by the role.

Inactivate(c). $c \in ROLE^A(a,t)$, $ROLE^A(a, t + 1) = ROLE^A(a, t) \setminus \{c\}$, and $ROLE^I(a, t + 1) = ROLE^I(a, t) \bigcup \{c\}$. That means that the agent will make the role inactive and behaviors of the agent will not be affected by the role.

As presented in Figure 3, in zombie-city model, agents play different roles (indicated by different colors) and the same agent could dynamically play various roles for adapting to different situations.

3. H7N9 Spreading Based on the Flocking Birds

3.1. Modeling with the Zombie-City Model. The processes of the spread of H7N9 include the infectious disease transmitting among these flocking birds, and then the dense infected birds may transmit H7N9 to the human. In this case, there are mainly four roles: *susceptible_bird*, *infected_bird*, *susceptible_person*, and *infected_person*.

The phenomenon of flocking birds is based on some simple rules without external or central controls. This process is a self-organized process. These simple rules could be constructed as follows.

(1) *Rule_Cohesion.* If the bird is far away from its neighbors (flockmates) (*max_distance* is the threshold of the max

distance from its neighbors), then this bird will turn towards its neighbors. The parameter *average_flockmates* means the average direction of the nearest neighbors, and *max_cohesion* means the adjusting degree of the direction of this bird. This rule could be described as follows: *Distance(self, nearest-neighbor)* > *max_distance* → *turn_towards(average_flockmates, max_cohesion)*.

(2) *Rule_Separation.* If the bird is too close to the nearest neighbor (*min_separation* is the threshold of the min distance from the nearest neighbor), then turn away from this neighbor. This rule could be described as follows: *Distance(self, nearest-neighbor)* < *min_separation* → *turn_away(nearest_neighbor, max_separation)*.

(3) *Rule_Alignment.* Keep the direction of the bird with the flockmates, and then turn towards its neighbors. The parameter *max_ alignment* means the adjusting degree of the direction of this bird. This rule could be described as follows: *Distance(self, nearest-neighbor)* < *max_distance* || *Distance(self, nearest-neighbor)* > *min_separation* → *turn_towards(average_flockmates, max_alignment)*.

As shown in Figure 4, based on these three rules, the flocking will appear.

As we know, H7N9 is highly pathogenic for birds; that is, the infectious disease H7N9 could easily infect the birds. If some birds interact with the bird infected with H7N9 and the distance between these birds is much closed, then all of these birds will be infected with H7N9. So the rule of the disease spreading between birds could be described as follows.

(4) *Rule_Birds_Infected.* If the infected bird is closed with other birds and the distance from the infected bird (*Infected_bird*) to other birds without infection (*Susceptible_bird*) is less than a threshold (*min_distance*), then all these birds without infection will be infected with H7N9, that is, $\forall a \in_t$ *Infected_bird* $\forall b \in_t$ *Susceptible_bird*

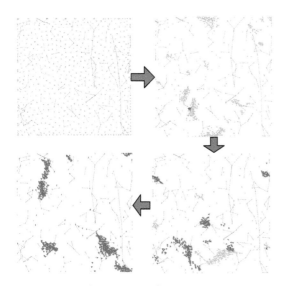

FIGURE 5: The processes of H7N9 transmission.

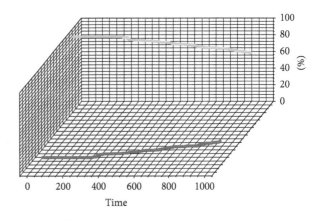

- Susceptible birds
- Infected birds

FIGURE 7: The epidemic status of the flocking birds.

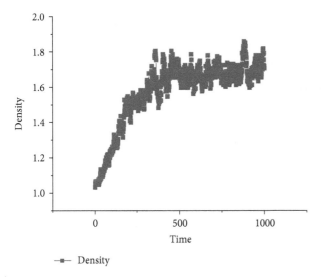

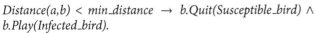

-■- Density

FIGURE 6: Density of the flocking birds.

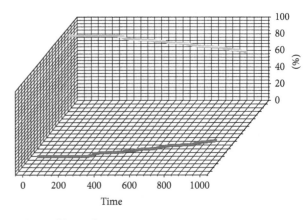

- Susceptible people
- Infected people

FIGURE 8: The epidemic status of the human.

$Distance(a,b) < min\_distance \rightarrow b.Quit(Susceptible\_bird) \wedge b.Play(Infected\_bird)$.

As the recent research shows, the infectious disease H7N9 has almost spreaded from the wild birds to the human, and there is no evidence of ongoing human-to-human infection [5, 7, 8]. It could be assumed that human-to-human transmission is only happening between intimate people and the probability of infection is very small. For people, the number of strong social relationships of a person is also very small, and in this case we assume the number to be 1. Usually, these intimate people live nearby. So the rule of this social network of artificial society could be described as follows.

(5) *Rule_Social_Network*. This social network is an undirected graph, and an agent connects with the nearest agent which has not connected with it, that is, $Average\_degree < 1 \rightarrow (\forall a, c \in_t$

$(Infected\_person \vee Susceptible\_person) \exists b \in_t (Infected\_person \vee Susceptible\_person) (a,c) \notin LINK^t(a,t) \wedge (a,b) \notin LINK(a,t) \wedge Distance(a,b) < Distance(a,c) \rightarrow Create(a,b))$.

Compared with the flocking birds, the positions of people in the environment could be seen as static. The wild flocking birds with H7N9 viruses will infect the human, but there are some conditions: in the unit grid of a person living, there are a number of infected birds (the number is *threshold_infected_human*).

(6) *Rule_Birds_Human_Infected*. If the agent without infection is habiting in a gird and in the gird there are enough infected birds (*threshold_infected_human*), then the agent will be infected, that is, $\forall a \in_t Susceptible\_person \exists b \in Environment (Habit(a,b) \wedge Count(Infected\_birds,b) \geq threshold\_infected\_human) \rightarrow a.Quit(Susceptible\_person) \wedge a.Play(Infected\_person)$.

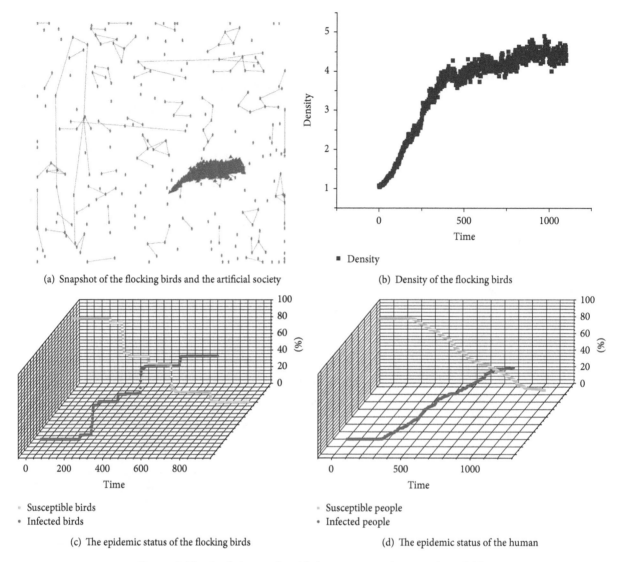

(a) Snapshot of the flocking birds and the artificial society

(b) Density of the flocking birds

- Susceptible birds
- Infected birds

- Susceptible people
- Infected people

(c) The epidemic status of the flocking birds

(d) The epidemic status of the human

FIGURE 9: The simulation results with the parameter *min_separation* = 0.25.

Although there is no evidence of ongoing human-to-human transmission, we could not exclude the small probability of human-to-human transmission through the intimate social network.

(7) *Rule_Human_to_Human.* If an infected agent a has connected with a susceptible agent b and the randomly produced number is less than the threshold (*infected_chance*), then this agent b will be infected with H7N9, that is, $\forall a \in_t$ *Infected_person* $\forall b \in_t$ *Susceptible_person* $((a,b) \in LINK(a,t) \wedge Random() < infected\_chance) \rightarrow b.Quit(Susceptible\_person) \wedge b.Play(Infected\_person)$.

3.2. *Experiments.* Based on these defined rules, we could do simulations and see the situations of the spread of this infectious disease H7N9.

(i) *Agents.* The population of agents is 750. The number of the humans is 250, and the number of birds is 500.

(ii) *Environments.* 32 × 32 grids.

(iii) *Role. Susceptible_bird (yellow color), susceptible_person (green color), infected_bird (red color), and infected_person (red color).*

We define the parameters as follows: *min_separation = max_distance = 0.5, max_cohesion = 3, max_alignment = 5, max_separation = 1.5, infected_chance = 0.1, threshold_infected_human = 5*, and the average of the social network of the human is 1. Figure 5 shows the processes of H7N9 transmission between the flocking birds and the human.

As shown in Figure 6, the density of the flocking birds firstly linearly increases, and then it fluctuates around 1.7. This density is related to the parameter *min_separation*.

Figure 7 shows the status of the H7N9 spreading between the flocking birds. At the ticks (200), a bird was infected with H7N9, and then the viruses transmitted among these birds quickly. At the ticks (400), all of these birds were infected with H7N9.

After about 80 ticks of the first bird infection with H7N9, the first person was infected with H7N9 by the dense flocking birds. The number of the infected people is increasing slowly. The birds-to-human transmission is the main way for H7N9 transmitting from birds to the human, and the epidemic status of the human could be shown in Figure 8.

How does the parameter *min_separation* affect the flocking birds and even the transmission of H7N9? We could adjust the parameter *min_separation* to 0.25. It means that the flocking birds will fly closed and the density of birds will increase. As shown in Figure 9, (a) presents the screenshot of the simulation; (b) shows the density of the flocking birds, and the density linearly increased and fluctuated around 4.5; (c) and (d) show the epidemic statuses of the flocking birds and the human, respectively.

As shown in Figure 9, we could clearly see that after the first bird was infected with H7N9 at the 200 ticks and at the 755 ticks, all of the birds were infected with H7N9. Because a small number of birds were fling separately and very closly, the birds in some small flocking were not infected with H7N9 until these birds met with the bigger flocking. Moreover, in human, more people were infected with H7N9 for the bigger density of birds or the denser flocking birds. During a same time, the number of infected people with *min_separation* = 0.25 is four times that of the number of infected people with *min_separation* = 0.5. Above all, we could know that the density of the flocking birds is related to the H7N9 epidemic in the human.

4. Conclusion

The phenomenon of the flocking is a natural beautiful scene. This phenomenon is organized by the birds without external and central controls. However, the flocking also has some problems, for example, the infectious disease H7N9 transmission. In order to aid analysis and modeling of the flocking and the disease transmission, this paper proposes a new artificial society model, zombie-city model, which includes five key concepts: agent, role, environment, social network, and rule. Based on this model, three simple rules of the flocking and other rules have been described. Then, this paper has studied the infectious disease H7N9 transmission among the flocking birds and the human. The simulation results show that a larger density of the flocking could accelerate the spread of the infectious disease H7N9 transmission from the flocking to the human and could slow down the spread of the H7N9 in the flocking birds.

The next works will include the following. (1) We will continue to perfect this zombie-city model, especially the description of an emergence. (2) We will continue with the flocking algorithm based on the zombie-city model and its effects on the human.

Acknowledgments

The National Nature and Science Foundation of China under Grants nos. 91024030, 61133001, and 61070034, the Program for New Century Excellent Talents in University, and the China Scholarship Council (CSC) support this work. The authors also gratefully express their sincere thanks to Professor Xiaogang Qiu, Dr. Bin Chen, and Dr. Yuanzheng Ge in College of Information System and Management, the National University of Defense Technology.

References

[1] G. Spedding, "The cost of flight in flocks," *Nature*, vol. 474, no. 7352, pp. 458–459, 2011.

[2] A. Bellaachia and A. Bari, "Flock by leader: a novel machine learning biologically inspired clustering algorithm," in *Advances in Swarm Intelligence*, vol. 7332 of *Lecture Notes in Computer Science*, pp. 117–126, Springer, Berlin, Germany, 2012.

[3] M. Nagy, Z. Ákos, D. Biro, and T. Vicsek, "Hierarchical group dynamics in pigeon flocks," *Nature*, vol. 464, no. 7290, pp. 890–893, 2010.

[4] J. R. Usherwood, M. Stavrou, J. C. Lowe, K. Roskilly, and A. M. Wilson, "Flying in a flock comes at a cost in pigeons," *Nature*, vol. 474, no. 7352, pp. 494–497, 2011.

[5] WHO, "Human infection with avian influenza A(H7N9) virus in China—update," http://www.who.int/csr/don/2013_04_19/en/index.html.

[6] M. Tang, X. Mao, and H. Zhou, "Zombie-city: a new artificial soceity model," *Journal of Computational Information Systems*, vol. 9, no. 12, pp. 4989–4996, 2013.

[7] R. Gao, B. Cao, Y. Hu et al., "Human infection with a novel avian-origin influenza A, (H7N9) virus," *The New England Journal of Medicine*, vol. 368, no. 20, pp. 1888–1897, 2013.

[8] T. M. Uyeki and N. J. Cox, "Global concerns regarding novel influenza A (H7N9) virus infections," *The New England Journal of Medicine*, vol. 368, no. 20, pp. 1862–1864, 2013.

5

Classification in Networked Data with Heterophily

Zhenwen Wang, Fengjing Yin, Wentang Tan, and Weidong Xiao

College of Information System and Management, National University of Defense Technology, Changsha 410073, China

Correspondence should be addressed to Zhenwen Wang; wang_zhen_wen@163.com

Academic Editors: J. Pavón and J. H. Sossa

In the real world, a large amount of data can be described by networks using relations between data. The data described by networks can be called networked data. Classification is one of the main tasks in analyzing networked data. Most of the previous methods find the class of the unlabeled node using the classes of its neighbor nodes. However, in the networks with heterophily, most of connected nodes belong to different classes. It is hard to get the correct class using the classes of neighbor nodes, so the previous methods have a low level of performance in the networks with heterophily. In this paper, a probabilistic method is proposed to address this problem. Firstly, the class propagating distribution of the node is proposed to describe the probabilities that its neighbor nodes belong to each class. After that, the class propagating distributions of neighbor nodes are used to calculate the class of the unlabeled node. At last, a classification algorithm based on class propagating distribution is presented in the form of matrix operations. In empirical study, we apply the proposed algorithm to the real-world datasets, compared with some other algorithms. The experimental results show that the proposed algorithm performs better when the networks are of heterophily.

1. Introduction

Classification is one of the main tasks in the data mining field. Most traditional classification methods assume the data instances are independent and assign class labels to the data instances using their attribute values. Besides the attribute information, the connections between data instances can be observed. These connections can be used to classify the data instances. For example, in the field of social network analyzing, it is requested to infer the missing community information of individuals using the interactions between them and other individuals whose community information is observed. This problem can be taken as classification in networked data. Networked data is a name for a group of data that can be described as networks where nodes represent the data instances and edges the connections between them. Classification in networked data is to predict the classes of unlabeled nodes based on the network and the classes of labeled nodes [1].

Many methods have been developed for classification in networked data, including collective inference [2–5] and random walk on graphs [6–8]. These methods predict classes of unlabeled nodes based on the classes of their neighbor nodes. In fact, they are the homophily-based methods. The phenomenon of homophily, nodes with similar characters having tendency to interconnect with each other, exists in many real-world networks [9]. Therefore, these methods can return the reasonable results in the networks with high homophily degree. However, there are many heterophilous networks, in which the homophily degrees are low and most of connected nodes have the different class labels. Consequently, those homophily-based methods, which use the classes of neighbor nodes to predict classes of nodes, cease to be effective.

A probabilistic method for classification in networked data is presented in this study. This method calculates the class of the unlabeled nodes based on a probabilistic approach. The main idea is that the class of the unlabeled node is influenced by their neighbor nodes and the influence from a node is measured by the probabilities that its neighbor nodes belong to each class. A classification algorithm is proposed based on this idea. In empirical study, we compare the proposed algorithm with three classification algorithms on six real-world networks. The experimental results show that the proposed algorithm provides better performance on the networks with heterophily.

2. Related Works

The classification problem in networked data is studied in this work. $G = \langle V, E \rangle$ represents a network, where V is the set of nodes and E is the set of edges. This problem can be described as finding the categories of those unlabeled nodes given G and the categories of labeled nodes. The research works related to this problem include collective inference, random walk on graphs, and the methods based on the feature extraction.

Collective inference is a group of methods that are based on a Markov assumption:

$$p(y_i \mid G) = p(y_i \mid \mathcal{N}_i), \qquad (1)$$

where y_i is the category of node v_i and $\mathcal{N}_i$ is the neighbor of node v_i. Many collective inference methods have been developed based on local classifiers including Bayesian classifier [2], normalized Logistic regression [3], maximum entropy model [4], and relational probability trees [5]. These methods based on classifiers have to train a classifier before classifying nodes. Weighted-vote relational neighbor classifier (wvRN) is a simple collective inference method, which does not require the training process and directly computes the categories of unlabeled nodes in the manner of iteration.

The MultiRankWalk (MRW) utilizes random walk on graphs to compute the categories of unlabeled nodes [6]. MRW still uses the neighbor nodes to compute the categories of unlabeled nodes. In MRW, the weighted transition matrix is calculated based on the adjacency matrix and the categories of unlabeled nodes are computed by

$$\mathbf{S^{t+1}} = (1-d) \cdot \mathbf{u} + d \cdot \mathbf{Y} \cdot \mathbf{S^t}. \qquad (2)$$

The matrix $\mathbf{Y}$ is the weighted transition matrix. The matrix $\mathbf{u}$ is the initial matrix of node category. The matrix $\mathbf{S^t}$ is the matrix representing the probabilities that each node belongs to each category. d is a constant. The method in [7] computes the classes of unlabeled nodes by utilizing a random walk on symmetric normalized Laplacian matrix. [8] considers the probabilities of classes during a random walk.

Collective inference and random walk on graphs both calculate the class labels of unlabeled nodes based on their neighbor nodes. These methods can be viewed as the group of homophily-based methods. Homophily is the phenomenon revealed in the studies of social networks [10]. Nodes connected by an edge have great possibility to possess the same classes, according to homophily. These methods can realize accurate classification on the networks with high homophily degree. However, in the networks with heterophily, most connected nodes have different class labels, and previous methods encounter accuracy decline. To overcome this problem, Tang and Liu propose SocioDim method, which trains an SVM classifier based on the latent node attributes extracted from the topology of networks [9]. However, the latent node attributes, which are obtained by paying great effort, may not reflect the real character of nodes. It makes it hard for SocioDim to ensure that nodes are classified into correct classes. In this study, a simple method is proposed to classification in the networks with heterophily by introducing a probabilistic approach.

3. A Method Based on Class Propagating Distributions

In the networks with heterophily, most of connected nodes have different classes. In this case, those classification methods based on the classes of the neighbor nodes lose their effectiveness. In this study, the scope on which we focus is expanded to the neighbors of their neighbor nodes and a probabilistic approach is utilized to calculate the class labels of unlabeled nodes. Let P_{ic} denote the probability that the node v_i has the class L_c. The vector $\mathbf{P_i} = \{P_{ic}\}_{c=1}^M$ is the class distribution of v_i where M is the number of classes. $\sum_{c=1}^M P_{ic} = 1$. The probabilities $\{P_{ic}\}_{c=1}^M$ can represent the class of the node v_i. In the network G, some nodes are labeled while others are unlabeled. For the labeled nodes, the class distribution is the vector in which only one element is 1 and the rest are 0. Calculating the classes of unlabeled nodes is to calculate the class distributions of unlabeled nodes.

The class of a node can be influenced by its neighbor nodes, but the influence is not determined by the classes of its neighbor nodes in this approach. Assume that the node v_i and v_j are connected by an edge. When calculating the class of the nodes v_i, the influence I_j from v_j is determined by the classes of the neighbor nodes of v_j. If the number of nodes labeled with L_c is larger in the neighbor nodes of the node v_j, I_j will make v_i labeled with the class L_c with greater probability. Consider a network G with N nodes. Let $\mathbf{W}$ denote the adjacency matrix of G and $\boldsymbol{\delta_i}$ the influence from the neighbor nodes of v_i. $\boldsymbol{\delta_i} = \{I_j\}_{j=1, W_{ij}=1}^N$. This approach calculates the label of the unlabeled node v_i based on the following assumption:

$$P_{ic} = p(y_i = c \mid \boldsymbol{\delta_i}). \qquad (3)$$

According to this assumption, the class distributions of unlabeled nodes are calculated based on $\{I_j\}_{j=1}^N$. To measure the influence I_j quantitatively, the class propagating distribution is proposed here. Let q_{jc} denote the fraction of the nodes that have the class L_c in the neighbor nodes of v_j. The vector $\mathbf{q_j} = [q_{j1}, \ldots, q_{jc}, \ldots, q_{jM}]$ is called the class propagating distribution of v_j. q_{jc} can be calculated by

$$q_{jc} = \frac{\sum_{i=1}^N P_{ic} W_{ij}}{\sum_{k=1}^N W_{jk}}. \qquad (4)$$

The vector $\mathbf{q_j}$ is used to measure the influence I_j, where the c'th element of $\mathbf{q_j}$ is larger and the probability that the neighbor nodes of v_j are labeled with the class L_c is greater. Considering all the neighbor nodes of v_i, the probability that the node v_i has the class L_c is proportional to the sum of the class propagating distributions of all the neighbor nodes. After normalization, P_{ic} can be described by

$$P_{ic} = p(y_i = c \mid \boldsymbol{\delta_i}) = \frac{\sum_{j=1}^N q_{jc} W_{ij}}{\sum_{k=1}^N W_{ik}}. \qquad (5)$$

The classes of unlabeled nodes are calculated in an iterative manner. At the beginning, all class distributions of unlabeled nodes are initialized with the vectors in which all elements are equal to a constant $1/M$, since the classes of these nodes are unknown. Then, the class propagating distributions of all nodes are calculated using (4). The class distributions of unlabeled nodes are then calculated using (5). Repeat the above two steps while the class distributions are not stable. When the class distributions are stable, the final class distributions of unlabeled nodes are obtained. The class label, to which the maximal element in the class distribution of the node v_i corresponds, is assigned to the node v_i.

The class distributions and the class propagating distributions are written in the matrix form, denoted by $\mathbf{P}$ and $\mathbf{Q}$,

$$\mathbf{P} = \left[\mathbf{P}_1^T, \ldots, \mathbf{P}_i^T, \ldots, \mathbf{P}_N^T\right]^T,$$
$$\mathbf{Q} = \left[\mathbf{q}_1^T, \ldots, \mathbf{q}_i^T, \ldots, \mathbf{q}_N^T\right]^T. \tag{6}$$

Equations (4) and (5) are written in matrix form

$$\mathbf{Q} = \mathrm{nrow}\,(\mathbf{W})\,\mathbf{P},$$
$$\mathbf{P} = \mathrm{nrow}\,(\mathbf{W})\,\mathbf{Q}, \tag{7}$$

where the function nrow() is the normalization for each row. The classification algorithm is displayed in Algorithm 1, where y_i denotes the classes of the node v_i. Let the matrix $\mathbf{Y}$ denote $\{y_i\}_{i=1}^N$. The matrix $\mathbf{Y}$ has some unknown elements, which are the classes of the unlabeled nodes. This algorithm calculates these elements. For convenience, the algorithm in Algorithm 1 is called CPD for short.

CPD algorithm is similar to MRW and wvRN, which calculate the classes of unlabeled nodes in an iterative manner. MRW and wvRN calculate the class of a node based on the classes of its neighbor nodes. CPD calculates the node class using a probabilistic approach, instead of the classes of neighbor nodes.

4. Experiments and Results

4.1. Experiment Setup. Six real networks are used to examine the performance of the proposed CPD algorithm, including Citeseer, Cora, and four networks in WebKB dataset [11]. WebKB dataset has four networks, including Texas, Cornell, Wisconsin, and Washington. In these networks, nodes are web pages of the four universities and edges are hyperlinks between them. Citeseer and Cora are paper citation networks built with citation relationship. The information of the experimental data is listed in Table 1.

In the experiments, micro-*F1* and macro-*F1* are used as the evaluation metrics. micro-*F1* and macro-*F1* are real numbers between 0 and 1; the larger they are the better the classification algorithms are. We calculate micro-*F1* and macro-*F1* with (8) and (9) used in [9]. t_{ic} indicates the true class label in original datasets while y_{ic} indicates the class label returned by classification algorithms. If the true class label of the node v_i is L_c, t_{ic} is equal to 1, otherwise $t_{ic} = 0$.

```
Algorithm CPD(W, Y)

For each unlabeled node v_i
    P_ic ← 1/M;
End for
For each labeled node v_i
    P_ic ← 1, if y_i = L_c;
End for
S_0 ← P;
k ← 0;
Repeat
    k ← k + 1;
    S_k ← nrow(nrow(W)nrow(W)S_{k-1});
Until max |S_k − S_{k-1}| ≤ ε
P ← S_k;
For each unlabeled node v_i
    y_i ← L_c, if c = arg max_r(P_ir);
End for
```

ALGORITHM 1: The classification algorithm based on class propagating distributions.

TABLE 1: The information about experimental data.

Name	Number of nodes	Number of edges
Texas	187	578
Cornell	195	569
Wisconsin	265	938
Washington	230	783
Citeseer	3312	4598
Cora	2708	10556

If the v_i's label returned by classification algorithms is L_c, y_{ic} is equal to 1, otherwise $y_{ic} = 0$.

$$\mathrm{micro\text{-}}F1 = 2\,\frac{\sum_{i,c}\left(y_{ic}t_{ic}\right)}{\sum_{i,c}\left(y_{ic} + t_{ic}\right)}, \tag{8}$$

$$\mathrm{macro\text{-}}F1 = \frac{2}{M}\sum_{c=1}^{M}\frac{\sum_{i,c}\left(y_{ic}t_{ic}\right)}{\sum_{i,c}\left(y_{ic} + t_{ic}\right)}. \tag{9}$$

4.2. Experiment Results

4.2.1. Classification Performance. In order to test the classification performance of the proposed CPD algorithm, CPD is compared with four methods on real networks. The four baseline methods are BLC, wvRN, MRW, and SocioDim. BLC is a collective inference method based on Bayesian local classifier. wvRN is the collective inference method without training classifiers. MRW is a classification method based on random walk. SocioDim is a classification method based on extracting latent attributes of nodes. CPD, wvRN, and MRW calculate the node classes in an iterative manner. In the realization of them, the termination condition of iterations is $\varepsilon = 10^{-5}/N$ and the maximal iteration number is 500.

Let r denote the proportion of the labeled nodes in all nodes of a network. According to the value of r, the labeled

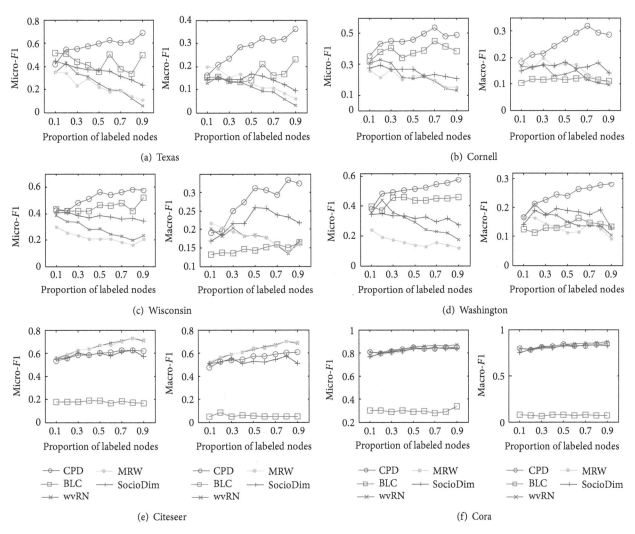

FIGURE 1: Results of comparison experiments.

nodes of a network are picked out randomly. The rest nodes are used as the test data, whose classes are calculated by classification methods. In this way, the labeled nodes of a network are produced for 10 times at a value of r. The average micro-$F1$ and macro-$F1$ are plotted in Figure 1.

Figure 1 displays that the performance of CPD is better than that of the other four methods on the first four networks. On Citeseer and Cora networks, CPD underperforms the other four methods. These experimental results can be explained by the homophily degree of these networks. According to [11], the homophily degree of a network can be indicated by the average percentage by which a node's neighbor is of the same class label. Consequently, the homophily degree of a network can be calculated using

$$\text{homophily} = \frac{\sum_{i=1}^{N} \left(s_i / d_i \right)}{N}, \tag{10}$$

where d_i denotes the number of nodes that connect to the node v_i and s_i denotes the number of nodes that connect to the node v_i and have the same class with v_i. The homophily degrees of the networks in Table 1 are calculated and

TABLE 2: The homophily degrees of the networks in Table 1.

Name	Homophily degree
Texas	0.1068
Cornell	0.1212
Wisconsin	0.1868
Washington	0.2698
Citeseer	0.7256
Cora	0.8252

the results are listed in Table 2. The homophily degrees of first four networks are very low, so they are the networks with heterophily.

MRW and wvRN are homophily-based methods, which calculate the classes of unlabeled nodes using the classes of their neighbor nodes, so they perform better on the Citeseer network and the Cora network, which are both of high homophily. The first four networks are of heterophily, where most of connected nodes have different classes, so the homophily-based methods performance declines. BLC,

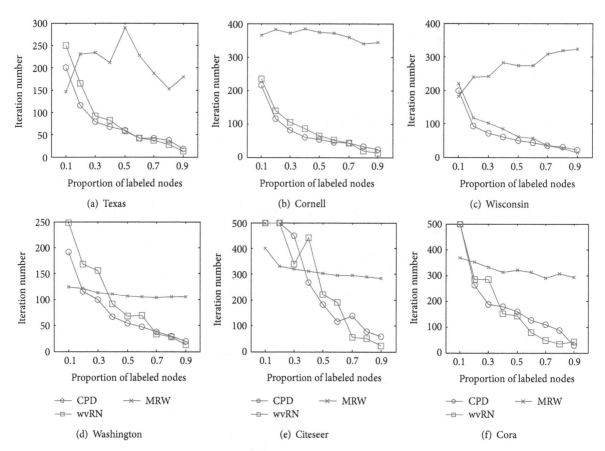

FIGURE 2: The comparison of iteration number.

SocioDim, and CPD abandon the homophily assumption, so they achieve better performance than MRW and wvRN. These experiments show that CPD has better performance on the networks with heterophily.

4.2.2. Convergence. CPD calculates class labels of nodes in the iterative manner and 500 iterations are used in the above experiments. The issue that concerns us is whether CPD is able to converge within 500 iterations. In this subsection, the convergence of CPD is studied through experiments. We use $\varepsilon = 10^{-5}/N$ as the termination condition of iterations, and the maximum iteration number is 500. The iteration numbers when CPD terminates are plotted in Figure 2.

Because MRW and wvRN require iterative calculation, their iteration numbers are also plotted in Figure 2 for comparison. Figure 2 shows that CPD can satisfy the termination condition of iterations on the first four networks and its iteration number is less than those of wvRN and MRW. It means that CPD is convergent on the networks with heterophily.

5. Conclusions

Many classification methods in networked data classify nodes based on homophily assumption using their neighbor nodes. In real world, there are many networks with heterophily, in which the classes of unlabeled nodes are hardly calculated using their neighbor nodes. This paper focuses on such problem to develop a novel approach, which utilizes a probabilistic approach to measure the class influence between two connected nodes. The experiments on real datasets show that the proposed method has better performance on the networks with heterophily.

References

[1] S. A. Macskassy and F. Provost, "Classification in networked data: a toolkit and a univariate case study," *Journal of Machine Learning Research*, vol. 8, pp. 935–983, 2007.

[2] J. Neville and D. Jensen, "Iterative classification in relational data," in *Proceedings of the 15th AAAI Workshop on Learning Statistical Models from Relational Data*, pp. 42–49, AAAI, Menlo Park, Calif, USA, 2000.

[3] Q. Lu and L. Getoor, "Link-based classification," in *Proceedings of the 20th International Conference on Machine Learning*, pp. 496–503, ACM, New York, NY, USA, August 2003.

[4] V. R. Carvalho and W. W. Cohen, " On the collective classification of email, 'speech acts'," in *Proceeding of the 28th Annual International ACM SIGIR Conference on Research and Development in Information Retrieval*, pp. 345–352, ACM, New York, NY, USA, 2005.

[5] J. Neville and D. Jensen, "Collective classification with relational dependency networks," in *Proceedings of the 2nd Workshop on*

Multi-Relational Data Mining at KDD-2003, pp. 77–91, ACM, New York, NY, USA, 2003.

[6] F. Lin and W. W. Cohen, "Semi-supervised classification of network data using very few labels," in *Proceedings of the International Conference on Advances in Social Network Analysis and Mining (ASONAM '10)*, pp. 192–199, IEEE Computer Society, Washington, DC, USA, August 2010.

[7] D. Zhou, O. Bousquet, T. N. Lal, J. Weston, and B. Schölkopf, "Learning with local and global consistency," in *Proceedings of the 16th Neural Information Processing Systems*, MIT, Cambridge, UK, 2004.

[8] J. He, J. Carbonell, and Y. Liu, "Graph-based semi-supervised learning as a generative model," in *Proceedings of the 20th International Joint Conference on Artificial Intelligence*, AAAI, Menlo Park, Calif, USA, 2007.

[9] L. Tang and H. Liu, "Leveraging social media networks for classification," *Journal of Data Mining and Knowledge Discovery*, vol. 23, no. 3, pp. 447–478, 2011.

[10] M. McPherson, L. Smith-Lovin, and J. M. Cook, "Birds of a feather: homophily in social networks," *Annual Review of Sociology*, vol. 27, pp. 415–444, 2001.

[11] P. Sen, G. M. Namata, M. Bilgic, L. Getoor, B. Gallagher, and T. Eliassi-Rad, "Collective classification in network data," *AI Magazine*, vol. 29, no. 3, pp. 93–106, 2008.

6

Order Batching in Warehouses by Minimizing Total Tardiness: A Hybrid Approach of Weighted Association Rule Mining and Genetic Algorithms

Amir Hossein Azadnia,[1] **Shahrooz Taheri,**[2] **Pezhman Ghadimi,**[3]
Muhamad Zameri Mat Saman,[1] **and Kuan Yew Wong**[1]

[1] *Department of Manufacturing and Industrial Engineering, Faculty of Mechanical Engineering, Universiti Teknologi Malaysia,*
Johor Bahru, 81310 UTM Skudai, Malaysia
[2] *Department of Computer Science, Faculty of Computer Science, Universiti Teknologi Malaysia, Johor Bahru,*
81310 UTM Skudai, Malaysia
[3] *Enterprise Research Centre, University of Limerick, Limerick, Ireland*

Correspondence should be addressed to Amir Hossein Azadnia; azadnia.ie@gmail.com

Academic Editors: Y.-P. Huang and P. Melin

One of the cost-intensive issues in managing warehouses is the order picking problem which deals with the retrieval of items from their storage locations in order to meet customer requests. Many solution approaches have been proposed in order to minimize traveling distance in the process of order picking. However, in practice, customer orders have to be completed by certain due dates in order to avoid tardiness which is neglected in most of the related scientific papers. Consequently, we proposed a novel solution approach in order to minimize tardiness which consists of four phases. First of all, weighted association rule mining has been used to calculate associations between orders with respect to their due date. Next, a batching model based on binary integer programming has been formulated to maximize the associations between orders within each batch. Subsequently, the order picking phase will come up which used a Genetic Algorithm integrated with the Traveling Salesman Problem in order to identify the most suitable travel path. Finally, the Genetic Algorithm has been applied for sequencing the constructed batches in order to minimize tardiness. Illustrative examples and comparisons are presented to demonstrate the proficiency and solution quality of the proposed approach.

1. Introduction

Based on ELA/AT Kearney [1], about twenty percent of the logistic costs of the surveyed companies were incurred due to warehousing in 2003. A vital part of the logistics system of a company is involved with its warehouses. Optimization of operations within every facility must be considered as an important part of its policies in order to promptly deliver goods or services to its customers at the least cost [2]. Responsiveness is a critical success factor in a warehousing system. Product movement within a warehouse can be facilitated effectively by consolidating orders into batches which can be done before picking customer orders [3].

In order picking systems, certain due dates are assigned to customer orders which should not be violated. In order to avoid production delays, item retrieval from the warehouse needs to be done at its appropriate time. In these cases, the tardiness of customer orders should be involved with order batching instead of using the total processing time as a measure for the solution quality [4]. Henn et al. [5] defined the tardiness of a customer order as the positive value between the completion time of a customer order with its due date. The time that an order picker finishes her/his tour of gathering all required items and comes back to the starting point is called completion time. Obviously, one of the factors that can influence the completion time is

Order Batching in Warehouses by Minimizing Total Tardiness: A Hybrid Approach of Weighted Association Rule
Mining and Genetic Algorithms

55

the processing time of the orders. According to the above explanation, reducing the processing time and travel time for constructing a batch is an important fact in reducing the costs and minimizing delays of the customer responses. On the other hand, not considering the order's due date in the process of order batching can cause a huge dissatisfaction in customer expectations regarding the efficient responsiveness of the company. For explanation purposes, assume that we have some orders with different due dates, considering just processing time or traveling time in the process of order batching regardless of their due dates may consolidate orders with different due dates in a same batch. So, this issue may cause a problem for meeting customers' demand in a certain due date. Consequently, it is highlighted that order due dates should be considered as an important factor for order batching.

Based on the above illuminated problem, this research paper attempts to develop a novel model to overcome the aforementioned issue in the multiple parallel aisles with manual order picking system. In our proposed model, it was assumed that orders with similar items are grouped together. Therefore, batching orders with higher resemblance can reduce the order pickers' traveled distance. Also, for considering the due dates in our model, the due date of each order is defined as a weight parameter in calculating the association between orders in terms of support. The association information integrates the bathing process with various data regarding each order. For calculating the association between orders in terms of support, mining association rules with weighted items (MINWAL) were utilized. Then, a clustering approach based on a binary integer programming model has been used in order to maximize the customer demand association which is called support. Next, the Genetic Algorithm (GA) has been utilized to solve the Traveling Salesman Problem (TSP) to minimize the travelling time for collecting all items in a constructed batch. This process was followed by a batch sequencing process which utilized a GA in order to minimize the average tardiness of all orders. This paper copes with integrating batch ordering, picker routing, and the batch sequencing problem regarding orders' due date in order to minimize the average tardiness of all orders. We believe that the proposed approach, namely, ATGH is not considered in any existing published paper. In the next section, a comprehensive literature survey is presented in order to review the existing research activities related to the current research paper.

2. Literature Review

2.1. Order Batching Problem. Order picking is an action which takes place to fulfill a customer demand (internal/external) that is normally done by retrieving items from buffer locations inside the warehouse [6–8]. In practice, there are two types of systems for order picking: systems which are totally manual and involved with human order pickers and the systems that are entirely computerized in case of retrieving items from the warehouse. Picker-to-parts and parts-to-picker systems can be categorized as the systems that belong to the first group of warehousing systems [5, 9].

Picker-to-parts systems are the most commonly used systems in warehousing in which picking the items is done by an operator that drives or walks along the aisles [10, 11]. This scenario is different in parts-to-picker systems. Order pickers do not move in this system and are located in the depot. Pallets or bins (unit load) from the warehouse are retrieved by automated storage and retrieval systems (AS/RS) and delivered to them at the depot. After that, the requested items are detached by the operators stationed in the depot and the pallets or bins are returned to its spot in the warehouse by the AS/RS [5].

In a large amount of orders, a single order picking policy might be applied in which one order can be picked in each picking tour. However, in a small amount of orders, picking loads in a single picking tour can lead to a decrease in travel times [12]. Order batching is classified as a NP-hard problem which can be done to improve warehouse efficiency by reducing operational costs [12, 13]. Thus, many heuristic algorithms are proposed in the literature which help to solve this problem. Savings and seed algorithms are the most commonly used order batching heuristics in the case of manual picking systems. Seed algorithms were introduced by [14] in which a seed order would be selected for each batch. With respect to the picking device capacity, other orders would be assigned to the seed orders. Clarke and Wright [15] first developed the savings algorithms inspired by a vehicle routing algorithm. This algorithm works based on the saving that would be achieved in travel distance or travel time. After that, a pair of batches would be selected iteratively by the algorithm and combined with each other until a capacity constraint threshold is reached that stops combining of the batches.

In the current literature review, it was tried to review all existing papers which are involved in order batching problems considering the minimization of due dates, total travel distance, and processing time. First, Vinod [16] suggested that integer programming can be used as a flexible method for grouping any kind of objects. Armstrong et al. [17] also presented an integer programming model based on predetermined batch sizes considering proximity batching.

They tried to minimize the total processing time of all batches. Ratliff and Rosenthal [18] tried to minimize travel distance based on a procedure which helps to find the best picking tour traveled. By means of a distinguished TSP, a tour was formed in a 50 aisles warehouse. Kusiak et al. [19] used a quadratic integer programming model to obtain batches from eight orders. In their proposed model, it was tried to minimize the total sum of distances.

One of their limitations was related to their model range of applicability which is not well suited for large numbers of orders. Gibson and Sharp [20] presented an order batching procedure integrated with a computer simulation which resulted in minimization of travel distance for each tour. Rosenwein [21] utilized Centre of Gravity (COG) and Minimum Additional Aisle (MAA) for order batching in order to measure travel distance. It was shown that the MAA metric performed better than the COG metric regarding travel tour generation. Gademann et al. [22] targeted to minimize the total travel time for all batches using a branch-and-bound algorithm. They tested their model by several test sets with a maximum order number of 32 which were compared together regarding their CPU times. Hsu et al. [3] applied Genetic Algorithms (GAs) to deal with order batching problems with any kind of configuration. In their proposed approach, they endeavored to minimize the total travel distance. In another research activity done by Chen and Wu [23]; data mining and integer programming were combined to form a solution approach regarding the order batching problem. They have tried to maximize the similarity between orders in a batch in terms of support without considering orders' due dates. Based on the presented results which was attempted to compare first-come first-served (FCFS), MAA, COG, and Gibson and Sharp's method (GSM), the authors stated that the proposed approach is effective in solving the order batching problems in terms of reducing traveling distances. Based on the analysis done by Gademann and van de Velde [24], the authors stated that the order batching problem is NP-hard to a great extent provided that no batch has more than two orders. They developed a branch-and-price algorithm to formulate the problem in order to minimize the total travel distance. Three years later, a mixed-integer programming model was developed by Bozer and Kile [25] in order to minimize the length of trips or travel distance. They stated that acquiring minimum travel distance for a large number of orders requires substantial computational time. Kulak et al. [26] proposed a solution approach to reduce the mathematical burden of order batching and picker routing problems. They proved the efficiency of their cluster-based tabu search approaches by running several test examples. They have focused on minimizing the travel distance between locations.

In practice, certain completion due dates are assigned to customer orders. For instance, in distribution warehouses, the scheduled departure of trucks has to be done by certain due dates to ensure the on time delivery of the requested items to the customers [22]. In material warehouses, avoiding production delays can be guaranteed, if retrieving the items from the warehouse is done based on their schedules. In these cases, assessing the tardiness of the customer orders needs to be focused in the process of batching customer orders into picking orders [4]. The tardiness is the difference between the order finish time and the due date, if this difference is positive. So, it is very important to consider the orders' due dates when batching processes are being done. To our knowledge, there are few papers that consider due dates or minimize tardiness in their model. Elsayed et al. [4] and Elsayed and Lee [27] focused on developing minimization models of order tardiness and their incurred costs. The solution approaches proposed by these two research papers are of limited applicability to manual picker-to-parts systems. Single processing times are used in both solution approaches in order to determine a sequence of batches. Therefore, they will not yield competitive results in the situation described in our paper. Won and Olafsson [28] endeavored to integrate order batching and picker routing problems together in order to minimize the travel time. They compared their proposed heuristics with other existing algorithms such as FCFS. It can be perceived that their simulation results improvement is reduced when the numbers of items for each order increase. Tsai et al. [29] attempted to solve a batch picking model considering earliness and tardiness penalty using a multiple-GA method for obtaining the best possible batch picking plans. They tried to develop a flexible model to cope with the current dynamic environment in terms of responsiveness. Upon studying their proposed method, it was determined that the orders were split which causes items in an order to be collected in different tours. Also, their proposed model allocates penalty to batches overweight (when the batch volume exceeds the picker capacity) which is not applicable in practice.

2.2. Picker Routing Problem. The picker routing problem is defined as the process of identifying the minimum distance which would be traveled by the order picker in a warehouse upon identifying which order should be picked first [30, 31]. There are some existing heuristics for picker routing such as return, s-shape, largest gap, and combined routing. De Koster et al. [32] tried to solve order batching problems by evaluating two groups of heuristic methods such as seed algorithms and time savings algorithms by means of s-shape and largest gap strategies as two different routing strategies. According to the obtained results, integrating the s-shape strategy and an outsized capacity pick device together with seed algorithms can yield better performance. In contrast, the largest gap strategy using a small capacity pick device gives best performance when it integrated with time savings algorithms. Ho and Tseng [33] considered the largest gap routing strategy together with a simulated annealing optimization method not only to optimize the total travel distance but also to find alternative routes that are better than ones found by just the largest gap strategy. In a research activity done by Theys et al. [34], s-shape, largest gap and some other routing heuristics were compared with the Lin-Kernighan-Helsgaun TSP heuristic. Based on their results, this TSP heuristic helps to reduce travel distance up to the rate of 48% on average. In the current research activity, a GA_{TSP} model has been used in order to solve the picker routing problem.

2.3. Batch Sequencing Problem. The problem of batch sequencing can be defined as finding the orders of constructed batches to be processed further. Henn and Schmid [35] used metaheuristics to solve their proposed model of order batching and sequencing to minimize the orders' tardiness. Iterated Local Search and Attribute-Based Hill Climber are the two employed metaheuristics in their model. According to different test problems, the efficiency of their proposed methods was illustrated. Provided solutions can be improved by 46% on average in comparison with the ones obtained by standard constructive heuristics such as an application of the Earliest Due Date rule. They conducted their proposed method for a maximum of 80 items.

Other sections of this paper are as follows. First, the proposed model is described in Section 3 which covers all the aspects that are involved with it. After that, Section 4 presents the research methodology of this paper. This is followed by Section 5 which encompasses the numerical examples, results, and discussion of this research activity.

Finally, Section 6 gives an end to the paper with a brief conclusion.

3. Model Description

The assumptions of this research are described as follows.

(1) A manual picker to part system in a parallel aisle warehouse is considered in this research.

(2) There is only one location for storing each type of item and vice versa.

(3) Multiple picker devices are not allowed. Therefore the maximum number of pickers is only one.

(4) The volume for each order should not exceed the capacity of the picker.

(5) Batch size does not exceed the capacity of picker.

(6) The storage size in each location is identical.

(7) All customer orders are known in advance.

3.1. Weighted Association Rule Mining Binary Integer Clustering Model. In this section, an association based clustering model developed by Chen and Wu [23] was modified in order to create the batch structure regarding orders' due date. First, the association between customers' demand will be calculated based on the similarity of items in orders with respect to their due date using MINWAL. Orders' due dates are considered as the weight of association rule mining. Although batching orders with higher associations generated by similarity between their items can decrease the distance travelled by order pickers, not considering the due dates would cause the orders to be batched inappropriately with different due dates. Some problems may occur by the aforementioned issue such as shortage or excess inventory costs. In order to solve this problem, the order due date has been considered as a weight of each order for calculating the support between orders. Relationship maximization of customer orders based on similar items within each order and due dates of each order can be done with the weighted association rules. Travel distance would be reduced by taking into account batching of orders with higher relationships. Other than that, higher associations can batch orders with similar due dates in order to minimize tardiness. This is followed by utilizing a binary integer programming model integrated with a clustering algorithm which assembles the orders into their respective batches.

3.1.1. Weighted Association Mining for Determining Customer Order Relationships. Association rule mining can be defined as a data mining method which tries to distinguish interrelations of variables where large databases exist [36]. Some rules are involved with the association rule model where there is an association between some set of items with another set of items [37]. In order to calculate rule interestingness, support and confidence can be considered as the two most appropriate measures in association rule mining. The support for an itemset is the percentage of transactions that contain the itemset

TABLE 1: Order-item data.

Order	Items	Due date
O_1	A(3) B(4)	10
O_2	A(2) C(3)	30
O_3	A(1) B(3)	5
O_4	A(2) B(4) C(2)	50

TABLE 2: Item-order data.

Item	Order
A	O_1, O_2, O_3, O_4
B	O_1, O_3, O_4
C	O_2, O_4

in the database. A probability shows how frequently the rule head occurs among all the groups containing the rule body which can be defined as the confidence of an association rule (body $\Rightarrow$ head) [38, 39].

Based on the definition by Agrawal et al. [36], the association rule mining problem is addressed as follows: items are described as $I = \{i_1, i_2, \ldots, i_n\}$ which is a set of n binary attributes. The database is represented as $D = \{t_1, t_2, \ldots, t_m\}$ which is a set of transactions. An exclusive transaction ID belongs to each transaction in D together with a subset of the items in I. A rule is defined as an implication of the form $X \Rightarrow Y$, where $X, Y \subseteq I$, and $X \bigcap Y = \phi$. The association rule, $X \Rightarrow Y$ [support = s%, confidence = c%], holds in the item-order data D with confidence c if c% of Order Identifiers in D contain orderset X and also contains orderset Y. The rule $X \Rightarrow Y$ has support s if s% of the item-order D contains both X and Y. For instance, upon batching the orders by taking into account the customer order patterns, association rule mining involves finding out the amount of support between demands of customers from the order database. In order batching, Table 1 which shows the order-item data is transposed to the item-order data form shown in Table 2 since the order associations are demanded and the product item associations is not necessary. In this example, association rule mining can perform its job to define the associations between customer orders that can be perceived from information presented in Table 2.

In the area of order batching, association rule mining was first used by Chen and Wu [23]. In their research paper, association rule mining was used to calculate the correlations between customers' demands in terms of support. They pointed out that orders with similar items should be consolidated together in order to minimize the total travel distance traversed by the picker. An Apriori algorithm has been used in their proposed method to calculate the association between orders. It should be highlighted that they only considered the relationships between orders in terms of similarities between items. However, in batch processing, each order has a due date which can be considered as the weight but this weight is not considered by any other existing method in the literature.

The classical Apriori algorithm [40] extracts binary association rules based on the downward closure property which

TABLE 3: Weight of each order.

Order	Weight
O_1	0.5827
O_2	0.1979
O_3	0.7634
O_4	0.0672

proves that subsets of a frequent itemset are also frequent [41]. However, the Apriori algorithm cannot be applied because it cannot handle the weighted case. Therefore, in this research activity, the MINWAL algorithm is applied in order to extract the weighted supports among the pair of orders to fulfill the task of considering both the support and the weights factors.

In order to use MINWAL [42] for mining weighted association rules, the weight should be in the range of the 0 to 1 interval. Based on the aforementioned fact, larger weights should be assigned to orders with smaller due dates in a comparison with other orders that have lots of time to be delivered in order to minimize the average tardiness of all orders. Therefore, in this study, (1) has been used to calculate the appropriate weights for each order as following:

$$\text{Weight}(O_i) = e^{(-0.1 * \beta * d_{O_i}/\text{Maximume Due Date})}, \quad (1)$$

where O_i denotes an order and d_{O_i} refers to the due date of order O_i. β is a constant value that is used to normalize the due dates which is considered as 30 (30 minute) in this study. Also, the maximum due date of the orders was used in order to provide an appropriate interval for the weights. For example, the weight of each order is tabulated in Table 3 which is calculated by (1).

Given a set of orders $O = \{o_1, o_2, \ldots, o_m\}$, a weight w_j for each order o_j, within the values of 0 to 1 is assigned by (1) via its due date, where $j = \{1, 2, \ldots, m\}$ shows the importance of it. The weighted support for the weighted association orders of O_1 and O_2 as $O_1 \Rightarrow O_2$ is defined, if the weighted support of such a pair of orders is no less than the minimum weighted support (minsup) threshold. In this study, the minimum support threshold is considered as 0 in order to identify all the associations among orders. Equation (2) shows the support of an association for any pair of orders as following:

$$\left(\sum \sum_{w_j \in (O_1 \cup O_2)} w_j \right) * \text{Support}(O_1 \cup O_2). \quad (2)$$

Algorithm 1 shows the MINWAL steps in order to mine weighted association rules. This algorithm consists of 6 subroutines such as, Search, Counting, Join, Prune, Checking and Rules. The search subroutine provides the size of the largest itemsets in database. Counting is responsible for counting every 1-itemset inside the database. The Join step is responsible for generating the k-itemsets (Ck) from ($k - 1$)-itemsets ($Ck - 1$). The Prune step removes inappropriate itemsets which do not exist. The Checking step updates the count of k-itemsets inside the transaction and prunes itemsets which do not meet the minimum support threshold. In the Rules step, every association rule will be extracted. Table 4 shows the notations of Algorithm 1.

```
(1)  Main Algorithm (wminsup, mincon f, D, w)
(2)     size = Search (D)
(3)  L = 0;
(4)        for (i = 1; i ≤ size; i++)
(5)           Cᵢ = Lᵢ = 0;
(6)        for each transaction do
(7)           (SC, C₁, size) = Counting (D, w);
(8)        k = 1;
(9)        while (|Ck| ≥ k)
(10)          k++;
(11)             Cₖ = Join (Cₖ₋₁);
(12)             Cₖ = Prune (Cₖ);
(13)             (Cₖ, Lₖ) = Checking (Cₖ, D);
(14) L = L ∪ Lₖ;
(15) Rules (SC, L);
(16) ends;
```

ALGORITHM 1: MINWAL algorithm [42].

TABLE 4: Notations of Algorithm 1.

D	The database
w	The set of item weights
L_k	Set of large k-itemsets
C_k	Set of k-itemsets which may be k-subsets of large j-itemsets for $j \geq k$
$SC(X)$	No. of transactions containing itemset X
wminsup	Weighted support threshold
minconf	Confidence threshold
Size	Maximum possible large weighted itemsets

3.1.2. Association Based Binary Integer Programming for Orders Batching. In order to create the batch structure, a binary integer clustering model which has been developed by Chen and Wu [23] was applied. They developed a binary integer programming model for maximizing similarity between orders in terms of support in order to minimize the total traveling distance. In this research activity, support between orders was calculated based on weighted association mining using MINWAL which was described in Section 3.1.1. The binary integer model for order batching is described as follows.

Parameters

S_{ij} Support between order i and j determined by MINWAL

C_v Capacity of picking vehicle

V_i Weight of order i

K Number of batches

$X_{ij} \begin{cases} 1 & \text{if order } i \text{ is assigned to batch } j; \\ 0 & \text{otherwise}; \end{cases}$

$$Y_i \begin{cases} 1 & \text{if order } j \text{ is chosen as a batch median;} \\ 0 & \text{otherwise;} \end{cases}$$

$$\text{Maximize} \quad \sum_{i=1}^{N}\sum_{j=1}^{N} S_{ij} * X_{ij} \qquad (3)$$

$$\text{Subject to} \quad \sum_{j=1}^{N} X_{ij} = 1 \quad \text{for } i, j = 1, 2 \ldots, N \qquad (4)$$

$$X_{ij} \leq Y_j \quad \text{for } i, j = 1, 2 \ldots, N \qquad (5)$$

$$\sum_{j=1}^{N} Y_j = K \qquad (6)$$

$$\sum_{i=1}^{N} V_i X_{ij} \leq C_v \quad \text{for } j = 1, 2 \ldots, N \qquad (7)$$

$$X_{ij} = 0, 1 \quad \text{for } i, j = 1, 2 \ldots, N \qquad (8)$$

$$Y_j = 0, 1 \quad \text{for } j = 1, 2 \ldots, N. \qquad (9)$$

In the current model, the objective function (3) maximizes the sum of support from all orders to their relevant batch medians as K orders are selected as batch medians. This model will maximize the support between orders in the batches. Membership of each order in just one batch would be guaranteed by constraint (4). The number of batches with K is limited using constraints (5) and (6). The total quantity in a tour is also represented as a limitation in constraint (7). It cannot exceed the capacity of order picker C_v. For the order batching model to have a binary solution would be ensured by constraints (8) and (9). For calculating the initial numbers of batches (10) will be used where $\sum V_i$ represents total volume of all orders as following:

$$K_{\text{initial}} = \left\lceil \frac{\sum V_i}{C_v} \right\rceil. \qquad (10)$$

3.2. Picker Routing

3.2.1. Genetic Algorithms. In this research, GAs which were introduced by Holland [43] have been used in order to solve the picker routing and batch sequencing problem. The biological evolution process is used as a base fact in a GA for problem solving to a great extent. The main steps of a GA can be described as follows [44, 45]:

(i) populating a series of solutions,

(ii) solutions assessment,

(iii) picking the most appropriate solutions,

(iv) generating new solutions based on some genetic operation.

In step (iii), selection forms the main part of a GA. The bad solutions are removed by selection and the good ones remain. Random generation over the feasible or infeasible

solution space of a problem is used as a basis for creating the population. Each solution is evaluated using the fitness function. Selection would be done according to certain selections of fitness together with the probability that is assigned to it. Generating a fresh population and a better solution are involved with recombination of the individual solution. Crossover and mutation are the most used GA operators for generating new offspring from the old generation of parents. Parameters of the GA are originated from the probabilities of mutation and crossover. Exploration of the sample space is diversified by these operators. In this research, the GA has been utilized in two steps. First, the GA has been used in order to solve the picker routing problem. Consider that in the warehouse a set of items should be picked by a picker in one tour. Therefore, the picker routing problem in the warehouse could be categorized as a TSP. The goal in the picker routing problem as a TSP in the warehouse is to find an optimal path for minimizing the travel distance traversed by the picking machine where each node is visited at least once. In this research, for a given number of itemset in a batch, $\text{GA}_{\text{-TSP}}$ has been used to find the minimum travel distance which is traversed by the picking machine. Second, a GA has been utilized in order to sequence all batches, namely, $\text{GA}_{\text{-sequencing}}$ which would be further processed. The batches are sequenced based on a fitness function which minimizes the tardiness of all orders. The detailed procedures of $\text{GA}_{\text{-TSP}}$ and $\text{GA}_{\text{-sequencing}}$ are illustrated in Sections 3.2.3 and 3.2.4.

3.2.2. Warehouse Layout. The warehouse discussed throughout this research is assumed to have a 3D multi-parallel-aisle warehouse layout. The picker will start the tour from the depot which is located in front of the leftmost aisle and returns back to it. A picker leaves the depot. After that, it travels to a certain buffer spot where it picks the requested order(s) and puts the order(s) into a certain picker. Then, it continue on its way to another spot. These procedures would be repeated again and again so that all the requested orders are picked. Then, it is time for the picker to return to the depot.

The graphic layout of the warehouse zone involved in this research activity is pictorially displayed in Figure 1. It shows the x and y dimensions of the 3D warehouse layout. Each item in the warehouse has a specific location. For example, the location of item i can be addressed by $L_i = (x_i, y_i, z_i)$. Consider two locations as $L_a = (x_a, y_a, z_a)$ and $L_b = (x_b, y_b, z_b)$. If two locations are located in the same sub-aisles of the same block, the distance between these two items locations, $(D_{a,b})$, will be calculated using

$$D_{a,b} = |x_a - x_b| + |y_a - y_b| + |z_a - z_b|. \qquad (11)$$

Equation (11) is not applicable if the two storage locations belong to different subaisles that are from the same block [34]. In order to solve this problem, distances of all possible paths between two locations have been calculated and the shortest one was considered.

3.2.3. $\text{GA}_{\text{-TSP}}$ for the Picker Routing Problem. In order to determine the optimal route of a picker related to a given

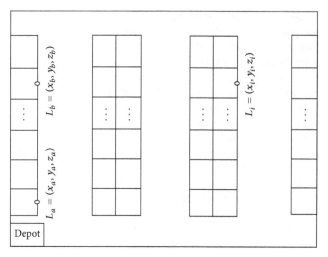

FIGURE 1: Warehouse layout.

1	2	3	4	5	6	7	8	9
L_0	L_1	L_8	L_{11}	L_9	L_{13}	L_{12}	L_{10}	L_0

FIGURE 2: A feasible chromosome encoding in GA_{TSP}.

set of items in a batch, a GA has been used to solve the TSP problem to minimize travelling time. In a GA, each solution is considered as a chromosome. The steps of GA_{TSP} are described as follows:

(1) for each batch establishing the structure of a chromosomes,

(2) generate initial feasible chromosomes,

(3) evaluate each chromosome based on the GA_{TSP} fitness function,

(4) apply the Selection operation,

(5) apply the Crossover operation,

(6) apply the Mutation operation,

(7) evaluate each offspring based on the fitness function,

(8) go to step 4, if the termination criterion is not satisfied, otherwise terminate and return the best solution as the optimal path.

At the first step of GA_{TSP}, the structure of the chromosome should be established. In the GA_{TSP}, the location of an item that should be visited is presented by the value of a gene. Accordingly, the sequence of visiting the item location is denoted by the order of a gene in a chromosome. Therefore, the total number of items locations in a specific batch is considered equal to the length of a chromosome. For example, if the length of a chromosome is nine it means nine places should be visited by the picker as shown in Figure 2. If L_i represents the item location in the warehouse, $i = \{1, \ldots, n\}$, it shows that the picker leaves the depot (L_0 denotes the location of a depot), goes to $L_1, L_8, L_{11}, L_9, L_{13}, L_{12}, L_{10}$, and then comes back to the depot.

In the second step, the initial number of feasible chromosomes should be generated randomly for each batch.

The number of initial chromosomes could be different based on the complexity of the problem. It should be considered that the first and the last gene of each chromosome should be assigned individually to the location of a depot. In step three, each chromosome will be evaluated based on the GA_{TSP} fitness function which is formulated as follows:

$$\text{fitness} = \text{Min} \sum_{j=1}^{n-1} D_{j,j+1}, \qquad (12)$$

where $D_{j,j+1}$ denotes the distance between two subsequent genes in a chromosome, $j = 1, \ldots, n-1$ represents the order of the genes, and n is number of genes.

Subsequently, step four is involved with the selection operation. In each iteration, the selection operator uses fitness values to select the parents of the next generation. In this research, the roulette wheel selection policy has been used to guarantee that the most appropriate pairs of chromosomes have been selected to generate offspring. It means that a higher probability of being selected to create a new population will be assigned to the chromosomes with higher fitness values.

Steps five and six are involved with conducting the crossover and mutation operation. The construction of the offspring is realized by the crossover and the diversity of the individuals is maintained by the mutation operator. Blocks of genes between chromosomes are traded by means of the crossover operation in which the exploitation of a particularly profitable portion of the parameter space is allowed to the block. Here, permutation order based crossover (POP) as a variation of the distinguished order crossover has been used. As shown in Figure 3, the original idea is about choosing two parents and a point for cutting. The first portion of offspring 2 contains the first portion of parent 1 up to the cut point. To form the second portion of offspring 2, consider all genes in parent 2 except those genes that already exist in the first portion of the offspring 2.

As shown in Figure 4, two positions are randomly selected in a chromosome and exchanged with each other; namely, the order based mutation approach, SWAP, is adopted for solving GA_{TSP}. Step six is followed by step seven which includes the evaluation of each offspring that has been generated in the previous step based on the GA_{TSP} fitness function. In step eight, termination criteria will be checked. If the termination condition is met, then the process will be terminated. After that, the best chromosome will be selected as the optimal solution. Otherwise, the selection process is to be conducted again to generate a new population.

3.2.4. GA for Sequencing the Batches. Sequencing the batches should be conducted in order to minimize the average tardiness of all orders. The problem of batch sequencing can be defined as finding the orders of batches which should be processed further. For this purpose, the $\text{GA}_{\text{sequencing}}$ method has been utilized. In this research, all of the batches which were constructed using binary integer programming and GA_{TSP} will be sequenced by using the GA. The population generation, selection, mutation, and stopping threshold in the $\text{GA}_{\text{sequencing}}$ are identical to those in the GA_{TSP}. However,

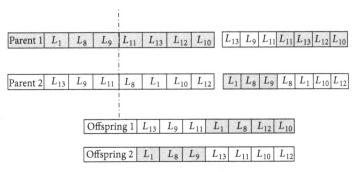

FIGURE 3: Crossover operation.

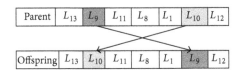

FIGURE 4: Mutation operation.

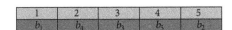

FIGURE 5: Chromosome structure.

the fitness function and chromosome structure are different than that of $GA_{\text{-TSP}}$. In contrast with $GA_{\text{-TSP}}$ chromosomes structure, batch number is presented by the value of a gene. Accordingly, the sequence of batch is denoted by the order of a gene in a chromosome. For instance, Figure 5 shows the chromosome structure. If $b_i \in B$ denotes a set of batches, Figure 5 shows that b_1, b_4, b_3, b_5, b_2 should be processed, respectively. Therefore, the length of a chromosome is equal to the number of the batches. The $GA_{\text{-sequencing}}$ fitness function for chromosome y is described in

$$\text{fitness}_y = \frac{1}{N} \sum_{k=1}^{n} \sum_{i \in b_k} CT(b_k) - Du(o_i), \qquad (13)$$

$$CT(b_k) = CT(b_{k-1}) + P_t(b_k), \qquad (14)$$

$$P_t(b_k) = \frac{\text{Opt}(b_k)}{VS}, \qquad (15)$$

where N denotes for the total number of orders. $k = \{1, \ldots, n\}$ represents the batch sequence in which n is the total number of batches. o_i stands for the order i in which $i \in b_k$. b_k denotes the batch in kth position of a sequence for specific chromosome. $CT(b_k)$ stands for the completion time of a batch in the kth position of a sequence. $Du(o_i)$ is the symbol for due date of order i which belongs to b_k. $P_t(b_k)$ is the process time of b_k. $\text{Opt}(b_k)$ is the optimal path solution for b_k. Finally, VS is the moving speed of the picker.

4. Research Methodology

In this research, the proposed methodology consists of five steps. These steps are described as follows and shown pictorially in Figure 6.

Step 1. It is involved with utilizing the MINWAL algorithm in order to determine the associations between orders in terms of support considering their due dates. In this step, an order due date will be considered as the weight of an order. It means orders that are similar in items and due date should have more support for being batched together.

Step 2. It encompasses determining the initial number of batches. In this step, the initial number of batches will be calculated by (10).

Step 3. It includes the problem of modeling and solving; first, the binary integer programming model for order clustering and batching will be modeled. Next, this model will be solved in order to determine the structures of batches.

Step 4. It is about the picker routing problem. The optimal path for a picker within each batch will be determined by solving a TSP using GA.

Step 5. It is about sequencing the batches based on the fitness function which minimizes the average tardiness of all orders. In this step, GA algorithm will be utilized in order to solve the batch sequencing problem regarding the fitness function.

5. Computational Experiments and Results

5.1. Test Problems and Parameter Setting. In this section, five numerical test problems with different settings and parameters have been carried out in order to illustrate the proficiency of the proposed method with respect to average tardiness of all orders. Table 5 summarizes the description of these test problems. This table includes information with regard to number of items, number of orders, capacity of the picker, total weight of all the items in an order, and minimum number of batches.

In these test problems, the quantity of items, quantity of orders, capacity of the picker device (C_v), and amount of each item are predetermined. Each order contains a certain

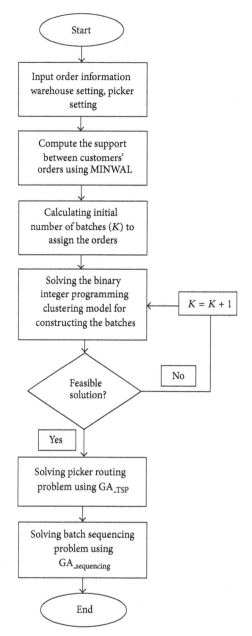

FIGURE 6: Methodology framework.

quantity of items and also each item has a certain quantity. These quantities are produced randomly. The distribution function type for the number of items in each order is Normal [5, 10]. Also, the distribution function type for each item quantity in an order is uniform [1, 10]. The picker moving speed is set as $VS = 2$ (m/s). The warehouse has 3000 item location. The GA control parameters for solving the TSP and sequencing problem are tabulated in Table 6.

All of the proposed approaches are coded using MATLAB version 7.9.0 and Java 1.5 programming language. Also, the IBM ILOG CPLEX optimization studio version 12.4 software was utilized jointly with MATLAB in order to facilitate the process of solving the binary integer programming problem. Examples are run by means of a computer featured by

4 Gigabytes random access memory (RAM) and a 2.20 Gigahertz Intel processor (T6600).

5.2. Computational Results and Discussion. In order to reveal the competency of the proposed solution approach, it was compared with the other existing methods in the literature. One of the latest published research activities in the literature which deals with minimization of tardiness has been conducted by Henn and schmid [35]. They utilized the Earliest Due Date (EDD) approach as their constructive algorithm for comparing with their proposed approaches. They proposed two heuristics. Iterated Local Search and Attribute-Based Hill Climber are the two employed metaheuristics in their model. According to different test problems, the efficiency of their

TABLE 5: Test problems description.

	Example 1	Example 2	Example 3	Example 4	Example 5
Number of orders	40	60	80	100	150
Number of items	80	120	160	200	200
Capacity of picker	200	200	300	400	550
Total weight	2212	3668	4393	6110	8369
Minimum number of batch	11	19	15	16	16
Due dates range	60	90	120	180	240

TABLE 6: GA control parameters.

	GA$_{\text{-TSP}}$	GA$_{\text{-sequencing}}$
Population size	500	200
Cross over strategy	Permutation order based crossover (POP)	Permutation order based crossover (POP)
Cross over probability	0.8	0.8
Mutation strategy	SWAP	SWAP
Mutation probability	0.2	0.2
Iteration number	10000	10000
Parent selection method	Roulette wheel	Roulette wheel

proposed methods was illustrated. Their obtained results from their proposed approaches showed a 46% improvement on tardiness compared to EDD. They used an s-shape and largest gap routing strategy for their proposed method. In order to make a reasonable comparison with their proposed method, EDD was integrated with the s-shape routing strategy and GA$_{\text{-sequencing}}$. Then, based on improvement on EDD, we can compare our proposed method with their proposed method. In the EDD approach, due dates play an important role in sorting all orders. Based on an ascending sequence, assigning the orders to batches ensures that no capacity violation can happen for the picking device.

For the warehouse condition which is described in Section 3.2.3, our proposed approach, EDD integrated with GA$_{\text{-TSP}}$ and GA$_{\text{-sequencing}}$ and EDD integrated with s-shape algorithm and GA$_{\text{-sequencing}}$ have been evaluated in terms of average tardiness for all orders (T) which is calculated based on (13), number of batches (K), total process time (P_t), and average process time for each batch (A_{P_t}). All of the GA setting for the TSP and sequencing problems are considered the same for all methods. Also, the settings which have been mentioned in Section 5.1 were considered for all of the compared methods.

The results for all of the test problems for the three approaches are tabulated in Tables 7, 8, and 9. As it is illustrated in Table 10, EDD integrated with GA$_{\text{-TSP}}$ and GA$_{\text{-sequencing}}$ has a 31.76% improvement on average in terms of average tardiness of all orders than EDD integrated with the s-shape algorithm and GA$_{\text{-sequencing}}$. It can be perceived that GA$_{\text{-TSP}}$ performs better than s-shape. Also, the ATGH method has a 68.11% improvement in average tardiness off all orders than EDD integrated with s-shape algorithm

and GA$_{\text{-sequencing}}$. Consequently, the ATGH method achieves much improvement against Henn and Schmid's [35] proposed method. According to Tables 7 and 8, it is also worth to mention that GA$_{\text{-TSP}}$ performs better than the s-shape routing strategy in terms of process time. The improvements which have been achieved in this research could be justified based on the following reasons.

The problem of order batching deals with several significant drivers in which the number of batches can be considered as a key factor [23]. As a justification to this matter, it is worth to mention that total travel distance may not decrease directly due to a decline in the number of batches. But a decline in the number of batches will increase batch sizes which may lead to an increase in the distance travelled by order picker. However, an advanced exploitation of picker capacity to load efficiently may reduce the number of constructed batches together reducing the total travel distance. Improving the total travel distance traversed by the picker can minimize the average tardiness of all orders. In terms of number of the batches according to Tables 7, 8, and 9, it can be perceived that our proposed method assigns the orders to the batches optimally. The ATGH method assigns the orders to batches based on their item similarity and their due dates and it uses the picker capacity efficiently. But the EDD method allocates the orders to batches based on an ascending sequence of their due date and it should be ensured that no capacity violation will happen for the picking device which may lead to an inefficient order batching. To highlight the problem, an example can be made based on the results tabulated in Tables 7 and 8. The number of batches for example 1 in our method is 11 in comparison with 13 obtained from EDD method. 13 batches can be justified based on this scenario that two subsequent orders, say, the first order is 100 kg and the other is 150 kg, cannot be batched together due to violated batch capacity which is set to be 200 kg. The number of batches would increase due to the aforementioned issue which affects the total process time to have an increasing manner. This situation will rarely happen in the ATGH method because of the weighted association based binary integer programming utilized which batches the orders in order to maximize the association between them which is calculated based on the item similarity of orders and the weight of their corresponding due dates. The ATGH method uses the picker capacity efficiently.

Obviously, one of the factors that can influence the completion time and the average tardiness of all orders is the processing time of the orders. Reducing the processing time

TABLE 7: Computational results of ATGH.

	Example 1	Example 2	Example 3	Example 4	Example 5
T	5.6204	29.948	9.0202	1.63	5.8898
P_t	60.5833	121.7833	105.833	121.033	133.9
K	11	19	15	16	16
A_{P_t}	5.5076	6.409	7.055	7.564	8.368

TABLE 8: Computational results of EDD integrated with $GA_{\_TSP}$ and $GA_{\_sequencing}$.

	Example 1	Example 2	Example 3	Example 4	Example 5
T	12.4550	42.976	18.222	5.981	15.47
P_t	66.7333	133.516	116.083	131.85	141.916
K	13	21	16	17	16
A_{P_t}	5.1333	6.357	7.255	7.775	8.869

TABLE 9: Computational results of EDD integrated with s-shape algorithm and $GA_{\_sequencing}$.

	Example 1	Example 2	Example 3	Example 4	Example 5
T	16.51	62.677	28.25	13.365	17.593
P_t	75.266	166.36	133.23	143.33	149.26
K	13	21	16	17	16
A_{P_t}	5.789	8.92	8.33	8.431	9.32

TABLE 10: Comparison results.

	EDD + s-shape + $GA_{\_sequencing}$	EDD + $GA_{\_TSP}$ + $GA_{\_sequencing}$		ATGH	
	Tardiness (min)	Tardiness (min)	Improvement (%)	Tardiness (min)	Improvement (%)
(1)	16.51	12.4550	24.56%	5.6204	65.96%
(2)	62.677	42.976	31.43%	29.948	52.22%
(3)	28.25	18.222	35.50%	9.0202	68.07%
(4)	13.365	5.981	55.25%	1.627	87.83%
(5)	17.593	15.47	12.06%	5.8898	66.52%
Average improvement			31.76%		68.11%

and travel time for constructing a batch is an outstanding fact in reducing the costs and minimizing delays of the customer responses. In our proposed model, orders with similar items are consolidated together. Therefore, batching orders with more similarity can reduce the distance traversed by the picker facility. Also, the due date of each order is defined as a weight parameter in calculating the association between orders in terms of support which was done for considering the due dates in our model. Thereupon, the model considers due date and the process time in an integrated manner which simultaneously affected the average tardiness of all orders. This spoken issue is different in the EDD approach in which the orders' due dates are just considered. Example 5 can be considered as evidence of this matter in which the total and average process time for ATGH is lower than EDD integrated with $GA_{\_TSP}$ and $GA_{\_sequencing}$ with respect to the fact that number of constructed batches for both approaches are happened to be equal after obtaining the results.

6. Conclusion

One of the most important concerns of warehouse managers is involved with finding the best optimal and cost efficient way to pick orders placed by customers in order to be known as a responsible company with satisfied customers in terms of on time delivery. In the current research activity, order batching, picker routing, and batch sequencing problems of warehouse processes were addressed which are to be solved jointly as they are mixed up with many manufacturing industries. Mathematical solutions of these NP-hard problems might be available for problems that are small in nature. But, these kinds of solutions may not be applicable to be considered by warehouse managers. Hence, we presented novel solution approach, namely, ATGH, to solve this issue in accordance with minimizing the average tardiness of all customers' orders which can be considered as a major objective of this research activity. A weighted association rule mining algorithm, namely, MINWAL, was utilized to determine the customers' orders association regarding similarity between items and orders' due dates. Actually, in our proposed method the due date of each order is defined as a weight parameter in calculating the association between orders. So, orders with similar items and due dates have more chance to be in a same batch. This issue is not considered in most of the research activities in the literature related to our work and considering this issue in the order batching problem is the main contribution of our research activity. The previous step was followed by a binary integer clustering model in order to solve the order batching problem which maximizes the similarity between orders in terms of support. After that, a GA was applied to solve a TSP in order to find the optimal routing path.

Finally, a batch sequencing problem was addressed in conjunction with a GA.

The other research objective of this research addresses whether the proposed ATGH algorithm can further improve the solution quality for a multiple parallel aisle warehouse with manual picking system. Hence, comparisons were made considering ATGH, EDD integrated GA_{TSP} and $GA_{sequencing}$, and EDD integrated s-shape and $GA_{sequencing}$ algorithms. As demonstrated by the obtained results, ATGH comes out to be the most striking solution approach in terms of tardiness. In spite of the fact that considering all customer orders, as discussed in this paper, would lead to have a static case, being involved with dynamic cases in which different points of time are assigned to customer's orders arrival would be beneficial. So, there might be some potential room of research to extend our discussed approach with respect to dynamic orders.

Conflict of Interests

The IBM ILOG CPLEX optimization studio version 12.4 software is not used for financial gain and there is no conflict of interests with any party as it is only a student version.

References

[1] ELA/AT Kearney, *Excellence in Logistics*, ELA, Brussels, Belgium, 2004.

[2] Y.-C. Ho, T.-S. Su, and Z.-B. Shi, "Order-batching methods for an order-picking warehouse with two cross aisles," *Computers & Industrial Engineering*, vol. 55, no. 2, pp. 321–347, 2008.

[3] C.-M. Hsu, K.-Y. Chen, and M.-C. Chen, "Batching orders in warehouses by minimizing travel distance with genetic algorithms," *Computers in Industry*, vol. 56, no. 2, pp. 169–178, 2005.

[4] E. A. Elsayed, M.-K. Lee, S. Kim, and E. Scherer, "Sequencing and batching procedures for minimizing earliness and tardiness penalty of order retrievals," *The International Journal of Production Research*, vol. 31, no. 3, pp. 727–738, 1993.

[5] S. Henn, S. Koch, and W. Gerhard, *Order Batching in Order Picking Warehouses: A Survey of Solution Approaches*, Springer, London, UK, 2012.

[6] J. Drury, *Towards More Efficient Order Picking*, IMM Monograph no. 1, The Institute of Materials Management, Cranfield, UK, 1988.

[7] M. Goetschalckx and J. Ashayeri, "Classification and design of order picking systems," *Logistics World*, pp. 99–106, 1989.

[8] J. A. Tompkins, J. A. White, Y. A. Bozer, E. H. Frazelle, and J. M. A. Tanchoco, *Facilities Planning*, John Wiley & Sons, Hoboken, NJ, USA, 2003.

[9] S. Henn and G. Wäscher, "Tabu search heuristics for the order batching problem in manual order picking systems," *European Journal of Operational Research*, vol. 222, no. 3, pp. 484–494, 2012.

[10] S. Henn, "Algorithms for on-line order batching in an order picking warehouse," *Computers and Operations Research*, vol. 39, no. 11, pp. 2549–2563, 2012.

[11] R. de Koster, "How to assess a warehouse operation in a single tour," Tech. Rep., RSM Erasmus University, Rotterdam, The Netherlands, 2004.

[12] R. de Koster, T. Le-Duc, and K. J. Roodbergen, "Design and control of warehouse order picking: a literature review," *European Journal of Operational Research*, vol. 182, no. 2, pp. 481–501, 2007.

[13] R. A. Ruben and F. R. Jacobs, "Batch construction heuristics and storage assignment strategies for walk/ride and pick systems," *Management Science*, vol. 45, no. 4, pp. 575–596, 1999.

[14] E. A. Elsayed, "Algorithms for optimal material handling in automatic warehousing systems," *International Journal of Production Research*, vol. 19, no. 5, pp. 525–535, 1981.

[15] G. Clarke and J. W. Wright, "Scheduling of vehicles from a central depot to a number of delivery points," *Operations Research*, vol. 12, no. 4, pp. 568–581, 1964.

[16] H. D. Vinod, "Integer programming and the theory of grouping," *Journal of the American Statistical Association*, vol. 64, no. 326, pp. 506–519, 1969.

[17] R. D. Armstrong, W. D. Cook, and A. L. Saipe, "Optimal batching in a semi-automated order picking system," *Journal of the Operational Research Society*, vol. 30, no. 8, pp. 711–720, 1979.

[18] H. D. Ratliff and A. S. Rosenthal, "Order-picking in a rectangular warehouse: a solvable case of the traveling salesman problem," *Operations Research*, vol. 31, no. 3, pp. 507–521, 1983.

[19] A. Kusiak, A. Vannelli, and R. K. Kumar, "Clustering analysis: models and algorithms," *Cybernetics*, vol. 15, pp. 139–154, 1986.

[20] D. R. Gibson and G. P. Sharp, "Order batching procedures," *European Journal of Operational Research*, vol. 58, no. 1, pp. 57–67, 1992.

[21] M. B. Rosenwein, "A comparison of heuristics for the problem of batching orders for warehouse selection," *International Journal of Production Research*, vol. 34, no. 3, pp. 657–664, 1996.

[22] A. J. R. M. Gademann, J. P. van den Berg, and H. H. van der Hoff, "An order batching algorithm for wave picking in a parallel-aisle warehouse," *IIE Transactions*, vol. 33, no. 5, pp. 385–398, 2001.

[23] M.-C. Chen and H.-P. Wu, "An association-based clustering approach to order batching considering customer demand patterns," *Omega*, vol. 33, no. 4, pp. 333–343, 2005.

[24] N. Gademann and S. van de Velde, "Order batching to minimize total travel time in a parallel-aisle warehouse," *IIE Transactions*, vol. 37, no. 1, pp. 63–75, 2005.

[25] Y. A. Bozer and J. W. Kile, "Order batching in walk-and-pick order picking systems," *International Journal of Production Research*, vol. 46, no. 7, pp. 1887–1909, 2008.

[26] O. Kulak, Y. Sahin, and M. E. Taner, "Joint order batching and picker routing in single and multiple-cross-aisle warehouses using cluster-based tabu search algorithms," *Flexible Services and Manufacturing Journal*, vol. 24, no. 1, pp. 52–80, 2012.

[27] E. A. Elsayed and M.-K. Lee, "Order processing in automated storage/retrieval systems with due dates," *IIE Transactions*, vol. 28, no. 7, pp. 567–577, 1996.

[28] J. Won and S. Olafsson, "Joint order batching and order picking in warehouse operations," *International Journal of Production Research*, vol. 43, no. 7, pp. 1427–1442, 2005.

[29] C.-Y. Tsai, J. J. H. Liou, and T.-M. Huang, "Using a multiple-GA method to solve the batch picking problem: considering travel distance and order due time," *International Journal of Production Research*, vol. 46, no. 22, pp. 6533–6555, 2008.

[30] Y. Kao, M. H. Chen, and Y. T. Huang, "A hybrid algorithm based on ACO and PSO for capacitated vehicle routing problems," *Mathematical Problems in Engineering*, vol. 2012, Article ID 726564, 17 pages, 2012.

[31] X. Gan, Y. Wang, S. Li, and B. Niu, "Vehicle routing problem with time windows and simultaneous delivery and pick-up service based on MCPSO," *Mathematical Problems in Engineering*, vol. 2012, Article ID 104279, 11 pages, 2012.

[32] M. B. M. de Koster, E. S. van der Poort, and M. Wolters, "Efficient orderbatching methods in warehouses," *International Journal of Production Research*, vol. 37, no. 7, pp. 1479–1504, 1999.

[33] Y.-C. Ho and Y.-Y. Tseng, "A study on order-batching methods of order-picking in a distribution centre with two cross-aisles," *International Journal of Production Research*, vol. 44, no. 17, pp. 3391–3417, 2006.

[34] C. Theys, O. Bräysy, W. Dullaert, and B. Raa, "Using a TSP heuristic for routing order pickers in warehouses," *European Journal of Operational Research*, vol. 200, no. 3, pp. 755–763, 2010.

[35] S. Henn and V. Schmid, *Metaheuristics for Order Batching and Sequencing in Manual Order Picking Systems*, Univ., Fak. für Wirtschaftswiss, 2011.

[36] M. Hahsler, B. Grün, and K. Hornik, "Arules—a computational environment for mining association rules and frequent item sets," *Journal of Statistical Software*, vol. 14, 2005.

[37] R. Agrawal, T. Imieliński, and A. Swami, "Mining association rules between sets of items in large databases," *ACM SIGMOD Record*, vol. 22, no. 2, pp. 207–216, 1993.

[38] S. Encheva, Y. Kondratenko, M. Z. Solesvik, and S. Tumin, "Decision support systems in logistics," in *Proceeding of International electronic conference on computer science*, pp. 254–256, 2007.

[39] M.-C. Chen, "Configuration of cellular manufacturing systems using association rule induction," *International Journal of Production Research*, vol. 41, no. 2, pp. 381–395, 2003.

[40] R. Srikant and R. Agrawal, "Mining generalized association rules," *Future Generation Computer Systems*, vol. 13, no. 2-3, pp. 161–180, 1997.

[41] J. Wu and X. M. Li, "An effective mining algorithm for weighted association rules in communication networks," *Journal of Computers*, vol. 3, no. 10, pp. 20–27, 2008.

[42] C. H. Cai, A. W. C. Fu, C. H. Cheng, and W. W. Kwong, "Mining association rules with weighted items," in *Proceedings of the International Symposium on Database Engineering & Applications*, pp. 68–77, Cardiff, UK, 1998.

[43] J. Holland, *Adaptation in Natural and Artificial Systems*, University of Michigan Press, Ann Arbor, Mich, USA, 1975.

[44] A. A. Taleizadeh, F. Barzinpour, and H.-M. Wee, "Meta-heuristic algorithms for solving a fuzzy single-period problem," *Mathematical and Computer Modelling*, vol. 54, no. 5-6, pp. 1273–1285, 2011.

[45] H. Yang, J. Yi, J. Zhao, and Zh. Dong, "Extreme learning machine based genetic algorithm and its application in power system economic dispatch," *Neurocomputing*, vol. 102, pp. 154–162, 2013.

7

Attribute Index and Uniform Design Based Multiobjective Association Rule Mining with Evolutionary Algorithm

Jie Zhang,[1,2] Yuping Wang,[1] and Junhong Feng[2]

[1] School of Computer Science and Technology, Xidian University, Xi'an 710071, China
[2] Department of Computer Science and Technology, Guangzhou University Sontan College, Zengcheng, Guangzhou 511370, China

Correspondence should be addressed to Jie Zhang; 290813268@qq.com and Yuping Wang; ywang@xidian.edu.cn

Academic Editors: F. J. Cabrerizo, Y.-P. Huang, and P. Melin

In association rule mining, evaluating an association rule needs to repeatedly scan database to compare the whole database with the antecedent, consequent of a rule and the whole rule. In order to decrease the number of comparisons and time consuming, we present an attribute index strategy. It only needs to scan database once to create the attribute index of each attribute. Then all metrics values to evaluate an association rule do not need to scan database any further, but acquire data only by means of the attribute indices. The paper visualizes association rule mining as a multiobjective problem rather than a single objective one. In order to make the acquired solutions scatter uniformly toward the Pareto frontier in the objective space, elitism policy and uniform design are introduced. The paper presents the algorithm of attribute index and uniform design based multiobjective association rule mining with evolutionary algorithm, abbreviated as IUARMMEA. It does not require the user-specified minimum support and minimum confidence anymore, but uses a simple attribute index. It uses a well-designed real encoding so as to extend its application scope. Experiments performed on several databases demonstrate that the proposed algorithm has excellent performance, and it can significantly reduce the number of comparisons and time consumption.

1. Introduction

Data mining is a very active and rapidly growing research area in the field of computer science. Its aim is to extract interesting and useful knowledge from a huge number of data stored in the databases. Association rule mining is one of the most well-known data mining technologies. It can find out effectively interesting relations among attributes.

Existing algorithms for mining association rules are mainly based on the approach suggested by Agrawal and Srikant [1, 2]. Apriori [2], SETM [3], AIS [2], Pincer search [4, 5], DIC [6], and so forth are some of the popular algorithms based on this approach.

The above algorithms can find out massive amount of possible rules. However, a large number of rules will increase the complexity and make the rule set harder to understand by users. That is to say, the greater the number of rules in

the results is, the greater the complexity for the users is [7]. Therefore, generating the rules which are as valid and few as possible is our ultimate aim. How to select representative and useful rules and to remove those similar rules is our greatest concern. In order to deal with the above problems, this paper introduces elitism policy and uniform design.

In the meanwhile, the above algorithms depend on two user-predefined parameters, *minimum support* and *minimum confidence*. However, how to select them is not an easy issue. If the value of *minimum support* is too large, the number of frequent itemsets generated will be less, and thereby too few rules may be generated. By contrast, if the value is too small, then almost all possible itemsets will become frequent and thus a huge number of rules may be generated. Similarly, if the value of *minimum confidence* is too large, many generated rules will be removed, and thereby some useful rules may be missing. However, if the value is too small, then almost all possible rules will become *strong rules* and thus a huge number of rules may be generated. Therefore, multiobjective rule mining with evolutionary algorithm is introduced, which visualizes rule mining problem as a multiobjective problem rather than a single objective problem. It need not specify those two user-predefined parameters any further [8–10].

Association rule mining algorithms can be taken into two steps. First they find the frequent itemsets and then extract the important association rules from the frequent itemsets. Among the two steps, the first step is the most time-consuming [7]. The reason is that in order to evaluate an association rule of the form $X \rightarrow Y$, we need to repeatedly scan the database to compare to the whole database with X, Y, and $X \cup Y$ itemsets [11]. In this paper, we present an attribute index method to decrease the number of comparisons. It is remarkable that the proposed method scans database only once.

The rest of this paper is organized as follows. Section 2 states the preliminaries of the proposed method. Section 3 presents our method in detail. Section 4 gives the numerical results of the proposed method. The conclusion of the work is made in Section 5.

2. Preliminaries

In this section, we describe some concepts concerning association rule, multiobjective evolutionary algorithms, uniform design, and multiobjective association rule mining.

2.1. Association Rules and Metrics. Let $I = \{i_1, i_2, i_3, \ldots, i_m\}$ be a set of items or itemset. Let $D = \{T_1, T_2, \ldots, T_n\}$ be the set of transactions, called the *transaction database*, where each transaction $T_i \in D$ is an itemset such that $T_i \subseteq I$. An association rule is of the form $X \rightarrow Y$ where $X \subseteq I, Y \subseteq I$, and $X \cap Y = \Phi$. The itemsets X, Y are respectively called the antecedent and consequent of the association rule.

A transaction T_i contains an itemset X, $T_i \supseteq X$, if and only if, for any item $i \in X$, then $i \in T_i$, namely, T_i, contains each item in X.

Support count of an itemset I_1 is denoted by $\mathrm{SUP}(I_1)$, which is the number of transactions that contain I_1 in D:

$$\mathrm{SUP}(I_1) = |\{t \in D \wedge t \supseteq I_1\}|. \quad (1)$$

Support count of an association rule $X \rightarrow Y$ is denoted by $\mathrm{SUP}(X \rightarrow Y)$, which is the number of transactions compatible with both X and Y, namely, the number of transactions that contain $X \cup Y$:

$$\mathrm{SUP}(X \rightarrow Y) = \mathrm{SUP}(X \cup Y). \quad (2)$$

In a similar way, $\mathrm{SUP}(X)$ and $\mathrm{SUP}(Y)$ are the number of transactions compatible with only X and Y, respectively.

Support of an itemset I_1 is denoted by support (I_1), which is the ratio of transactions that contain I_1 in D, namely,

$$\mathrm{support}(I_1) = \frac{\mathrm{SUP}(I_1)}{|D|}, \quad (3)$$

where $|D|$ indicates the total number of transactions in the database D.

Support of an association rule $X \rightarrow Y$ is denoted by support$(X \rightarrow Y)$:

$$\mathrm{support}(X \longrightarrow Y) = \frac{\mathrm{SUP}(X \longrightarrow Y)}{|D|} = \frac{\mathrm{SUP}(X \cup Y)}{|D|}. \quad (4)$$

An itemset, X, in a transaction database, D, is called a large (frequent) itemset if its Support is larger than or equal to a threshold of minimum support (minsupp), which is given by users or experts.

The *confidence* or *predictive accuracy* of a rule $X \rightarrow Y$, written as confidence$(X \rightarrow Y)$, is to measure specificity or consistency. It indicates the probability of creating the rule dependent on the antecedent part, and is defined as follows:

$$\mathrm{confidence}(X \longrightarrow Y)$$
$$= \frac{\mathrm{support}(X \longrightarrow Y)}{\mathrm{support}(X)} = \frac{\mathrm{SUP}(X \cup Y)}{\mathrm{SUP}(X)}. \quad (5)$$

That is, *support* implies frequency of cooccurring patterns, and *confidence* means the strength of a rule. The *support-confidence framework* is as follows [1, 2].

The minimal support, minsupp, and the minimal confidence, minconf, are given by users or experts. Then rule $X \rightarrow Y$ is valid if

$$\mathrm{support}(X \longrightarrow Y) \geq \mathrm{minsupp},$$
$$\mathrm{confidence}(X \longrightarrow Y) \geq \mathrm{minconf}. \quad (6)$$

Generally speaking, only those rules with *support* and *confidence* larger than or equal to a given threshold are interesting. These rules are called *strong rules*.

Mining association rules can be taken into the following two subproblems.

(1) Generating all itemsets whose *support* are greater than or equal to the user-specified minimum support, that is, generating all frequent itemsets.

(2) Generating all the rules which satisfy the minimum confidence constraint. If the confidence of a rule is greater than or equal to the minimum confidence, then the rule can be extracted as a valid rule [8–10].

Apart from the above metrics, other several important metrics are illustrated as follows.

Coverage of an association rule $X \rightarrow Y$, denoted by coverage$(X \rightarrow Y)$, is to measure the extent to which the consequent part is covered by the rule (the maximum value is reached when all the elements that satisfy Y are covered by the rule) [7]. It shows the probability of creating the rule dependent on the consequent part, and is defined as follows:

$$\mathrm{coverage}(X \longrightarrow Y) = \frac{\mathrm{support}(X \longrightarrow Y)}{\mathrm{support}(Y)} = \frac{\mathrm{SUP}(X \cup Y)}{\mathrm{SUP}(Y)}. \quad (7)$$

Both the *confidence* and *coverage* are two important measuring factors for the rule quality or rule interest, but if we use them separately we will reach bad conclusions [7].

The generated rules may have a large number of attributes involved, which may make them difficult to understand [12]. If the generated rules are not understandable to the users, the users will never use them. A careful study of an association rule infers that if the number of conditions involved in the antecedent part is less, the rule is more comprehensible. Therefore, *comprehensibility* of a rule $X \rightarrow Y$ can be measured by the number of attributes involved in the rule. It is quantified by the following expression [8, 9]:

$$\text{comprehensibility} = \frac{\log(1 + |Y|)}{\log(1 + |X \cup Y|)}. \tag{8}$$

Here, $|Y|$ and $|X \cup Y|$ are the number of attributes involved in the consequent part and the whole rule, respectively.

Another *comprehensibility* of a rule is defined as follows [13]:

$$\text{comprehensibility} = 1 - \frac{n}{N}, \tag{9}$$

where n and N are, respectively, the numbers of attributes in antecedent part and in the whole dataset.

Comprehensibility of a rule tries to increase the readability by shortening the length of an association rule.

Interestingness of a rule, denoted by interestingness($X \rightarrow Y$), is used to quantify how much the rule is surprising for the users. As the most important purpose of rule mining is to find some hidden information, it should extract those rules that have comparatively less occurrence in the database. The following expression can be used to quantify the interestingness [8, 9, 14, 15]:

$$\text{Interestingness}(X \longrightarrow Y)$$

$$= \frac{\text{SUP}(X \cup Y)}{\text{SUP}(X)} \times \frac{\text{SUP}(X \cup Y)}{\text{SUP}(Y)} \tag{10}$$

$$\times \left(1 - \frac{\text{SUP}(X \cup Y)}{|D|}\right),$$

where $|D|$ indicates the total number of transactions in the database.

Yan et al. defined the relative confidence as the interestingness measure as follows [10]:

$$\text{rconf} = \frac{\text{supp}(X \cup Y) - \text{supp}(X)\,\text{supp}(Y)}{\text{supp}(X)\,(1 - \text{supp}(Y))}. \tag{11}$$

Here, supp indicates *support*.

Hipp et al. [16] compared the popular association rule mining approaches including Apriori [1, 2], Partition [17], and Eclat [18] and made conclusions that these approaches have shown similar runtime behavior. They found no algorithm that fundamentally outperforms others. For example, Apriori is superior in the market basket database, but it performs poorly with the car equipment database. The FP-growth algorithm is very efficient in many cases, but it requires a large amount of memory to store the FP-tree [19]. Although there may be differences with different implementations and datasets, association rule mining approaches have the same performance behavior with respect to the support threshold value. The experiments conducted in articles [1, 16, 20, 21] have shown that the decrease of the support threshold leads to an exponential increase on the number of frequent itemsets, which consequently results in an exponential increase in runtime and resource usage (i.e., memory and disk space) during the frequent itemset mining process [22].

2.2. Multiobjective Evolutionary Algorithms.

The notion of Pareto-optimality is one of the major approaches to multiobjective programming. For any two points x_1 and x_2 in Ω, if the following conditions hold:

$$f_i(x_1) \leq f_i(x_2), \quad \text{for all } i \in \{1, 2, \ldots, M\},$$
$$f_j(x_1) < f_j(x_2), \quad \text{for some } j \in \{1, 2, \ldots, M\}, \tag{12}$$

then x_1 is at least as good as x_2 with respect to all the objectives (the first condition), and x_1 is strictly better than x_2 with respect to at least one objective (the second condition). Therefore, x_1 is strictly better than x_2. If no other solution is strictly better than x_1, then x_1 is called a *Pareto-optimal solution*. A multiobjective programming problem may have multiple Pareto-optimal solutions, and these solutions can be regarded as the best compromise solutions. Different decision-makers may select different Pareto-optimal solutions in terms of the preference for themselves. It may be desirable to find all the Pareto-optimal solutions, so that the decision-makers can select the best one based on his preference. The set of all possible Pareto-optimal solutions constitutes a *Pareto frontier* in the objective space.

Many multiobjective programming problems have very large or infinite numbers of Pareto-optimal solutions. When it is not possible to find all these solutions, it may be desirable to find as many solutions as possible in order to provide more choices to the decision maker [23].

Evolutionary algorithms, EAs, simultaneously deal with a set of possible solutions, which allows finding several members of the Pareto optimal set in a single run of the algorithm. Additionally, they are not too susceptible to the shape or continuity of the Pareto front (e.g., they can easily deal with concave and discontinuous Pareto fronts).

Schaffer is generally considered as the first to design a Multiobjective Evolutionary Algorithms (MOEAs), during the mid-1980s [24]. However, it was until the mid-1990s that MOEAs started to attract serious attention from researchers. Nowadays, it is possible to find applications of MOEAs in almost all domains [25].

Schaffer's approach, called Vector Evaluated Genetic Algorithm (VEGA), consists of a simple genetic algorithm with a modified selection mechanism. After VEGA, there has been a growing interest in applying evolutionary algorithms to deal with multiobjective optimization. The researchers designed a first generation MOEAs where the main lesson learned was that successful MOEAs had to combine a good mechanism to select non-dominated individuals. The most representative algorithms of this generation MOEAs are as follows: Non-dominated Sorting Genetic Algorithm

TABLE 1: Values of the parameter σ for different number of factors and different number of levels per factor.

Number of levels per factors	Number of factors	σ
5	2~4	2
7	2~6	3
11	2~10	7
13	2	5
	3	4
	4~12	6
17	2~16	10
19	2~3	8
	4~18	14
23	2, 13~14, 20~22	7
	8~12	15
	3~7, 15~19	17
29	2	12
	3	9
	4~7	16
	8~12, 16~24	8
	13~15	14
	25~28	18
31	2, 5~12, 20~30	12
	3~4, 13~19	22

(NSGA) [26], Niched-Pareto Genetic Algorithm (NPGA) [27], and Multi-Objective Genetic Algorithm (MOGA) [28]. A second generation MOEAs started when elitism became a standard mechanism. In fact, the use of elitism is a theoretical requirement in order to guarantee convergence of a MOEA. Many MOEAs have been proposed during the second generation. The Strength Pareto Evolutionary Algorithm 2 (SPEA2) [29] and the NSGA-II [30] can be considered as the most representative MOEAs of the second generation [31]. There are many works about MOEAs published every year. Zhou et al. surveys the development of MOEAs primarily during the last eight years [32]. The paper indicates that more than 5600 publications have been published on evolutionary multiobjective optimization By January 2011. Among these papers, 66.8% have been published in the last eight years, 38.4% are journal papers, and 42.2% are conference papers.

2.3. Uniform Design. The main objective of uniform design is to sample a small set of points from a given set of points, such that the sampled points are uniformly scattered [23, 33–35].

Let there be n factors and q levels per factor. When n and q are given, the uniform design selects q from q^n possible combinations, such that these q combinations are uniformly scattered over the space of all possible combinaions. The selected q combinations are expressed as a uniform array $U(n, q) = [U_{i,j}]q \times n$, where $U_{i,j}$ is the level of the jth factor in the ith combination, and can be calculated by the following formula:

$$U_{i,j} = \left(i\sigma^{j-1} \bmod q\right) + 1, \tag{13}$$

where σ is a parameter given in Table 1.

2.4. Multiobjective Association Rule Mining with Evolutionary Algorithm. The rules produced by the rule mining approach need to be evaluated using various metrics like the support and confidence. There are also other metrics such as the comprehensibility and interestingness of the rules. These make the rules more usable. If these metrics are consistent, they can be merged. However, the metrics are conflicting sometimes. For example, a user may wish to have rules which are both novel and accurate. However, these two objectives are conflicting since if the accuracy of the rule increases its novelty will decrease. Thus the problem of constructing rules with specific metrics should be faced as a multiobjective optimization problem [36].

In the early years, some optimization methods for association rule mining have been proposed. However, the process is too much resource consuming, especially when there is not enough available physical memory for the whole database. A solution to this problem is to use evolutionary algorithm, which reduces both the cost and time of rule discovery. Evolutionary algorithm (EA), genetic algorithm (GA), ant colony optimization (ACO), and particle swarm optimization (PSO) are instances of single objective association rule mining algorithms. A few of these algorithms have been used for multiobjective problems [9].

Multiobjective association rule mining with EA is to use EA to solve the association rule mining problem. Those metrics mentioned in Section 2.1 can be taken as multiply objectives to optimize in multiobjective rule mining. The operators such as select, crossover, and mutate are used to evolve the chromosome representing an association rule.

2.5. Related Works. There have been some attempts and works for multiobjective association rule mining using evolutionary algorithms. Ghosh and Nath visualized an association rule mining as a multiobjective problem rather than a single objective one [8], where multiobjective genetic algorithm, MOGA, was applied to maximize the confidence, comprehensibility and interestingness of a rule. Khabzaoui et al. used a parallel MOGA to optimize the support, confidence, J-measure, interest, and surprise [37]. Dehuri et al. presented an elitist MOGA for mining classification rules, which take three conflicting metrics with each other, accuracy, comprehensibility, and interestingness, as multiply objectives [38]. Iglesia et al. used multiobjective evolutionary algorithm to search for Pareto-optimal classification rules with respect to support and confidence for partial classification [39]. A multiobjective evolutionary algorithm combined with improved niched Pareto genetic algorithm was applied to optimize two conflicting metrics with each other, predictive accuracy and comprehensibility of the rules in multiobjective rule mining [40]. Rule mining method with PSO, chaos rough particle swarm algorithm [41], and numeric rule mining method

TABLE 2: An example of transation database.

Transaction	Containing items
T_1	i_1, i_3, i_5
T_2	i_4, i_5
T_3	i_1, i_2, i_4, i_5
T_4	i_2, i_3, i_4, i_5
T_5	i_1, i_3, i_5, i_6
T_6	i_1, i_3, i_4, i_5, i_6

with simulated annealing [42] have been proposed. Alatas et al. proposed multiobjective differential evolution algorithm for mining numeric association rules [43]. Later, they proposed another numeric association rule mining method using rough particle swarm algorithm. Yan et al. proposed a method based on genetic algorithm without considering minimum support [10]. Qodmanan et al. applied MOGA to association rule mining without taking the minimum support and confidence into account by applying the FP-tree algorithm [9]. Hoque et al. presented a method to generate both frequent and rare itemsets using multiobjective genetic algorithm [14]. Fung et al. suggested a novel MOGA based rule mining method for affective product design, which can discover a set of rules relating design attributes with customer evaluation based on survey data [44].

3. The Proposed Method

Section 2.1 has described several import metrics for the evaluation of an association rule. As using separately the *confidence* and *coverage* of a rule can reach bad conclusions [7], the two metrics are selected together in the proposed method. If the generated rules are not understandable to the users, they will never use them. Therefore, the *comprehensibility* of a rule is selected. As the most important purpose of association rule mining is to find some hidden information, therefore the *interestingness* of a rule is selected to quantify how much the rule is surprising for the users. The proposed method selects the four metrics as multiple objectives to optimize. Namely, we need to optimize the following multiobjective problem:

$$\begin{aligned} &\text{Maximize} \quad \text{confidence} \\ &\text{Maximize} \quad \text{coverage} \\ &\text{Maximize} \quad \text{comprehensibility} \\ &\text{Maximize} \quad \text{interestingness.} \end{aligned} \qquad (14)$$

3.1. Attribute Index. In the above four metrics, 3 of them need to calculate the *support count* of a rule. The *support count* of an itemset X is the number of transactions that contain X in D. A transaction T_i contains an itemset X, if and only if, for any item $i \in X$, then $i \in T_i$, namely, T_i, contain all the items in X. Therefore, to evaluate an association rule $X \rightarrow Y$, the database D will be repeatedly scanned to compare each transaction $T_i \in D$ with an itemset X, Y and $X \cup Y$. In order to judge whether a transaction T_i contains an itemset X or not, we need to judge whether T_i contains each of the items of

itemset X. Namely, the number of comparisons for an itemset X is formulated as follows:

$$\text{NC}_X = |D| \times |X|, \qquad (15)$$

where NC_X indicates the number of comparisons for an itemset X, $|D|$ indicates the total number of transactions in the database D, and $|X|$ indicates the number of all items in the itemset X.

Therefore, the number of comparisons for a rule $X \rightarrow Y$ is formulated as follows:

$$\begin{aligned} \text{NC}_{X \rightarrow Y} &= \text{NC}_X + \text{NC}_Y + \text{NC}_{X \cup Y} \\ &= |D| \times (|X| + |Y| + |X \cup Y|). \end{aligned} \qquad (16)$$

In the above formula, $|X|$, $|Y|$, and $|X \cup Y|$ indicate the number of the items in the antecedent, consequent, and the whole rule, respectively. If any of them turns less, the number of comparisons for a rule will turn smaller. In the meanwhile, from (8) and (9), we can see that the *comprehensibility* of a rule will also turn smaller. Namely, the smaller the size of the itemsets in a rule is, the more easily comprehensible the rule is and the smaller the number of comparisons is. In other word, selecting the more easily comprehensible rule can decrease the number of comparisons.

As $|D|$ is fixed, we cannot decrease the number of comparisons through the parameter. However, if only by means of comparing a part of transactions rather than all transactions in D, we can still evaluate an association rule and calculate metrics values, then the number of comparisons can certainly decrease.

Hadian et al. presented a method that only compares the transactions the size of which is larger than or equal to the size of the itemset, which is in terms of the fact that a transaction contains an itemset only if the minimal size of the transaction is equal to size of the itemset [11]. This method can prevent some unnecessary comparisons by excluding the transactions whose size is less than the size of the itemset. However, a majority of transactions that do not contain the itemset are still compared. An example is illustrated as follows.

Example 1. Assume a transaction database D contain 6 transactions, as shown in Table 2. The universal itemset I contains 6 attributes $\{i_1, i_2, i_3, i_4, i_5, i_6\}$. For a rule of the form $i_1 i_3 i_5 \rightarrow i_4$, the above method can exclude T_1 and T_2 as their sizes are less than the size of the rule. It compares T_3, T_4, T_5 and T_6 with the rule. However, it is obvious that T_3, T_4, T_5, are unsuitable as they miss a certain item of the rule, are impossible to contain the rule.

In order to overcome the above problems, the work presents the strategy of the attribute index. It can prevent a great deal of unnecessary comparisons by only comparing those transactions directly related to the rule. Therefore, it can significantly improve the performance of an algorithm.

The strategy creates the attribute index for each attribute in database. Its index value is the successive link of all transactions containing the attribute. For example, T_1, T_2, T_3, T_4, T_5, and T_6 can be previously defined as 1, 2, 3, 4, 5, 6 or 0, 1, 2, 3, 4, 5, and so on. The attribute index

```
attrIdx(D, I): create the attribute index of each attribute.
Input: D indicates the transaction database; I indicates
       the universal itemset, namely I contains all attributes.
Output: The attribute indices of the each attribute in I.
    for each attribute i in the universal itemset I
        Idx(i) ← Φ;
    end for
    for each transaction T in database D
        define T as k;
        for each attribute i in the universal itemset I
            if i ∈ T
                Idx(i) ← Idx(i) ∪ {k};
            end if
        end for
    end for
    return Idx;
```

PSEUDOCODE 1: Pseudocode of creating the attribute index.

of the above example is as follows. The attribute index of the attribute i can be formulated as follows:

$$\text{Idx}(i) = \{k \mid i \in T \wedge T \in D \wedge T \text{ is defined as } k\}. \quad (17)$$

Example 2. For Table 2, the attribute index of each attribute is as follows:

$$\text{Idx}(i_1) = \{1, 3, 5, 6\};$$
$$\text{Idx}(i_2) = \{3, 4\};$$
$$\text{Idx}(i_3) = \{1, 4, 5, 6\};$$
$$\text{Idx}(i_4) = \{2, 3, 4, 6\}; \quad (18)$$
$$\text{Idx}(i_5) = \{1, 2, 3, 4, 5, 6\};$$
$$\text{Idx}(i_6) = \{5, 6\}.$$

In this method, the database is scanned once to create the attribute index of each attribute before rule generations. The pseudocode of creating the attribute index is shown in Pseudocode 1.

The created attribute indices make it easy to calculate the *support count* of the antecedent, consequent, and the whole rule. Therefore, several import metrics to evaluate a rule can also be easy to calculate as these calculations do not need scan a database anymore. The calculations of the *support count* of an itemset only acquire the same values of the attribute index of each item in the itemset. As the same values represent those transactions that contain the itemset, therefore, the number of the same values is just the *support count* of the itemset. The pseudocode of calculating the *support count* of an itemset is shown in the function SUPItem of Pseudocode 2.

To calculate the *support count* of an association rule $X \rightarrow Y$, we can take X, Y and $X \cup Y$ as an itemset or parameter to call the function SUPItem so as to calculate the *support count* of the antecedent, consequent, and the whole rule. The pseudocode of calculating the *support count* of an association rule is shown in the function SUPRule of Pseudocode 2.

Example 3. For a rule of the form $i_1 i_3 i_5 \rightarrow i_4$, the attribute indices of each item i_1, i_3, and i_5 in the antecedent part are $\text{Idx}(i_1) = \{1, 3, 5, 6\}$; $\text{Idx}(i_3) = \{1, 4, 5, 6\}$; $\text{Idx}(i_5) = \{1, 2, 3, 4, 5, 6\}$. The same values of them are $\{1, 5, 6\}$. This indicates T_1, T_5, and T_6 contain the antecedent of the rule, as can be verified from Table 2. Therefore, $\text{SUP}(i_1 i_3 i_5) = |\{1, 5, 6\}| = 3$. In the similar way, $\text{SUP}(i_4) = |\{2, 3, 4, 6\}| = 4$; $\text{SUP}(i_1 i_3 i_5 \rightarrow i_4) = \text{SUP}(i_1 i_3 i_5 \cup i_4) = |\{1, 5, 6\} \cup \{2, 3, 4, 6\}| = |\{6\}| = 1$.

If the *support count* of the antecedent, consequent, and the whole rule is known, the *confidence* and *coverage* of the rule can easily be acquired according to (5) and (7). Formula (8) or (9) can easily calculate the *comprehensibility* of the rule in terms of the number of attributes involving in the consequent part and the whole rule.

The *interestingness* of an association rule can be calculated by (10) or (11). However, we can obviously see that the acquired *interestingness* according to (11) may be less than 0 because it is possible that $\text{supp}(X \cup Y)$ is less than $\text{supp}(X) \text{supp}(Y)$. The negative *interestingness* does not meet our requirements. Therefore, (11) is not what we need. For (10), we can deduce it as follows:

interestingness $(X \longrightarrow Y)$

$$= \frac{\text{SUP}(X \cup Y)}{\text{SUP}(X)} \times \frac{\text{SUP}(X \cup Y)}{\text{SUP}(Y)} \times \left(1 - \frac{\text{SUP}(X \cup Y)}{|D|}\right)$$

$$= \text{confidence} \times \text{coverage} \times (1 - \text{support}). \quad (19)$$

From (19), we can obviously see that the *interestingness* of an association rule consists of 3 parts, the *confidence*, *coverage*, and complement of the *support*. Among them, the confidence and coverage are both larger than 0 and less than or equal to 1, and their product is also larger than 0 and less than or equal to 1. However, if they are very small, their product will be a great deal less than any of them. For instance, confidence = 0.3, coverage = 0.5, their product 0.15 is much less than 0.3 and 0.5. Therefore, the interestingness of a rule is often rather small. This has been confirmed by the results of many works.

According to the definition of the interestingness of a rule, it is to extract the rules that have comparatively less occurrence in the database. Namely, the interestingness is to mine such association rules as low support but higher confidence. Therefore, we revise (19) as follows:

interestingness $(X \longrightarrow Y)$

$$= \alpha \times \text{confidence} + \beta \times \text{confidence} \times (1 - \text{support})$$

$$= \alpha \times \frac{\text{SUP}(X \cup Y)}{\text{SUP}(X)} + \beta \times \frac{\text{SUP}(X \cup Y)}{\text{SUP}(X)}$$

$$\times \left(1 - \frac{\text{SUP}(X \cup Y)}{|D|}\right), \quad \alpha + \beta = 1 \wedge \alpha, \ \beta > 0, \quad (20)$$

where α, β are two regulating coefficients with the interval $[0, 1]$.

```
SUPRule(rul, Idx): calculate the support count of a rule.
Input: rul indicates an association rule; Idx indicates the
        attribute indices of each attribute.
Output: SUP1, SUP2, and SUP3 indicate the support count of
        the antecedent, the consequent and the rule,
        respectively.
    X ← the antecedent of rul, Y ← the consequent of rul;
    SUP1 ← Call SUPItem(X, Idx);
    SUP2 ← Call SUPItem(Y, Idx);
    SUP3 ← Call SUPItem(X ∪ Y, Idx);
    return SUP1, SUP2, SUP3;
SUPItem(Iset, Idx): calculate the support count of an itemset.
Input: Iset indicates an itemset; Idx indicates the attribute
        indices of each attribute.
Output: the support count of Iset.
    same ← Φ;
    for each item a ∈ Iset in Iset
        same ← same ∩ Idx(a);
    end for
    num ← |same|;
    return num;
```

PSEUDOCODE 2: Pseudocode of calculating the support count.

From (20), we can see that the interestingness of a rule is the linear combination of the confidence and the complement of the support. As the two parts and two regulating coefficients all belong to the interval of $[0, 1]$, the interestingness of a rule lies also in the interval of $[0, 1]$. Meanwhile, it can also be seen that if the confidence keeps invariable, the support is the less, the interestingness is the larger, and vice versa; and when the support is fixed, the confidence is the larger, the interestingness is the larger, and vice versa. This is just in accordance with the definition of the interestingness of a rule.

From the above-mentioned, it can be seen that only by means of the attribute indices can all metrics to evaluate a rule be calculated out. Namely, the calculations of all metrics do not need to scan database any further, but only fetch from the created attribute indices. Therefore, there is no doubt that the proposed method can highly improve the performance of algorithm.

3.2. Fitness Function.

Evolutionary algorithm, EA, is a promising approach to find Pareto-optimal solutions. It uses a fitness function to guide the population members to converge toward the Pareto frontier. A well-known fitness function is the weighted sum of the objective function

$$\text{fitness} = \omega_1 f_1(x) + \omega_2 f_2(x) + \cdots + \omega_M f_M(x), \quad (21)$$

where $\omega_1, \omega_2, \ldots, \omega_M$ are nonnegative weights such that $\omega_1 + \omega_2 + \cdots + \omega_M = 1$. We call $w = (\omega_1, \omega_2, \ldots, \omega_M)$ a weight vector.

If an EA uses one weight vector to compose one fitness function, there is only one search direction. To overcome this shortcoming, multiple weight vectors can be used to compose multiple fitness functions, so that there are multiple search directions. Leung and Wang applied the uniform design to compose multiple fitness functions, such that multiple search directions are scattered uniformly toward the Pareto frontier in the objective space. This method is as follows [23].

Firstly, normalize each objective function as follows:

$$h_i(x) = \frac{f_i(x)}{\max_{y \in \psi} \{|f_i(y)|\}}, \quad (22)$$

where ψ is a set of points in the current population and $h_i(x)$ is the normalized objective function.

Then compose D fitness functions for any given D, where the ith fitness function is given by ($1 \leq i \leq D$):

$$\text{fitness}_i = \omega_{i,1} h_1(x) + \omega_{i,2} h_2(x) + \cdots + \omega_{i,M} h_M(x). \quad (23)$$

Let $w_i = (\omega_{i,1}, \omega_{i,2}, \ldots, \omega_{i,M})$. The uniform design is applied to select the weight vectors $w_1, w_2, \ldots, w_D$ as follows. In the objective space, each objective function is treated as one factor and hence there are M factors. Assume D weight vectors and hence there are D levels. The uniform array $U(M, D)$ is applied to determine $\omega_{i,j}$ for any and $1 \leq i \leq D$ and $1 \leq j \leq M$ as follows:

$$\omega_{i,j} = \frac{U_{i,j}}{\sum_{j=1}^{M} U_{i,j}}. \quad (24)$$

The equation can ensure the square sum of the weight for each fitness function to be one.

The D weight vectors $w_1, w_2, \ldots, w_D$ can provide D search directions. Using the uniform design to select the D weight vectors can ensure the D search directions to be scattered uniformly toward the Pareto frontier in the objective space.

```
decode(chrom): decode from chrom to generate the antecedent and the consequent.
Input: chrom indicates a chromosome.
Output: the antecedent and the consequent of an association rule.
    antecedent ← Φ;
    consequent ← Φ;
    for the ith gene chrom(i) ∈ chrom
        if chrom(i) = 1
            antecedent ← antecedent ∪ {i};
        end if
        if chrom(i) = 2
            consequent ← antecedent ∪ {i};
        end if
    end for
    return antecedent, consequent;
```

PSEUDOCODE 3: Pseudocode of decoding.

In the proposed method, there are 4 objective functions, namely, $M = 4$, and (23) can be modified as follows:

$$\text{fitness}_i = \omega_{i,1}\text{confidence} + \omega_{i,2}\text{coverage}$$

$$+ \omega_{i,3}\text{comprehensiblity} \qquad (25)$$

$$+ \omega_{i,4}\text{interestingness}.$$

3.3. Encoding and Decoding. An association rule of the form $X \rightarrow Y$ can be represented as a chromosome, among which, each gene represents an attribute in the database. The itemset X and Y are, respectively, called the antecedent and consequent of a association rule. In general, a rule only contains a part of attributes, and the length, antecedent, and consequent, of the various rules are all variable. Therefore, it is a very urgent issue how to code a chromosome for the various rules.

However, from the viewpoint of each attribute, the above problem can be easily handled. The existence of an attribute in an association rule can be classified into three situations as follows.

(i) The attribute does not exists in the rule;

(ii) the attribute exists in the antecedent X;

(iii) the attribute exists in the consequent Y.

It can be noted that there is not the situation that the attribute exists in both the antecedent and consequent, the reason of which is $X \cap Y = \Phi$ in the definition of an association rule.

If the above situations are, respectively, coded as 0, 1, and 2, then the chromosome representing a rule can contain each attribute whose value is 0, 1, or 2. Therefore, the length of the chromosome is fixed and is equal to the number of attributes in the database.

The decoding of a chromosome is the reverse process of the coding. Namely, each gene, whose value is 0, 1 or 2, is translated as one of the above three situations. The index of the gene whose value is equal to 1 or 2, respectively, decoded

as the antecedent and the consequent. The pseudocode of decoding is illustrated in Pseudocode 3.

An example of coding and decoding is described as follows.

Example 4. Assume the database with 6 attributes (A, B, C, D, E, F). An association rule $BC \rightarrow E$ can be coded as 011020. A chromosome 101022 can be decoded as the antecedent $\{1, 3\}$ and consequent of $\{5, 6\}$, namely, the corresponding rule is $AC \rightarrow EF$.

3.4. Initialization. Assume the size of the population and the number of attributes in the database to be M_P and N, an M_P-by-N integer matrix is randomly generated. In the matrix, the value of each element is equal to 0, 1, or 2, which present three situations mentioned in Section 3.3. The matrix is the initialized population. The pseudocode of the initialization of a population is shown in Pseudocode 4.

In Pseudocode 4, the function *isvalid* is to judge whether a chromosome representing a rule is valid or not. A valid rule is that the size of the antecedent and consequent of a rule are both larger than 0. Namely a chromosome is valid, if and only if the genes whose value is 1 and 2 in the chromosome are both larger than 0. For instance, the chromosomes such as 22000, 00000, and 01010 are all invalid, and those such as 11020 and 01012 are all valid.

3.5. Crossover Operator of Variable Length. In order to ensure that each gene in chromosome has as many chances as possible to implement crossover operation, a crossover operator with variable lengths and positions is designed as follows.

First generate a random integer N_1, which represents the number to exchange genes, where $N_1 < N$, N is the number of attributes in a database or the number of the genes in a chromosome. Then generate two random integer vectors of length N_1, which represent the positions to exchange genes. Lastly, the genes of the corresponding positions in two chromosomes are exchanged with each other to generate two novel offspring.

```
population initialize(P_size, N)
Input: P_size indicates the size of the population; N indicates the number
    of the attributes in the database.
Output: an M_P-by-N integer matrix indicates the initial population.
    pop ← Φ; indiv ← Φ;
    while sizeof(pop) < P_size
        while sizeof(indiv) < N
            temp ← generate a random integer whose value is 0, 1, or 2;
            indiv = indiv ∪ temp;
        end while
        if isvalid(indiv)
            pop = pop ∪ indiv;
        end if
    end while
    return pop;
```

PSEUDOCODE 4: Pseudocode of the initialization.

TABLE 3: An example of crossover of variable length and positions.

(a) Before crossover

C_1	A_1	A_2	A_3	A_4	A_5	A_6	A_7	A_8	A_9	A_{10}
pos_1		2		4			7	8		10
C_2	B_1	B_2	B_3	B_4	B_5	B_6	B_7	B_8	B_9	B_{10}
pos_2	1		3	4		6		8		

(b) After crossover

C_1	A_1	B_1	A_3	B_3	A_5	A_6	B_4	B_6	A_9	B_8
pos_1		*		*			*	*		*
C_2	A_2	B_2	A_4	A_7	B_5	A_8	B_7	A_{10}	B_9	B_{10}
pos_2	*		*	*		*		*		

For example, two chromosomes C_1 and C_2 containing 10 genes are illustrated in Table 3(a). The steps of implementing crossover operator on two chromosomes C_1 and C_2 are as follows.

(i) Generate a random integer $N_1 = 5$ which is less than 10.

(ii) Two random integer vectors $\text{pos}_1 = \{2, 4, 7, 8, 10\}$ and $\text{pos}_2 = \{1, 3, 4, 6, 8\}$ are generated.

(iii) Those genes whose positions are pos_1 in C_1, and those genes whose positions are pos_2 in C_2, are exchanged with each other.

The results of implementing crossover operation are illustrated in Table 3(b). Notice those genes located at the asterisk have been exchanged.

The pseudocode of the crossover function is shown in Pseudocode 5. Here, the function *isvalid* can be referred to Section 3.4. Only valid rule can be taken into the offspring.

3.6. Selection Scheme for Crossover Operation. The above crossover operation needs to firstly select some chromosomes from the population. A new selection scheme is designed as follows. For each pair chromosomes, one is selected randomly, another is chosen as the best one of chromosomes from various directions. These directions are provided by the weight vectors selected using the uniform design. The detailed steps are as follows.

First randomly select K_1 chromosomes to a set A from the population according to the probability of crossover. Assume the number of the needed weight vectors is D_1, where D_1 is a prime number. If $K_1 \geq D_1$, any D_1 of the K_1 chromosomes remain, the others are discarded. If $K_1 < D_1$, randomly select $D_1 - K_1$ chromosomes to A in order that A contain D_1 chromosomes. Next, apply the uniform design to select $D_1 - M$ weight vectors. The remainder M weight vectors are single objective weight vectors for M objective functions. Then, use (25) to generate D_1 fitness functions, which can provide D_1 search directions. Finally, adopt each fitness function to evaluate the quality of each chromosome in the population, and select the best one chromosome. Therefore, a total of D_1 chromosomes are selected as another part of chromosomes to a set B.

Each pair of A and B can be used to perform crossover operator. The pseudocode of the selection scheme for crossover operation is illustrated in Pseudocode 6.

3.7. Mutation Operator. The function *mutate* is to handle the mutation operator. Its steps are as follows. Firstly fetch a chromosome according to the probability of mutation from a population and perform mutate operator on the chromosome in order to acquire a new one by calling the function mut. If the new chromosome is invalid, call the function mut again till the newly generated chromosome is valid. Next, the valid chromosome is taken as one of the offspring. Then, return to the first step and continue. Finally, return the generated offspring. The pseudocode of the mutation function is shown in Pseudocode 7.

In Pseudocode 7, *mutate* function is used to handle mutation for the population contained many chromosomes by calling mut function. The mut function is used to handle mutation for the chromosome in the population. It firstly generates a random number. If the random number is less

population crossover(pop,p_c, M, N_1)
Input: pop indicates the population; p_c indicates the probability of
           crossover; M indicates the number of the objective function; N_1
           indicates the number of the wanted weight vectors.
Output: offspring indicates the offspring after crossover.
   offspring $\leftarrow \Phi$;
   $A, B \leftarrow$ **call** seleforcross(pop, p_c, M, N_1)
   $C_1 \in A, C_2 \in B, C_1 \neq C_2$;
   Nexch $\leftarrow \forall$ random integer$r_{temp} \wedge r_{temp} < \text{length}(C_1)$;
   $pos_1, pos_2 \leftarrow \forall$ two random integer vectors with length of Nexch;
   $C_3, C_4 \leftarrow (C_1(pos_1) \leftrightarrow C_2(pos_2))$;
   while $C_3 = C_1$ or $C_3 = C_2$ or not isvalid(C_3)
      $pos_1, pos_2 \leftarrow \forall$ two random integer vectors with length of Nexch;
      $tmp_1, tmp_2 \leftarrow (C_1(pos_1) \leftrightarrow C_2(pos_2))$;
      $C_3 \leftarrow$ isvalid(tmp_1), $C_3 \leftarrow$ isvalid(tmp_2);
   end while
   while $C_4 = C_1$ or $C_4 = C_2$ or isvalid(C_4) is false
      $pos_1, pos_2 \leftarrow \forall$ two random integer vectors with length of Nexch;
      $tmp_1, tmp_2 \leftarrow (C_1(pos_1) \leftrightarrow C_2(pos_2))$;
      $C_4 \leftarrow$ isvalid(tmp_1), $C_4 \leftarrow$ isvalid(tmp_2)
   end while
   offspring $\leftarrow$ offspring $\cup \{C_1, C_2\}$;
   return offspring;

PSEUDOCODE 5: Pseudocode of the crossover operator.

population seleforcross(pop, p_c, M, D_1)
Input: pop indicates the population; p_c indicates the probability of
           crossover; M indicates the number of the objective function; D_1
           indicates the number of the wanted weight vectors.
Output: A indicates the randomly select chromosomes; B indicates the
            chromosomes selected by the uniform design.
   $A \leftarrow \Phi; B \leftarrow \Phi$;
   for $\forall$ chrom $\in$ pop
      $r \leftarrow$ generate a random;
      if $r < p_c$
         $A \leftarrow A \cup$ chrom;
      end if
   end for
   $K_1 \leftarrow \text{length}(A)$;
   if $K_1 \geq D_1$
      $A \leftarrow$ take out D_1 from A;
   else
      $A \leftarrow A \cup \{$randomly select $D_1 - K_1$ chromosomes$\}$
   end if
   $w \leftarrow$ apply the uniform design to select $D_1 - M$ weight vectors;
   $w \leftarrow w \cup \{M$ single objective weight vectors$\}$;
   for $\forall wv \in w$
      Fitn$V \leftarrow \Phi$;
      fitness $\leftarrow$ generate fitness functions;
      for $\forall$ chrom $\in$ pop
         Fitn$V \leftarrow$ Fitn$V \cup$ fitness(chrom);
      end for
      $B \leftarrow B \cup \max(\text{Fitn}V)$;
   end for
   return A, B;

PSEUDOCODE 6: Pseudocode of the selection scheme for crossover operation.

```
population mutate(pop, p_m)
Input: pop indicates the population; p_m indicates
        the probability of mutation.
Output: offspring indicates the offspring after mutatation.
    offspring ← Φ;
    for ∀ chrom ∈ pop
        r ← generate a random;
        if r < p_m
            chrom2 ← mut(chrom, p_m);
            while not isvalid(chrom2)
                chrom2 ← mut(chrom, p_m);
            end while
            offspring ← offspring ∪ chrom2;
        end if
    end for
    return offspring;
```

PSEUDOCODE 7: Pseudocode of the mutate operator.

```
population mut(chrom, p_m)
Input: chrom indicates a chromosome in the population;
        p_m indicates the probability of mutation.
Output: chrom2 indicates a chromosome after mutatation.
    chrom2 ← chrom;
    for the jth gene ∈ chrom
        r ← generate a random;
        if r < p_m
            gene ← ∀ t ∈ {0, 1, 2} ∧ t ≠ gene;
            chrom2(j) ← gene;
        end if
    end for
    Return chrom2;
```

PSEUDOCODE 8: Pseudocode of the mut function.

than the probability of mutation, the gene is changed into one of the remainder values in the set $\{0, 1, 2\}$. The pseudocode of the mut function is shown in Pseudocode 8.

3.8. Elitist Selection or Elitism. Elitism means that elite individuals cannot be excluded from the mating pool of the population. A strategy presented can always include the best individual of the current population into the next generation in order to prevent the loss of good solutions that have been found. This strategy can be extended to copy the best n individuals to the next generation. This is explanation of the elitism. In evolutionary multiobjective optimization, elitism plays an important role [45]. Elitism can speed significantly up the performance of the genetic algorithm and help to achieve better convergence in multiobjective evolutionary algorithms, MOEAs [46]. MOEAs using elitist strategies tend to outperform their non-elitist counterparts [47]. Elitism usually has positive effects on both the convergence of

solutions toward the Pareto front and the diversity along the Pareto front in MOEAs [48].

MOEAs often use two strategies to implement elitism. One maintains elitist solutions in the population, the other stores elitist solutions into an external secondary list and reintroduces them to the population. The former copies all non-dominated solutions in the current population to the next population, then fills the rest of the next population by selecting from the remaining dominated solutions in the current population. The latter uses an external secondary list to store the elitist solutions. The external list stores the non-dominated solutions found, and the list is updated in the next generation by means of removing elitist solutions dominated by a new solution or adding the new solution if it is not dominated by any existing elitist solution.

The work adopts the second strategy, namely storing elitist solutions to an external secondary list. Its advantage is that it can preserve and dynamically adjust all the non-dominated solutions set till the current generation. The pseudocodes of

```
population paretocreate(pop)
Input: pop indicates the population.
Output: pareto indicates the non-dominated solutions.
    pareto ← pop;
    for ∀ chr1 ∈ pop;
        for ∀ chr2 ∈ pareto ∧ chr2 ≠ chr1;
            if chr1 dominate chr2
                pareto ←pareto − chr2;
            end if
        end for
    end for
    return pareto;
```

PSEUDOCODE 9: Pseudocode of selecting elitist.

```
population paretoupdate(offspring, pareto)
Input: offspring indicates the offsprings after performing the crossover
        operator and mutation operator; pareto indicates the non-dominated
        solutions.
Output: pareto indicates the non-dominated solutions.
    offspring ← call paretocreate(offspring);
    for ∀ chr1 ∈ offspring;
        nondominated ← true;
        for ∀ chr2 ∈ pareto;
            if chr1 dominate chr2
                pareto ←pareto − chr2;
            else if chr2 dominate chr1
                nondominated ← false;
            else
                continue
            end if
        end for
        if nondominated
            pareto ← pareto ∪ chr1
        end if
    end for
    return pareto;
```

PSEUDOCODE 10: Pseudocode of updatting elitist.

selecting elitist and updating elitist are, respectively, shown in Pseudocodes 9 and 10.

3.9. Selection Scheme for Next Generation Combined with Elitism. After performing the crossover operator and mutation operator, we need to select some of the potential offspring to generate the new generation. Combining the elitism with the uniform design, the proposed algorithms design a new algorithm as follows.

We call the external secondary list the *elitist pool*. It stores the non-dominated solutions found till the current generation. Assume the size of the population and elitist pool, respectively, are N_p and N_{pt}. If $N_p \leq N_{pt}$, then N_p nondominated solutions are randomly selected from the elitist pool as the next generation. Otherwise, all N_{pt} solutions in the elitist pool are taken as a part of the next generation, and the remainder $G = N_p - N_{pt}$ chromosomes are selected as follows.

Among the parents and the offspring generated by crossover and mutation, we select G of them to append to the next generation. In this selection, we adopt D_2 fitness functions in order to realize D_2 search directions, where D_2 is a design parameter and it is prime. For each fitness function, each chromosome in the parents and offspring is evaluated using this fitness function and then the best $\lfloor G/D_2 \rfloor$ or $\lceil G/D_2 \rceil$ of them are selected, where $\lfloor G/D_2 \rfloor$ mean the nearest integer less than or equal to G/D_2, and $\lceil G/D_2 \rceil$ mean the nearest integer larger than or equal to G/D_2. Overall, a total of G chromosomes are selected to append to the next generation. Therefore, a total of N_p chromosomes are selected for the next generation.

3.10. The Steps of the Proposed Algorithm. The work proposes the attribute index and uniform design based multiobjective association rule mining with evolutionary algorithm,

TABLE 4: The specifications of data sets.

Dataset	Number transactions	Number attributes
Balance scale	625	23
Solar flare	1066	48
Chess	3196	75
Mushroom	8124	119
Nursery	12960	32
T40I10D100K	100000	942

abbreviated as IUARMMEA. The steps of this algorithm are as follows.

Step 1. Firstly, load the whole database or a sample of records in the database D according to the capacity of the computer memory. Then, create the attribute index of each attribute in database by calling the function attrIdx described in Section 3.1. Finally, unload D to release the computer memory.

Step 2. Generate the initial population by calling the function "initialize" described in Section 3.4.

Step 3. Calculate several metrics values of the confidence, coverage, comprehensibility, and interestingness using (5), (7), (8), and (20), respectively. Choose all non-dominated solutions to the elitist pool from the initial populations by calling the function "paretocreate" described in Section 3.8.

Step 4. Select some chromosomes for performing the crossover operation from the population by calling the function "seleforcross" described in Section 3.6.

Step 5. Perform the crossover operation on the selected chromosomes by calling the function "crossover" described in Section 3.5.

Step 6. Perform the mutate operation on the selected chromosomes from the population in term of the probability of mutation by calling the function "mutate" described in Section 3.7.

Step 7. Regulate and update the non-dominated solutions in the elitist pool by calling the function "paretoupdate" described in Section 3.8. This step will compare the non-dominated solutions and the generated offspring after performing the crossover operator and mutation operator.

Step 8. Select some of the potential offspring to form the new generation by the selection scheme described in Section 3.9.

Step 9. Go to Step 4 and continue if the stop criterion is not met. Otherwise, go to Step 10.

Step 10. Decode all non-dominated solutions in the elitist pool to acquire the final association rules by calling the function "decode" described in Section 3.3.

4. Numerical Results

The proposed algorithm IUARMMEA is performed to test its performance and compare with the algorithm ARMMEA, which does not use the attribute index and uniform design.

4.1. Test Problems. We use six datasets to show the effectiveness and performance of IUARMMEA. The specifications of six datasets are described in Table 4. They represent various kinds of domains and include both dense and non-dense datasets, as well as various numbers of items. The first five datasets are from UCI repository [49]. The last dataset was generated using the generator from the IBM Almaden Quest research group. It can be acquired from the workshop on frequent itemset mining implementations [50].

For each dataset, the categorical attribute is converted or divided into boolean attribute in terms of each attribute and its various values. For instance, assume an attribute x can take any of the set $\{"a","b","c","d","e"\}$ in a categorical dataset. Therefore, x can be divided into 5 attributes, such as x_1, x_2, x_3, x_4, x_5. For each transaction, if $x = a$, then $x_1 = 1$, otherwise $x_1 = 0$; If $x = b$, then $x_2 = 1$, otherwise $x_2 = 0$, and so on.

However, it can be noted that the gene in the chromosome only take one of the divided attributes, namely, only one attribute can be larger than 0 in the divided attributes. This is because the divided attributes are mutually exclusive. Therefore, the evolution, initialization, and evaluation of the population must consider the situation.

4.2. Parameter Values. The parameters of the proposed algorithm are as follows.

(i) *Population Size*: the population size is 100.

(ii) *Parameters for Crossover and Mutation*: we adopt $p_c = 0.9$, $N_1 = 23$ and $p_m = 0.5$.

(iii) *Parameters for Interestingness*: the regulating coefficient α is 0.5.

(iv) *Parameters for Selection*: $D_1 = 31$.

(v) *Stopping Condition*: the algorithm terminates if the number of iterations is larger than the given maximal value 10.

4.3. Results. For each test problem, we perform 3 independent executions and calculate the average values of the following results, the number of scanning database, the number of comparing transactions, the number of comparing attribute indices, and execution times. Tables 5 and 6, respectively, show these average values of two algorithms.

Tables 5 and 6 indicate that IUARMMEA compared with ARMMEA, the number of scanning database is very little and can be disregarded. This is because in ARMMEA algorithm, each chromosome and each offspring generated by crossover and mutation need to scan database to calculate the support count of the antecedent, consequent, and the whole rule, while in IUARMMEA algorithm, all chromosomes and offsprings do not need to scan database any further, and only need to scan database once to create the attribute index.

TABLE 5: The averages of several results for IUARMMEA.

Dataset	Number scanning database	Number comparing transactions	Number comparing indices	Execution times (sec)
Balance scale	1	625	8406	52.04
Solar Flare	1	1066	17047	99.36
Chess	1	3196	43683	282.81
Mushroom	1	8124	27123	363.05
Nursery	1	12960	9121	296.87
T40I10D100K	3	300000	85447	712.62

TABLE 6: The averages of several results for ARMMEA.

Dataset	Number scanning database	Number comparing transactions	Number comparing indices	Execution times (sec)
Balance scale	2380	1487500	0	121.39
Solar flare	2326	2479516	0	232.66
Chess	2320	7414720	0	626.78
Mushroom	2320	18847680	0	1183.06
Nursery	2378	30818880	0	1312.82
T40I10D100K	6885	229500000	0	1937.53

For the dataset T40I10D100, as the number of transactions and attributes is very large, it is loaded in three batches according to the capacity of the computer memory. Therefore, the number of scanning database is 3.

The number of comparing transactions is the product of the number of scanning database and the number of transactions in database, since scanning database once is to compare each transaction in database with each part of the rule. As the algorithm ARMMEA has not the attribute index, the number of comparing indices is certainly 0. From Table 5, it can be seen that there is a relationship between the number of comparing indices and the number of the undivided attributes. This is because several metrics of a rule need to compare the attribute indices of the undivided attributes.

Tables 5 and 6 also indicate that the execution times of IUARMMEA are significantly less than those of ARMMEA. The former really outperforms the latter. In the meanwhile, it can be seen that the execution times have relation to not only the number of comparing the indices but also the lengths of attribute index. For example, the dataset mushroom compared with chess, the number of comparing indices is less, but the execution times are even longer. This is because the length of attribute index is much larger.

5. Conclusion and Future Work

In this paper, we present a method of multiobjective association rule mining based on the attribute index and uniform design. The proposed method only scans database once to create the attribute index and uses it to replace repeatedly scanning database. This significantly reduces the number of comparisons and time consumption, and improves the performance of the algorithms.

This algorithm is going on for further enhancement and improvement. Attempt is to extend it to immediately use the categorical or numeric dataset rather than converting them into Boolean dataset.

Acknowledgments

This work is supported by the National Natural Science Foundation of China (no. 61272119, no. 61203372), and the Fundamental Research Funds for the Central Universities (no. K50510030014).

References

[1] R. Agrawal and R. Srikant, "Fast algorithms for mining association rules," in *Proceedings of the 20th International Conference on Very Large Data Bases (VLDB '94)*, pp. 487–499, 1994.

[2] R. Agrawal, T. Imieliński, and A. Swami, "Mining association rules between sets of items in large databases," in *Proceedings of the ACM SIGMOD International Conference on Management of Data*, pp. 207–216, May 1993.

[3] M. Houtsma and A. Swami, "Set-oriented mining for association rules in relational databases," in *Proceedings of the IEEE 11th International Conference on Data Engineering*, pp. 25–33, March 1995.

[4] D.-I. Lin and Z. M. Kedem, "Pincer-search: an efficient algorithm for discovering the maximum frequent set," *IEEE Transactions on Knowledge and Data Engineering*, vol. 14, no. 3, pp. 553–566, 2002.

[5] D. I. Lin and Z. Kedem, "Pincer-search: a new algorithm for discovering the maximum frequent set," in *Proceedings of the 6th International Conference Extending Database Technology (EDBT '98)*, pp. 103–119, March 1998.

[6] S. Brin, R. Motwani, J. D. Ullman, and S. Tsur, "Dynamic itemset counting and implication rules for market basket data," in *Proceedings of the ACM SIGMOD International Conference on Management of Data (SIGMOD '97)*, pp. 255–264, 1997.

[7] N. Marin, C. Molina, J. M. Serrano, and M. A. Vila, "A complexity guided algorithm for association rule extraction on fuzzy datacubes," *IEEE Transactions on Fuzzy Systems*, vol. 16, no. 3, pp. 693–714, 2008.

[8] A. Ghosh and B. Nath, "Multi-objective rule mining using genetic algorithms," *Information Sciences*, vol. 163, no. 1–3, pp. 123–133, 2004.

[9] H. R. Qodmanan, M. Nasiri, and B. Minaei-Bidgoli, "Multi objective association rule mining with genetic algorithm without specifying minimum support and minimum confidence," *Expert Systems with Applications*, vol. 38, no. 1, pp. 288–298, 2011.

[10] X. Yan, C. Zhang, and S. Zhang, "Genetic algorithm-based strategy for identifying association rules without specifying actual minimum support," *Expert Systems with Applications*, vol. 36, no. 2, pp. 3066–3076, 2009.

[11] A. Hadian, M. Nasiri, and B. Minaei-Bidgoli, "Clustering based multi-objective rule mining using genetic algorithm," *International Journal of Digital Content Technology and its Applications*, vol. 4, no. 1, pp. 37–42, 2010.

[12] M. V. Fidelis, H. S. Lopes, and A. A. Freitas, "Discovering comprehensible classification rules with a genetic algorithm," in

Proceedings of the Congress on Evolutionary Computation (CEC '00), pp. 805–810, July 2000.

[13] Y. H. Chan, T. C. Chiang, and L. C. Fu, "A two-phase evolutionary algorithm for multiobjective mining of classification rules," in *Proceedings of the IEEE Congress on Evolutionary Computation (CEC '10)*, Barcelona, Spain, July 2010.

[14] N. Hoque, B. Nath, and D. K. Bhattacharyya, "A new approach on rare association rule mining," *International Journal of Computer Applications*, vol. 53, no. 3, pp. 1–6, 2012.

[15] M. Kaya, "Autonomous classifiers with understandable rule using multi-objective genetic algorithms," *Expert Systems with Applications*, vol. 37, no. 4, pp. 3489–3494, 2010.

[16] J. Hipp, U. Güntzer, and G. Nakhaeizadeh, "Algorithms for association rule mining-a general survey and comparison," *ACM SIGKDD Explorations Newsletter*, vol. 2, no. 1, pp. 58–64, 2000.

[17] A. Savasere, E. R. Omiecinski, and S. B. Navathe, "An efficient algorithm for mining association rules in large databases," in *Proceedings of the International Conference on Very Large Data Bases (VLDB '95)*, 1995.

[18] M. J. Zaki, S. Parthasarathy, M. Ogihara, and W. Li, "New algorithms for fast discovery of association rules," in *Proceedings of the 3rd International Conference on Knowledge Discovery and Data Mining*, pp. 283–286, 1997.

[19] B. Goethals, "Memory issues in frequent itemset mining," in *Proceedings of the ACM Symposium on Applied Computing (SAC '04)*, pp. 530–534, Cyprus, March 2004.

[20] J. Han, J. Pei, Y. Yin, and R. Mao, "Mining frequent patterns without candidate generation: a frequent-pattern tree approach," *Data Mining and Knowledge Discovery*, vol. 8, no. 1, pp. 53–87, 2004.

[21] J. Han, J. Pei, and Y. Yin, "Mining frequent patterns without candidate generation," in *Proceedings of the ACM SIGMOD International Conference on Management of Data (SIGMOD '00)*, pp. 1–12, 2000.

[22] T. D. Do, S. C. Hui, A. C. M. Fong, and B. Fong, "Associative classification with artificial immune system," *IEEE Transactions on Evolutionary Computation*, vol. 13, no. 2, pp. 217–228, 2009.

[23] Y. W. Leung, "Multiobjective programming using uniform design and genetic algorithm," *IEEE Transactions on Systems, Man and Cybernetics C*, vol. 30, no. 3, pp. 293–304, 2000.

[24] J. D. Schaffer, "Multiple objective optimization with vector evaluated genetic algorithms," in *Proceedings of the 1st international Conference on Genetic Algorithms*, pp. 93–100, Pittsburgh, PA, USA, 1985.

[25] C. A. C. Coello, "Evolutionary multi-objective optimization: basic concepts and some applications in pattern recognition," in *Pattern Recognition*, vol. 6718 of *Lecture Notes in Computer Science*, pp. 22–33, Springer, Berlin, Germany, 2011.

[26] N. Srinivas and K. Deb, "Muiltiobjective optimization using nondominated sorting in genetic algorithms," *Journal of Evolutionary Computation*, vol. 2, no. 3, pp. 221–248, 1994.

[27] J. Horn, N. Nafpliotis, and D. E. Goldberg, "Niched Pareto genetic algorithm for multiobjective optimization," in *Proceedings of the 1st IEEE Conference on Evolutionary Computation*, pp. 82–87, June 1994.

[28] C. M. Fonseca and P. J. Fleming, "Genetic algorithms for multiobjective optimization: formulation, discussion and generalization," in *Proceedings of the 5th International Conference on Genetic Algorithms*, p. 416, 1993.

[29] E. Zitzler, M. Laumanns, and L. Thiele, "SPEA2: improving the strength Pareto evolutionary algorithm," TIK-Report 103, Eidgenössische Technische Hochschule Zürich (ETH), Institut für Technische Informatik und Kommunikationsnetze (TIK), 2001.

[30] K. Deb, A. Pratap, S. Agarwal, and T. Meyarivan, "A fast and elitist multiobjective genetic algorithm: NSGA-II," *IEEE Transactions on Evolutionary Computation*, vol. 6, no. 2, pp. 182–197, 2002.

[31] D. Martin, A. Rosete, J. Alcala-Fdez, and F. Herrera, "A multiobjective evolutionary algorithm for mining quantitative association rules," in *Proceedings of the 11th International Conference on Intelligent Systems Design and Applications (ISDA '11)*, pp. 1397–1402, Córdoba, Spain, 2011.

[32] A. Zhou, B.-Y. Qu, H. Li, S. Z. Zhao, P. N. Suganthan, and Q. Zhangd, "Multiobjective evolutionary algorithms: a survey of the state of the art," *Swarm and Evolutionary Computation*, vol. 1, no. 1, pp. 32–49, 2011.

[33] J. Zhang, Y. Wang, and J. Feng, "Parallel multi-swarm PSO based on K-medoids and uniform design," *Research Journal of Applied Sciences, Engineering and Technology*, vol. 5, no. 7, pp. 2576–2585, 2013.

[34] Y. Wang, C. Dang, H. Li, L. Han, and J. Wei, "A clustering multi-objective evolutionary algorithm based on orthogonal and uniform design," in *Proceedings of the IEEE Congress on Evolutionary Computation (CEC '09)*, pp. 2927–2933, Trondheim, Norway, May 2009.

[35] L. Jia, Y. Wang, and L. Fan, "Uniform design based hybrid genetic algorithm for multiobjective bilevel convex programming," in *Proceedings of the 7th International Conference on Computational Intelligence and Security (CIS '11)*, pp. 159–163, Hainan, China, 2011.

[36] S. Srinivasan and S. Ramakrishnan, "Evolutionary multi objective optimization for rule mining: a review," *Artificial Intelligence Review*, vol. 36, no. 3, pp. 205–248, 2011.

[37] M. Khabzaoui, C. Dhaenens, and E. G. Talbi, "Parallel genetic algorithms for multi-objective rule mining," in *Proceedings of the 6th Metaheuristics International Conference (MIC '05)*, pp. 571–576, 2005.

[38] S. Dehuri, S. Patnaik, A. Ghosh, and R. Mall, "Application of elitist multi-objective genetic algorithm for classification rule generation," *Applied Soft Computing Journal*, vol. 8, no. 1, pp. 477–487, 2008.

[39] B. d. l. Iglesia, M. S. Philpott, A. J. Bagnall, and V. J. Rayward-Smith, "Data mining rules using multi-objective evolutionary algorithms," in *Proceedings of the Congress on Evolutionary Computation (CEC '03)*, vol. 3, pp. 1552–1559, 2003.

[40] S. Dehuri and R. Mall, "Predictive and comprehensible rule discovery using a multi-objective genetic algorithm," *Knowledge-Based Systems*, vol. 19, no. 6, pp. 413–421, 2006.

[41] B. Alatas and E. Akin, "Rough particle swarm optimization and its applications in data mining," *Soft Computing*, vol. 12, no. 12, pp. 1205–1218, 2008.

[42] M. Nasiri, L. S. Taghavi, and B. Minaee, "Numeric multiobjective rule mining using simulated annealing algorithm," *International Journal of Operational Research*, vol. 1, no. 2, pp. 37–48, 2011.

[43] B. Alatas, E. Akin, and A. Karci, "MODENAR: multi-objective differential evolution algorithm for mining numeric association rules," *Applied Soft Computing Journal*, vol. 8, no. 1, pp. 646–656, 2008.

[44] K. Y. Fung, C. K. Kwong, K. W. M. Siu, and K. M. Yua, "A multi-objective genetic algorithm approach to rule mining for affective product design," *Expert Systems with Applications*, vol. 39, no. 8, pp. 7411–7419, 2012.

[45] M. Laumanns, E. Zitzler, and L. Thiele, "Unified model for multi-objective evolutionary algorithms with elitism," in *Proceedings of the Congress on Evolutionary Computation (CEC '00)*, vol. 1, pp. 46–53, July 2000.

[46] E. Zitzler, K. Deb, and L. Thiele, "Comparison of multiobjective evolutionary algorithms: empirical results.," *Evolutionary computation*, vol. 8, no. 2, pp. 173–195, 2000.

[47] A. Konak, D. W. Coit, and A. E. Smith, "Multi-objective optimization using genetic algorithms: a tutorial," *Reliability Engineering and System Safety*, vol. 91, no. 9, pp. 992–1007, 2006.

[48] H. Ishibuchi and Y. Nojima, "Multiobjective genetic fuzzy systems," *Computational Intelligence*, vol. 1, no. 2, pp. 131–173, 2009.

[49] "UCI repository of machine learning databases," 1998, http://www.ics.uci.edu/~mlearn/MLRepository.html.

[50] Frequent Itemset Mining Implementations (FIMI '03) Workshop, 2003, http://fimi.cs.helsinki.fi.

8

An Improved Marriage in Honey Bees Optimization Algorithm for Single Objective Unconstrained Optimization

Yuksel Celik[1] and Erkan Ulker[2]

[1] *Department of Computer Programming, Karamanoglu Mehmetbey University, Karaman, Turkey*
[2] *Computer Engineering Department, Selcuk University, Konya, Turkey*

Correspondence should be addressed to Yuksel Celik; celik_yuksel@hotmail.com

Academic Editors: P. Agarwal, V. Bhatnagar, and Y. Zhang

Marriage in honey bees optimization (MBO) is a metaheuristic optimization algorithm developed by inspiration of the mating and fertilization process of honey bees and is a kind of swarm intelligence optimizations. In this study we propose improved marriage in honey bees optimization (IMBO) by adding Levy flight algorithm for queen mating flight and neighboring for worker drone improving. The IMBO algorithm's performance and its success are tested on the well-known six unconstrained test functions and compared with other metaheuristic optimization algorithms.

1. Introduction

Optimization means to find the best among the possible designs of a system. In other words, for the purpose of minimizing or maximizing a real function, selecting real or integer values from an identified range, placing these into the function and systematically examining or solving the problem is referred to as optimization. For the solution of optimization problems, mathematical and heuristic optimization techniques are used. In problems with wide and large solution space, heuristic algorithms heuristically produce the closest results to the solution, without scanning the whole solution space and within very short durations. Metaheuristic algorithms are quite effective in solving global optimization problems [1]. The main metaheuristic algorithms are genetic algorithm (GA) [2], simulated annealing (SA) [3], particle swarm optimization (PSO) [4], ant colony optimization (ACO) [5], differential evolution (DE) [6], marriage in honey bees optimization (MBO) [7, 8], artificial bee colony algorithm (ABC) [9] and evolutionary algorithms (EAs) [9, 10].

Performance of algorithms carrying out nature-inspired or evolutionary calculations can be monitored with their application on the test functions of such algorithms. Karaboga and Basturk implemented the artificial bee colony (ABC) algorithm, which they proposed from the inspiration of the food searching activities of honey bees, on unconstrained test functions [11]. Digalakis and Margaritis developed two algorithms titled as the generational replacement model (GRM) and the steady state replacement model by making modifications on the genetic algorithm and monitored their performances on unconstrained test functions [12]. By combining the GA and SA algorithms, Hassan et al. proposed the geno-simulated annealing (GSA) algorithm and implemented it on the most commonly used unconstrained test functions [13]. In order to obtain a better performance in the multidimensional search space, Chatterjee et al. suggested the nonlinear variation of the known PSO, the non-PSO algorithm, and measured its performance on several unconstrained test functions [14]. By integrating the opposition-based learning (OBL) approach for population initialization and generation jumping in the DE algorithm, Rahnamayan et al. proposed the opposition-based DE (ODE) algorithm and compared the results they obtained from implementing the algorithm on the known unconstrained test functions with DE [15]. It is difficult to exhibit a good performance on all test functions. Rather than expecting the developed algorithm to provide accurate results on all types of problems, it is more reasonable to determine the types of problems where the algorithm functions well and decide on the algorithm to be used on a specific problem.

Test functions determine whether the algorithm will be caught to the local minimum and whether it has a wide search function in the search space during the solution.

In 2001, Abbass [8] proposed the MBO algorithm, which is a swarm intelligence based and metaheuristic algorithm predicated on the marriage and fertilization of honey bees. Later on, Abbass and Teo used the annealing approach in the MBO algorithm for determining the gene pool of male bees [16]. Chang made modifications on MBO for solving combinatorial problems and implemented this to the solution. Again, for the solution of infinite horizon-discounted cost stochastic dynamic programming problems, he implemented MBO on the solution by adapting his algorithm he titled as "Honey Bees Policy Iteration" (HBPI) [17]. In 2007, Afshar et al. proposed MBO algorithm as honey bee mating optimization (HBMO) algorithm and implemented it on water resources management applications [18]. Marinakis et al. implemented HBMO algorithm by obtaining HBMOTSP in order to solve Euclidan travelling salesman problem (TSP) [19]. Chiu and Kuo [20] proposed a clustering method which integrates particle swarm optimization with honey bee mating optimization. Simulations for three benchmark test functions (MSE, intra-cluster distance, and intercluster distance) are performed.

In the original MBO algorithm, annealing algorithm is used during the queen bee's mating flight, mating with drones, generation of new genotype, and adding these into the spermatheca. In the present study, we used Levy flight [1] instead of the annealing algorithm. Also, during the improvement of the genotype of worker bees, we applied single neighborhood and single inheritance from the queen. We tested the IMBO algorithm we developed on the most commonly known six unconstrained numeric test functions, and we compared the results with the PSO and DE [21] algorithms from the literature.

This paper is organized as follows: in Section 2, the MBO algorithm and unconstrained test problems are described in detail. Section 3 presents the proposed unconstrained test problems solution procedure using IMBO. Section 4 compares the empirical studies and unconstrained test results of IMBO, MBO, and other optimization algorithms. Section 5 is the conclusion of the paper.

2. Material and Method

2.1. The Marriage in Honey Bee Optimization (MBO) Algorithm

2.1.1. Honey Bee Colony. Bees take the first place among the insects that can be characterized as swarm and that possess swarm intelligence. A typical bee colony is composed of 3 types of bees. These are the queen, drone (male bee), and workers (female worker). The queen's life is a couple of years old, and she is the mother of the colony. She is the only bee capable of laying eggs.

Drones are produced from unfertilized eggs and are the fathers of the colony. Their numbers are around a couple of hundreds. Worker bees are produced from fertilized eggs, and all procedures such as feeding the colony and the queen,

maintaining broods, building combs, and searching and collecting food are made by these bees. Their numbers are around 10–60 thousand [22].

Mating flight happens only once during the life of the queen bee. Mating starts with the dance of the queen. Drones follow and mate with the queen during the flight. Mating of a drone with the queen depends of the queen's speed and their fitness. Sperms of the drone are stored in the spermatheca of the queen. The gene pool of future generations is created here. The queen lays approximately two thousand fertilized eggs a day (two hundred thousand a year). After her spermatheca is discharged, she lays unfertilized eggs [23].

2.1.2. Honey Bee Optimization Algorithm. Mating flight can be explained as the queen's acceptance of some of the drones she meets in a solution space, mating and the improvement of the broods generated from these. The queen has a certain amount of energy at the start of the flight and turns back to the nest when her energy falls to minimum or when her spermatheca is full. After going back to the nest, broods are generated and these are improved by the worker bees crossover and mutation.

Mating of the drone with the queen bee takes place according to the probability of the following annealing function [8]:

$$\text{prob}\, f\,(Q, D) = e^{-\text{difference/speed}}, \qquad (1)$$

where (Q, D) is the probability of the drone to be added to the spermatheca of the Q queen (probability of the drone and queen to mate) and $\Delta(f)$ is the absolute difference between D's fitness and Q's fitness. $f(Q)$ and $S(t)$ are the speed of the queen at t time. This part is as the annealing function. In cases where at first the queen's speed is high or the fitness of the drone is as good as the queen's fitness, mating probability is high. Formulations of the time-dependent speed $S(t)$ and energy $E(t)$ of the queen in each pass within the search space are as follows:

$$\begin{aligned} S\,(t+1) &= \alpha \times S\,(t), \\ E\,(t+1) &= E\,(t) - \gamma. \end{aligned} \qquad (2)$$

Here, α is the factor of $\in [0, 1]$ and γ is the amount of energy reduction in each pass. On the basis of (1) and (2), the original MBO algorithm was proposed by Abbas [8] as shown in Algorithm 1.

2.2. Unconstrained Numerical Benchmark Functions. Performance of evolutionary calculating algorithms can be monitored by implementing the algorithm on test functions. A well-defined problem set is useful for measuring the performances of optimization algorithms. By their structures, test functions are divided into two groups as constrained and unconstrained test functions. Unconstrained test functions can be classified as unimodal and multimodal. While unimodal functions have a single optimum within the search space, multimodal functions have more than one optimum. If the function is predicated on a continuous mathematical objective function within the defined search space, then it

Initialize workers
Randomly generate the queens
Apply local search to get a good queen
For a pre-defined maximum number of mating-flights
    For each queen in the queen list
        Initialize energy (E), speed (S), and position
        The queen moves between states
        And probabilistically chooses drones $\text{prob}f\,(Q,D) = e^{-(\text{difference}/\text{speed})}$
        If a drone is selected, then
            Add its sperm to the queen's spermatheca
            $S(t + 1) = \alpha \times S(t)$
            $E(t + 1) = E(t) - \gamma$
        End if
        Update the queen's internal energy and speed
    End for each
    Generate broods by crossover and mutation
    Use workers to improve the broods
    Update workers' fitness
    While the best brood is better than the worst queen
        Replace the least-fittest queen with the best brood
        Remove the best brood from the brood list
    End while
End for

ALGORITHM 1: Original MBO algorithm [8].

is a continuous benchmark function. However, if the bit strings are not defined and continuous, then the function is described as a discreet benchmark function [24]. Alcayde et al. [25] approach a novel extension of the well-known Pareto archived evolution strategy (PAES) which combines simulated annealing and tabu search. They applied this several mathematical problems show that this hybridization allows an improvement in the quality of the nondominated solutions in comparison with PAES Some of the most commonly known test functions are as follows. We have solved well-known six unconstrained single objective numeric benchmark function. The details of the benchmark functions are given in Table 1.

3. IMBO for Unconstrained Test Functions

In the original MBO mating possibility of the queen bee in the mating flight is calculated through the annealing function. In the proposed study Improved MBO (IMBO) algorithm was obtained by improving the MBO algorithm through the replacement of the annealing algorithm with the Levy flight algorithm in order to enable the queen to make a better search in the search space. Flight behaviors of many animals and insects exhibited the typical characteristics of Levy flight [26]. In addition, there are many studies to which Levy flight was successfully adapted. Pavlyukevich solved a problem of nonconvex stochastic optimization with the help of simulated annealing of Levy flights of a variable stability index [27]. In biological phenomena, Viswanathan et al. used Levy flight in the search of biologic organisms for target organisms [28]. Reynolds conducted a study by integrating Levy flight

algorithm with the honey bees' strategies of searching food [29]. Tran et al. proposed Levy flight optimization (LFO) for global optimization problems, implemented it on the test functions, and compared the results they obtained with simulated annealing (SA) [30]. By adapting Levy flight algorithm instead of the gaussian random walk in the group search optimizer (GSO) algorithm developed for Artificial neural network (ANN), Shan applied the algorithm on a set of 5 optimization benchmark functions [31].

In general terms, Levy flight is a random walk. The steps in this random walk are obtained from Levy distribution [1]. Levy flight is implemented in 2 steps. While the first is a random selection of direction, the second is the selection of a step suitable for Levy distribution. While direction has to be selected from a homogenous distribution region, step selection is a harder process. Although there are several methods for step selection, the most effective and simplistic one is the Mantegna algorithm.

Mantegna algorithm is calculated as shown in the following equation:

$$s = \frac{u}{|v|^{1/\beta}}. \tag{3}$$

Here, the v is obtained by taking the magnitude of the genotype as basis.

u on the other hand is calculated as shown in the following equation;

$$\sigma_u = \left\{ \frac{\Gamma\,(1 + \beta)\,\sin(\pi\beta/2)}{\Gamma\,[(1 + \beta)\,/2]\,\beta 2^{(\beta-1)/2}} \right\}^{1/\beta}, \quad \sigma_u = 1. \tag{4}$$

TABLE 1: Unconstrained test functions.

No.	Function name	Formula	Range	Optimum $f(x)$
1	Sphere	$f(x) = \sum_{i=1}^{n} x^2$	$[5.12, 5.12]^n$	0
2	Rosenbrock	$f(\vec{x}) = \sum_{i=1}^{n-1} 100\left(x_{i+1} - x^2\right)^2 + \left(x_i - 1\right)^2$	$[-2.04, 2.048]^n$	0
3	Rastrigin	$f(\vec{x}) = 10 \cdot n + \sum_{i=1}^{n} \left(x_i^2 - 10 \cdot \cos\left(2\pi x_i\right)\right)$	$[-5.12, 5.12]^n$	0
4	Griewank	$f(\vec{x}) = \sum_{i=1}^{n} \frac{x_i^2}{4000} - \prod \cos\left(\frac{x_i}{\sqrt{i}}\right) + 1$	$[-600, 600]^n$	0
5	Schwefel	$f(\vec{x}) = 418.9829 \cdot n + \sum_{i=1}^{n} x_i \cdot \sin\left(\sqrt{|x_i|}\right)$	$[-500, 500]^n$	$-418.9829 * n$
6	Ackley	$f(\vec{x}) = 20 + e - 20 \cdot e^{-0.2 \cdot \sqrt{(1/n)\sum_{i=1}^{n} x_i^2}} - e^{(1/n)\sum_{i=1}^{n} \cos(2\pi x_i)}$	$[-32.768, 32.768]^n$	0

While in this equation β is $0 \leq \beta \leq 2$, is the Γ is the Gamma function, and calculated as follows:

$$\Gamma(z) = \int_0^{\infty} t^{z-1} e^{-t} dt. \tag{5}$$

In consequence, the direction of the next step is determined with the u and v parameters, and step length is found by placing u and v into their place in the Mantegna algorithm (3). Based on S, new genotype is generated as much as random genotype size, and the generated genotype is added to the previous step. Consider

$$s = \propto_0 \left(x_j^{(t)} - x_i^{(t)}\right) \oplus \text{Lévy}(\beta) \sim 0.01 \frac{u}{|v|^{1/\beta}} \left(x_j^{(t)} - x_i^{(t)}\right). \tag{6}$$

Creation of the new genotype of this step is completed by subjecting the new solution set obtained, that is, the genotype to the maximum and minimum controls defined for the test problem and adjusting deviations if any. Accordingly, through these implemented equations, the queen bee moves from the previous position to the next position, or towards the direction obtained from Levy distribution and by the step length obtained from Mantegna algorithm as follows:

$$L_{ij} = x_{ij} + s * \text{rand}\left(\text{size}\left(x_{ij}\right)\right). \tag{7}$$

In the crossover operator, the genotype of the queen bee and all genotypes in the current population are crossed over. Crossover was carried out by randomly calculating the number of elements subjected to crossover within Hamming distance on the genotypes to be crossed over.

In the improvement of the genotype (broods) by the worker bees single neighborhood and single inheritance from the queen was used. Consider

$$W_{ij} = x_{ij} + \left(x_{ij} - x_{kj}\right) \emptyset_{ij}, \tag{8}$$

where $\emptyset_{ij}$ is a random $(0, 1)$ value, x_i is the current brood genotype, x_k is the queen genotype, j is a random value number of genotype. In this way, and it was observed that the developed IMBO algorithm exhibits better performance than the other metaheuristic optimization algorithms.

The MBO algorithm we modified is shown in Algorithm 2.

4. Experimental Results

In this study, we used Sphere, Rosenbrock, Rastrigin, Griewank, Schwefel, and Ackley unconstrained test problems; a program in the MatLab 2009 programming language was developed for the tests of MBO and IMBO. Genotype sizes of 10, 50, 100, 300, 500, 800, and 1000 were taken for each test. Population size (Spermatheca Size) was accepted as $M = 100$. At the end of each generation, mean values and standard deviations were calculated for test functions. Each genotype was developed for 10,000 generations. Each improvement was run for 30 times. Global minimum variance graphs of each test function for IMBO are presented in Figure 1.

Examining the six test functions presented in Figure 1 shows that, at first, global optimum values were far from the solution value in direct proportion to genotype size. Accordingly, for large genotypes, or in other words in cases where the number of entry parameters is high, convergence of the proposed algorithm to the optimum solution takes a longer time. The test results for MBO and IMBO are given in Tables 2 and 3.

When Tables 2 and 3 were examined, it is seen that genotype size increases in all functions of MBO IMBO algorithms and the global minimum values get away from the optimal minimum values. In Table 2, the MBO algorithm Sphere function, 10, 50, 100 the size of genotype reached an optimum value while the other genotype sizes converge to the optimal solution. It was observed that Rosenbrock function minimum is reached optimal sizes in all genotypes. It was observed that rastrigin function 10, 50, 100, Griewank function 50, 100 genotype sizes in the optimal solution was reached. It was observed that except Schwefel function, other function and genotype sizes, the optimal solution was reached close to values.

When Table 3 was examined, it was seen that, while the size of genotype increased, IMBO algorithm Sphere, Rastrigin, Griewank, Schwefel, and Ackley function, were getting away from the optimal minimum. It was seen that Sphere function, 10, 50, 100 the size of genotype reached an optimum value while the other genotype sizes converges to the optimal solution. It was observed that, except for the size of 10 genotypes Rosenbrock function, but all other

```
Initialize
Randomly generate the queens
Apply local search to get a good queen
For a pre-defined maximum number of mating-flights (Maximum Iteration)
    While spermatheca not full
        Add its sperm to the queen's spermatheca by Levy Flight (7)
    End while
    Generate broods by crossover and mutation
    Use workers to improve the broods by single inheritance single neighborhood (8)
    Update workers' fitness
    While the best brood is better than the worst queen
        Replace the least-fittest queen with the best brood
        Remove the best brood from the brood list
    End while
End for
```

ALGORITHM 2: Proposed IMBO algorithm.

TABLE 2: Test results of the MBO algorithm for the genotype sizes of 10, 50, 100, 300, 500, 800, and 1000; number of runs = 30; SD: standard deviation, AV: global minimum average; generation = 10000.

Genotype size		10	50	100	300	500	800	1000
Sphere	AV	0	0	0	$1.97E-26$	$1.21E-13$	$2.06E-06$	$8.26E-04$
	SD	$9.81E-01$	$3.36E+01$	$1.41E+02$	$1.19E+03$	$2.66E+03$	$6.82E+03$	$1.84E+04$
Rosenbrock	AV	0	0	0	0	0	0	0
	SD	$4.73E-03$	$8.67E-03$	$8.29E-03$	$1.55E-02$	$7.28E-03$	$8.09E-03$	0
Rastrigin	AV	0	0	0	$6.0633E-13$	$7.88048E-12$	$3.33194E-05$	0.002606
	SD	0	0	0	$3.95279E-13$	$1.80594E-12$	$3.09109E-05$	0.002843
Griewank	AV	0.010377126	0	0	$3.40468E-16$	$7.26498E-08$	$1.1388E-06$	0.000141
	SD	0.026549182	0.32563139	1.09610828	8.02049039	70.78602045	36.67034057	108.177558
Schwefel	AV	$-9.99E+223$	$-2.96E+211$	$-1.00E+183$	$-2.37E+306$	$-1.02E+305$	$-1.10E+305$	$-1.10E+305$
	SD	$3.81E+22$	$1.94E+16$	$5.13E+26$	$4.31E+35$	$7.31E+35$	$3.39E+32$	$7.89E+35$
Ackley	AV	$4.08562E-15$	$8.23045E-15$	$7.3922E-09$	$8.49609E-14$	$9.13234E-10$	0.000227233	0.000452387
	SD	0.006649746	0.01783530	0.61180347	0.05005151	0.507695929	1.288113922	0.287375496

TABLE 3: Test results of the IMBO algorithm for the genotype sizes of 10, 50, 100, 300, 500, 800, and 1000; number of runs = 30; SD: standard deviation, AV: global minimum average; generation = 10000.

Genotype size		10	50	100	300	500	800	1000
Sphere	AV	0	0	0	$1.38E-28$	$1.47E-13$	$2.78E-07$	0.0001224
	SD	0	0	0	$8.97E-29$	$1.90E-15$	$8.50E-08$	$3.09E-05$
Rosenbrock	AV	$2.25E-07$	0	0	0	0	0	0
	SD	$2.24E-06$	0	0.1425029	0	0	0.2440021	0
Rastrigin	AV	0	0	$4.54E-15$	$5.68E-13$	$3.60E-12$	$6.13E-07$	0.0002386
	SD	0	0	$3.18E-14$	$4.78E-13$	$1.25E-12$	$3.14E-07$	$9.13E-05$
Griewank	AV	0.0002219	0	0	$3.48E-16$	$9.15E-13$	$1.78E-07$	$3.26E-05$
	SD	0.0012617	0	0	$3.85E-17$	$1.88E-14$	$5.43E-08$	$6.73E-06$
Schwefel	AV	$-1.21E+23$	$-1.08E+25$	$-6.17E+29$	$-1.21E+40$	$-1.76E+36$	$-2.96E+39$	$-1.64E+39$
	SD	$7.28E+44$	$1.06E+26$	$3.52E+30$	$6.52E+40$	$5.78E+36$	$2.14E+40$	$1.49E+40$
Ackley	AV	$3.73E-15$	$8.13E-15$	$1.57E-14$	$7.49E-14$	$1.76E-05$	$3.30E-05$	0.0006221
	SD	$1.42E-15$	$9.94E-16$	$2.30E-15$	$5.11E-15$	$3.09E-05$	$9.57E-06$	0.0001513

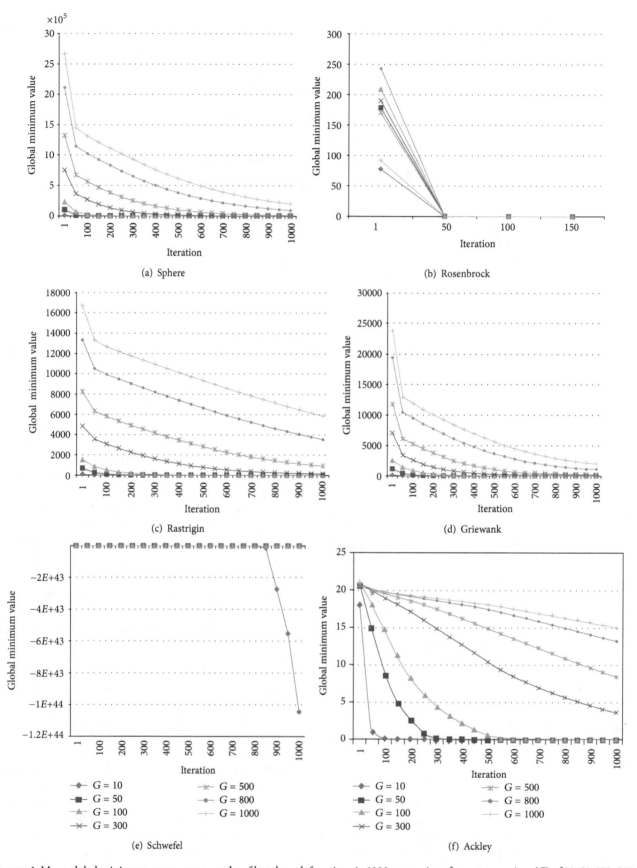

FIGURE 1: Mean global minimum convergence graphs of benchmark functions in 1000 generations for genotype sizes (G) of 10, 50, 100, 300, 500, 800 and 1000.

TABLE 4: Success rates of MBO when compared with those of the IMBO algorithm. + indicates that the algorithm is better while − indicates that it is worse than the other. If both algorithms show similar performance, they are both +.

Genotype size	10		50		100		300		500		800		1000	
Function	MBO	IMBO	MBO	IMBO	MBO	IMBO	MBO	IMBO	MBO	IMBO	MBO	IMBO	MBO	IMBO
Sphere	+	+	+	+	+	+	−	+	+	−	−	+	−	+
Rosenbrock	+	−	+	+	+	+	+	+	+	+	+	+	+	+
Rastrigin	+	+	+	+	+	−	−	+	−	+	−	+	−	+
Griewank	−	+	+	+	+	+	+	−	−	+	−	+	−	+
Schwefel	−	+	−	+	−	+	−	+	−	+	−	+	−	+
Ackley	−	+	−	+	−	+	−	+	+	−	−	+	+	−
Total	3	5	4	6	4	5	2	5	3	4	1	6	2	5

TABLE 5: CPU time results of the MBO algorithm for the genotype sizes of 10, 50, 100, 300, 500, 800, and 1000; number of runs = 1; iteration = 10000.

Genotype size	Sphere	Rosenbrock	Rastrigin	Griewank	Schwefel	Ackley
10	02:45:095	02:36:827	03:12.552	05:00.894	03:25.141	03:20.882
50	05:39:832	05:35.729	06:15.572	08:22.590	07:30.842	06:20.845
100	15:47:269	17:13.912	17:36.329	18:34.517	17:29.746	15:55:318
300	1:09:07:083	1:07:07.602	1:12:21.617	1:16:02.748	1:17:11.700	1:16:04.994
500	2:03:31:669	2:03:54.118	2:08:22.112	2:03:11.670	2:06:25.689	2:09:27.164
800	3:23:52:834	2:51:14.834	2:53:25.547	3:00:11.898	3:06:41.792	2:52:34.737
1000	4:31:56.752	3:35:18.224	3:40:03.753	3:45:45.894	3:54:20.884	3:38:12.446

TABLE 6: CPU time results of the IMBO algorithm for the genotype sizes of 10, 50, 100, 300, 500, 800, and 1000; number of runs = 1; iteration = 10000.

Genotype size	Sphere	Rosenbrock	Rastrigin	Griewank	Schwefel	Ackley
10	35.303	31.949	40.716	01:08.110	46.831	42.245
50	43.134	39.749	49.592	01:20.714	01:21.869	48.141
100	54.475	50.466	01:00.980	01:36.439	01:57.109	58.983
300	1:42.213	01:39.778	01:52.445	02:45.033	04:41.472	01:41.151
500	2:32.662	02:11.836	02:31.180	03:26.841	07:30.062	02:26.812
800	3:49.415	03:16.452	03:49.633	05:00.754	11:15.094	03:49.227
1000	4:48.789	4:02:082	04:37.822	06:05.650	14:15.259	04:42.845

genotypes sizes optimal minimum was reached. Rastrigin function 10, 50, Griewank function 50, 100 to the optimal solution was observed to have reached the optimal solution. The other functions and sizes of genotype were observed to have reached the values close to the optimal solution.

Comparative results of the best and mean solutions of the MBO and IMBO algorithms are presented in Table 4.

According to Table 4, it is seen that, when compared with the MBO algorithm and IMBO algorithm according to genotype, IMBO exhibited better performance than MBO in all genotypes sizes. When it was thought that total better or equal cases were represented with "+" mark, MBO algorithm, a total of 19 "+" available, and IMBO algorithm, a total of 36 pieces of the "+" were available. Accordingly, IMBO's MBO algorithm demonstrates a better performance.

CPU time results of the all genotype sizes for MBO are given in Table 5 and for IMBO are given in Table 6.

In Tables 5 and 6, it was seen that, when CPU time values were analyzed, depending upon the size in the same proportion as genotype problem, solving time took a long time. Again in these tables, when solution CPU time of MBO and IMBO algorithm was analyzed, IMBO algorithm solves problems with less CPU time than MBO algorithm.

For 10, 50, 100, and 1000 problem sizes of unconstrained numeric six benchmark functions, comparisons were made between test results of IMBO algorithm and the algorithms in literature, including DE, PSO, ABC [32], bee swarm optimization, (BSO) [33], bee and foraging algorithm (BFA) [34], teaching-learning-based optimization (TLBO) [35], bumble bees mating optimization (BBMO) [36] and honey bees mating optimization algorithm (HBMO) [36]. Table 7 presents the comparison between experimental test results obtained for 10-sized genotype (problem) on unconstrained test functions of IMBO algorithm and the results for the same problem size in literature including PSO, DE, ABC, BFA and BSO optimization algorithms; while the comparison of success of each algorithm and IMBO algorithm is given in Table 8. Table 9 shows the comparison between experimental

TABLE 7: The mean solutions obtained by the PSO, DE, ABC, BFA, BSO, and IMBO algorithms for 6 test functions over 30 independent runs and total success numbers of algorithms. Genotype size: 10; (—): not available value, SD: standard deviation, AV: global minimum average.

Problem		PSO	DE	ABC	IMBO	BFA	BSO
Sphere	ORT	$4.13E-17$	$4.41E-17$	$4.88E-17$	0	0.000031	$8.475E-123$
	SD	$7.71E-18$	$8.09E-18$	$5.21E-18$	0	0.00024	$3.953E-122$
Rosenbrock	ORT	0.425645397	$4.22E-17$	0.013107593	$2.25E-07$	7.2084513	$3.617E-7$
	SD	1.187984439	$1.09E-17$	0.008658828	$2.24E-06$	9.436551	$5.081E-5$
Rastrigin	ORT	7.362692992	0.099495906	$4.76E-17$	0	0.003821	$4.171E-64$
	SD	2.485404145	0.298487717	$4.40E-18$	0	0.006513	$7.834E-64$
Griewank	ORT	0.059270504	0.008127282	$5.10E-19$	0.000221881	3.209850	$3.823E-46$
	SD	0.03371245	0.009476456	$1.93E-19$	0.00126167	4.298031	$6.679E-46$
Schwefel	ORT	-2654.033431	-4166.141206	-4189.828873	$-1.21E+23$	—	—
	SD	246.5263242	47.37533385	$9.09E-13$	$7.289E+44$	—	—
Ackley	ORT	$4.67E-17$	$4.86E-17$	$1.71E-16$	$3.73E-15$	0.000085	$7.105E-19$
	SD	$8.06E-18$	$6.55E-18$	$3.57E-17$	$1.42E-15$	0.000237	$5.482E-18$

TABLE 8: Comparative results of IMBO with PSO, DE, ABC, BFA, and BSO algorithms over 30 independent runs for genotype size 50. + indicates that the algorithm is better while − indicates that it is worse than the other, (—): not available value. If both algorithms show similar performance, they are both +.

Problem	IMBO-PSO		IMBO-DE		IMBO-ABC		IMBO-BFA		IMBO-BSO	
	IMBO	PSO	IMBO	DE	IMBO	ABC	IMBO	BFA	IMBO	BSO
Sphere	+	−	+	−	+	−	+	−	+	−
Rosenbrock	+	−	−	+	+	−	+	−	+	−
Rastrigin	+	−	+	−	+	−	+	−	+	−
Griewank	+	−	+	−	−	+	+	−	−	+
Schwefel	−	+	−	+	−	+	—	—	—	—
Ackley	−	+	−	+	−	+	+	−	−	+
Total	4	2	3	3	3	3	5	0	3	2

TABLE 9: The mean solutions obtained by the TLBO, HBMO, BBMO, and IMBO algorithms for 6 test functions over 30 independent runs and total success numbers of algorithms. Genotype size: 50; (—): not available value, SD: standard deviation, AV: global minimum average.

Problem		IMBO	TLBO	HBMO	BBMO
Sphere	AV	0	0.00	0.67	0.00
	SD	0	0.00	—	—
Rosenbrock	AV	0	47.0162	46.07	24.37
	SD	0.142502861	$3.56E-01$	—	—
Rastrigin	AV	$4.54747E-15$	$2.03E-12$	4.03	$1.59E-08$
	SD	$3.18323E-14$	$5.46E-12$	—	—
Griewank	AV	0	0.00	$1.44E-02$	0.00
	SD	0	0.00	—	—
Schwefel	AV	$-6.17561E+29$	-20437.84	—	—
	SD	$3.52272E+30$	$1.48E+02$	—	—
Ackley	AV	$1.57E-14$	$3.55E-15$	—	—
	SD	$2.30E-15$	$8.32E-31$	—	—

test results obtained for 50-sized genotype (problem) on unconstrained test functions of IMBO algorithm and the results for the same problem size in literature including TLBO, HBMO and BBMO optimization algorithms, while the comparison of success of each algorithm and IMBO algorithm is given in Table 10. Table 11 shows the comparison between experimental test results for 100-sized genotype (problem) on unconstrained test functions of IMBO algorithm and the results for the same problem size in literature including PSO, DE, and ABC optimization algorithms, while the comparison of success of each algorithm and IMBO algorithm is given in Table 12. Table 13 shows the comparison between experimental test results obtained for 1000-sized genotype (problem) on unconstrained test functions of

TABLE 10: Comparative results of IMBO with TLBO, HBMO, and BBMO algorithms over 30 independent runs for genotype size 50. + indicates that the algorithm is better while − indicates that it is worse than the other, (—): not available value. If both algorithms show similar performance, they are both +.

Problem	IMBO-TLBO		IMBO-HBMO		IMBO-BBMO	
	IMBO	TLBO	IMBO	HBMO	IMBO	BBMO
Sphere	+	−	+	−	+	+
Rosenbrock	+	−	+	−	+	−
Rastrigin	+	−	+	−	+	−
Griewank	+	+	+	−	+	+
Schwefel	−	+	—	—	—	—
Ackley	−	+	—	—	—	—
Total	4	3	4	0	4	2

TABLE 11: The mean solutions obtained by the DE, PSO, ABC, and IMBO algorithms for 6 test functions over 30 independent runs and total success numbers of algorithms. Genotype size: 100; (—): not available value, SD: standard deviation, AV: global minimum average.

Problem		PSO	DE	ABC	IMBO
Sphere	AV	$5.14E-16$	$8.84E-17$	$1.08E-15$	0
	SD	$3.12E-16$	$4.29E-17$	$1.04E-16$	0
Rosenbrock	AV	113.143751	132.3488752	0.054865327	0
	SD	48.99432331	41.72265261	0.045566135	0.142502861
Rastrigin	AV	148.2486456	133.1138439	$1.08E-15$	$4.54747E-15$
	SD	17.76489083	106.6728854	$8.99E-17$	$3.18323E-14$
Griewank	AV	0.048643996	0.000739604	$4.92E-17$	0
	SD	0.063166266	0.002218812	$4.25E-18$	0
Schwefel	AV	−20100.36156	−31182.49983	−41898.28873	$-6.17561E+29$
	SD	1763.156655	2078.47339	$3.30E-10$	$3.52272E+30$
Ackley	AV	0.732022399	$2.14E-16$	$4.21E-15$	$1.57E-14$
	SD	0.755456829	$4.53E-17$	$3.09E-16$	$2.30E-15$

TABLE 12: Comparative results of IMBO with DE, PSO, and ABC algorithms over 30 independent runs for genotype size 100. + indicates that the algorithm is better while − indicates that it is worse than the other. If both algorithms show similar performance, they are both +.

Problem	IMBO-PSO		IMBO-DE		IMBO-ABC	
	IMBO	PSO	IMBO	DE	IMBO	ABC
Sphere	+	−	+	−	+	
Rosenbrock	+	−	+	−	+	
Rastrigin	+	−	+	−	−	+
Griewank	+	−	+	−	+	−
Schwefel	−	+	−	+	−	+
Ackley	+	−	+	−	−	+
Total	5	1	5	1	3	3

IMBO algorithm and the results for the same problem size in the literature including PSO, DE, and ABC optimization algorithms, while the comparison of success of each algorithm and IMBO algorithm is given in Table 14.

Tables 7, 11, and 13 demonstrate that, as the problem size increases in ABC, DE, and PSO, the solution becomes more distant and difficult to reach. However, the results obtained with IMBO showed that, despite the increasing problem size, optimum value could be obtained or converged very closely. There are big differences among the results obtained for 10, 100, and 1000 genotype sizes in DE and PSO; however, this difference is smaller in IMBO algorithm, which indicates that IMBO performs better even in large problem sizes. In Tables 7 and 8, it is seen that IMBO performs equally to DE and ABC and better than PSO, BFA and BSO. In Tables 9 and 10 showing the comparison of IMBO with LBO, HBMO, and BBMO for genotype (problem) size 50, it is seen that IMBO performs better than all the other algorithms. In Tables 11 and 12 showing the comparison of IMBO with DE, PSO and ABC algorithms on problem size 100, it is seen that IMBO performs equally to ABC and better than DE and PSE. In Tables 13 and 14 showing the comparison of IMBO with DE, PSO and ABC

TABLE 13: The mean solutions obtained by the DE, PSO, ABC, and IMBO algorithms for 6 test functions over 30 independent runs and total success numbers of algorithms. Genotype size: 1000; (—): not available value, SD: standard deviation, AV: global minimum average.

Problem		PSO	DE	ABC	IMBO
Sphere	AV	9723.034942	329214.6744	0.058275686	0.000122371
	SD	3920.944041	917847.3604	0.021093306	$3.09627E-05$
Rosenbrock	AV	1679629.019	14373397912	2603.968539	0
	SD	648462.4744	361340776.6	599.4022496	0
Rastrigin	AV	2722.799729	1674.782779	735.8480014	0.000238574
	SD	83.14754621	96.86409615	24.75231998	$9.13969E-05$
Griewank	AV	86.03568115	266.1639753	0.10290266	$3.2663E-05$
	SD	29.1502045	335.3504904	0.068217103	$6.73212E-06$
Schwefel	AV	−187704.1438	−252854.5198	−350890.8062	$-1.64729E+39$
	SD	11097.95553	17724.02042	2279.801625	$1.49786E+40$
Ackley	AV	8.741445965	17.47129372	3.200412604	0.000622099
	SD	0.784830594	3.815946124	0.133628837	0.000151332

TABLE 14: Comparative results of IMBO with DE, PSO, and ABC algorithms over 30 independent runs for genotype size 1000. + indicates that the algorithm is better while − indicates that it is worse than the other. If both algorithms show similar performance, they are both +.

Problem	IMBO-PSO		IMBO-DE		IMBO-ABC	
	IMBO	PSO	IMBO	DE	IMBO	ABC
Sphere	+	−	+	−	+	−
Rosenbrock	+	−	+	−	+	−
Rastrigin	+	−	+	−	+	−
Griewank	+	−	+	−	+	−
Schwefel	−	+	−	+	−	+
Ackley	+	−	+	−	+	−
Total	5	1	5	1	5	1

on problem size 1000, IMBO is seen to perform better than all the other algorithms.

5. Conclusion

In the proposed study, we developed a new IMBO by replacing annealing algorithm in the queen bee's mating flight with the Levy flight algorithm and using single inheritance and single neighborhood in the genotype improvement stage. We tested the MBO algorithm we improved on the most commonly known six unconstrained numeric benchmark functions. We compared the results obtained with the results of other metaheuristic optimization algorithms in the literature for the same test functions.

In order to observe the improvement of IMBO, the experimental test results of MBO and IMBO were compared for 10, 50, 100, 300, 500, 800, and 1000 problem sizes. Consequently, IMBO algorithm was concluded to perform better than MBO algorithm. Furthermore, according to CPU time of problem solving process, IMBO algorithm works in shorter CPU times. The test results obtained with IMBO were compared with the results of DE, ABC, PSO, BSO, BFA; TLBO, BBMO and HBMO in the literature.

Accordingly, IMBO is observed to perform equally to or a little better than other algorithms in comparison with small genotype size, while IMBO performs much better than other algorithms with large genotype size. A total of 14 comparisons were made between experimental results of IMBO and other optimization algorithms in literature, and it showed better performances in 11 comparisons, and equal performances in 3 comparisons.

In future studies, different improvements can be made on the MBO algorithm and tests can be made on different test functions. Also, comparisons can be made with other metaheuristic optimization algorithms not used in the present study.

References

[1] X.-S. Yang, "Levy flight," in *Nature-Inspired Metaheuristic Algorithms*, pp. 14–17, Luniver Press, 2nd edition, 2010.

[2] D. Bunnag and M. Sun, "Genetic algorithm for constrained global optimization in continuous variables," *Applied Mathematics and Computation*, vol. 171, no. 1, pp. 604–636, 2005.

[3] H. E. Romeijn and R. L. Smith, "Simulated annealing for constrained global optimization," *Journal of Global Optimization*, vol. 5, no. 2, pp. 101–126, 1994.

[4] J. Kennedy and R. Eberhart, "Particle swarm optimization," in *Proceedings of the IEEE International Conference on Neural Networks*, pp. 1942–1948, December 1995.

[5] J. Holland, *Adaptation in Natural and Artificial Systems*, University of Michigan Press, 1975.

[6] R. Storn and K. Price, "Differential evolution—a simple and efficient heuristic for global optimization over continuous spaces," *Journal of Global Optimization*, vol. 11, no. 4, pp. 341–359, 1997.

[7] O. B. Haddad, A. Afshar, and M. A. Mariño, "Honey-bees mating optimization (HBMO) algorithm: a new heuristic approach for water resources optimization," *Water Resources Management*, vol. 20, no. 5, pp. 661–680, 2006.

[8] H. A. Abbass, "MBO: Marriage in honey bees optimization a haplometrosis polygynous swarming approach," in *Proceedings of the Congress on Evolutionary Computation (CEC '01)*, pp. 207–214, May 2001.

[9] T. Thomas, *Evolutionary Algorithms in Theory and Practice: Evolution Strategies, Evolutionary Programming, Genetic Algorithms*, Oxford University Press, New York, NY, USA, 1996.

[10] C. Coello Coello and G. B. Lamont, *Evolutionary Algorithms for Solving Multi-Objective Problems*, Genetic Algorithms and Evolutionary Computation, Kluwer Academic Publishers, Boston, Mass, USA, 2nd edition, 2007.

[11] D. Karaboga and B. Basturk, "On the performance of artificial bee colony (ABC) algorithm," *Applied Soft Computing Journal*, vol. 8, no. 1, pp. 687–697, 2008.

[12] J. G. Digalakis and K. G. Margaritis, "On benchmarking functions for genetic algorithms," *International Journal of Computer Mathematics*, vol. 77, no. 4, pp. 481–506, 2001.

[13] M. M. Hassan, F. Karray, M. S. Kamel, and A. Ahmadi, "An integral approach for Geno-Simulated Annealing," in *Proceedings of the 10th International Conference on Hybrid Intelligent Systems (HIS '10)*, pp. 165–170, August 2010.

[14] A. Chatterjee and P. Siarry, "Nonlinear inertia weight variation for dynamic adaptation in particle swarm optimization," *Computers and Operations Research*, vol. 33, no. 3, pp. 859–871, 2006.

[15] R. S. Rahnamayan, H. R. Tizhoosh, and M. M. A. Salama, "Opposition-based differential evolution," *IEEE Transactions on Evolutionary Computation*, vol. 12, no. 1, pp. 64–79, 2008.

[16] H. A. Abbass and J. Teo, "A true annealing approach to the marriage in honey-bees optimization algorithm," *International Journal of Computational Intelligence and Aplications*, vol. 3, pp. 199–208, 2003.

[17] H. S. Chang, "Converging marriage in honey-bees optimization and application to stochastic dynamic programming," *Journal of Global Optimization*, vol. 35, no. 3, pp. 423–441, 2006.

[18] A. Afshar, O. Bozorg Haddad, M. A. Mariño, and B. J. Adams, "Honey-bee mating optimization (HBMO) algorithm for optimal reservoir operation," *Journal of the Franklin Institute*, vol. 344, no. 5, pp. 452–462, 2007.

[19] Y. Marinakis, M. Marinaki, and G. Dounias, "Honey bees mating optimization algorithm for the Euclidean traveling salesman problem," *Information Sciences*, vol. 181, no. 20, pp. 4684–4698, 2011.

[20] C.-Y. Chiu and T. Kuo, "Applying honey-bee mating optimization and particle swarm optimization for clustering problems," *Journal of the Chinese Institute of Industrial Engineers*, vol. 26, no. 5, pp. 426–431, 2009.

[21] D. Karaboga and B. Basturk, "A powerful and efficient algorithm for numerical function optimization: artificial bee colony (ABC) algorithm," *Journal of Global Optimization*, vol. 39, no. 3, pp. 459–471, 2007.

[22] R. F. A. Moritzl and C. Brandesl, "Behavior genetics of honeybees (Apis mellifera L.)," in *Neurobiology and Behavior of Honeybees*, pp. 21–35, Springer, Berlin, Germany, 1987.

[23] R. F. A. Moritz and E. E. Southwick, *Bees as Super-Organisms*, Springer, Berlin, Germany, 1992.

[24] B. Bilgin, E. Özcan, and E. E. Korkmaz, "An experimental study on hyper-heuristics and exam scheduling," in *Practice and Theory of Automated Timetabling VI*, vol. 3867 of *Lecture Notes in Computer Science*, pp. 394–412, Springer, 2007.

[25] A. Alcayde, R. Baños, C. Gil, F. G. Montoya, J. Moreno-Garcia, and J. Gómez, "Annealing-tabu PAES: a multi-objective hybrid meta-heuristic," *Optimization*, vol. 60, no. 12, pp. 1473–1491, 2011.

[26] X.-S. Yang and S. Deb, "Multiobjective cuckoo search for design optimization," *Computers and Operations Research*, vol. 40, no. 6, pp. 1616–1624, 2013.

[27] I. Pavlyukevich, "Lévy flights, non-local search and simulated annealing," *Journal of Computational Physics*, vol. 226, no. 2, pp. 1830–1844, 2007.

[28] G. M. Viswanathan, F. Bartumeus, and S. V. Buldyrev, "Levy Flight random searches in biological phenomena," *Physica A*, vol. 314, pp. 208–213, 2002.

[29] A. M. Reynolds, "Cooperative random Lévy flight searches and the flight patterns of honeybees," *Physics Letters A*, vol. 354, no. 5-6, pp. 384–388, 2006.

[30] T. T. Tran, T. T. Nguyen, and H. L. Nguyen, "Global optimization using levy flight," in *Proceedings of the 3rd National Symposium on Research, Development and Application of Information and Communication Technology (ICT.rda '06)*, Hanoi, Vietnam, September 2004.

[31] S. He, "Training artificial neural networks using lévy group search optimizer," *Journal of Multiple-Valued Logic and Soft Computing*, vol. 16, no. 6, pp. 527–545, 2010.

[32] B. Akay, *Nimerik Optimizasyon Problemlerinde Yapay Arı Kolonisi (Artifical Bee Colony, ABC) Algoritmasının Performans Analizi*, Kayseri Üniversitesi, Fen Bilimleri Enstitüsü, Kayseri, Turkey, 2009.

[33] R. Akbari, A. Mohammadi, and K. Ziarati, "A novel bee swarm optimization algorithm for numerical function optimization," *Communications in Nonlinear Science and Numerical Simulation*, vol. 15, no. 10, pp. 3142–3155, 2010.

[34] K. Sundareswaran and V. T. Sreedevi, "Development of novel optimization procedure based on honey bee foraging behavior," in *Proceedings of the IEEE International Conference on Systems, Man and Cybernetics (SMC '08)*, pp. 1220–1225, October 2008.

[35] R. Venkata Rao and V. Patel, "An improved teaching-learning-based optimization algorithm for solving unconstrained optimization problems," *Scientia Iranica*. In press.

[36] Y. Marinakis, M. Marinaki, and N. Matsatsinis, "A bumble bees mating optimization algorithm for global unconstrained optimization problems," *Studies in Computational Intelligence*, vol. 284, pp. 305–318, 2010.

9

PRESEE: An MDL/MML Algorithm to Time-Series Stream Segmenting

Kaikuo Xu,[1] Yexi Jiang,[2] Mingjie Tang,[3] Changan Yuan,[4] and Changjie Tang[5]

[1] College of Computer Science & Technology, Chengdu University of Information Technology, Chengdu 610225, China
[2] School of Computing and Information Sciences, Florida International University, Miami, IN 33199, USA
[3] Department of Computer Science, Purdue University, West Lafayette, FL 47996, USA
[4] Guangxi Teachers Education University, Nanning 530001, China
[5] School of Computer Science, Sichuan University, Chengdu 610065, China

Correspondence should be addressed to Changan Yuan; yca@gxtc.edu.cn

Academic Editors: R. Haber, S.-S. Liaw, J. Ma, and R. Valencia-Garcia

Time-series stream is one of the most common data types in data mining field. It is prevalent in fields such as stock market, ecology, and medical care. Segmentation is a key step to accelerate the processing speed of time-series stream mining. Previous algorithms for segmenting mainly focused on the issue of ameliorating precision instead of paying much attention to the efficiency. Moreover, the performance of these algorithms depends heavily on parameters, which are hard for the users to set. In this paper, we propose PRESEE (parameter-free, real-time, and scalable time-series stream segmenting algorithm), which greatly improves the efficiency of time-series stream segmenting. PRESEE is based on both MDL (minimum description length) and MML (minimum message length) methods, which could segment the data automatically. To evaluate the performance of PRESEE, we conduct several experiments on time-series streams of different types and compare it with the state-of-art algorithm. The empirical results show that PRESEE is very efficient for real-time stream datasets by improving segmenting speed nearly ten times. The novelty of this algorithm is further demonstrated by the application of PRESEE in segmenting real-time stream datasets from ChinaFLUX sensor networks data stream.

1. Introduction

Time series stream is everywhere in our daily life. It is widely used in fields such as ecology, medical care, and environment. These applications make time series stream type be possibly the most frequently encountered type for data mining problems [1]. Hence, in recent years, a large number of works focus on time series stream mining.

In order to process massive data efficiently, the method of time series stream segmenting is employed. The primary purpose of time series segmenting is dimensionality reduction. To achieve the goal of accelerating later mining tasks, time-series stream segmenting decomposes the time series stream into smaller number of segments. After segmenting, each segment can be described by a simple model like linear segment and monotonic segment [2]. An example of time-series segmenting can be seen in Figure 1.

There are several time series stream fitting models proposed, including symbolic mappings [3], adaptive multivariate spline [4], hybrid adaptive [5], wavelets [6], Fourier transforms [7], and piecewise linear representation [8, 9]. However, neither of them could handle different types of time series streams or is parameter free.

For real-time series application, the algorithm should be able to handle continuously real-time stream, which means that the stream could only be scanned once. A lot of real applications such as sensor network data [10], stock market trading data [11], or intensive-care unit (ICU) data [12] are in this form since the data are generated very fast and the processing time is limited. So, for time series stream segmentation, the issues of scalability, numerical stability, and efficiency cannot be avoided.

In this paper, we propose PRESEE to segment time series stream based on MDL/MML method [13, 14]. MDL/MML is

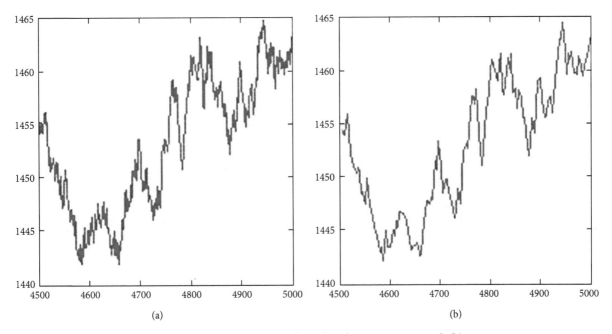

FIGURE 1: Time series original data (a) and its segmenting result (b).

an information expressing method in the field of information theory. By capturing the characteristics of information distribution in data, it can reduce the size of data while retaining most of the critical information. PRESEE the following characteristics has

(1) High scalability. It can process time series stream in linear time. PRESEE adopts slide window to process data with the size of gigabytes or even larger scale.

(2) Parameter free. Parameter settings are not essential in PRESEE for an entry-level user. This may avoid the trouble of misleading the algorithm by setting any improper parameters. Of course, if the end users are the domain experts and have confidence to set proper parameters, they can set some optional parameters to accelerate the segmenting speed.

(3) Adaptive. PRESEE can segment the time series data according to the characteristic of data. Since the segmenting strategy is based on MDL/MML, it can segment time series automatically. Violating place requires more characteristic points while elsewhere requires less.

(4) Pipeline. PRESEE can output the earlier data while processing the newly arrived data. Thus, the later time series stream mining algorithm and PRESEE can run simultaneously.

The rest of this paper is organized as follows. The related work is described in Section 2. Some necessary concepts are introduced in Section 3. A time series stream segmenting algorithm named PRESEE is presented in Section 4. The result of experiments is evaluated in Section 5. Finally, the paper is concluded and future work is discussed in Section 6.

2. Related Work

2.1. Time Series Stream Mining. Time series stream mining is possibly the most frequent mining task in recent data mining community. In particularly, in the last several years, a large number of papers are related to this area [15–17]. Time series stream mining derives from traditional time-series mining [1–4, 11, 18]. As a further requirement of deep understanding of the time series, it turns into high-dimensional data mining problem.

2.1.1. Segmenting. Segmenting is one of the major tasks in time-series stream mining. In order to process time-series data efficiently and effectively, segmenting is a key step for other time-series mining tasks. A lot of algorithms focus on finding good global segmenting of the time-series data.

There are mainly three characteristics of these algorithms. Firstly, these methods are mainly based on dynamic programming [19, 20], top-down [21], and bottom-up [22] strategies. Secondly, they require domain expert knowledge to set the parameters, either the parameter to measure the error [2, 22] or parameter k ($k \ll n$) to control the number of segments [19, 21]. Thirdly, these algorithms can at most handle millions of data, and they can hardly to handle stream data (gigabytes at least) due to the limitation of the algorithms.

Segmenting with slide window can handle large-scale data. This method is attractive because it can be easily implemented as an online algorithm. Some existing slide-window-based algorithms work well, but their performances are parameter dependent. Since different time-series data types such as electrocardiogram (ECG), water level, and stock market own quite different characteristics, it is hard to find a general set of parameters for all these data types.

2.1.2. MDL/MML. The theory of minimum message length (MML) and minimum description length (MDL) first appears in the computation complexity community [23, 24] then in the categorization community [25]. Its application in data mining community is the work of climate data segmentation [26], trajectory clustering [27], and social network mining [28]. So far, to the best of our knowledge, our work segmenting time-series stream with MDL/MML is the work with the most features.

3. Preliminary

This section reviews the concepts for time-series data mining. Section 3.1 introduces terminology about the time series. Section 3.2 presents the distance function used in this paper. Section 3.3 is the problem statement.

3.1. Terminology. We first begin with the definition of the time-series data type.

Definition 1. Time-series: let R_d denote a set of the observed values for given variables in the research domain. Let $s_i \in R_d$ be an element observed at time i. Time-series $S = \langle s_1 s_2 s_3 \cdots s_n \rangle$ is an ordered sequence of n such elements. From the stream view, the length of S is infinite.

Slide window may be a general and effective way to handle massive data that cannot be processed in whole. Thus we employ slide window idea to do the segmenting task.

Definition 2. Slide window: let B be a user-defined buffer to hold elements and w be the size of elements that B can hold. The slide window $W = \langle w_1 w_2 \cdots w_w \rangle$ is the buffer to hold a continuous subsequence of S at any time. All the data in slide window can be processed by the algorithm in one time.

3.2. Distance Function for Time Series Segments. For the ease of segmenting, some data transformation work should be done. Almost all kinds of time series data can be discretized and transformed in the form of lines. For example, the original time-series data $S = \langle s_1 s_2 \cdots s_n \rangle$ can be discretized into $n-1$ lines: $s_1 s_2, s_2 s_3, \ldots, s_{n-1} s_n$. The goal of segmenting is to generate m $(m < n)$ lines that can represent most of the characteristics of original lines. There should be a distance function to measure the distance between the original time-series line L_o and the candidate segment L_s. In order to better measure the distance between original time-series stream and its segmenting result, firstly, the distance function should be simple so that the stream can be processed very fast. Additionally, the measurement should consider the shape of stream and its segmenting result. Finally, the focus of factor in measurement can vary according to different application. After delving into the character of time-series data, we find that the best way to measure the distance between time-series by considering the conciseness and preciseness is to use *Hausdorff metric*. *Hausdorff metric* has been previously used in the area of pattern recognition and trajectory mining [27, 29]. Previous works proved that it is precise in the scenario

of shape similarity measurement. In the scenario of time-series segmenting, we represent the *segmenting distance* by considering the perpendicular and angle space relationship based on *Hausdorff metric*.

Segmenting distance is a quantitative criterion to measure the quality of segmenting. Smaller distance represents better segment result for the original stream. The final form of distance between the original line and the segment it belongs to is defined in Definition 3.

Definition 3. Segmenting distance. Let L_o be the original line, L_s be the candidate segment, l_{p1} and l_{p2} be the distances from the start point and end point of L_o to L_s, respectively (Formula (1)), and $\theta (L_o, L_s)$ be the smaller intersection angle between two lines. Then the following can be considered.

(1) The perpendicular distance between two lines is defined as $d_p(L_o, L_s)$ in Formula (2). In Formula (1), (x_{ps}, y_{ps}) and (x_{pe}, y_{pe}) represent the start point and end point of each original time-series line, respectively; (x_s, y_s) and (x_e, y_e) represent the coordinates of the start point and end point of a candidate segment time-series line (one possible segment solution in the process of segmenting computation), respectively.

(2) The angle distance between two lines is defined as $d_a(L_o, L_s)$ in Formula (3).

(3) The segmenting distance between two lines is defined as $d(L_o, L_s)$ in Formula (4): the weighted sum of perpendicular distance and angle distance.

Consider

$$l_{p1(2)} = \frac{\left| k \times x_{ps(pe)} - y_{ps(pe)} + b \right|}{\sqrt{k^2 + 1}},$$
$$\left(k = \frac{y_s - y_e}{x_s - x_e}, b = y_s - k \times x_s \right), \tag{1}$$

$$d_p(L_o, L_s) = \frac{l_{p1}^2 + l_{p2}^2}{l_{p1} + l_{p2}}, \tag{2}$$

$$d_a(L_o, L_s) = L_o \times \sin(\theta(L_o, L_s)), \tag{3}$$

$$d(L_o, L_s) = w_p \cdot d_p + w_a \cdot d_a. \tag{4}$$

The sum of weight w_p and w_a should be 1, and they can both be set to 1/2 if there is no special requirement. Figure 2 and Example 4 show an example of how to compute the distance.

Example 4. As shown in Figure 2, there are 3 original lines L_{o1}(line $s_1 s_2$), L_{o2}(line $s_2 s_3$), and L_{o3}(line $s_3 s_4$) and one segment L_s(line $s_1 s_4$). Since it can be observed that the start point of L_{o1} and L_s is the same point, the distance $d(L_{o1}, L_s) = w_p \cdot l_{p2} + w_a \cdot (L_o \cdot \sin \theta_1)$. The distance between L_{o2} and L_s is $d(L_{o2}, L_s) = w_p \cdot (l_{p2}^2 + l_{p3}^2)/(l_{p2} + l_{p3}) + w_a \cdot (L_o \cdot \sin \theta_2)$, and between L_{o3} and L_s is $d(L_{o3}, L_s) = w_p \cdot l_{p3} + w_a \cdot (L_o \cdot \sin \theta_3)$.

3.3. Problem Statement. Given a time series S with length n (i.e., $S = \langle s_1 s_2 s_3 \cdots s_n \rangle$, n can be infinite), our algorithm

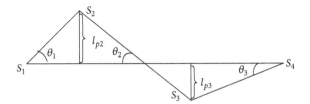

FIGURE 2: Distance between 3 original lines and one segment that they belong to.

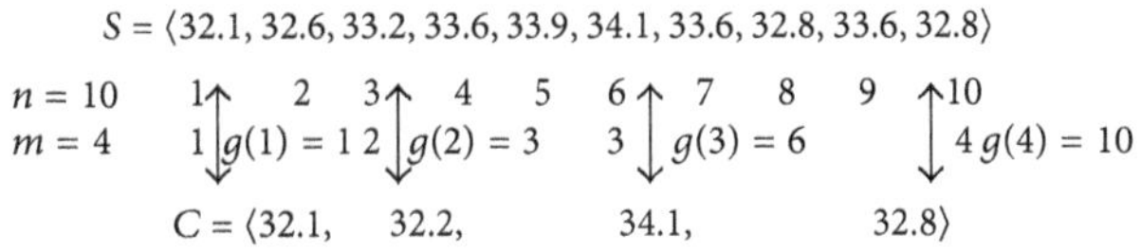

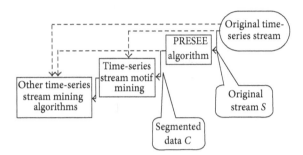

FIGURE 3: The comparison between original time-series S and the character points C.

generates a sequence of character points $C = \langle c_1, c_2, c_3 \ldots c_m \rangle$. For sequence C, each pair c_i to s_j has a projection relationship: $g(i) = j$. This means that each c_i located at i in C has a counterpart located at j in S. For each consecutive character point $c_x, c_y \in C$, there exist several points $(s_i, \ldots, s_j)$ in S such that $g(x) < i < j < g(y)$. Every pair of c_x, c_y represents a segment which is an approximation of lines represented by several pairs of consecutive points in the original time series stream S. Thus, these m character points partition the original stream into $m-1$ continuous segments. And for each $s_x \in S$, if s_x is just the start or end point of one segment, it belongs to two segments; otherwise, it only belongs to one segment. Figure 3 shows lines representing S compared with lines representing C.

The segmenting algorithm is implemented under a pipeline framework shown in Figure 4. Besides the segmenting algorithm, we had already implemented the time-series stream motif mining algorithm. This framework is designed specifically for handling time-series stream mining. It owns several advantages as follows.

(1) Data stream is only scanned once. When data flow out of the slide window, it would never turn back to slide window again.

(2) Mining tasks can be processed simultaneously. Earlier data that have been segmented before can be processed by following mining task while the later data is under processing by segmenting task.

4. PRESEE Algorithm

This section first introduces how to use segmenting strategy based on MDL/MML in our algorithm PRESEE, and then introduces this algorithm in detail.

4.1. Information-Theory-Based Segmenting Strategy. Our algorithm aims at finding the best segments for time-series. As for the problem of segmenting, there are two properties to measure the quality: *preciseness* and *conciseness*. *Preciseness* measures the distance between the lines represented by consecutive points of the character point c_i, c_j in set C and lines represented by consecutive points of original time series in stream S between the corresponding two character points c_i, c_j. Smaller distance indicates better *preciseness*. *Conciseness* measures how less the character points are used to depict the certain length of data points in original stream. Less character points represents better conciseness.

FIGURE 4: The pipeline for time-series mining. All data are processed as stream. At first the original data are flowed into PRESEE and then flowed into any other time-series stream mining algorithms.

It is easy to get the conclusion that, when every point in original stream is the character point, *preciseness* gets its maximum. However, such kind of segmenting is meaningless since it in fact just lets the stream go through the slide window and does not do any work to compress the stream. *Conciseness* reaches the maximum when there are only two character points for the stream, the start point and the end point.

The best *preciseness* and best *conciseness* cannot be satisfied at the same time because they are contradictory. Therefore, we need to do some work to find the optimum tradeoff between *preciseness* and *conciseness*, which generates the best segmenting L_{opt}.

In order to find the optimum tradeoff, we intend to solve this problem in information perspective by employing the MDL/MML principle in information theory area. We use MDL/MML in our algorithm because it is parameter free. MDL/MML can automatically find a proper estimate of original information. If no proper segmenting solution exists, the data S are deemed as random data. In our scenario, we simply keep all the information.

The code of MDL/MML is composed of two parts: $I = H : D$ [30, 31]. H specifies the hypothesis about the information (normally selected from a limited set of possible hypotheses), while D specifies the code for the information based on the hypothesis. The shortest code I in all the H and D combinations are the optimum solution for the piece of information. In our scenario, it are the optimum for stream segmenting.

The cost of code is represented by its length. In *Shannon's theory*, the length of coding an event E in optimum condition is given by $-\log_2(E)$. In time-series segmenting scenario, the computation of the formula is as follows:

$$L(H) = \sum_{i=1}^{w-1} \log_2 \left(len \left(s_{c_i} s_{c_{i+1}} \right) \right), \tag{5}$$

$$L(S \mid H)$$

$$= \sum_{i=1}^{w-1} \sum_{k=c_i}^{c_{i+1}-1} \left\{ \log_2 w_p d_p \left(s_{c_i} s_{c_{i+1}}, s_k s_{k+1} \right) \right. \tag{6}$$

$$\left. + \log_2 w_a d_a \left(s_{c_i} s_{c_{i+1}}, s_k s_{k+1} \right) \right\},$$

$$L_{\text{opt}} = \operatorname{argmin} \left\{ L(H) + L(S \mid H) \right\}. \tag{7}$$

In the first two formulas, w represents the size of data S, $c_x \in C$ represents the character points. The optimum segmenting is the minimum value of sum of $L(H)$ and $L(S \mid H)$. The following is a concrete computation example for Figure 3. Line $s_1 s_4$ is the optimum segmenting for point s_1 through s_4.

Consider

$$L(H) = \log_2 \left(len \left(s_1 s_4 \right) \right),$$

$$L(S \mid H)$$

$$= \left\{ \log_2 \frac{1}{2} d_p \left(s_1 s_2, s_1 s_4 \right) + \log_2 \frac{1}{2} d_a \left(s_1 s_2, s_1 s_4 \right) \right\}$$

$$+ \left\{ \log_2 \frac{1}{2} d_a \left(s_2 s_3, s_1 s_4 \right) + \log_2 \frac{1}{2} d_p \left(s_2 s_3, s_1 s_4 \right) \right\} \tag{8}$$

$$+ \left\{ \log_2 \frac{1}{2} d_a \left(s_3 s_4, s_1 s_4 \right) + \log_2 \frac{1}{2} d_p \left(s_3 s_4, s_1 s_4 \right) \right\}.$$

4.2. Algorithm Details. Finding global optima requires computing all partitions possibilities of the points, which is prohibitive for real applications. We present a greedy algorithm to find local optima.

Algorithm 1 shows the details of the segmenting process. At first, only the data flowed into slide window are processed. In lines 5 and 6, the costs of MDL_{seg} and $\text{MDL}_{\text{noseq}}$ are computed, respectively. $\text{MDL}_{\text{seq}}(s_i, s_j)$ denotes the MDL cost by considering s_i and s_j as the character points for points s_x $(i < x < j)$. It equals to $L(H) + L(D \mid H)$. $\text{MDL}_{\text{noseq}}(s_i, s_j)$ denotes the MDL cost by assuming that there are no character points between s_i and s_j. It equals to $L(H)$. In the greedy strategy, the local optimum solution is the longest segment that satisfies the inequality (9).

In the algorithm shown previously, the points in slide window are scanned sequentially only once. The candidate segmenting (segment with $s_{startIndex}$ and $s_{curIndex}$ as start point, and end point resp.) grows once per time to test whether it satisfies inequality (9).

There is a parameter *batchSize* for this algorithm. The default value is 1, and the user can set it as a larger integer. The algorithm will return *batchSize* + 1 character points per time. Thus, the algorithm can run faster.

Consider

$$\text{MDL}_{\text{seq}} \left(s_i, s_j \right) < \text{MDL}_{\text{noseq}} \left(s_i, s_j \right). \tag{9}$$

PRESEE algorithm calls Algorithm 1 every time when slide window is full. Algorithm 2 describes PRESEE algorithm in the form of pseudocode.

In line 2, the slide window is filled at the first time. Then the method *ReadIn()* is called in *while* loop. *ReadIn()* takes the response of filling slide window and checking whether there is new data. It returns *false* when no new data exists. In line 4, Algorithm 1 is called to provide the local optima segmenting result based on the data in slide window. It is possible that no proper segment exists. Thus the size of *tmpSet* is less than 2. In this scenario, we simply put all the data in slide window into *apprSet* and empty the slide window. Otherwise, add *at most* first *batchSize* + 1 points in *tmpSet* into *apprSet*. We use "at most" here because it is possible that all the points in slide window may be generated less than in *batchSize* segments.

From the pseudocode, we can see that the data are input and output simultaneously (line 4 and line 13), which guarantees that the earlier data can be processed by later mining algorithm. Additionally, it is obvious that the stream is only scanned once and processed once. Thus the time complexity of both algorithms is $O(n)$, where n is the length of time-series stream.

5. Empirical Comparison of the Segmenting Algorithms

In this section, we demonstrate the effectiveness and efficiency of the proposed algorithm through several sets of experiments on large collections of real and synthetic time-series datasets. For the effectiveness test, the precision of the proposed method is compared with nonstream segmenting algorithm. Then the speed and scalability of the algorithm are tested with a different scale of datasets ranging from 10 M to 10 G.

All the experiments are performed on a laptop computer with 2 GHz Intel Core 2 Duo CPU and 3G main memories. The C++ implementation of the algorithm and the related source code are all available at http://code.google.com/p/ots-sm/.

5.1. Benchmark Algorithm. The performance of the proposed algorithm is compared with well-known benchmark algorithms. A good candidate is the BU (bottom-up) algorithm [22]. It is used as a counterpart in precision algorithm. Since BU cannot handle stream-like datasets and the time complexity is uncertain for large datasets, we use slide-window-based bottom-up (SWBU for short) segmenting algorithm in the part of efficiency and scalability experiment instead.

5.2. Dataset. Real Datasets. We consider two sets of real datasets to evaluate our algorithm. The first set includes three classical datasets: IBM stock price dataset from 1.2.1961 to 1.6.2010 [32], "Dodgers," and "ICU" from UCI Machine Learning Repository [33] used by most of the papers in data mining and machine learning community. The second set of real-time stream data is collected from Chinese Terrestrial Ecosystem Flux Research Network (ChinaFLUX) [34], which is a long-term national network of micrometeorological flux measurement sites that measures the net exchange of carbon dioxide, water vapor, and energy. In this paper, we only choose part of the flux data from one wild filed survey site

Input: points in $slideWindow$ Seg = $\langle p_1, p_2, p_3 \cdots p_{len} \rangle$,
$\quad\quad$ $batchSize$
Output: character points set $C = \langle c_{i1}, c_{i2} \cdots \rangle$
(1) $\quad$ Put p_1 into C
(2) $\quad$ $curSize = 0$, $startIndex = 1$, $length = 1$;
(3) $\quad$ **While** $startIndex + length < len$ **do**
(4) $\quad\quad$ $curIndex = startIndex + length$;
(5) $\quad\quad$ $Cost_{seg} = \mathrm{MDL}_{seg}(S_{startIndex}, s_{curIndex})$; $Cost_{noseg} =$
$\quad\quad$ $\mathrm{MDL}_{noseg}(c_{startIndex}, c_{curIndex})$;
(6) $\quad\quad$ **If** $cost_{seg} > cost_{noseg}$ **then**
(7) $\quad\quad\quad$ Put $p_{curIndxe-1}$ into C;
(8) $\quad\quad\quad$ $++curSize$;
(9) $\quad\quad\quad$ **If** $curSize == batchSize$ **then**
$\quad\quad\quad$ // enough batch has been processed
(10) $\quad\quad\quad\quad$ **Return** C;
(11) $\quad\quad\quad$ **Else** $startIndex = curIndex - 1$; $length = 1$;
(12) $\quad\quad$ **Else** $length = length + 1$;
(13) $\quad$ **If** C has only one point **do**
(14) $\quad\quad$ **Return** NULL;
(15) $\quad$ **Else** Put$_{plen}$ into C;

ALGORITHM 1: Segment in slide window.

Input: windowSize, $S = \langle s_1, s_2 \cdots \rangle$, $batchSize$
Output: $C = \langle c_1, c_2 \cdots \rangle$
(1) $\quad$ $slideWindow = \{\}$, $apprSet = \{\}$
(2) $\quad$ Read data into $slideWindow$
(3) $\quad$ **While** $ReadIn()$ **do**
(4) $\quad\quad$ $tmpSet = \mathrm{MDLSlideWindow}(slideWindow,$
$\quad\quad$ $batchSize)$;
(5) $\quad\quad$ **If** $tmpSet.size() < 2$ **do**
$\quad\quad$ // no proper hypothesis is found,
$\quad\quad\quad$ data deemed as random noise
(6) $\quad\quad\quad$ Add all data in $slideWindow$ into $apprSet$
(7) $\quad\quad\quad$ Empty $slideWindow$
(8) $\quad\quad$ **Else**
(9) $\quad\quad\quad$ Add at most first $batchSize + 1$ points in
$\quad\quad\quad$ $tmpSet$ into $apprSet$
(10) $\quad\quad\quad$ Take out used points from $slideWindow$
(11) $\quad\quad$ Output apprSet

ALGORITHM 2: PRESEE.

located in Yucheng, Shandong, China. The data is stored from 2009-03-04 to 2009-11-12 with the number of 38850980.

Synthetic Datasets. The synthetic datasets are generated according to Formula (10) with parameters in Table 1. The data is in the format of index, value, where index represents the timestamp of the record. The monotonically increasing record serial number is also available. In our experiments, without loss of generalization, we simply use the latter one.

For synthetic data, the range of values is bounded within $[lb, ub]$. The current record value fluctuates (increases, decreases, or remains the same) according to previous record value.

Consider

$$\Delta = \mathrm{sign} \times (\mathrm{random}\,() \bmod (lb - \mathrm{previous\_value}))$$
$$\times \mathrm{sharpness}. \tag{10}$$

The *sign* is randomly selected as either + or −, and *sharpness* is a parameter to control the power of fluctuation. It is easy to observe that when the value would suffer more resistance when it goes far away from the mean $((ub - lb)/2)$.

TABLE 1: Parameters for synthetic datasets.

Number	Data size	Lower bound (lb)	Upper bound (ub)	Sharpness
1	10,000 (10 k)	0	3000	0.001
2	100,000 (100 k)	0	3000	0.001
3	1,000,000 (1 M)	0	3000	0.001
4	10,000,000 (10 M)	0	3000	0.001
5	10,000,000 (10 M)	0	3000	0.002
6	10,000,000 (10 M)	0	3000	0.0005
7	10,000,000 (10 M)	0	3000	0.0002
8	10,000,000 (10 M)	0	3000	0.0001
9	100,000,000 (100 M)	0	3000	0.00005
10	1,000,000,000 (1 G)	0	5000	0.00001
11	10,000,000,000 (10 G)	0	5000	0.00001

6. Results

Visualization of Segmenting Result. For the ease of observing the segmenting result, Figure 5 presents the visualization of three real datasets (IBM stock, ICU, and Dodger). The first row is the original datasets; the second row is the segmenting result generated by BU; and the last row is generated by PRESEE. It is obvious that the charts in the first row seem to be the most complex because they contain the most detailed information about the time-series. For the other two rows, the charts seem to be more concise because segmenting algorithm removes some of the unimportant information from original time-series. Nevertheless, the main trends in the charts are reserved. This means that both algorithms keep the characteristics of original time-series data.

Precision. We compare our algorithm with BU, which can process general types of time-series datasets and can find the global optimum segmenting solution. We evaluate the result of segmenting algorithm via the *error rate* measure in Formula (11). Let w be the number of segments and n be the number of points in segment i. The error rate is computed as follows:

$$\text{error\_rate} = \frac{1}{w}\sum_{i=1}^{i<w}\frac{1}{n}\sum_{o_j \in s_i} d\left(L_{o_j}, L_{s_i}\right). \quad (11)$$

Error rate for fifteen datasets is reported in Table 2. It is evident that, for generating approximately the same number of segments, the error rate of bottom-up and PRESEE stays in the same level. That means that PRESEE can generate segments based on partial data (data only in slide window) no worse than segments generated in global perspective.

Problem of Getting Proper Number of Segments. In Table 2, for the real datasets ChinaFLUX, BU fails to find a proper number of segments because this kind of data changes tremendously. This is the flaw of BU. One significant advantage of PRESEE over BU is that users do not need to set any threshold parameter. The parameter of BU is hard to set. A little deviation would generate a quite different number of segments. In order to find out the relationship between segment size and the parameter error threshold that BU

requires, we run each dataset 100 times to find a proper parameter that can generate the same number of segments as PRESEE. Figure 6 shows their relationship for BU. In the experiment, all three real datasets encounter a big drop of segments number when the error threshold increases. In particular, for Dodgers datasets, the number of segments drops from 6082 to 1958 when the value changes from 1.0 to 1.1, which is very significant. Further experiments show that, even we only increase the threshold with 0.001, the change is also tremendous. Such phenomenon indicates that we should be careful to the error threshold parameter of BU. Such puzzle can be well avoided by the user of PRESEE.

Efficiency and Scalability. We only test the relative speed of algorithms since the absolute speed (running time) is varied according to machines. The speed of synthetic-dataset-generated algorithm is used as a benchmark. It reflects the maximum processing speed that a certain running machine can reach.

Since the IBM stock, ICU, and Dodger datasets are too small and not suitable for horizontal comparison in efficiency and scalability test, we use real-time ChinaFLUX datasets and the synthetic datasets 1–4 and 9–11 in this experiment. At first, we compare the efficiency among data generator, SWBU, and PRESEE. The error rate threshold of SWBU set as 1.1 means that SWBU can generate comparatively the same number of segments with PRESEE. Figure 7 shows the efficiency of different algorithms in logarithmic plot for synthetic datasets 1–4 and 9–11. It is certain that data generator owns the best speed since it just generates data without any extra processing. In this figure, we can find that the curve of PRESEE is very near to the curve of data generator and these two are far from the curve of SWBU (near one order of magnitude). Figure 8 shows its efficiency on different datasets (datasets ChinaFLUX). Figure 8 indicates that the efficiency would not be affected by characters of datasets. Table 3 shows the relative speed of two segmenting algorithms' relative speed (with t_{seg} representing the time cost of segmenting algorithm and t_{gen} representing the time cost of data generator). PRESEE is just a little slower than data generator with the value 1.1311, while SWBU is nearly one order of magnitude slower. This is because PRESEE is an $O(n)$

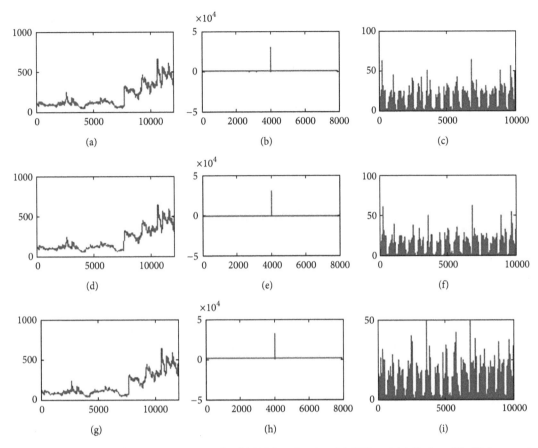

FIGURE 5: Time-series streams with their segmenting results: (a) IBM stock price, (b) ICU, and (c) Dodger. (d)–(f) Segmenting result with bottom-up. (g)–(i) Segmenting result with PRESEE.

TABLE 2: Precision of datasets.

Number	Data size	Error rate (BU)	Error rate (PRESEE)
1	10,000 (10 k)	2.00201	2.58561
2	100,000 (100 k)	1.75349	2.45916
3	1,000,000 (1 M)	1.67456	4.03172
4	10,000,000 (10 M)	1.65483	2.28419
5	10,000,000 (10 M)	1.66074	2.28695
6	10,000,000 (10 M)	1.65577	2.28768
7	10,000,000 (10 M)	1.65978	2.28862
8	10,000,000 (10 M)	1.66243	2.28124
9	100,000,000 (100 M)	1.67212	2.29100
10	100,000,000 (1 G)	N/A	2.27872
11	100,000,000 (10 G)	N/A	2.27984
12	IBM stock price from 1.2.1961 to 1.6.2010 (12087 records)	1.57696	2.38069
13	ICU (7931 records)	0.696307	0.893313
14	Dodger (10082 records)	1.34914	1.08395
15	ChinaFLUX (38850980 records)	N/A	1.76781

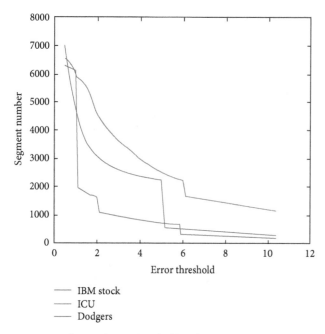

── IBM stock
── ICU
── Dodgers

FIGURE 6: Relative of error threshold and segments number for BU.

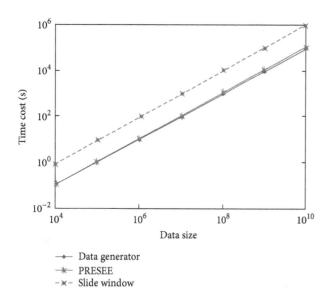

── Data generator
──✱── PRESEE
──✗── Slide window

FIGURE 7: Efficiency and scalability of different algorithms.

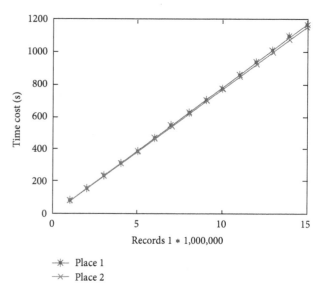

──✱── Place 1
──✗── Place 2

FIGURE 8: Efficiency of PRESEE for different datasets. Datasets are gathered from different places by ChinaFLUX.

TABLE 3: Relative speed of SWBU and PRESEE compared with data generated by the data generator.

Algorithm	Relative speed (t_{seg}/t_{gen})
SWBU	9.7114
PRESEE	1.1311

algorithm, but SWBU uses BU, an $O(n \log n)$ algorithm, as the base algorithm in slide window. With larger error rate threshold set, slower SWBU would run.

Features Affecting Algorithm Efficiency. In this section, we do some experiments to explore the characteristic of our algorithm. There are two optional parameters for PRESEE: window size and batch size. Window size controls the number of points to process at once; batch size controls how many result segments are output per time. As is mentioned before, there is no necessary parameter in PRESEE, so the user can directly use default values for the two parameters. In order to see how the two parameters affect the algorithm's efficiency,

we run synthetic dataset number 3 for 100 times, set window size from 100 to 1000 and batch size from 1 to 10. Figure 9 shows the triple relationship among the efficiency, window size, and batch size. This figure indicates that the time cost decreases while the batch size increases, but if the batch size is too large, the efficiency of algorithm decreases. The reason is that more segments output per time can accelerate the speed of algorithm and let the slide window move faster at first. Gradually, the efficiency begins to decrease with segments size increases. There are two reasons why this phenomenon happens: firstly, the points in slide window do not have such many segments, the efficiency cannot increase forever. Secondly, the algorithm would cost extra time to identify the character points of each segment.

Compress Rate. There is no parameter to control the precision of result since MDL/MML owns the self-adaptive property. We do an experiment to see the *compress rate* (*compress rate = size of result/size of original dataset*) on different kinds of datasets. We choose ChinaFLUX datasets, IBM stock price, ICU and Dodgers datasets, and synthetic datasets 4–8 to do the experiments. The four real datasets are quite different in their appearance and they are different in cyclical/noncyclical, sharp/smooth, degree of noise, dimensions, and length. The synthetic datasets 4–8 have the same parameter on data size and range, and they are generated in the same way. The only difference is the degree of *sharpness*.

From Table 4, we can conclude that, for the same kind of data and with different *sharpness*, the compress rate is steady.

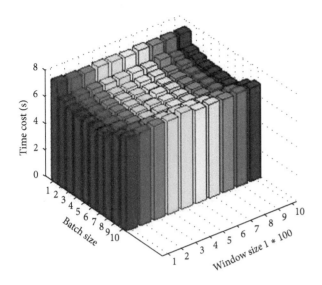

FIGURE 9: Relationship among efficiency, window size, and batch size.

TABLE 4: Compress rate of datasets.

Number	Data size	Compress rate
4	10,000,000 (10 M)	1 : 0.27548
5	10,000,000 (10 M)	1 : 0.27536
6	10,000,000 (10 M)	1 : 0.27537
7	10,000,000 (10 M)	1 : 0.27531
8	10,000,000 (10 M)	1 : 0.27536
12	IBM stock price	1 : 0.43779
13	ICU	1 : 0.48468
14	Dodgers	1 : 0.35540
15	ChinaFLUX	1 : 0.48194

7. Conclusion and Future Work

In this paper, we have proposed a new algorithm for time-series stream segmenting that is parameter free, scalable and self-adaptive. We also undertake several sets of time-series experiments on a variety of time series data types and compare them with the state-of-the art algorithms to evaluate our algorithm. The empirical results prove that PRESEE can generate a proper number of segments for time-series streams. Moreover, it can handle large dataset up to gigabytes. Finally, the parameters of PRESEE would only affect the efficiency but not the segmenting result.

In the future, we plan to design a series of time-series stream mining algorithms under the pipeline framework. Those algorithms should be able to well concatenate to the segmenting algorithm. Another direction is to design the algorithms that can do time-series mining tasks across multiple streams in real time.

Acknowledgments

This work was supported by NSF under Grant no. 31071700, the Natural Science Key Foundation of Guangxi under Grant no. 2011GXNSFD018025, and the Development Foundation of CUIT under Grant no. KYTZ201108. The authors would like to thank Dr. Yue Wang for discussing an early version of this paper.

References

[1] J. F. Roddick and M. Spiliopoulou, "A survey of temporal knowledge discovery paradigms and methods," *IEEE Transactions on Knowledge and Data Engineering*, vol. 14, no. 4, pp. 750–767, 2002.

[2] M. Brooks, Y. Yan, and D. Lemire, "Scale-based monotonicity analysis in qualitative modelling with flat segments," in *Proceedings of the 19th International Joint Conference on Artificial Intelligence (IJCAI '05)*, pp. 400–405, 2005.

[3] C. S. Perng, H. Wang, S. R. Zhang, and D. S. Parker, "Landmarks: a new model for similarity-based pattern querying in time series databases," in *Proceedings of the 16th IEEE International Conference on Data Engineering (ICDE '00)*, pp. 33–42, March 2000.

[4] J. Friedman, "Multivariate adaptive regression splines," *Annals of Statistics*, vol. 19, pp. 1–141, 1991.

[5] Z. Luo and G. Wahba, "Hybrid adaptive splines," *Journal of the American Statistical Association*, vol. 92, no. 437, pp. 107–116, 1997.

[6] D. B. Percival and A. T. Walden, *Wavelet Methods for Time Series Analysis*, Cambridge University Press, New York, NY, USA, 2000.

[7] R. A. C. Faloutsos and A. Swami, "Efficient similarity search in sequence databases," in *Proceedings of the 4th Conference on Foundations of Data Organization and Algorithms*, pp. 69–84, 1993.

[8] V. Lavrenko, M. Schmill, D. Lawrie, P. Ogilvie, D. Jensen, and J. Allan, "Mining of concurrent text and time series," in *Proceedings of the 6th International Conference on Knowledge Discovery and Data Mining*, pp. 37–44, 2000.

[9] X. Ge and P. Smyth, "Segmental semi-Markov models for endpoint detection in plasma etching," *IEEE Transactions on Semiconductor Engineering*. In press.

[10] K. Teymourian, M. Rohde, and A. Paschke, "Knowledge-based processing of complex stock market events," in *Proceedings of the 15th International Conference on Extending Database Technology (EDBT '12)*, pp. 594–597, 2012.

[11] L. A. Tang, X. Yu, S. Kim, J. Han, C. C. Hung, and W. C. Peng, "Tru-alarm: trustworthiness analysis of sensor networks in cyber-physical systems," in *Proceedings of the 10th IEEE International Conference on Data Mining (ICDM '10)*, pp. 1079–1084, Sydney, Australia, December 2010.

[12] ICU USER GUIDE, 2012, http://userguide.icu-project.org/icu-data.

[13] J. David and C. Mackay, *Information Theory, Inference & Learning Algorithms*, Cambridge University Press, New York, NY, USA, 2003.

[14] P. Grünwal, *The Minimum Description Length Principle*, MIT Press, Boston, Mass, USA, 2007.

[15] X. Lian and L. Chen, "Efficient similarity search over future stream time series," *IEEE Transactions on Knowledge and Data Engineering*, vol. 20, no. 1, pp. 40–54, 2008.

[16] M. Kontaki, A. N. Papadopoulos, and Y. Manolopoulos, "Continuous trend-based classification of streaming time series," in

Advances in Databases and Information Systems, vol. 3631 of *Lecture Notes in Computer Science*, pp. 294–308, 2005.

[17] X. S. Wang, L. Gao, and M. Wang, "Condition evaluation for speculative systems: a streaming time series case," in *Proceedings of the 2nd Workshop on Spatio-Temporal Database Management (STDBM '04)*, pp. 65–72, 2004.

[18] P. P. Rodrigues, J. Gama, and J. P. Pedroso, "ODAC: hierarchical clustering of time series data streams," in *Proceedings of the 6th SIAM International Conference on Data Mining*, pp. 499–503, Bethesda, Md, USA, April 2006.

[19] E. Bingham, A. Gionis, N. Haiminen, H. Hiisilä, H. Mannila, and E. Terzi, "Segmentation and dimensionality reduction," in *Proceedings of the 6th SIAM International Conference on Data Mining*, pp. 372–383, April 2006.

[20] E. Terzi and P. Tsaparas, "Efficient algorithms for sequence segmentation," in *Proceedings of the 6th SIAM International Conference on Data Mining*, pp. 316–327, April 2006.

[21] D. Lemire, "A better alternative to piecewise linear time series segmentation," in *Proceedings of the 7th SIAM International Conference on Data Mining*, pp. 545–550, April 2007.

[22] J. Hunter and N. Mcintosh, "Knowledge-based event detection in complex time series data," in *Proceedings of the Joint European Conference on Artificial Intelligence in Medicine and Medical Decision Making (AIMDM '99)*, pp. 271–280, 1999.

[23] A. R. Barron and T. M. Cover, "Minimum complexity density estimation," *IEEE Transactions on Information Theory*, vol. 37, no. 4, pp. 1034–1054, 1991.

[24] J. Rissanen, "Modeling by shortest data description," *Automatica*, vol. 14, no. 5, pp. 465–471, 1978.

[25] C. S. Wallace and D. M. Boulton, "An information measure for classification," *Computer Journal*, vol. 11, no. 2, pp. 185–194, 1968.

[26] Q. Q. Lu, "An MDL approach to the climate segmentation problem," *Annals of Applied Statistics*, vol. 4, no. 1, pp. 299–319, 2010.

[27] J. G. Lee, J. Han, and K. Z. Whang, "Trajectory clustering: a partition-and-group framework," in *Proceedings of the ACM SIGMOD International Conference on Management of Data (SIGMOD '07)*, pp. 593–604, June 2007.

[28] K. Xu, C. Tang, C. Li, Y. Jiang, and R. Tang, "An MDL approach to efficiently discover communities in bipartite network," in *Database Systems for Advanced Applications*, vol. 5981 of *Lecture Notes in Computer Science*, pp. 595–611, 2010.

[29] C. S. Wallace and D. L. Dowe, "Minimum message length and Kolmogorov complexity," *Computer Journal*, vol. 42, no. 4, pp. 281–283, 1999.

[30] P. Grunwald, I. J. Myung, and M. Pitt, *Advances in Minimum Description Length: Theory and Applications*, MIT Press, Boston, Mass, USA, 2005.

[31] IBM Stock Price, http://finance.yahoo.com.

[32] A. Asuncion and D. J. Newman, *UCI Machine Learning Repository*, Irvine, University of California, School of Information and Computer Science, 2007, http://archive.ics.uci.edu/ml/datasets.

[33] G. R. Yu, X. F. Wen, X. M. Sun, B. D. Tanner, X. Lee, and J. Y. Chen, "Overview of ChinaFLUX and evaluation of its eddy covariance measurement," *Agricultural and Forest Meteorology*, vol. 137, no. 3-4, pp. 125–137, 2006.

[34] J. Cheng, Y. Zhou, B. Wang, X. Wang, and J. Li, "SROS: sensor-based real-time observing system for ecological research," in *Proceedings of the International Conference on Web Information Systems and Mining (WISM '09)*, pp. 396–400, Shanghai, China, November 2009.

10

A New Logistic Dynamic Particle Swarm Optimization Algorithm Based on Random Topology

Qingjian Ni[1,2] and Jianming Deng[1]

[1] *School of Computer Science and Engineering, Southeast University, Nanjing 211189, China*
[2] *Provincial Key Laboratory for Computer Information Processing Technology, Soochow University, Suzhou 215006, China*

Correspondence should be addressed to Qingjian Ni; niqingjian@gmail.com

Academic Editors: P. Agarwal, S. Balochian, and V. Bhatnagar

Population topology of particle swarm optimization (PSO) will directly affect the dissemination of optimal information during the evolutionary process and will have a significant impact on the performance of PSO. Classic static population topologies are usually used in PSO, such as fully connected topology, ring topology, star topology, and square topology. In this paper, the performance of PSO with the proposed random topologies is analyzed, and the relationship between population topology and the performance of PSO is also explored from the perspective of graph theory characteristics in population topologies. Further, in a relatively new PSO variant which named logistic dynamic particle optimization, an extensive simulation study is presented to discuss the effectiveness of the random topology and the design strategies of population topology. Finally, the experimental data are analyzed and discussed. And about the design and use of population topology on PSO, some useful conclusions are proposed which can provide a basis for further discussion and research.

1. Introduction

Particle swarm optimization (briefed as PSO) is a kind of bionic evolutionary algorithm which rooted in imitation of behavioral mechanisms in populations such as birds and fish stocks and has been widely used in engineering field as optimization method [1–3].

In the PSO algorithms, the particles evolve according to their own experience and the experience of the neighborhood particles. During the evolutionary process, particles identify their own neighborhood according to the population topology and then learn from each other and update the positions of the particles. Therefore, population topology determines the form of information sharing among particles and thus has a very important impact on the solving performance of PSO algorithms. Therefore, it is important to explore the population topologies of PSO algorithms. This will produce a deep understanding of the working mechanism of PSO algorithms and thus improve the solving performance.

In the PSO algorithms, the most common used static population topologies are the fully connected topology (Gbest model) and the ring topology (lbest model) which are also first proposed [4]. Since then, researchers have proposed different population topologies in succession. Kennedy carried out a preliminary analysis of four static population topologies [5]. Suganthan adjusted the neighborhood structure of particles through calculating distances between particles in the evolutionary process [6]. Mendes et al. detailly analyzed the relationship between the population topology and a class of PSO variant [7–9]. Clerc initially attempted to adopt the random topology [10]. However, these studies concerned population topologies paid more attention to the static classic population topology, and research of random population topologies is relatively small. As the population topology directly affect the exchange of information between the particles, it is necessary to design the suitable population topology according to the characteristics of different types of applications. Therefore, it is necessary to explore the population topologies in depth from a theoretical and experimental point of view.

In this paper, in a relatively new PSO variant which named logistic dynamic particle optimization, we analyze the linkages between population topologies and the performance of PSO algorithms from graph theory and experimental point of view. The rest of the paper is organized as follows. In Section 2, we describes the PSO variant which are used in the paper. Section 3 describes the classic population topologies and introduces the proposed random population topologies. In Section 4, we have presented the experimental analysis and comparative performance between the classic and the proposed random population topologies. Section 5 concludes the paper.

2. The PSO Variants

PSO is a population-based method which is similar to other evolutionary computation methods. The individual in the PSO population is called the particle, and particles generally have the speed and position in most PSO variants.

2.1. The Canonical PSO. Based on the earlier version of PSO, Clerc developed the PSO with the compression factor [11]. This PSO variants have been widely used in practical applications, and the velocity and position update of particles in this variant are as follows:

$$v_{id} = \chi * \left[v_{id} + c_1 * \mathrm{rand}\,() * \left(p_{id} - x_{id} \right) \right.$$
$$\left. + c_2 * \mathrm{Rand}\,() * \left(p_{gd} - x_{id} \right) \right], \tag{1}$$

$$\chi = \frac{2}{\left| 2 - \varphi - \sqrt{\varphi^2 - 4\varphi} \right|}, \tag{2}$$

$$x_{id} = x_{id} + v_{id}. \tag{3}$$

In (1), v_{id} is the dth dimensional component of particle *i*s velocity attribute, c_1 and c_2 are two positive acceleration factors, rand() and Rand() are random number generating functions between 0 and 1, x_{id} is the dth dimensional component of the particle *i*s position property, p_{id} is the dth dimensional component of the best position that particle i obtained, and p_{gd} is the dth dimensional component of the best position that the whole population obtained. In actual use, usually χ in (2) is set to 0.729, and φ is often set to 4.1.

The right part of the equation1 can be understood as particle's memory, cognitive and social cognition. Velocity of particles is precisely through this three-part interaction effects thereby, position of particles is updated.

2.2. The Dynamic Probabilistic Particle Swarm Optimization. In the previous PSO variants, particles usually have both velocity attribute and position attribute. Kennedy first proposed a new PSO variant without velocity attribute, which named Gaussian dynamic particle swarm optimization [12]. Ni and Deng carried out a further study on the PSO variants without velocity [13]. This type of algorithm variants can be called dynamic probabilistic particle swarm optimization (briefed as DPPSO). In the DPPSO algorithms, particles have

no velocity attributes, and the update of particles' positions is reorganized as follows:

$$X_i(t+1) = X_i(t) + \alpha * \left(X_i(t) - X_i(t-1) \right)$$
$$+ \beta * \mathrm{CT}_i(t) + \gamma * \mathrm{Gen}\,() * \mathrm{OT}_i(t), \tag{4}$$

$$\mathrm{CT}_{id}(t) = \sum_{k=1}^{K} \frac{P_{kd}}{K - X_{id}(t)}, \tag{5}$$

$$\mathrm{OT}_{id}(t) = \sum_{k=1}^{K} \frac{|P_{id} - P_{kd}|}{K}. \tag{6}$$

In (4), (5), and (6), t represents the current evolution generation of particle, i is the index number of particle, k is the index number of particle's neighborhood, K represents the number of particle's neighborhood particles, P_k is the optimum position of the particle's neighborhood that numbered k, and d is the number of the particles *is* dimension. $\mathrm{CT}_i(t)$ is an abbreviation of centralized tendency, which is a D-dimensional vector and is determined by the particle's current location and neighborhood particles' optimal positions. $\mathrm{OT}_i(t)$ is an abbreviation of outlier trend, which is also a D-dimensional vector and is determined by the particle's current location and neighborhood particles' optimal positions. In (4), α, β, and γ are generally preferable to positive constants. Gen() is a dynamic probabilistic evolutionary operator which is the random number generator function which satisfies a specific distribution, and this particular distribution may be provided by a Gaussian distribution or a logistic distribution and so forth.

In (4), the calculation of particle's position in new generation is decided jointly by the right four parts. The first part is the memory of particles on the self-position. The second part is the trend of the particles along the previous direction of movement of the "flying." The third part means the influence of neighborhood particles' experience to the new generation position, this part of the calculations needs neighborhood particles' experience, and this part determines the degree of influence of the neighborhood particles' experience. The part IV reflects the impact of differences in best position between particles on the next generation position.

The performance of DPPSO variants is different when using different dynamic probabilistic evolutionary operator Gen() [13]. DPPSO-Gaussian (briefed as GDPS) has faster convergence speed in the early evolution. DPPSO-Cauchy may get better solutions on certain issues, but the performance is unstable. DPPSO-Logistic (logistic dynamic particle swarm optimization, briefed as LDPSO) still shows good exploration ability in the later evolution. For DPPSO variants, the calculation of $\mathrm{CT}_i(t)$ and $\mathrm{OT}_i(t)$ will use the experience of each neighborhood particles which can also be seen from (5) and (6). The optimal information of neighborhood particles could be fully utilized, so the research of population topology in DPPSO variants is more important.

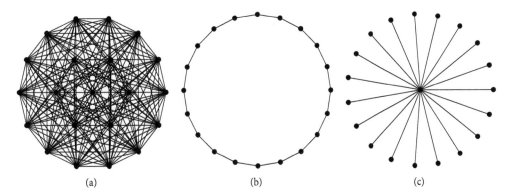

FIGURE 1: (a) Fully connected topology; (b) ring topology; (c) star topology.

3. Population Topologies

3.1. The Classic Population Topologies. Figure 1 shows the fully connected topology, ring topology, and star topology. Fully connected topology and ring topology are two commonly used topologies which are also called Gbest model and Lbest model. In the fully connected topology, particle's neighborhood contains all particles in the population. And in the evolutionary process, only the particle that obtains the optimal position is considered in the entire population. PSO algorithms with this topology converge very fast but easy to fall into local optimum.

For a ring topology, typically particle's neighborhood includes the particles on both sides of one or a few particles. In this topology, the exchange of information is relatively slow within the population, but once a particle searched for an optimal location, the information eventually will slowly spread to the entire population.

For a star topology, one particle is connected with all the other particles, and other particles only connect with the particle. In addition to a central particle, other particles are independent of each other, the dissemination of information must be passed through the central particle.

However, the information dissemination mechanism of the social groups is not static throughout the whole evolutionary process, and tends to have a certain degree of randomness and dynamic characteristics. Mendes studied random population topology and confirmed that population topology directly affects the execution performance of PSO algorithms [9].

3.2. Graph Theory Characteristics of Population Topology. The population topology of the PSO algorithm can be abstracted into a connected undirected graph, represented by the symbol $G(V, E)$, where V is the set of vertices, E is the set of edges, and the number of vertices is denoted by n. For any two points u and v in G, $d(u, v)$ denotes the distance from u to v, that is, the length of the shortest path between two points.

Definition 1 (average degree). The degree of the vertex v is the number of its adjacent vertices, denoted by k_v. Average degree k of undirected connected graph is calculated by

$$K = \sum_{v \in V} \frac{k_v}{n}. \tag{7}$$

Definition 2 (average clustering coefficient). The local clustering coefficient $c(v)$ of vertex v, equals to the number of edges which can be connected between vertices associated with vertex v, divided by the maximum number of edges between these vertices. The average clustering coefficient c of a graph is the arithmetic mean of the local clustering coefficient of all vertices, which can be calculated by

$$c = \sum_{v \in V} \frac{c(v)}{n}. \tag{8}$$

The average degree of population topology means the average number of particles' neighborhood particles; it represents the degree of socialization of population. A small number of neighborhood particles means that the particle is both difficult to obtain information from the population and difficult to influence other particles. On the contrary, a particle which have large number of neighborhood particles can get a lot of information available in the population, and such a particle has a greater influence in the population. In the common used population topologies, fully connected topology has the largest average degree which is equal to the population size minus 1. The ring topology has the minimum average degree; the average degree of a ring topology such as in Figure 1 is equal to 2. The local clustering coefficient is the ratio of the number of connections between the actual existence and the possible existence, and the average clustering coefficient represents the degree of aggregation of the vertices in a graph which is the average of the local clustering coefficient of all vertices. In this paper, we will analyze the role of the population topology based on the previous graph theory characteristics.

3.3. Random Population Topologies. Clerc initially attempted to proposed a method of random population topology [10]. The basic idea is to generate a random topology by selecting the neighborhood particles randomly for each particle. The concrete steps could be described as Algorithm 1.

In the resulting matrix L of Algorithm 1, $L(u, v) = 1$ means that the particles u and v are connected. By this

---

(1) For the population that the size is S, build a $S * S$ matrix, and let $L(i, i) = 1$;
(2) Select a K value, for each row i of the matrix L, generate a uniformly distributed random number
    m from $\{1, \ldots, m\}$ (m may be selected repeatedly), let $L(i, m) = 1$;
(3) For the matrix L, If $L(i, m) = 1$, then let $L(m, i) = 1$;

ALGORITHM 1: Clerc's generating method of random population topology.

---

(1) For the population that the size is S, build a $S * S$ matrix, and let $L(i, i) = 1$;
(2) Select a K value, for each row i of the matrix L, generate a uniformly distributed random number
    m ($m \neq i$) from $\{1, \ldots, m\}$ (m may be selected repeatedly), let $L(i, m) = L(m, i) = 1$;
(3) Use the Dijkstra algorithm to calculate the distance between the particles and stored in the $S * S$ matrix D;
(4) **While** *The graph corresponding to the generating random topology is not connected* **do**
(5)   Scan the matrix D;
(6)   IF two particles u and v are not connected;
(7)   Let $L(u, v) = 1$;

ALGORITHM 2: The proposed generating method of random population topology.

---

method, a random topology could be generated with an average degree slightly larger than K. In the random topology by this method, the distribution of degree is the sum of $S - 1$ independent Bernoulli random variables which is described in [10]

$$\text{prob}(Y = n) = C_{S-1}^{n-1} \left(\frac{K}{S}\right)^{n-1} \left(1 - \frac{K}{S}\right)^{s-n}. \quad (9)$$

In this paper, in order to ensure the connectivity of undirected graph which is corresponding to the generating random topology, we proposed a new generating method of random topology based on Clerc's method. The basic idea is: in selecting the neighborhood particles for each particle if the selection is itself, reselect in order to reduce the probability of particles isolated; after the random population is generated, use the Dijkstra algorithm to compute the distance between the particles if there exist the unconnected particles in the generated topology, then add an edge between these unconnected particles, and retest. The improved random population topology generating method is as Algorithm 2.

4. Experiment and Analysis

4.1. Experiment Setting. Two sets of experiments were conducted which used the canonical PSO (briefed as CPSO) and the DPPSO-Logistic, respectively, that are described in Section 2. For CPSO, set $c_1 = c_2 = 2.05$, $\chi = 0.7298$. For DPPSO-Logistic, set $\alpha = 0.729$, $\beta = 2.187$, and $\gamma = 0.5$.

The algorithms were used to solve five benchmark functions, which is defined in Table 1. These functions consist of Ackley, Schwefel, Schaffer's F6, Rastrigin, and Sphere. Table 2 shows the settings of these functions.

In the experiment, the population size is set to 20, in addition to the the Schaffer's F6 function of the dimension 2, the remaining functions are carried out in the case of 30-dimensional test, and the frequency of repeated experiments is 50.

The performance of the algorithms will be evaluated by the following aspects:

(i) in the case of a certain number of iterations, compare the accuracy (briefed as Perform.) of the optimal fitness value in each case. These values reflect the quality of the optimal solution obtained in the last;

(ii) in the case of a certain number of iterations, compare the success rates (briefed as Prop.) which means that the algorithms achieve the accuracy (accepted error) that is defined in Table 2. These data reflect the stability of the algorithms;

(iii) in the case of a certain number of iterations, compare the evolutionary trends of various algorithms, these figures reflect the evolution of the optimal solution in the evolutionary process.

4.2. Comparison between Random Topologies and Different Average Degrees. For the random topology, the first set of experiments used the canonical PSO algorithm to solve the five benchmark functions. By changing the K value, we generated random topologies with different average degrees for comparison and evaluation. Experimental results are shown in Table 3.

As can be seen from Table 3, with the increase in the value of K, the indicators of Perform. and Prop. have improved. For multimodal functions such as Schwefel, Schaffer's F6, Rastrigin, and Ackley function, with the increase in the value of K, when the K value is from 3 to 4 (i.e., the average degree of the random topology is between 5 and 7, substantially in about 6), the PSO algorithm could get better performance. And when the K value is larger, the performance is usually poor. For multimodal functions, when a particle has found a local optimal solution, if the interaction between particles is more, the dissemination of information will be very quickly, and the entire population is susceptible to rapid convergence to the local optimal solution. Therefore, too large average

TABLE 1: Definition of benchmark functions.

Benchmark function	Formula
Sphere	$F(\vec{x}) = \sum_{i=1}^{n} x_i^2$
Schaffer's F6	$F(\vec{x}) = 0.5 + \dfrac{\left(\sin^2 \sqrt{x^2 + y^2}\right) - 0.5}{\left(1.0 + 0.001\left(x^2 + y^2\right)\right)^2}$
Rastrigin	$F(\vec{x}) = 10 * n + \sum_{i=1}^{n}(x_i^2 - 10\cos(2\pi x_i))$
Schwefel	$F(\vec{x}) = 418.9829 * n + \sum_{i=1}^{n} x_i \sin(\sqrt{|x_i|})$
Ackley	$F(\vec{x}) = -20 \cdot \exp\left(-0.2\sqrt{\dfrac{1}{n} \cdot \sum_{i=1}^{n} x_i^2}\right) - \exp\left(\dfrac{1}{n} \cdot \sum_{i=1}^{n} \cos\left(2\pi x_i\right)\right) + 20 + \exp(1)$

TABLE 2: Settings of benchmark functions.

Benchmark function	Dimension	Optimal value	Optimal solution	Range	Accepted error
Sphere	30	0	$(0, 0, 0, \ldots, 0)$	$(-100, 100)$	0.01
Schaffer's F6	2	0	$(0, 0)$	$(-100, 100)$	0.00001
Rastrigin	30	0	$(0, 0, 0, \ldots, 0)$	$(-5.12, 5.12)$	100
Schwefel	30	0	$(0, 0, 0, \ldots, 0)$	$(-500, 500)$	6000
Ackley	30	0	$(0, 0, 0, \ldots, 0)$	$(-30, 30)$	5

degree of population topology is not conducive to find the global optimal solution for a multimodal function.

Taking these factors together, when the value of K is at about 4, the PSO algorithm has a more satisfactory performance for most benchmark functions. Accordingly, the following experiments will generate random topologies which the K value is 4, and compare these topologies with other classic static population topologies.

4.3. Comparison between Random Topologies and Classic Topologies. The second set of experiments used the DPPSO-Logistic algorithm to solve the five benchmark functions on the fully connected topology, ring topology, star topology, and random topology, wherein K value is set to 4 to generate random topologies. Comparison and evaluation are conducted by the evolutionary trends of algorithms with various population topologies. In the figures of evolutionary trends, different line types expressed different DPPSO-Logistic algorithms with various population topologies.

For Sphere function (Figure 2), the performance of ring topology and star topology is poor, and the fully connected topology and random topology show better search ability. For Schaffer's F6 function (Figure 2), random topology is significantly better than the three classic neighborhood topologies.

For Rastrigin function (Figure 3), random topology is superior to the three classic population topologies; in the early stages of evolution, the convergence speed of the random topology is almost the same as the fully connected topology; however, in the later stage of evolution, random topology shows a larger advantage, and the end result is better than the fully connected topology.

For Schwefel function (Figure 3), the performance of the ring topology is poor; the fully connected topology convergence fast in the early stage of evolution, but the end result is poor; the star topology has achieved good results; the convergence speed of random topology is second only to the fully connected topology in the early evolution stage, and the final result of random topology is better than the other classic topologies.

For Ackley function (Figure 4), the fully connected topology and the star topology show poor performance; the ring topology performs better; the random topology shows obvious advantage in both the convergence speed and the final result.

Overall, according to the convergence speed, random topology is relatively stable in the early stages of evolution, faster in the midstages of evolution, and shows a distinct advantage in the late stages of evolution. From the view of final result, the PSO algorithms using random topology demonstrate remarkable performance.

For unimodal function (such as Sphere function), because there is no problem of falling into a local optimum, the close ties between particles can make faster convergence and achieve better results. Therefore, the performance of the fully connected topology and random topology with a relatively high average degree is ideal. In the case of random topology for unimodal function, the convergence speed and the solution will be better with the greater average degree of population topology.

For multimodal function, it can be seen that the convergence speed will be faster when the average degree of population topology is increasing. If the average degree of population topology is too high, it is easy to fall into local optimum. On the average degree after 6, the optimal solution

TABLE 3: Comparison between random topologies with different average degrees.

Benchmark function	K	Average degree	Clustering coefficient	Perform.	Prop.
Sphere	1	1.958	0.753	$1.38E - 15$	0.768507
	2	3.700	0.541	$1.53E - 30$	0.817693
	3	5.244	0.498	$3.70E - 32$	0.82624
	4	6.640	0.510	$5.92E - 33$	0.833993
	5	7.928	0.534	$4.15E - 33$	0.836973
	6	9.040	0.568	$8.09E - 34$	0.84178
	7	10.116	0.606	$1.00E - 33$	0.84702
	8	11.092	0.641	$1.68E - 34$	0.84278
	9	11.814	0.671	$9.18E - 34$	0.84446
Schaffer's F6	1	1.942	0.753	0.002915	0.497393
	2	3.700	0.545	0.001757	0.63916
	3	5.228	0.497	0.001749	0.681847
	4	6.626	0.508	0.00136	0.716053
	5	7.926	0.530	0.001943	0.6303
	6	8.998	0.563	0.003303	0.558613
	7	10.070	0.602	0.00272	0.59538
	8	11.078	0.643	0.003313	0.542707
	9	11.854	0.673	0.002915	0.558667
Rastrigin	1	1.956	0.751	63.65224	0.868587
	2	3.688	0.546	58.10571	0.923933
	3	5.198	0.500	58.64275	0.915993
	4	6.694	0.507	62.68228	0.934207
	5	7.940	0.532	58.80197	0.94144
	6	9.018	0.565	62.54299	0.93782
	7	10.118	0.608	59.10044	0.944673
	8	10.982	0.638	61.90622	0.908687
	9	11.916	0.674	63.51805	0.925493
Schwefel	1	1.956	0.752	4773.649	0.91388
	2	3.694	0.548	4366.848	0.942427
	3	5.234	0.500	4388.532	0.9436
	4	6.616	0.502	4399.952	0.943533
	5	7.922	0.532	4286.961	0.950633
	6	9.046	0.571	4397.724	0.950987
	7	10.074	0.602	4412.291	0.932327
	8	11.016	0.641	4420.19	0.951007
	9	11.734	0.667	4397.566	0.933313
Ackley	1	1.948	0.751	1.224299	0.960753
	2	3.690	0.549	1.030908	0.969733
	3	5.282	0.493	0.985613	0.972333
	4	6.672	0.507	1.256866	0.97304
	5	7.872	0.539	1.238158	0.973947
	6	9.028	0.568	1.593962	0.974087
	7	10.134	0.611	1.755415	0.97432
	8	10.922	0.640	1.919407	0.974847
	9	11.876	0.671	1.962931	0.97564

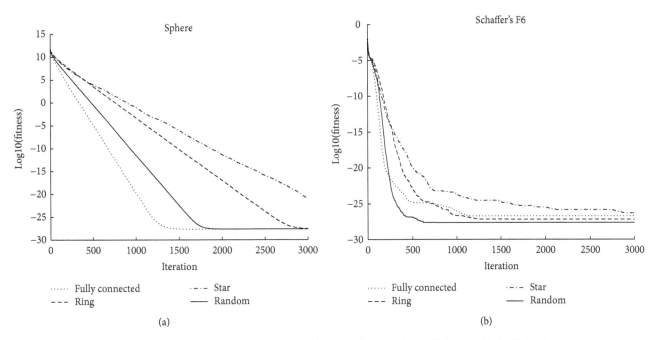

FIGURE 2: Comparison of evolutionary trend between four topologies (Sphere and Schaffer's F6).

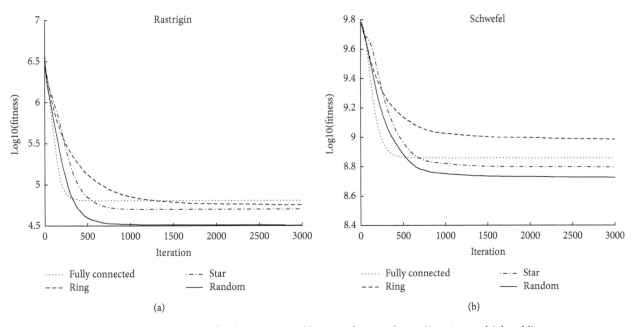

FIGURE 3: Comparison of evolutionary trend between four topologies (Rastrigin and Schwefel).

quality of most algorithms begins to decrease. When the average degree is between 5 and 7 (K is set to 4), the performance of algorithms is usually ideal.

5. Conclusion

In this paper, we propose an improved method of generating random topology based on previous research. And we carry out in-depth research of the performance of the algorithms using random topology based on the canonical PSO and DPPSO-Logistic, respectively. Combined with experimental results, we conduct the analysis and interpretation of the performance of the algorithms from the perspective of graph theory. And empirical laws in generating random topologies are given according to our experimental results and theoretical analysis.

On the whole, relative to the three classic population topologies (fully connected topology, ring topology, and star topology), the algorithm has obvious advantages which is using the proposed random topology. Further work will include the theoretical analysis of different population topologies, as well as dynamic population topology strategy

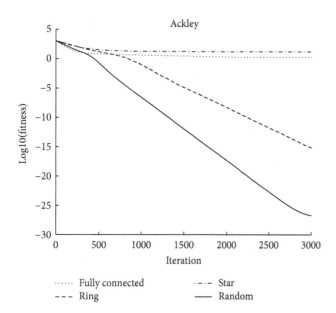

FIGURE 4: Comparison of evolutionary trend between four topologies (Ackley).

which is designed in accordance with the conclusions of this paper.

Acknowledgments

This paper is supported by Provincial Key Laboratory for Computer Information Processing Technology, Soochow University, Suzhou, China, and NSFC (Grant no. 61170164).

References

[1] M. R. AlRashidi and M. E. El-Hawary, "A survey of particle swarm optimization applications in electric power systems," *IEEE Transactions on Evolutionary Computation*, vol. 13, no. 4, pp. 913–918, 2009.

[2] A. A. Esmin, R. A. Coelho, and S. Matwin, "A review on particle swarm optimization algorithm and its variants to clustering highdimensional data," *Artificial Intelligence Review*, 2013.

[3] R. V. Kulkarni and G. K. Venayagamoorthy, "Particle swarm optimization in wireless-sensor networks: a brief survey," *IEEE Transactions on Systems, Man and Cybernetics C*, vol. 41, no. 2, pp. 262–267, 2011.

[4] J. Kennedy and R. Eberhart, "Particle swarm optimization," in *Proceedings of the IEEE International Conference on Neural Networks*, vol. 4, pp. 1942–1948, December 1995.

[5] J. Kennedy, "Small worlds and mega-minds: effects of neighborhood topology on particle swarm performance," in *Proceedings of the Congress on Evolutionary Computation (CEC '99)*, vol. 3, IEEE, 1999.

[6] P. N. Suganthan, "Particle swarm optimiser with neighbourhood operator," in *Proceedings of the Congress on Evolutionary Computation (CEC '99)*, vol. 3, IEEE, 1999.

[7] R. Mendes, J. Kennedy, and J. Neves, "The fully informed particle swarm: simpler, maybe better," *IEEE Transactions on Evolutionary Computation*, vol. 8, no. 3, pp. 204–210, 2004.

[8] M. A. M. de Oca and T. Stützle, "Convergence behavior of the fully informed particle swarm optimization algorithm," in *Proceedings of the 10th Annual Genetic and Evolutionary Computation Conference (GECCO '08)*, pp. 71–78, ACM, July 2008.

[9] R. Mendes, *Population topologies and their influence in particle swarm performance [Ph.D. dissertation]*, Universidade do Minho, 2004.

[10] M. Clerc, "Back to random topology," Tech. Rep. 2007, 2007.

[11] M. Clerc and J. Kennedy, "The particle swarm-explosion, stability, and convergence in a multidimensional complex space," *IEEE Transactions on Evolutionary Computation*, vol. 6, no. 1, pp. 58–73, 2002.

[12] J. Kennedy, "Dynamic-probabilistic particle swarms," in *Proceedings of the Conference on Genetic and Evolutionary Computation Conference*, pp. 201–207, ACM, June 2005.

[13] Q. Ni and J. Deng, "Two improvement strategies for logistic dynamic particle swarm optimization," in *Adaptive and Natural Computing Algorithms*, pp. 320–329, Springer, 2011.

11

Feature Selection Method Based on Artificial Bee Colony Algorithm and Support Vector Machines for Medical Datasets Classification

Mustafa Serter Uzer,[1] **Nihat Yilmaz,**[1] **and Onur Inan**[2]

[1] *Electrical-Electronics Engineering, Faculty of Engineering, Selcuk University, Konya, Turkey*
[2] *Computer Engineering, Faculty of Engineering, Selcuk University, Konya, Turkey*

Correspondence should be addressed to Mustafa Serter Uzer; msuzer@selcuk.edu.tr

Academic Editors: J. Yan and Y. Zhang

This paper offers a hybrid approach that uses the artificial bee colony (ABC) algorithm for feature selection and support vector machines for classification. The purpose of this paper is to test the effect of elimination of the unimportant and obsolete features of the datasets on the success of the classification, using the SVM classifier. The developed approach conventionally used in liver diseases and diabetes diagnostics, which are commonly observed and reduce the quality of life, is developed. For the diagnosis of these diseases, hepatitis, liver disorders and diabetes datasets from the UCI database were used, and the proposed system reached a classification accuracies of 94.92%, 74.81%, and 79.29%, respectively. For these datasets, the classification accuracies were obtained by the help of the 10-fold cross-validation method. The results show that the performance of the method is highly successful compared to other results attained and seems very promising for pattern recognition applications.

1. Introduction

Pattern recognition and data mining are the techniques that allow for the acquirement of meaningful information from large-scale data using a computer program. Nowadays, these techniques are extensively used, particularly in the military, medical, and industrial application fields, since there is a continuously increasing amount and type of data in these areas, due to advanced data acquisition systems. For this reason, for the obtained data set, data reduction algorithms are needed for filtering, priority sorting, and providing redundant measurements to detect the feature selection. By using these algorithms, quality data is obtained, which in turn raises the quality of the analyzing systems or the success of the recognition systems. In particular, medical applications with ever-increasing popularity and use of advanced technology are the most important field in which these algorithms are used. Many new algorithms developed in the field of medicine are tested on the disease data presented for the common use of all the scientists, and their performances are compared.

The datasets from UCI database are very popular for this purpose. The algorithm developed and tested on hepatitis, liver disorders, and diabetes data from UCI was compared with studies in the literature that use the same datasets. These data sets consist of diseases that are commonly encountered in society and significantly reduce the quality of life of patients. The selected data sets are comprised of a variety of test and analysis device data and personal information about the patients. The main objective our work is the integration of the developed systems to these test and analysis devices and to provide a fully automatic assistance to the physician in the creation of diagnosis systems for the diseases. The diagnosis systems, which can be easily used during routine controls, will make the timely information and the early treatment of patients possible.

For the dataset recognition aiming diagnosis of the diseases, we propose a two-stage approach. The first stage has used the clustering with ABC algorithm as selection criteria for feature selection, and, thus, more effective feature selection methods have been constituted. Hence, it has been made possible both to select the related features faster and to reduce the feature vector dimensions. In the second stage, the reduced data was given to the SVM classifier and the accuracy rates were determined. The k-fold cross-validation method was used for improving the classifier reliability. The datasets we have worked on have been described in the Background section. As it is seen from the results, the performance of the proposed method is highly successful compared to other results attained and seems very promising for pattern recognition applications.

1.1. Background. The developed approach has been tested for the diagnosis of liver diseases and diabetes, which are commonly seen in the society and both reduce the quality of life. In the developed system, the hepatitis and liver disorders datasets were used for the diagnosis of liver disease, and the Diabetes dataset was used for the diagnosis of diabetes.

The liver disease diagnostics studies using the Hepatitis dataset were as follows: Polat and Güneş [1] proposed a new diagnostic method of hepatitis disease based on a hybrid feature selection (FS) method and artificial immune recognition system (AIRS) using fuzzy resource allocation mechanism. The obtained classification accuracy of the proposed system was 92.59%. A machine learning system studied by Polat and Güneş [2] was conducted to identify hepatitis disease. At first, the feature number of dataset on hepatitis disease was reduced from 19 to 10 by using in the feature selection (FS) subprogram and C4.5 decision tree algorithm. Then, fuzzy weighted preprocessing was used for weighting the dataset after normalizing between 0 and 1. AIRS classifier system was used while classifying the weighted input values. The classification accuracy of their system was 94.12%. Principal component analysis (PCA) and artificial immune recognition system (AIRS) were conducted for hepatitis disease prediction in the study by Polat and Güneş [3]. Classification accuracy, 94.12%, was obtained with the proposed system using 10-fold cross-validation. A method which had an accuracy value of 96.8% for hepatitis dataset was proposed by Kahramanli and Allahverdi [4], and in this method extracting rules from trained hybrid neural network was presented by using artificial immune systems (AISs) algorithm. An automatic diagnosis system using linear discriminant analysis (LDA) and adaptive network based on fuzzy inference system (ANFIS) was proposed by Dogantekin et al. [5] for hepatitis diseases. This automatic diagnosis system of hepatitis disease diagnostics was obtained with a classification accuracy of about 94.16%. Bascil and Temurtas [6] realized a hepatitis disease diagnosis based on a multilayer neural network structure that used the Levenberg- Marquardt algorithm as training algorithm for the weights update with a classification accuracy of 91.87% from 10-fold cross-validation.

The studies for the diagnosis of liver disease in using the liver disorders dataset were as follows: by Lee and Mangasarian [7], smoothing methods were applied to generate and solve an unconstrained smooth reformulation of the support vector machine for pattern classification using a completely arbitrary kernel. They termed such reformulation a smooth support vector machine (SSVM). Correct classification rate of the proposed system with CV-10 was 70.33% for liver disorders dataset. In Van Gestel et al.'s [8] article, the Bayesian evidence framework was combined with the LS-SVM classifier formulation. Correct classification rate of proposed system with CV-10 was 69.7% for liver disorders dataset. Gonçalves et al. [9] a new neuro-fuzzy model, especially created for record classification and rule extraction of databases, named as inverted hierarchical neuro-fuzzy BSP System (HNFB). Correct classification rate of this system was 73.33% for liver disorders dataset. Özşen and Güneş [10] aimed to contribute to an artificial immune system AIS by attaching this aspect and used the Euclidean distance, Manhattan distance, and hybrid similarity measure with simple AIS. Correct classification rate of the proposed system with AWAIS was 70.17%, with hybrid similarity measure 60.57%, with the Manhattan distance 60.21%, with the Euclidean distance 60.21% for liver disorders. Li et al. [11] proposed a nonlinear transformation method based on fuzzy to find classification information in the original data attribute values for a small dataset and used a support vector machine (SVM) as a classifier. Correct classification rate of the proposed system was 70.85% for liver disorders. Chen et al. [12] proposed an analytical approach by taking an integration of particle swarm optimization (PSO) and the 1-NN method. Correct classification rate of proposed system with 5-fold cross-validation was 68.99% for liver disorders dataset. A hybrid model based on integrating a case-based reasoning approach and a particle swarm optimization model were proposed by Chang et al. [13] for medical data classification.

Another disease that we selected is diabetes. Some of the most important studies conducted on this dataset are as follows: Şahan et al. [14] proposed attribute weighted artificial immune system (AWAIS) with weighting attributes due to their important degrees in class discrimination and using them for the Euclidean distances calculation. AWAIS had a classification accuracy of 75.87 using 10-fold cross-validation method for diabetes dataset. Polat and Güneş [15] worked on diabetes disease using principal component analysis (PCA) and adaptive neuro-fuzzy inference system (ANFIS). The obtained test classification accuracy was 89.47% by using the 10-fold cross-validation. Polat et al. [16] proposed a new learning system which is cascade and used generalized discriminant analysis and least square support vector machine. The classification accuracy was obtained as 82.05%. Kahramanli and Allahverdi [17] presented a hybrid neural network that achieves accuracy value of 84.24% using artificial neural network (ANN) and fuzzy neural network (FNN) together. Patil et al. [18] proposed hybrid prediction model (HPM) which uses Simple k-means clustering algorithm for verifying the chosen class labels and then using the classification algorithm on the result set. Accuracy value of HPM was 92.38%. Isa and Mamat [19] presented a modified hybrid multilayer perceptron (HMLP) network for improving the conventional one, and the average correct classification rate of the proposed system was 80.59%. Aibinu et al. [20] proposed a new biomedical signal classification method using complex-valued pseudo autoregressive (CAR) modeling approach. The presented technique obtained a classification accuracy of 81.28%.

Feature Selection Method Based on Artificial Bee Colony Algorithm and Support Vector Machines for
Medical Datasets Classification

115

```
(1) Start with the empty set $Y_0 = \{\varnothing\}$
(2) Select the next best feature
    $x^+ = \arg\max[J(Y_k + x)]; \ x \notin Y_k$
(3) Update $Y_{k+1} = Y_k + x^+; \ k = k + 1$
(4) Goto 2
```

PSEUDOCODE 1: Pseudo code for SFS [22].

2. Preliminaries

2.1. Feature Selection. Feature selection provides a smaller but more distinguishing subset compared to the starting data, selecting the distinguishing features from a set of features and eliminating the irrelevant ones. Reducing the dimension of the data is aimed by finding a small important features set. This results in both reduced processing time and increased classification accuracy.

The algorithm developed in this study was based on the sequential forward selection (SFS) algorithm, which is popular in these algorithms. SFS is a method of feature selection offered by Whitney [21]. Sequential forward selection is the simplest greedy search algorithm which starts from the empty set and sequentially adds the feature x^+ for obtaining results in the highest objective function $J(Y_k + x^+)$ when combined with the features Y_k that have already been selected. Pseudo code is given Pseudocode 1 for SFS [22].

In summary, SFS begins with zero attributes and then evaluates the whole feature subsets with only one feature, and the best performing one adds this subset to the best performing feature for subsets of the next larger size. This cycle repeats until there is no improvement in the current subset [23].

The objection function is critical for this algorithm. Finding the highest value of this function is an optimization problem. Clustering is an ideal method for the detection of feature differentiation. The developed method can be summarized using the ABC algorithm for feature selection aiming clustering problem adaptation.

2.1.1. Clustering with Optimization. Clustering is a grouping process running on the multi-dimensional data by using similarities. Distance criteria are used to evaluate similarities in samples set. Clustering problems can be expressed as the placement of every object into one K cluster for a given N number of objects and minimizing the sum of squares of the Euclidean distances between the centers of these objects in the cluster to which they belong. The function that uses the clustering algorithm is given in (1) [24] for minimizing:

$$J(w, z) = \sum_{i=1}^{N} \sum_{j=1}^{K} w_{ij} \left\| x_i - z_j \right\|^2. \tag{1}$$

Here, N is the number of samples, K is the number of clusters, x_i ($i = 1, \ldots, N$) is the place of the ith sample, and

the center of the jth sample z_j ($j = 1, \ldots, N$) can be obtained by (2):

$$z_j = \frac{1}{N_j} \sum_{i=1}^{N} w_{ij} x_i. \tag{2}$$

Here, N_j is the number of samples in the jth cluster, and w_{ij} is the relationship of j cluster and x_i sample with a value of 1 or 0. If the sample i (x_i) belongs to the j cluster, w_{ij} is 1, otherwise that it is 0.

The clustering process that separates objects into groups can be performed by supervised or unsupervised learning. Training data in unsupervised clustering (also known as automatic clustering) does not need to set class tags. In supervised clustering, however, it should be specified so that the classes can learn the tags. In this study, the datasets used should contain class information since supervised clustering was used. Therefore, the optimization aims to find the centers of clusters by making the objective function minimize, which is the total of the samples distances to centers [24]. In this study, the sum of distances between all training cluster samples and the cluster center ($p_i^{\text{CL}_{\text{known}}(x_j)}$) that samples belong to in the n-dimensional Euclidean space are minimized for adaptation [24]. Consider the following:

$$f_i = \frac{1}{D_{\text{Train}}} \sum_{j=1}^{D_{\text{Train}}} d\left(x_j, p_i^{\text{CL}_{\text{known}}(x_j)} \right). \tag{3}$$

Here, D_{Train} is the number of training samples, and the total expression in the cost function is for normalizing the number to a value between 0.0 and 1.0. The $p_i^{\text{CL}_{\text{known}}(x_j)}$ value indicates the center of the class that belongs to the sample that is used according to training data. Here, the ABC algorithm was chosen as the optimization method for clustering. Thus, ABC, as a new clustering method, can also be used in the feature selection algorithms.

2.2. Artificial Bee Colony (ABC) Algorithm. Artificial bee colony (ABC) algorithm, as a population-based stochastic optimization proposed by Karaboga in [24–26], realize the intelligent foraging behavior of honey bee swarms. It can be used for classification, clustering and optimization studies. Pseudocode of the ABC algorithm is given as Pseudocode 2.

An artificial group of bees in the ABC algorithm consists of three different groups: employed bees, onlooker bees, and scout bees. In this algorithm, the number of bees employed in the colony also equals the number of onlooker bees. Additionally, the number of employed bees or onlooker bees equals the number of solutions in the population. An onlooker bee is the bee that waits in the dance area to make the food source selection decision. An onlooker bee is named employed bee once it goes to a food source. An employed bee that has consumed the food source turns into a scout bee, and its duty is to perform a random search to discover new resources. Food supply position—which represents the solution to the optimization problem—and the amount of nectar

```
(1) Load training samples
(2) Generate the initial population z_i, i = 1, ..., SN
(3) Evaluate the fitness (f_i) of the population
(4) set cycle to 1
(5) repeat
(6)   FOR each employed bee {
          Produce new solution v_i by using (6)
          Calculate the value f_i
          Apply greedy selection process}
(7) Calculate the probability values p_i for the solutions (z_i) by (5)
(8) FOR each onlooker bee {
      Select a solution z_i depending on p_i
      Produce new solution v_i
      Calculate the value f_i
      Apply greedy selection process}
(9) If there is an abandoned solution for he scout
          then replace it with a new solution which will
          be randomly produced by (7)
(10) Memorize the best solution so far
(11) cycle = cycle + 1
(12) until cycle = MCN
```

PSEUDOCODE 2: Pseudo-code of the ABC algorithm [24].

in the food source depends on the quality of the associated solution. This value is calculated in (4).

$$\text{fit}_i = \frac{1}{1 + f_i} \qquad (4)$$

SN in the algorithm indicates the size of the population. At first, the ABC algorithm produces a distributed initial population $P(C = 0)$ of SN solutions (food source positions) randomly, where SN means the size of population. Each z_i solution is a D-dimensional vector for $i = 1, 2, 3, \ldots, \text{SN}$. Here, D is the numbers of cluster products and input size for each dataset. After startup, an investigation is repeated on employed bees, onlooker bees, and scout bees processes until the number of population of positions ($C = 1, 2, \ldots, \text{MCN}$) is completed. Here, MCN is the maximum cycle number.

An employed bee makes a small change in position due to the local knowledge in its memory, and a new source is generated. This bee makes a comparison of the nectar amount (fitness amount) of a new source with the nectar amount of previous source and decides which one is higher. If the new position is higher than the old one then it is assimilated into its memory and the old one is forgotten. Otherwise, the position of the previous one stays in its memory. All employed bees that complete the task of research share the position and nectar food source information with the onlooker bees that are in the dance area.

An onlooker bee evaluates the nectar information of all employed bees and chooses a food source depending on the probability of the nectar amount. This probability value (p_i) is calculated in (5). Just like the employed bees, the onlooker bee modifies the situation from memory and it checks the nectar amount of the candidate source. If its nectar amount is higher than the previous one and the new position is assimilated into memory and the old one is forgotten, then

$$p_i = \frac{\text{fit}_i}{\sum_{n=1}^{\text{SN}} \text{fit}_n}, \qquad (5)$$

where SN is the number of food sources which is equal to the number of employed bees and the fitness of the fit_i solution given in (4). The f_i given in (3) is the cost function of the cluster problem. ABC uses (6) for producing a candidate food position:

$$v_{ij} = z_{ij} + \phi_{ij} \left(z_{ij} - z_{kj} \right). \qquad (6)$$

Here, $k \in \{1, 2, \ldots, \text{SN}\}$ and $j \in \{1, 2, \ldots, D\}$ are randomly selected indexes. k is a random value different from i. ϕ_{ij} is a random number between $[-1, 1]$ which controls the production of neighboring food sources around z_{ij} and represents comparison of two food sources to a bee.

While onlooker and employed bees perform exploitation in the search area, scout bees control the discovery process and replace the consumed nectar food source with a new food source in the ABC algorithm. If the position cannot be improved as a previously determined cycle number, this food source is accepted as abandoned. The previously determined cycle number is defined as the "*limit*" for abandonment. In this case, there are three control parameters in ABC: the number of food sources (SN) which is equal to the number of employed and onlooker bees, the maximum cycle number (MCN), and the limit value.

If an abandoned source is assumed to be z_i and $j \in \{1, 2, \ldots, D\}$, the scout looks for a new source to replace z_i. This process is described by (7):

$$z_i^j = z_{\min}^j + \text{rand}(0, 1) \left(z_{\max}^j - z_{\min}^j \right). \qquad (7)$$

Feature Selection Method Based on Artificial Bee Colony Algorithm and Support Vector Machines for
Medical Datasets Classification

117

After (v_{ij}) which is each candidate position is produced, the position is evaluated by ABC and its performance is compared with previous one. The performance is compared with the previous one. If the new food source has an equal amount or more nectar than the old one, the new one takes place instead of the old food source in memory. Otherwise, the old one stays in its place in memory. So a greedy selection mechanism is used to make selections among the old source and one of the candidates.

2.3. Support Vector Machines (SVMs). SVM is an effective supervised learning algorithm used in classification and regression analyses for applications like pattern recognition, data mining, and machine learning application. SVM was developed in 1995 by Cortes and Vapnik [27]. Many studies have been conducted on SVM: a flexible support vector machine for regression, an evaluation of flyrock phenomenon based on blasting operation by using support vector machine [28, 29].

In this algorithm, there are two different categories separated by a linear plane. The training of the algorithm is determining the process for the parameters of this linear plane. In multiclass applications, the problem is categorized into groups as belonging either to one class or to others. SVM's use in pattern recognition is described below.

An n-dimensional pattern (object) x has n coordinates, $x = (x_1, x_2, \ldots, x_n)$, where each x is a real number, $x_i \in R$ for $i = 1, 2, \ldots, n$. Each pattern x_j belongs to a class $y_j \in \{-1, +1\}$. Consider a training set T of m patterns together with their classes, $T = \{(x_1, y_1), (x_2, y_2), \ldots, (x_m, y_m)\}$. Consider a dot product space S, in which the patterns x are embedded, $x_1, x_2, \ldots, x_m \in S$. Any hyperplane in the space S can be written as

$$\{x \in S \mid w \cdot x + b = 0\}, \quad w \in S, \ b \in R. \tag{8}$$

The dot product $w \cdot x$ is defined by

$$w \cdot x = \sum_{i=1}^{n} w_i x_i. \tag{9}$$

A training set of patterns can be separated as linear if there exists at least one linear classifier expressed by the pair (w, b) which correctly classifies all training patterns as can be seen in Figure 1. This linear classifier is represented by the hyperplane $H (w \cdot x + b = 0)$ and defines a region for class $+1$ patterns $(w \cdot x + b > 0)$ and another region for class -1 patterns $(w \cdot x + b < 0)$.

After the training process, the classifier becomes ready for prediction of the class membership on new patterns, different from training. The class of a pattern x_k is found from the following equation:

$$\text{class} (x_k) = \begin{cases} +1 & \text{if } w \cdot x_k + b > 0 \\ -1 & \text{if } w \cdot x_k + b < 0. \end{cases} \tag{10}$$

Thus, the classification of new patterns relies on only the sign of the expression $w \cdot x + b$ [30].

Sequential Minimal optimization is used in the training stage of SVM. SMO algorithm is a popular optimization

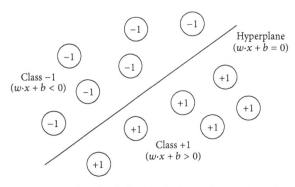

FIGURE 1: Linear classifier defined by the hyperplane $H (w \cdot x + b = 0)$.

method used to train the support vector machine (SVM). The dual presentation of an SVM primal optimization problem is indicated in (11):

$$\max_{\alpha} \quad \Psi (\alpha) = \sum_{i=1}^{N} \alpha_i - \frac{1}{2} \sum_{i=1}^{N} \sum_{j=1}^{N} y_i y_j k (x_i, x_j) \alpha_i \alpha_j$$

$$\text{subject to} \quad \sum_{i=1}^{N} y_i \alpha_i = 0, \quad 0 \le \alpha_i \le C, \ i = 1, \ldots, n, \tag{11}$$

where x_i is a training sample, $y_i \in \{-1, +1\}$ is the corresponding target value, α_i is the Lagrange multiplier, and C is a real value cost parameter [31].

2.4. Performance Evaluation. Four criteria for performance evaluation of hepatitis, liver disorders and diabetes datasets were used. These criteria are classification accuracy, confusion matrix, analysis of sensitivity and specificity, and k-fold cross-validation.

2.4.1. Classification Accuracy. In this study, the classification accuracies for the datasets are measured with the following the equation:

$$\text{accuracy} (T) = \frac{\sum_{i=1}^{N} \text{assess} (t_i)}{N}, \quad t_i \in T,$$

$$\text{assess} (t_i) = \begin{cases} 1, & \text{if classify} (t_i) \equiv \text{correctclassification}, \\ 0, & \text{otherwise}, \end{cases} \tag{12}$$

where T is the classified set of data items (the test set) and N is the number of testing samples of the dataset. We will also show the accuracy of our performed k-fold cross-validation (CV) experiment.

2.4.2. Confusion Matrix. The confusion matrix includes four classification performance indices: true positive, false positive, false negative, and true negative as given in Table 1. They are also usually used in the two-class classification problem to evaluate the performance.

2.4.3. Analysis of Sensitivity and Specificity. The following expressions were used for calculating sensitivity, specificity,

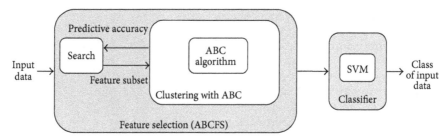

FIGURE 2: Block diagram of the proposed system.

TABLE 1: The four classification performance indices included in the confusion matrix.

Actual class	Predicted class	
	Positive	Negative
Positive	True positive (TP)	False negative (FN)
Negative	False positive (FP)	True negative (TN)

positive predictive value, and negative predictive value; we use [32]:

$$\text{Sensitivity (\%)} = \frac{\text{TP}}{\text{TP} + \text{FN}} \times 100,$$

$$\text{Specificity (\%)} = \frac{\text{TN}}{\text{TN} + \text{FP}} \times 100,$$

$$\text{Positive predctive value (\%)} = \frac{\text{TP}}{\text{TP} + \text{FP}} \times 100,$$

$$\text{Negative predicitive value (\%)} = \frac{\text{TN}}{\text{TN} + \text{FN}} \times 100.$$

$$(13)$$

2.4.4. k-Fold Cross-Validation. k-fold cross-validation is used for the test result to be more valuable [33]. In k-fold cross-validation, the original sample is divided into random k subsamples, one of which is retained as the validation data for model testing and the remaining k-1 sub-samples are used for training The cross-validation process is then repeated k times (the folds), with each of the k sub-samples used exactly once as the validation data. The process is repeated k times (the folds), with each of the k sub-samples used only once as the validation data. The average of k results from the folds gives the test accuracy of the algorithm [34].

3. Experimental Work

Less distinctive features of the data set affect the classification negatively. Such data especially decrease the speed and the system performance significantly. With the proposed system, using the feature selection algorithm, the features with less discriminant data were eliminated. The reduced data set increased the testing success of the classifier and the rate of the system. From Figure 2, the proposed system has two phases. At the first phase, as selection criteria, clustering with ABC algorithm was used for feature selection, and, thus, a more effective feature selection method was constituted. Hence, it has been made possible both to select the related

features in a shorter period of time and to reduce the dimension of the feature vector. At second stage, the obtained reduced data is supplied to the SVM classifier to determine the accuracy rates. The k-fold cross-validation was used for the classifier reliability improvement.

In this study, ABCFS + SVM system is suggested in order to solve the three classification problem named as Hepatitis dataset, Liver Disorders dataset, Diabetes dataset, respectively.

3.1. Datasets. We used the dataset from the UCI machine learning database [35], which is commonly used among researchers for classification, that gives us a chance to compare the performance of our method with others. The datasets of this work can be defined shortly as follows.

3.1.1. Hepatitis Dataset. This dataset was donated by Jozef Stefan Institute, Yugoslavia. The purpose of the dataset is to predict the presence or absence of hepatitis disease from the different medical tests results of a patient. This database contains 19 attributes. There are 13 binary and 6 discrete values. Hepatitis dataset includes 155 samples from two different classes (32 "die" cases, 123 "live" cases). This dataset contains missing attribute values. We substituted the missing data by frequently encountered values of own class. Attributes of symptoms that are obtained from patient are given in Table 2 [3, 35].

3.1.2. Liver Disorders Dataset. The liver disorders dataset is named as BUPA liver disorders. The liver disorders database includes 6 features, that is, MCV, alkphos, SGPT, SGOT, gammaGT and drinks. There are 345 data in total and each sample is taken from an unmarried man. Two hundred of them are chosen for one class with the remaining 145 are in the other. The first 5 features are all blood tests which are sensitive to liver disorders that arise from excessive alcohol consumption. This dataset is donated by Richard S. Forsyth et al. in 1990. The attributes are given in Table 3 [13].

3.1.3. Diabetes Dataset. This dataset contains 768 samples, where each sample has 8 features which are eight clinical findings. All patients of the dataset are Pima Indian women in which the youngest one is 21 years old and living near Phoenix, Arizona, USA. The binary target variable can take "0" or "1." If it takes "1," it means a positive test for Diabetes, or if it takes "0," it means a negative test. There are 268 different cases in class "1" and 500 different cases in class "0." The features and parameters are given in Table 4 [16].

Feature Selection Method Based on Artificial Bee Colony Algorithm and Support Vector Machines for
Medical Datasets Classification

119

TABLE 2: Range values and attribute names for hepatitis dataset [35].

The number of attribute	The name of attribute	Interval of attribute
1	Age	7–78
2	Sex	Male, Female
3	Steroid	No, Yes
4	Antivirals	No, Yes
5	Fatigue	No, Yes
6	Malaise	No, Yes
7	Anorexia	No, Yes
8	Liver big	No, Yes
9	Liver firm	No, Yes
10	Spleen palpable	No, Yes
11	Spiders	No, Yes
12	Ascites	No, Yes
13	Varices	No, Yes
14	Bilirubin	0.3–8
15	Alk phosphate	26–295
16	SGOT	14–648
17	Albumin	2.1–6.4
18	Protime	0–100
19	Histology	No, Yes

TABLE 3: Range values and attribute names for liver disorders dataset [35].

The number of attribute	The name of attribute	Description of the attribute	Interval of attribute
1	MCV	Mean corpuscular volume	65–103
2	Alkphos	Alkaline phosphatase	23–138
3	SGPT	Alamine aminotransferase	4–155
4	SGOT	Aspartate aminotransferase	5–82
5	gammaGT	Gamma-glutamyl transpeptidase	5–297
6	Drinks	Number of half-pint equivalents of alcoholic beverages drunk per day	0–20

TABLE 4: Features and parameters of the diabetes dataset.

Features	Mean	Standard deviation	Min	Max
Number of times pregnant	3.8	3.4	0	17
Plasma glucose concentration, 2 h in an oral glucose tolerance test	120.9	32.0	0	199
Diastolic blood pressure (mm Hg)	69.1	19.4	0	122
Triceps skinfold thickness (mm)	20.5	16.0	0	99
2-hour serum insulin (mu U/mL)	79.8	115.2	0	846
Body mass index (kg/m^2)	32.0	7.9	0	67.1
Diabetes pedigree function	0.5	0.3	0.078	2.42
Age (years)	33.2	11.8	21	81

TABLE 5: List of datasets.

Databases	Number of classes	Samples	Number of features	Number of selected features	Selected features
Hepatitis	2	155	19	11	12, 14, 13, 15, 18, 1, 17, 5, 16, 2, 4
Liver disorders	2	345	6	5	5, 3, 2, 4, 1
Diabetes	2	768	8	6	2, 8, 6, 7, 4, 5

TABLE 6: List of classification parameters.

Parameters	Value
Method	SVM
Optimization algorithm	SMO
Validation method	k-fold cross-validation (10-fold CV)
Kernel_Function	Linear
TolKKT	$1.0000e - 003$
MaxIter	15000
KernelCacheLimit	5000
The initial value	Random

TABLE 7: Performance of classification for the hepatitis, liver disorders, and diabetes datasets.

Performance criteria	Hepatitis dataset	Liver disorders dataset	Diabetes dataset
Classification accuracy (%)	94.92	74.81	79.29
Sensitivity (%)	97.13	88.22	89.84
Specificity (%)	88.33	56.68	59.61
Positive predictive value (%)	96.91	73.99	80.63
Negative predictive value (%)	88.33	78.57	75.65

3.2. Feature Selection with ABC. In the system, a searching process runs to find the best feature subset same like sequential forward selection algorithm. Prediction accuracy for feature selection is found by ABC clustering. Pseudocode of the developed feature selection algorithm based on ABC is given in Pseudocode 3.

In Pseudocode 3, n is sample count and p is desired feature count which is selected as providing the highest performance criteria. While *data* represents the entire dataset, *Data_all* includes the features that are considered chosen. *Train_data_all* is generated by taking 75% of the data found in all classes of *Data_all*. *Test_data_all* is generated by taking 25% of the data that are found in all classes of *Data_all*.

Thus, a uniform dispersion was obtained according to the classes. Train data that belongs to each class (*train_data_class*) is trained by the ABC algorithm, which has been modified to cluster. At the end of training, 10 feature vectors named food and representing each class are obtained. Goodness of the chosen feature cluster is described by the food values

```
n = sample_count;
Selected_features = {∅}
For p = 1 to desired_feature_count
  For c = 1 to feature_count
    Data_all = data(Selected_features + feature(c));
    For i = 1 to class_number
      Train_data_class(i) = partition(rand(Data_all(class == i)), 0.75)
      Test_data_class(i) = partition(rand(Data_all(class = i)), others);
        [foods(i)] = Modified_ABC_algortihm (train_data_class(i), performance_function);
    End for i
    Test_data_all = merge(test_data_class);
    For i = 1: size(Test_data_all)
      For k = 1: class_count
        For j = 1: count(foods(k))
          distance(k, j) = oklid_distance(foods(j, k)-test_data(i));
        End for j
        min_dist(k) = min(distance(k));
      End for k
      [result_of_test_data(i), class_of_test_data(i)] = min(min_dist);
    End for i
    Performance_criteria(feature(c))
  = sum(class_of_test_data(i) == class_of_test_data_expected);
    End for c
  Best_feature(c) = arg max(performance_criteria(feature(c))
  Selected_features = Selected_fetures + best_feature(c)
End for p
```

PSEUDOCODE 3: Pseudo-code of developed feature selection algorithm based on ABC.

TABLE 8: Classification accuracies obtained by our method and other classifiers for the hepatitis dataset.

Author (year)	Method	Classification accuracy (%)
Polat and Güneş (2006) [1]	FS-AIRS with fuzzy res. (10-fold CV)	92.59
Polat and Güneş (2007) [2]	FS-Fuzzy-AIRS (10-fold CV)	94.12
Polat and Güneş (2007) [3]	AIRS (10-fold CV)	76.00
	PCA-AIRS (10-fold CV)	94.12
Kahramanli and Allahverdi (2009) [4]	Hybrid system (ANN and AIS) (without k-fold CV)	96.8
Dogantekin et al. (2009) [5]	LDA-ANFIS	94.16
Bascil and Temurtas (2011) [6]	MLNN (MLP) + LM (10-fold CV)	91.87
Our study	ABCFS + SVM (10-fold CV)	**94.92**

TABLE 9: Classification accuracies obtained by our method and other classifiers for the liver disorders dataset.

Author (year)	Method	Classification accuracy (%)
Lee and Mangasarian (2001) [7]	SSVM (10-fold CV)	70.33
van Gestel et al. (2002) [8]	SVM with GP (10-fold CV)	69.7
Gonçalves et al. (2006) [9]	HNFB-1 method	73.33
	AWAIS (10-fold CV)	70.17
Özşen and Güneş (2008) [10]	AIS with hybrid similarity measure (10-fold CV)	60.57
	AIS with Manhattan distance (10-fold CV)	60.21
	AIS with Euclidean distance (10-fold CV)	60.00
Li et al. (2011) [11]	A fuzzy-based nonlinear transformation method + SVM	70.85
Chen et al. (2012) [12]	(PSO) + 1-NN method (5-fold CV)	68.99
Chang et al. (2012) [13]	CBR + PSO (train: 75%-test: 25%)	76.81
Our study	ABCFS + SVM (train: 75%-test: 25%)	**82.55**
	ABCFS + SVM (10-fold CV)	**74.81**

TABLE 10: Classification accuracies obtained by our method and other classifiers for diabetes dataset.

Author (year)	Method	Classification accuracy (%)
Şahan et al. (2005) [14]	AWAIS (10-fold CV)	75.87
Polat and Güneş (2007) [15]	Combining PCA and ANFIS	89.47
Polat et al. (2008) [16]	LS-SVM (10-fold CV)	78.21
	GDA-LS-SVM (10-fold CV)	82.05
Kahramanli andAllahverdi (2008) [17]	Hybrid system (ANN and FNN)	84.2
Patil et al. (2010) [18]	Hybrid prediction model (HPM) with reduced dataset	92.38
Isa and Mamat (2011) [19]	Clustered-HMLP	80.59
Aibinu et al. (2011) [20]	AR1 + NN (3-fold CV)	81.28
Our study	ABCFS + SVM (train: 75%-test: 25%)	**86.97**
	ABCFS + SVM (10-fold CV)	**79.29**

accuracy representing the test dataset. The error value is found by taking the difference between the test data class and the food value class having a minimum Euclidean distance to the test data class.

The performance value shows the suitability of the added property. The most appropriate property value does not belong to the chosen properties cluster. This process is repeated by starting from an empty cluster up until the desired feature number. The decline in the value of rising performance trend is for determining the maximum number of features. In summary, in ABCFS, it starts from selecting the feature set as empty, then adds the feature(c) that results in the highest objective function.

We selected colony size 20, maximum cycle/generation number (MCN) 300, and limit value 200. The algorithm was run 100 times. Performance value is found by taking the average of these algorithm results.

The datasets used for evaluating ABCFS performance and their features are as follows: the number of classes, the number of samples, the number of features and the number of selected features, which are given in Table 5.

3.3. SVM Classification Parameters. The reliability of the classifier was provided by the k-fold cross-validation method. While this classifier was used, the training was performed according to the parameters in Table 6.

4. Experimental Results and Discussion

ABCFS + SVM method test results developed for the hepatitis dataset, liver disorders dataset and diabetes datasets are given in Pseudocode 3. These test results contain the classification performance values achieved by the developed methodology by the help of 10-fold cross-validation. The performance values include average classification accuracy, sensitivity, specificity, positive predictive value, and negative predictive value of the proposed system which are given in Table 7. The results of the study show that the average correctness rate of the studies performed so far on all used datasets by employing the method of k-fold cross-validation is a very promising result.

For the hepatitis dataset, the comparisons with the other systems are given in Table 8.

For the liver disorders dataset, the comparisons with the other systems are given in Table 9.

For the diabetes dataset, the comparisons with the other systems are given in Table 10.

5. Conclusions

This study was designed for use in the diagnosis of liver and diabetes. In these databases that were used, there are some redundant and low-distinctive features. These features are very important factors affecting the success of the classifier and the system processing time. In the system we have developed, the elimination of these redundant features increased the system speed and success. The artificial bee Colony (ABC) algorithm, which is a very popular optimization method, was used for the feature selection process in the study. The ABC-based feature selection algorithm that was developed in this study is the first example of the ABC algorithm used in the field of feature selection. The databases that are subjected to feature selection are classified using SVM. In order to achieve a reliable performance of the classifier, the 10-fold cross-validation method was used. The system results were compared with the literature articles that use the same databases. Classification accuracy of the proposed system reached 94.92%, 74.81%, and 79.29% for hepatitis dataset, liver disorders dataset and diabetes dataset, respectively. Obtained results show that the performance of the proposed method is highly successful compared to other results attained and seems very promising for pattern recognition applications.

Acknowledgment

The authors would like to thank Selcuk University Scientific Research Projects Coordinatorship for the support of this paper.

References

[1] K. Polat and S. Güneş, "Hepatitis disease diagnosis using a new hybrid system based on feature selection (FS) and artificial immune recognition system with fuzzy resource allocation," *Digital Signal Processing*, vol. 16, no. 6, pp. 889–901, 2006.

[2] K. Polat and S. Güneş, "Medical decision support system based on artificial immune recognition immune system (AIRS), fuzzy

weighted pre-processing and feature selection," *Expert Systems with Applications*, vol. 33, no. 2, pp. 484–490, 2007.

[3] K. Polat and S. Güneş, "Prediction of hepatitis disease based on principal component analysis and artificial immune recognition system," *Applied Mathematics and Computation*, vol. 189, no. 2, pp. 1282–1291, 2007.

[4] H. Kahramanli and N. Allahverdi, "Extracting rules for classification problems: AIS based approach," *Expert Systems with Applications*, vol. 36, no. 7, pp. 10494–10502, 2009.

[5] E. Dogantekin, A. Dogantekin, and D. Avci, "Automatic hepatitis diagnosis system based on linear discriminant analysis and adaptive network based on fuzzy inference system," *Expert Systems with Applications*, vol. 36, no. 8, pp. 11282–11286, 2009.

[6] M. S. Bascil and F. Temurtas, "A study on hepatitis disease diagnosis using multilayer neural network with Levenberg Marquardt training algorithm," *Journal of Medical Systems*, vol. 35, no. 3, pp. 433–436, 2011.

[7] Y. J. Lee and O. L. Mangasarian, "SSVM: a smooth support vector machine for classification," *Computational Optimization and Applications*, vol. 20, no. 1, pp. 5–22, 2001.

[8] T. van Gestel, J. A. K. Suykens, G. Lanckriet, A. Lambrechts, B. de Moor, and J. Vandewalle, "Bayesian framework for least-squares support vector machine classifiers, Gaussian processes, and Kernel Fisher discriminant analysis," *Neural Computation*, vol. 14, no. 5, pp. 1115–1147, 2002.

[9] L. B. Gonçalves, M. M. B. R. Vellasco, M. A. C. Pacheco, and F. J. de Souza, "Inverted Hierarchical Neuro-Fuzzy BSP system: a novel neuro-fuzzy model for pattern classification and rule extraction in databases," *IEEE Transactions on Systems, Man and Cybernetics C*, vol. 36, no. 2, pp. 236–248, 2006.

[10] S. Özşen and S. Güneş, "Effect of feature-type in selecting distance measure for an artificial immune system as a pattern recognizer," *Digital Signal Processing*, vol. 18, no. 4, pp. 635–645, 2008.

[11] D. C. Li, C. W. Liu, and S. C. Hu, "A fuzzy-based data transformation for feature extraction to increase classification performance with small medical data sets," *Artificial Intelligence in Medicine*, vol. 52, no. 1, pp. 45–52, 2011.

[12] L. F. Chen, C. T. Su, K. H. Chen, and P. C. Wang, "Particle swarm optimization for feature selection with application in obstructive sleep apnea diagnosis," *Neural Computing and Applications*, vol. 21, no. 8, pp. 2087–2096, 2012.

[13] P. C. Chang, J. J. Lin, and C. H. Liu, "An attribute weight assignment and particle swarm optimization algorithm for medical database classifications," *Computer Methods and Programs in Biomedicine*, vol. 107, no. 3, pp. 382–392, 2012.

[14] S. Şahan, K. Polat, H. Kodaz, and S. Güneş, "The medical applications of attribute weighted artificial immune system (AWAIS): diagnosis of heart and diabetes diseases," in *Artificial Immune Systems*, vol. 3627 of *Lecture Notes in Computer Science*, pp. 456–468, 2005.

[15] K. Polat and S. Güneş, "An expert system approach based on principal component analysis and adaptive neuro-fuzzy inference system to diagnosis of diabetes disease," *Digital Signal Processing*, vol. 17, no. 4, pp. 702–710, 2007.

[16] K. Polat, S. Güneş, and A. Arslan, "A cascade learning system for classification of diabetes disease: generalized discriminant analysis and least square support vector machine," *Expert Systems with Applications*, vol. 34, no. 1, pp. 482–487, 2008.

[17] H. Kahramanli and N. Allahverdi, "Design of a hybrid system for the diabetes and heart diseases," *Expert Systems with Applications*, vol. 35, no. 1-2, pp. 82–89, 2008.

[18] B. M. Patil, R. C. Joshi, and D. Toshniwal, "Hybrid prediction model for type-2 diabetic patients," *Expert Systems with Applications*, vol. 37, no. 12, pp. 8102–8108, 2010.

[19] N. A. M. Isa and W. M. F. W. Mamat, "Clustered-hybrid multilayer perceptron network for pattern recognition application," *Applied Soft Computing Journal*, vol. 11, no. 1, pp. 1457–1466, 2011.

[20] A. M. Aibinu, M. J. E. Salami, and A. A. Shafie, "A novel signal diagnosis technique using pseudo complex-valued autoregressive technique," *Expert Systems with Applications*, vol. 38, no. 8, pp. 9063–9069, 2011.

[21] P. Pudil, J. Novovičová, and J. Kittler, "Floating search methods in feature selection," *Pattern Recognition Letters*, vol. 15, no. 11, pp. 1119–1125, 1994.

[22] L. Ladha and T. Deepa, "Feature selection methods and algorithms," *International Journal on Computer Science and Engineering*, vol. 3, no. 5, pp. 1787–1797, 2011.

[23] M. Sasikala and N. Kumaravel, "Comparison of feature selection techniques for detection of malignant tumor in brain images," in *Proceedings of the Annual IEEE INDICON '05*, pp. 212–215, December 2005.

[24] D. Karaboga and C. Ozturk, "A novel clustering approach: artificial bee colony (ABC) algorithm," *Applied Soft Computing Journal*, vol. 11, no. 1, pp. 652–657, 2011.

[25] D. Karaboga and B. Akay, "A comparative study of artificial bee colony algorithm," *Applied Mathematics and Computation*, vol. 214, no. 1, pp. 108–132, 2009.

[26] B. Akay and D. Karaboga, "A modified artificial bee colony algorithm for real-parameter optimization," *Information Sciences*, vol. 192, pp. 120–142, 2012.

[27] C. Cortes and V. Vapnik, "Support-vector networks," *Machine Learning*, vol. 20, no. 3, pp. 273–297, 1995.

[28] H. Amini, R. Gholami, M. Monjezi, S. R. Torabi, and J. Zadhesh, "Evaluation of flyrock phenomenon due to blasting operation by support vector machine," *Neural Computing and Applications*, vol. 21, no. 8, pp. 2077–2085, 2012.

[29] X. B. Chen, J. Yang, and J. Liang, "A flexible support vector machine for regression," *Neural Computing and Applications*, vol. 21, no. 8, pp. 2005–2013, 2012.

[30] O. Ivanciuc, *Reviews in Computational Chemistry*, edited by K. B. Lipkowitz and T. R. Cundari, 2007.

[31] T. W. Kuan, J. F. Wang, J. C. Wang, P. C. Lin, and G. H. Gu, "VLSI design of an SVM learning core on sequential minimal optimization algorithm," *IEEE Transactions on Very Large Scale Integration (VLSI) Systems*, vol. 20, no. 4, pp. 673–683, 2012.

[32] K. Polat and S. Güneş, "Breast cancer diagnosis using least square support vector machine," *Digital Signal Processing*, vol. 17, no. 4, pp. 694–701, 2007.

[33] D. François, F. Rossi, V. Wertz, and M. Verleysen, "Resampling methods for parameter-free and robust feature selection with mutual information," *Neurocomputing*, vol. 70, no. 7-9, pp. 1276–1288, 2007.

[34] N. A. Diamantidis, D. Karlis, and E. A. Giakoumakis, "Unsupervised stratification of cross-validation for accuracy estimation," *Artificial Intelligence*, vol. 116, no. 1-2, pp. 1–16, 2000.

[35] C. L. Blake and C. J. Merz, *University of California at Irvine Repository of Machine Learning Databases*, 1998, http://www.ics.uci.edu/~mlearn/MLRepository.html.

12

An Anonymous User Authentication with Key Agreement Scheme without Pairings for Multiserver Architecture Using SCPKs

Peng Jiang, Qiaoyan Wen, Wenmin Li, Zhengping Jin, and Hua Zhang

State Key Laboratory of Networking and Switching Technology, Beijing University of Posts and Telecommunications, Beijing 100876, China

Correspondence should be addressed to Peng Jiang; jiangpengbanana@163.com

Academic Editors: G. A. Gravvanis and G. Wei

With advancement of computer community and widespread dissemination of network applications, users generally need multiple servers to provide different services. Accordingly, the multiserver architecture has been prevalent, and designing a secure and efficient remote user authentication under multiserver architecture becomes a nontrivial challenge. In last decade, various remote user authentication protocols have been put forward to correspond to the multi-server scenario requirements. However, these schemes suffered from certain security problems or their cost consumption exceeded users' own constrained ability. In this paper, we present an anonymous remote user authentication with key agreement scheme for multi-server architecture employing self-certified public keys without pairings. The proposed scheme can not only retain previous schemes' advantages but also achieve user privacy concern. Moreover, our proposal can gain higher efficiency by removing the pairings operation compared with the related schemes. Through analysis and comparison with the related schemes, we can say that our proposal is in accordance with the scenario requirements and feasible to the multi-server architecture.

1. Introduction

In modern society, people's life is highly dependent on the Internet, but the exposure of networks often causes great loss to users, which brings about that a secure user authentication mechanism has become the key issue to preserve valid remote clients in safety from being attacked. There is no doubt that the user authentication with smart card is one of the most widely used and the simplest approaches. When taking only one sort of service into account, some password authentication schemes for single-server environment have been proposed [1, 2].

Later with the rapid development of technology, different servers are needed to offer service via the network, and conventional methods need users to register with various servers repetitively and remember different identities and passwords. It is obvious that these traditional schemes make authentication inconvenient and cost much. Consequently, an appropriate multiserver user authentication mechanism has

turned into a concern. In 2001, Li et al. [3] gave a remote user authentication scheme in neural networks for the first time, which opened up the gateway access to the multiserver architecture.

Considering the system environment without loss of generality, the multiserver architecture consists of multiple distributed service servers and remote clients with limited resource and capability. The service servers offer different access services such as e-commerce, online conference, network game, and remote medical system. If a remote client wants to access to these services, he/she needs to login these service servers through cellular network or wireless local area networks (WLANs).

Due to multiserver environment special characteristics and information security problem in public networks, designing a feasible user authentication scheme under multi-server architecture is a key issue, which can ensure the access of legitimate users and prevent invalid user from interfering with the service server. A practical user authentication scheme under the multiserver environment must address the following requirements. They consist of both the previous criteria [1] and new user anonymity issue.

(1) No repetitive registration is needed for the multiserver environments.

(2) No verification table is stored in the server.

(3) Mutual authentication and session key agreement can be achieved between the users and the service servers to carry on subsequent communications.

(4) Various possible attacks can be resisted.

(5) User can choose identity and password freely and change his/her password freely.

(6) The computational and communication cost is low since the energy resources and computing capability of a smart card are limited.

(7) The user is not allowed to expose his identity privacy information to eavesdroppers. Assume that the adversary obtains a valid user's identity, he/she can masquerade the user to enjoy the regular service without registration, which can cause losses for the valid user or even worse consequences. So the anonymous authentication should be implemented.

In order to satisfy all of these criteria, this paper proposes an anonymous remote user authentication scheme without pairings for multiserver architecture using self-certified public keys (SCPKs). We present public key-based user anonymous authentication scheme under the multiserver environment. Meanwhile, our proposal heightens efficiency increasingly accompanied by the removal of pairings operation; in contrast, the existing public key-based authentication schemes generally employ pairings function. Moreover, our proposal can avoid the server spoofing attack since the verification process relies on the server's private key. Through security and performance analysis, our proposal not only achieves anonymous authentication with key agreement securely but also results more efficiently, remedying the weaknesses of previous authentication schemes which either encounter some attacks or fail to protect user privacy or cost relatively more energy. Compared with other related achievements, ours is more suitable for the remote user whose resources and capability are constrained under multiserver architecture.

The rest of this paper is organized as follows. Section 2 briefly describes some related works. Some preliminaries are given in Section 3. Our proposed secure and efficient user authentication scheme for multiserver architecture and corresponding analysis are presented in Sections 4 and 5, respectively. Finally, some conclusions are drawn in Section 6.

2. Related Work

Until now, two categories of improved multiserver user authentication schemes, hash-based authentication and public key based authentication, have emerged successively. To hash-based authentication, some user password authentication suggestions [4–7] based on static ID have been proposed

to conquer the weaknesses of Li et al.'s, yet these were proven easy to be traced. In 2009, Liao and Wang [8] raised a dynamic identity authentication protocol for multiserver environment to advance previous work. In the following years, many researchers [9–12] have developed and enhanced the user authentication scheme step by step. To public key-based authentication, employing public key cryptosystem into the password authentication, Das et al. [13] first proposed a remote user authentication protocol with smart card using bilinear pairings. Yet theirs had an obvious disadvantage: no mutual authentication and key agreement. To improve the security, a series of user authentication schemes [14–16] with bilinear pairings have been presented. To improve the efficiency, Tseng et al. [17] gave a low-cost pairing-based user authentication protocol for wireless users and claimed that theirs was efficient, easy password changing, and suitable for multiserver environment in distributed networks. Unfortunately, in 2013, Liao and Hsiao [18] pointed out that Tseng et al.'s scheme also lacked mutual authentication with session key agreement, suffered from insider attack, password guessing attack, and replay attack, and advanced a pairings-based user authentication scheme using self-certified public keys. Liao and Hsiao claimed that their proposal could withstand various possible attacks and was well suited for multiserver environment.

Regretfully, most of the existing related public key based authentication schemes under multiserver architecture mentioned previously did not pay attention to user anonymity issue. Moreover, their authentication schemes needed excessive energy consumption employing pairings operation and suffered from the server spoofing attack, which was not conducive to communication running and trapped in DoS attack easily.

3. Preliminaries

We now briefly review some basic concepts used in this paper, including bilinear pairings [19], related complexity assumptions [20], and self-certified public keys [21, 22].

3.1. Admissible Bilinear Pairing. Let $\mathbb{G}$ be an additive group generated by P with prime order q and let $\mathbb{G}_T$ be a multiplicative group of the same order. A map $\hat{e} : \mathbb{G} \times \mathbb{G} \rightarrow \mathbb{G}_T$ is said to be an admissible bilinear pairing if the following three conditions hold true.

(1) Bilinearity: for all $a, b \in \mathbb{Z}_q^*$, we have $\hat{e}(aP, bP) = \hat{e}(P, P)^{ab}$.

(2) Nondegeneracy: $\hat{e}(P, P) \neq 1_{\mathbb{G}_T}$.

(3) Computability: $\hat{e}$ is efficiently computable.

We refer readers to [19] for more details of such pairings.

3.2. Complexity Assumption

(1) Computational discrete logarithm (CDL) assumption: given $Q = k \cdot P$, where $P, Q \in \mathbb{G}$, there exists no probabilistic polynomial-time algorithm which can determine k.

(2) Computational Diffie-Hellman (CDH) assumption: given two elements aP, bP in a group $\mathbb{G}$, where the unknown numbers $a, b \in \mathbb{Z}_q^*$ are selected at random, there exists no probabilistic polynomial-time algorithm which can compute abP.

(3) Elliptic curve factorization (ECF) assumption: given two elements P, Q, where $Q = aP + bP$ and $a, b \in \mathbb{Z}_q^*$, there exists no probabilistic polynomial-time algorithm which can obtain aP and bP.

3.3. Self-Certified Public Key. Here, we describe a self-certified public key process briefly; more details can be found in [21, 22].

(1) Initialization: given a group $\mathbb{G}$ on an elliptic curve E, P is a based point generator of prime order q, the system authority (SA) selects a random value $s \in \mathbb{Z}_q^*$ as its private key and computes the public key $P_{\text{pub}} = s \cdot P$. Publish the related parameters and keep s secret.

(2) Partial private key and private key generation: the user U_i chooses a number k_i randomly, computes $K_i = k_i \cdot P$, and sends (ID_i, K_i) to SA over a secure channel. SA calculates $W_i = K_i + w_i \cdot P$ as the witness using a random number w_i. Then, SA computes the user's partial private key $\bar{s}_i = H(\text{ID}_i \| W_i) \cdot s + w_i$ and submits $(\bar{s}_i, W_i)$ to U_i. U_i can obtain its private key $s_i = \bar{s}_i + k_i$.

(3) Public key extraction: U_i's public key can be computed by $\text{Pub}_i = s_i \cdot P$. Any entity, who communicates with U_i and receives the witness W_i, can authenticate U_i's public key Pub_i as long as he/she calculates the equation: $\text{Pub}_i = H(\text{ID}_i \| W_i) \cdot P_{\text{pub}} + W_i$.

4. The Proposed Scheme

In this section, we propose an anonymous remote user authentication scheme for multiserver environment without pairings, which consists of five phases: server registration phase, user registration phase, login phase, verification phase, and password change phase. Three entities are involved: user (U_i), service server (S_j), and registration center (RC). RC chooses the system private/public key pair s/P_{pub}, where s is a random number in $\mathbb{Z}_q^*$ and $P_{\text{pub}} = s \cdot P$. Then publish the system parameters $\text{Params} = \{\mathbb{G}, P, q, P_{\text{pub}}, H(\cdot)\}$ and keep s secret. The notations used in this section are listed in Table 1. Some detailed steps will be described as follows and shown in Figure 1.

4.1. Server Registration Phase. When the service server wants to access to the multiserver architecture, it needs to register first. In this phase, RC uses the self-certified public key (SCPK) to generate the related credentials.

Step S1. S_j chooses a random value $k_j \in \mathbb{Z}_q^*$, computes $K_j = k_j \cdot P$, and sends (SID_j, K_j) to RC.

TABLE 1: Notations used in proposed scheme.

Notations	Descriptions
RC	The registration center
S_j	The jth service server
U_i	The ith user with mobile device
s	The private key of RC
SID_j	The identity of S_j
ID_i	The identity of U_i
P	A generator of group G
$H(\cdot)$	A one-way hash function
PW_i	The password of U_i
SK	A session key shared between U_i and S_j
x	The secret value maintained by RC
$\oplus$	A simple Exclusive-OR operation
$\|$	The concatenation operation

Step S2. After receiving the message (SID_j, K_j), RC generates a $w_j \in \mathbb{Z}_q^*$ randomly, calculates $W_j = K_j + w_j \cdot P$, $\bar{s}_j = H(\text{SID}_j \| W_j) \cdot s + w_j$, and issues $(W_j, \bar{s}_j)$ to S_j.

Step S3. S_j can obtain its private key with $s_j = \bar{s}_j + k_j$ and verify the validity of the message by computing $\text{Pub}_j = s_j \cdot P = H(\text{SID}_j \| W_j) \cdot P_{\text{pub}} + W_j$.

If the equation holds, the issued values are valid, and vice versa.

4.2. User Registration Phase. Supposing that the user U_i wants to get service granted only from S_j, he/she needs to register to the same RC that S_j did, by submitting his identity ID_i and password PW_i to RC. Then, RC returns the smart card back to U_i. The communication between U_i and RC is through a secure channel. The steps are performed as follows.

Step U1. U_i freely chooses a password PW_i and a random number b_i to compute $A_i = H(\text{PW}_i \| b_i)$ and $I_i = H(\text{ID}_i \| b_i)$. Then, U_i submits (ID_i, A_i, I_i) to RC for user registration via a secure channel.

Step U2. RC calculates

$$B_i = s \cdot H(\text{ID}_i \| I_i) + x,$$
$$C_i = B_i \oplus H(A_i),$$
$$D_i = B_i \oplus H(\text{ID}_i) \oplus A_i,$$
$$X = x \cdot P,$$
$$E_i = H(\text{ID}_i \| A_i) \cdot P - X,$$

stores $(C_i, D_i, E_i, H(\cdot))$ in U_i's smart card, and submits it to U_i. Then U_i keys b_i into the smart card.

4.3. Login Phase. When U_i wants to login to the server S_j, he/she first inserts his/her own smart card to a card reader and then inputs the identity ID_i and password PW_i. The login details with respect to this smart card are as follows.

Step L1. The smart card computes $A_i' = H(\text{PW}_i \| b_i)$, $B_i' = D_i \oplus H(\text{ID}_i) \oplus A_i'$, and $C_i' = B_i' \oplus H(A_i')$ and checks whether

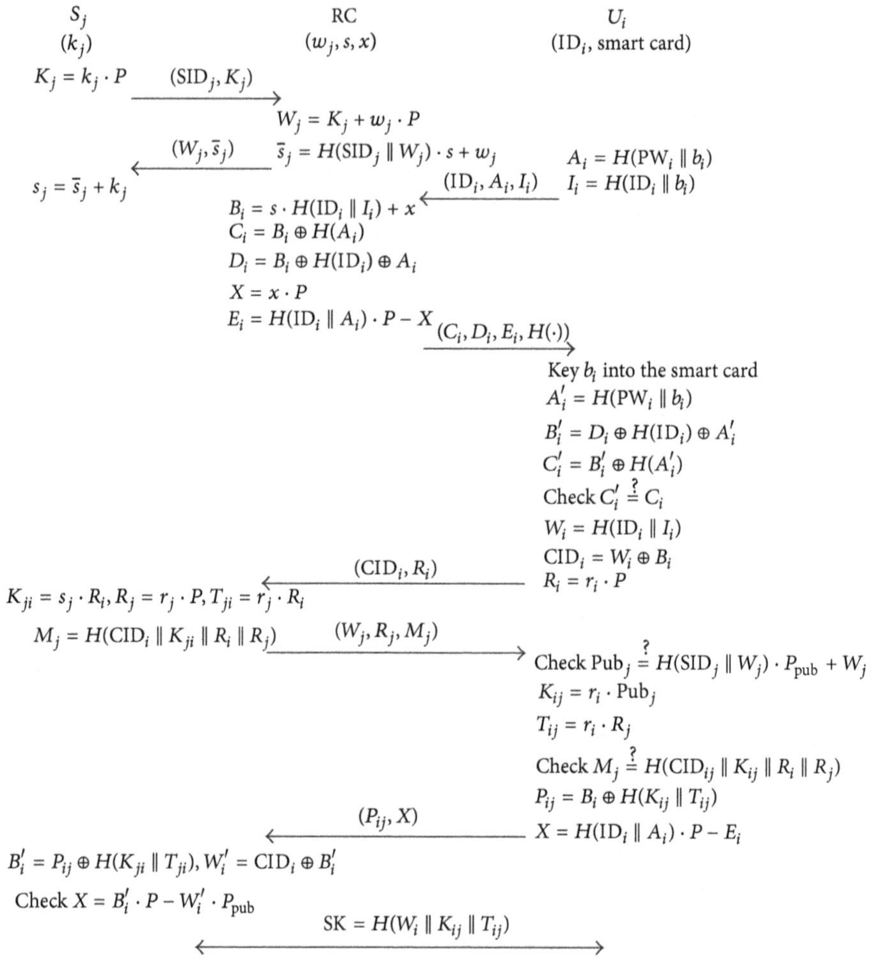

$$S_j \qquad\qquad RC \qquad\qquad U_i$$
$$(k_j) \qquad\qquad (w_j, s, x) \qquad\qquad (\text{ID}_i, \text{smart card})$$

$K_j = k_j \cdot P \quad \xrightarrow{\;(\text{SID}_j, K_j)\;}$

$\qquad\qquad W_j = K_j + w_j \cdot P$

$\qquad\quad \xleftarrow{\;(W_j, \bar{s}_j)\;} \bar{s}_j = H(\text{SID}_j \parallel W_j) \cdot s + w_j \qquad A_i = H(\text{PW}_i \parallel b_i)$

$s_j = \bar{s}_j + k_j \qquad\qquad\qquad\qquad \xleftarrow{\;(\text{ID}_i, A_i, I_i)\;} I_i = H(\text{ID}_i \parallel b_i)$

$\qquad\qquad B_i = s \cdot H(\text{ID}_i \parallel I_i) + x$

$\qquad\qquad C_i = B_i \oplus H(A_i)$

$\qquad\qquad D_i = B_i \oplus H(\text{ID}_i) \oplus A_i$

$\qquad\qquad X = x \cdot P$

$\qquad\qquad E_i = H(\text{ID}_i \parallel A_i) \cdot P - X \xrightarrow{\;(C_i, D_i, E_i, H(\cdot))\;}$

$\qquad\qquad\qquad\qquad\qquad\qquad\qquad\qquad\text{Key } b_i \text{ into the smart card}$

$\qquad\qquad\qquad\qquad\qquad\qquad\qquad\qquad A_i' = H(\text{PW}_i \parallel b_i)$

$\qquad\qquad\qquad\qquad\qquad\qquad\qquad\qquad B_i' = D_i \oplus H(\text{ID}_i) \oplus A_i'$

$\qquad\qquad\qquad\qquad\qquad\qquad\qquad\qquad C_i' = B_i' \oplus H(A_i')$

$\qquad\qquad\qquad\qquad\qquad\qquad\qquad\qquad \text{Check } C_i' \overset{?}{=} C_i$

$\qquad\qquad\qquad\qquad\qquad\qquad\qquad\qquad W_i = H(\text{ID}_i \parallel I_i)$

$\qquad\qquad\qquad\qquad\qquad\qquad\qquad\qquad \text{CID}_i = W_i \oplus B_i$

$K_{ji} = s_j \cdot R_i, R_j = r_j \cdot P, T_{ji} = r_j \cdot R_i \quad \xleftarrow{\;(\text{CID}_i, R_i)\;} R_i = r_i \cdot P$

$\quad M_j = H(\text{CID}_i \parallel K_{ji} \parallel R_i \parallel R_j) \xrightarrow{\;(W_j, R_j, M_j)\;}$

$\qquad\qquad\qquad\qquad\qquad\qquad\qquad\qquad \text{Check Pub}_j \overset{?}{=} H(\text{SID}_j \parallel W_j) \cdot P_{\text{pub}} + W_j$

$\qquad\qquad\qquad\qquad\qquad\qquad\qquad\qquad K_{ij} = r_i \cdot \text{Pub}_j$

$\qquad\qquad\qquad\qquad\qquad\qquad\qquad\qquad T_{ij} = r_i \cdot R_j$

$\qquad\qquad\qquad\qquad\qquad\qquad\qquad\qquad \text{Check } M_j \overset{?}{=} H(\text{CID}_{ij} \parallel K_{ij} \parallel R_i \parallel R_j)$

$\qquad\qquad\qquad\qquad\qquad\qquad\qquad\qquad P_{ij} = B_i \oplus H(K_{ij} \parallel T_{ij})$

$\qquad\qquad\qquad\quad \xleftarrow{\;(P_{ij}, X)\;} X = H(\text{ID}_i \parallel A_i) \cdot P - E_i$

$B_i' = P_{ij} \oplus H(K_{ji} \parallel T_{ji}), W_i' = \text{CID}_i \oplus B_i'$

$\qquad \text{Check } X = B_i' \cdot P - W_i' \cdot P_{\text{pub}}$

$\qquad\qquad\qquad\qquad\quad \xleftrightarrow{\;SK = H(W_i \parallel K_{ij} \parallel T_{ij})\;}$

FIGURE 1: The proposed scheme.

$C_i' = C_i$. If the answer is yes, it means that the smart card matches to U_i.

Step L2. The smart card generates a random value $r_i \in \mathbb{Z}_q^*$ and computes

$$W_i = H(\text{ID}_i \parallel I_i),$$
$$\text{CID}_i = W_i \oplus B_i,$$
$$R_i = r_i \cdot P.$$

Step L3. The smart card submits the login request message (CID_i, R_i) to S_j over a public channel.

4.4. Verification Phase. After receiving the login request message from U_i, S_j performs the following tasks to authenticate the user.

Step V1. S_j checks whether CID_i conforms to the fixed format. If the format is wrong, S_j outputs the reject message; otherwise it calculates

$$K_{ji} = s_j \cdot R_i,$$
$$R_j = r_j \cdot P,$$

$$T_{ji} = r_j \cdot R_i,$$

$$M_j = H(\text{CID}_i \parallel K_{ji} \parallel R_i \parallel R_j),$$

where r_j is a random value, chosen by S_j. Then S_j sends $(\text{SID}_j, W_j, R_j, M_j)$ to U_i.

Step V2. Receiving the message (W_j, R_j, M_j), U_i first verifies the public key of S_j by the equation $\text{Pub}_j = H(\text{SID}_j \parallel W_j) \cdot P_{\text{pub}} + W_j$. Only under the case the equation holds, U_i continues to calculate $K_{ij} = r_i \cdot \text{Pub}_j$, $T_{ij} = r_i \cdot R_j$. Then U_i needs to check whether $M_j \overset{?}{=} H(\text{CID}_{ij} \parallel K_{ij} \parallel R_i \parallel R_j)$. When the verification can pass, U_i authenticates S_j and computes

$$P_{ij} = B_i \oplus H(K_{ij} \parallel T_{ij}),$$

$$X = H(\text{ID}_i \parallel A_i) \cdot P - E_i.$$

Then U_i transmits (P_{ij}, X) to S_j.

Step V3. Next, S_j undoes $B_i' = P_{ij} \oplus H(K_{ji} \parallel T_{ji})$, $W_i' = \text{CID}_i \oplus B_i'$ and examines $X \overset{?}{=} B_i' \cdot P - W_i' \cdot P_{\text{pub}}$. If it is not the case,

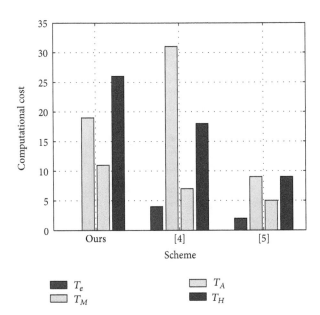

FIGURE 2: Performance comparison between our scheme and others.

S_j rejects the message and stops the session. Otherwise, S_j successfully authenticates U_i.

Step V4. Finally, the user U_i and the service server S_j agree on a common session key as

$$SK = H(W_i \parallel K_{ij} \parallel T_{ij}).$$

4.5. Password Change Phase. The password change phase is invoked when the user wants to change his/her password PW_i to a new password PW_i^*. The user first inserts his/her smart card into a card reader and enters ID_i, PW_i. The smart card computes $A_i = H(PW_i \parallel b_i)$, $B_i' = D_i \oplus H(ID_i) \oplus A_i$ and $C_i' = B_i' \oplus H(A_i)$. Then, the smart card checks if the C_i' is the same as C_i. If both values are the same, the user is asked to input a new password PW_i^*. The smart card calculates new information $A_i^* = H(PW_i^* \parallel b_i)$, $C_i^* = C_i \oplus H(A_i) \oplus H(A_i^*)$, $D_i^* = D_i \oplus A_i \oplus A_i^*$, $E_i^* = H(ID_i \parallel A_i^*) \cdot P + E_i - H(ID_i \parallel A_i) \cdot P$. At last, the smart card replaces C_i, D_i, E_i with the new C_i^*, D_i^*, E_i^* to accomplish changing password. In this phase, RC is not needed to participate and the user can freely complete changing password by himself.

5. Analysis of Our Scheme

In this section, we first analyze the functionality features of our proposed scheme based on the requirements of the remote user authentication for multiserver architecture, which have been presented in Section 1. Then we evaluate the performance of the proposed scheme and make comparisons with some related works [8, 9, 11, 12, 17, 18].

5.1. No Repetitive Registration. In our scheme, before the user wants to login to the server under multiserver environment, they must run the user registration with his/her information

to the registration center. Then, the user can access to all the service without submitting registration request once again.

5.2. No Verification Table. Throughout the protocol process, it is not difficult to find that RC and S_j have no need to maintain any verification or password table, which can cost much and whose leakage may cause serious disruption. Meanwhile, our scheme does not need to store the user's password or public key with certificate, too.

5.3. Mutual Authentication with Session Key Agreement. In the verification phase of the proposed scheme, the service server S_j can authenticate the validity of U_i by checking if $X = B_i' \cdot P - W_i' \cdot P_{pub}$ holds. U_i can verify the public key of S_j $Pub_j = H(SID_j \parallel W_j) \cdot P_{pub} + W_j$ with W_j to confirm that S_j is the objective service server; meanwhile check the equation $M_j' = M_j$ to affirm that the login message is received by S_j. Only when all previous equations are satisfied, the session continues and the communication parties agree on a shared session key $SK = H(W_i \parallel K_{ij} \parallel T_{ij})$. For the aforementioned analysis, our scheme can achieve mutual authentication with session key agreement.

5.4. No Synchronization Clock. In our scheme, both the user and the service server employ the random points R_i, R_j to interactive with each other. The timestamp does not appear in the proposed scheme; therefore the synchronization clock problem can also be abstained in the session key.

5.5. Anonymity. In the user registration phase, the identity of the remote user can be protected from disclosure by the secure channel between U_i and RC. In the login and authentication phase, U_i's identity is submitted with CID_i substituting ID_i, nobody can learn the user's real identity, and S_j can only verify the user's validity cannot obtain the real ID_i with the received message. To general adversary, he/she can extract the smart card and intercept the login message, but he can do nothing to crack the user's identity due to the resistance to collision of the hash function. Therefore, we claim that our scheme can provide the user anonymity.

5.6. Security of the Session Key

(1) *Perfect Forward Secrecy and Backward Secrecy.* In this scheme, the session key is established by W_i, K_{ij}, T_{ij}, where K_{ij} and T_{ij} rely on the random values r_i and r_j. r_i and r_j are independently generated in each session, are also changed for each authentication phase and are not correlated. The adversary cannot use current session key to derive forward and backward session key. Hence, we claim that our scheme achieves perfect forward secrecy and backward secrecy.

(2) *Known Session Key Security.* In this scheme, the session key $SK = H(W_i \parallel K_{ij} \parallel T_{ij})$ is composed of W_i, K_{ij} and T_{ij}. Assume that the adversary can seize a session key SK_{mn}; he cannot obtain the parameters W_m, K_{mn}, and T_{mn} attributed to the one-way hash function $H(\cdot)$. Since K_{mn} and T_{mn} consist of R_m, R_n, which are

independent for each session, no session keys rely on each other. Furthermore, though the adversary can intercept the current transmitted message R'_m, R'_n, he cannot compute the new session key SK'_{mn}'s components K'_{mn} without the server's private key or T'_{mn} due to the CDH problem's difficulty.

(3) *No Key Control.* In this scheme, the session key consists of W_i, K_{ij}, T_{ij}, where partial parameters K_{ij}, T_{ij} are generated by Diffie-Hellman key exchange form ; thereby the fairness of the session key can be guaranteed. More specifically, $K_{ij} = s_j \cdot R_i = r_i \cdot \text{Pub}_j$, $T_{ij} = r_j \cdot R_i = r_i \cdot R_j$, R_i and R_j are respectively provided by the user and the server; therefore either party is in vain attempting to preselect or control the session key.

5.7. Various Common Attacks. Our proposed remote user authentication scheme for multiserver architecture cannot only meet the previous security features, but also be against various known attacks, such as impersonation attack, and stolen smart card attack. We will discuss the following extra four attacks, the others can refer to [11, 18].

(1) *Impersonation Attack.* If an adversary tries to impersonate as a legitimate user to log into the server, he/she must first forge a valid login request message (CID_i, R_i). However, the adversary cannot compute a new and legal login message without knowing ID_i or B_i. Suppose that the adversary can steal the smart card of the user U_i by virtue of some approaches, he is still unable to calculate B_i for the reason that he has no information about A_i and ID_i. Moreover, even if the adversary utilizes (CID_i, R_i) to log into S_j, he cannot pass the verification $X \overset{?}{=} B'_i \cdot P - W'_i \cdot P_{pub}$ because he is unable to provide correct P_{ij} without B_i or K_{ij}. The adversary cannot obtain the valid session key. Under the situation, our proposed scheme can withstand the impersonation attack.

(2) *Stolen Smart Card Attack.* We assume that U_i's smart card is stolen or lost; the adversary picks it and has the ability to breach the information stored in the smart card $(C_i, D_i, E_i, H(\cdot), b_i)$. Yet on the one hand, it is impossible to guess A_i and ID_i correctly at the same time, on the other hand, s and x are, respectively, private key and secret value of RC, so the adversary cannot derive B_i. Consequently, the adversary cannot fabricate a valid login message or compute the session key. That is the reason that our proposed protocol is secure against the stolen smart card attack.

(3) *Off-Line Password Guessing Attack.* Assume that the adversary guesses a password PW' from the dictionary; he can compute $A_i = H(PW' \| b_i)$, $B_i = C_i \oplus H(A_i)$ but fails to calculate other information without ID_i or K_{ij}. The adversary cannot examine whether the guessed password PW' is correct without comparing parameters. Hence, the adversary can extract the smart card information and intercept the transmitted message in public channel, but our proposed scheme can resist the off-line password guessing attack.

(4) *Man-in-the-Middle Attack.* When an adversary wants to perform the man-in-the-middle attack, he can intercept the login message, communicate, and share the session key with the server. In the proposed scheme, even if the adversary gets the message in public channel, he cannot calculate W_i, K_{ij}, or T_{ij} without ID_i or other random values r_i, r_j. Consequently, our scheme can resist the man-in-the-middle attack.

(5) *Server Spoofing Attack.* When a valid but malicious server S_m wants to cheat U_i on behalf of S_j and obtain the session key, he needs to know both the witness and private key of S_j. In our scheme, S_m cannot provide the correct witness, and the user U_i cannot pass the server's public key verification. Even if S_m intercepts W_j, he cannot check the equation $X = B'_i \cdot P - W'_i \cdot P_{pub}$ since he does not obtain K_{ji} without knowing the private key s_j. Finally, the adversary fails to share the session key with the user U_i. Therefore, our scheme can resist the server spoofing attack.

5.8. Local Password Verification. In our scheme, U_i can account whether the used smart card matches with himself by checking $C'_i = C_i$ before logging into S_j, and thus accomplish the user password verification locally. Through the previous equation, U_i can avoid network resource wasting caused by wrong password. Because until the authentication phase S_j can authenticate user's validity and password appropriateness; in other words, wrong password cannot be detected until the authentication phase. Therefore, our scheme can achieve local password verification.

At last, the functionality comparisons among our and other previously proposed schemes, such as [8, 9, 11, 12, 17, 18], are listed in Table 2. In particular, we can clearly see that the other schemes do not assist in the impersonation attack except our proposed scheme. Thus, it is obvious that our proposed scheme is superior to the others in accordance with all of essential comparative items. In addition, unlike the other related public key-based multiserver authentication schemes [17, 18], ours can achieve the user anonymity and local password verification. On the whole, our proposal is the only one that can satisfy all the functionalities for the multiserver architecture.

5.9. Performance. Under multiserver architecture, the computational cost is a key issue to evaluate whether a remote user authentication scheme is efficient because of mobile devices' constrained resources and computing capability. Before analyzing the computational cost of each phase, define some notations and equivalence relationship first:

(i) T_e: the time to compute a bilinear pairing map;

(ii) T_M: the time to compute a point multiplication on the elliptic curve group;

(iii) T_A: the time to compute a point addition on the elliptic curve group;

TABLE 2: Functionality and security comparison with the related schemes.

Functionality	Ours	[18]	[17]	[12]	[11]	[9]	[8]
No repetitive registration	Y	Y	Y	Y	Y	Y	Y
No verification table	Y	Y	Y	Y	Y	Y	Y
Mutual authentication with key agreement	Y	Y	N	N	Y	N	N
No synchronization clock	Y	Y	N	Y	Y	N	Y
Change password freely	Y	Y	Y	Y	Y	Y	Y
Anonymity	Y	N	N	Y	Y	Y	Y
Perfect forward and backward secrecy	Y	Y	N	N	Y	N	N
No key control	Y	Y	Y	Y	Y	Y	Y
Known session key security	Y	Y	Y	Y	Y	Y	Y
Impersonation attack	Y	N	N	N	N	N	N
Stolen smart card attack	Y	Y	N	N	N	N	N
Off-line password guessing attack	Y	N	N	Y	N	N	N
Man-in-the-middle attack	Y	Y	N	Y	Y	N	N
Server spoofing attack	Y	N	N	Y	Y	Y	N
Local password verification	Y	N	N	Y	Y	Y	Y

TABLE 3: Cost comparison with the related schemes.

Phase	Ours	[18]	[17]
Server registration	$5T_M + 4T_A + 2T_H$	$5T_M + 4T_A + 2T_H$	—
User registration	$2T_M + 2T_A + 6T_H$	$3T_M + 2T_H$	$3T_M + 2T_H$
Login	$T_M + 4T_H$	$3T_M + T_A + 3T_H$	$3T_M + 2T_H$
Verification	$9T_M + 3T_A + 6T_H$	$2T_e + 8T_M + 2T_A + 5T_H$	$2T_e + T_M + T_A + 2T_H$
Password change	$2T_M + 2T_A + 8T_H$	$2T_e + 15T_M + 6T_H$	$2T_M + T_H$
Total	$19T_M + 11T_A + 26T_H$	$4T_e + 31T_M + 7T_A + 18T_H$	$2T_e + 9T_M + 5T_A + 9T_H$

(iv) T_H: the time to compute a hash function;

(a) $T_e = 20T_M$;

(b) $T_M = 6T_A$.

The XOR operation, modular multiplication, and modular addition operation are negligible during evaluating the performance. In the following, we will give the computational cost of five phases individually. In the server registration phase, the computational cost is $5T_M + 4T_A + 2T_H$. The user registration phase consumes $2T_M + 2T_A + 6T_H$. When the user logs into the server, it costs $T_M + 4T_H$. During verification of each other between the server and the user, $9T_M + 3T_A + 6T_H$ is demanded. The computational cost of the password change phase is $2T_M + 2T_A + 8T_H$. The detailed cost comparisons with the related authentication schemes [17, 18] are illustrated in Table 3. At the same time, we show the implementation result in Figure 2, which can show the computational cost contrast more intuitively. Table 3 and Figure 2 can clearly indicate that our proposal needs no pairing operation, while [18] contains $4T_e$ and [17] contains $2T_e$. Because the relative computational cost of a pairing is approximately 20 times higher than that of the point multiplication over elliptic curve group, we can find that the computational cost of ours is obviously much less than that of others by removing pairing operation.

From Tables 2 and 3, we can make a conclusion that our remote authentication scheme has more security features and lower computational cost among the existing related works, which satisfies the requirements for the multiserver architecture.

6. Conclusions

An anonymous and efficient remote user authentication scheme for the multiserver architecture is proposed in this paper and the self-certified public keys are employed. Our scheme can satisfy all of the requirements needed for achieving secure authentication in multiserver environments, as compared with the previously proposed schemes. Moreover, the proposal succeeds to both achieve the user's identity anonymity and remove the pairing operation, which makes that the proposed scheme can provide more advantages and be more practical for the actual applications. Additionally, we analyze the security and performance of our proposal and make comparisons with other related works. From these analysis and comparisons, we can reach a conclusion that our proposed scheme owns more functionalities and attains higher efficiency.

Acknowledgments

This work is supported by NSFC (Grant nos. 61272057, 61202434, 61170270, 61100203, 61003286, and 61121061) and the Fundamental Research Funds for the Central Universities (Grant nos. 2012RC0612 and 2011YB01).

References

[1] C. I. Fan, Y. C. Chan, and Z. K. Zhang, "Robust remote authentication scheme with smart cards," *Computers and Security*, vol. 24, no. 8, pp. 619–628, 2005.

[2] S. W. Lee, H. S. Kim, and K. Y. Yoo, "Efficient nonce-based remote user authentication scheme using smart cards," *Applied Mathematics and Computation*, vol. 167, no. 1, pp. 355–361, 2005.

[3] L. H. Li, I. C. Lin, and M. S. Hwang, "A remote password authentication scheme for multiserver architecture using neural networks," *IEEE Transactions on Neural Networks*, vol. 12, no. 6, pp. 1498–1504, 2001.

[4] C. C. Chang and J. S. Lee, "An efficient and secure multi-server password authentication scheme using smart cards," in *Proceedings of the International Conference on Cyberworlds (CW '04)*, pp. 417–422, Tokyo, Japan, November 2004.

[5] W. S. Juang, "Efficient multi-server password authenticated key agreement using smart cards," *IEEE Transactions on Consumer Electronics*, vol. 50, no. 1, pp. 251–255, 2004.

[6] J. L. Tsai, "Efficient multi-server authentication scheme based on one-way hash function without verification table," *Computers and Security*, vol. 27, no. 3-4, pp. 115–121, 2008.

[7] W. J. Tsaur, C. C. Wu, and W. B. Lee, "A smart card-based remote scheme for password authentication in multi-server Internet services," *Computer Standards and Interfaces*, vol. 27, no. 1, pp. 39–51, 2004.

[8] Y. P. Liao and S. S. Wang, "A secure dynamic ID based remote user authentication scheme for multi-server environment," *Computer Standards and Interfaces*, vol. 31, no. 1, pp. 24–29, 2009.

[9] H. C. Hsiang and W. K. Shih, "Improvement of the secure dynamic ID based remote user authentication scheme for multi-server environment," *Computer Standards and Interfaces*, vol. 31, no. 6, pp. 1118–1123, 2009.

[10] C. C. Lee, T. H. Lin, and R. X. Chang, "A secure dynamic ID based remote user authentication scheme for multi-server environment using smart cards," *Expert Systems with Applications*, vol. 38, no. 11, pp. 13863–13870, 2011.

[11] X. Li, Y. P. Xiong, J. Ma, and W. D. Wang, "An efficient and security dynamic identity based authentication protocol for multi-server architecture using smart cards," *Journal of Network and Computer Applications*, vol. 35, no. 2, pp. 763–769, 2012.

[12] S. K. Sood, A. K. Sarje, and K. Singh, "A secure dynamic identity based authentication protocol for multi-server architecture," *Journal of Network and Computer Applications*, vol. 34, no. 2, pp. 609–618, 2011.

[13] M. L. Das, A. Saxena, V. P. Gulati, and D. B. Phatak, "A novel remote user authentication scheme using bilinear pairings," *Computers and Security*, vol. 25, no. 3, pp. 184–189, 2006.

[14] T. Goriparthi, M. L. Das, and A. Saxena, "An improved bilinear pairing based remote user authentication scheme," *Computer Standards and Interfaces*, vol. 31, no. 1, pp. 181–185, 2009.

[15] Z. T. Jia, Y. Zhang, H. Shao, Y. Z. Lin, and J. Wang, "A remote user authentication scheme using bilinear pairings and ECC," in *Proceedings of the 6th International Conference on Intelligent Systems Design and Applications (ISDA '06)*, pp. 1091–1094, Jinan, China, October 2006.

[16] W. S. Juang and W. K. Nien, "Efficient password authenticated key agreement using bilinear pairings," *Mathematical and Computer Modelling*, vol. 47, no. 11-12, pp. 1238–1245, 2008.

[17] Y. M. Tseng, T. Y. Wu, and J. D. Wu, "A pairing-based user authentication scheme for wireless clients with smart cards," *Informatica*, vol. 19, no. 2, pp. 285–302, 2008.

[18] Y. P. Liao and C. M. Hsiao, "A novel multiserver remote user authentication scheme using selfcertified public keys for mobile clients," *Future Generation Computer Systems*, vol. 29, no. 3, pp. 886–900, 2013.

[19] D. Boneh and M. Franklin, "Identity-based encryption from the weil pairing," *SIAM Journal on Computing*, vol. 32, no. 3, pp. 586–615, 2003.

[20] J. H. Yang and C. C. Chang, "An ID-based remote mutual authentication with key agreement scheme for mobile devices on elliptic curve cryptosystem," *Computers and Security*, vol. 28, no. 3-4, pp. 138–143, 2009.

[21] Y. P. Liao and S. S. Wang, "A new secure password authenticated key agreement scheme for SIP using self-certified public keys on elliptic curves," *Computer Communications*, vol. 33, no. 3, pp. 372–380, 2010.

[22] W. J. Tsaur, "Several security schemes constructed using ECC-based self-certified public key cryptosystems," *Applied Mathematics and Computation*, vol. 168, no. 1, pp. 447–464, 2005.

13

A Cyber-ITS Framework for Massive Traffic Data Analysis Using Cyber Infrastructure

Yingjie Xia,[1,2] **Jia Hu,**[2] **and Michael D. Fontaine**[2]

[1] *Hangzhou Institute of Service Engineering, Hangzhou Normal University, 222 Wenyi Road, Hangzhou 310012, China*
[2] *Department of Civil and Environmental Engineering, University of Virginia, 351 McCormick Road, Charlottesville, VA 22903, USA*

Correspondence should be addressed to Yingjie Xia; xiayingjie@zju.edu.cn

Academic Editors: A. Chatzigeorgiou and A. Puliafito

Traffic data is commonly collected from widely deployed sensors in urban areas. This brings up a new research topic, data-driven intelligent transportation systems (ITSs), which means to integrate heterogeneous traffic data from different kinds of sensors and apply it for ITS applications. This research, taking into consideration the significant increase in the amount of traffic data and the complexity of data analysis, focuses mainly on the challenge of solving data-intensive and computation-intensive problems. As a solution to the problems, this paper proposes a Cyber-ITS framework to perform data analysis on Cyber Infrastructure (CI), by nature parallel-computing hardware and software systems, in the context of ITS. The techniques of the framework include data representation, domain decomposition, resource allocation, and parallel processing. All these techniques are based on data-driven and application-oriented models and are organized as a component-and-workflow-based model in order to achieve technical interoperability and data reusability. A case study of the Cyber-ITS framework is presented later based on a traffic state estimation application that uses the fusion of massive Sydney Coordinated Adaptive Traffic System (SCATS) data and GPS data. The results prove that the Cyber-ITS-based implementation can achieve a high accuracy rate of traffic state estimation and provide a significant computational speedup for the data fusion by parallel computing.

1. Introduction

The quantity and quality of sensor data collected dedicatedly for transportation systems have increased tremendously in the past few decades. This trend will continue in the foreseeable future and leads to a new research direction on traffic data analysis in intelligent transportation systems (ITS). Intelligent data analysis, supported by mathematical algorithms, is becoming an important tool for scientific discovery and decision making in many fields, for example, bioinformatics, geographic information systems, and ecology. By integrating intelligent data analysis into ITS, a research direction named data-driven ITS emerges to focus on algorithmic and intelligent analysis on multisensor heterogeneous traffic data. This new direction leads to a revolution in ITS development, which adopts vision, multi-source, and learning-based traffic data processing algorithms for performance optimization [1]. In recent years, data-driven ITS is becoming more feasible in

ITS since a variety of traffic sensors are widely deployed in the urban and suburban areas.

As data size and algorithmic complexity increase, data-driven ITS faces significant challenges in terms of solving computation-intensive problems. These problems lead to excessive lag in the execution time of the applications. A solution is proposed to migrate computation-intensive ITS applications from the conventional single-CPU architecture to the emerging Cyber Infrastructure (CI). CI is by nature a parallel-computing architecture and software environment, which is urgently needed by applications that must be run in real time.

In this paper, a new Cyber ITS framework is proposed to synergistically integrate data analysis algorithms into ITS and realize efficient processing of massive traffic data sets using CI. This framework is urgently needed for the following reasons: (i) ITS demands transformative breakthroughs to solve computationally intensive data processing problems; (ii) CI is now increasingly accessible to ITS and data analysis [2];

and (iii) some theoretical investigation on using CI for ITS has been conducted [3]. Cyber-ITS is technically designed to provide a traffic data and operation sharing framework based on parallel computing techniques. The framework is also designed following the component-and-workflow-based model, which enables different applications to assemble their relevant functionality components into workflows.

The rest of the paper is organized as follows. The next section reviews the past research relating data-driven ITS and CI. The design of the new Cyber-ITS framework is then introduced, and a case study of traffic state estimation using parallelized traffic data fusion is presented. Afterwards, the accuracy and efficiency tests are conducted on the studied case. Finally, conclusions and recommendations for future research are discussed.

2. Related Work

Conventional ITS is evolving into data-driven ITS, which focuses on processing data collected from multiple traffic sensors. Depending on the types of data and the fashion that the data is processed, the data-driven ITS is categorized into three types: vision-driven ITS, multisource-driven ITS, and learning-driven ITS. Vision-driven ITS takes video cameras as traffic sensors, which collect data for some representative applications, such as traffic object detection [4] and recognition [5], traffic behavior analysis [6], and vehicle trajectory construction [7]. However, vision-driven ITS suffers from some constraints, for example, weather, brightness, and camera positions. Therefore, to overcome the weakness of vision-driven ITS, multisource-driven ITS proposes to use multiple types of sensors, so that different kinds of sensor, can compensate each other's weaknesses. For example, the loop detectors deployed in-pavement are robust to environmental constraints, but have the drawbacks of a high failure ratio and potential inaccurate calculation of traffic state [8]. On the contrary, probe vehicles (e.g. GPS data) can provide true point-to-point travel times, but small sample size could result in poor statistical representation, and probes could be subject to errors in the map-matching process [9]. Multisource-driven ITS fuses heterogeneous data from video sensors, loop detectors, and probe vehicles to improve the accuracy and completeness of traffic data [10]. No matter what kinds of traffic sensors are used, it is always required to have the corresponding learning-based analytical tools to process data. This leads to the learning-driven ITS. Some commonly used learning algorithms, including rough set theory [11], online learning [12], fuzzy logic [13], are used to extract intrinsic rules from historical and real-time traffic data. These kinds of work always run into challenges of computational efficiency when dealing with large data sets. Luckily, this problem can be effectively solved by algorithmic parallelization executed on CI resources [14].

CI has been widely adopted in computer systems for its improved computing capability and cost effectiveness. Multinode, many-core, and general purpose graphics processing unit (GPGPU) are three major architectures of CI. Above the underlying hardware, the application-oriented

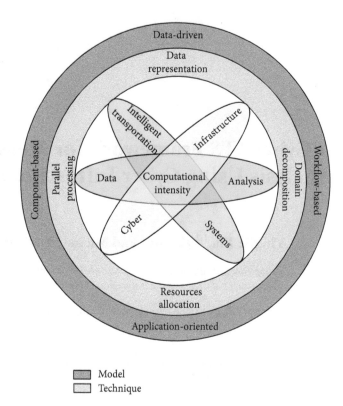

FIGURE 1: The Cyber-ITS framework synthesizes CI and data analysis in the context of ITS.

techniques, such as data decomposition [15] to generate multiple computing tasks, task scheduling to allocate computing nodes, nodes communication for tasks interaction, and computation synchronization [16] for results collection are leveraged to support computation-intensive and data-intensive problems solving. These techniques are integrated as a piece of middleware, which delivers interoperable and reusable services for efficient use of CI resources [17].

Recently, some research on the combination of data-driven ITS and CI has been published, such as parallel implementation of transportation network models [18], computationally efficient online identification of traffic control intervention measures [19], parallel traffic control and management [20], and Message Passing Interface (MPI)-based parallelized fusion for traffic state estimation [21]. However, these studies are just for specific applications and cannot be extended to build a generic framework. Nevertheless, current applications all show the need for data sharing and applications integration. Therefore, this research seeks to develop Cyber ITS as a framework that can perform heterogeneous data analysis on CI in the context of ITS.

3. Cyber-ITS Framework

The Cyber-ITS framework is designed to synthesize CI and data analysis in the context of ITS, as shown in Figure 1. These three fields are interlinked on computational intensity, which plays a central role in the framework. On the technique level, a collection of technical tools are equipped to complete the tasks of data representation, domain decomposition,

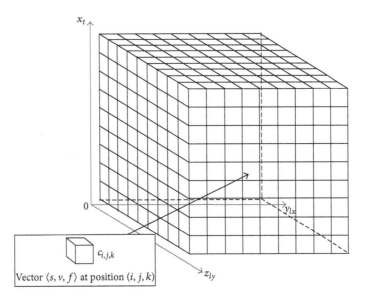

FIGURE 2: ITS computational domain projects heterogeneous traffic data into three-dimensional space.

resources allocation, and parallel processing based on the computational intensity. These tools, such as ITS computational domain, octree-based decomposition, and max-min tasks scheduling, can improve the computing performance of traffic data analysis by parallel computing. The techniques are organized as the models on the outside layer in Figure 1, such as data-driven, application-oriented, and component-and-workflow-based models. The details about computational intensity, techniques, and models of the Cyber-ITS framework are specified as follows.

3.1. Computational Intensity. Computational intensity is fundamental to the Cyber-ITS framework. The definition of computational intensity is derived from the traditional computational complexity theory, which focuses on assessing the algorithmic complexity in theoretical computer science [22]. However, the complexity theory only evaluates the algorithmic structure without adequately capturing the spatiotemporal characteristics of ITS data analysis. These characteristics, such as spatiotemporal clustering, neighborhood, autocorrelation, and interaction dynamics of massive traffic data, need to be considered in the transformed computational intensity and therefore can reinforce the algorithmic complexity in evaluating computing time, memory, and input/output (I/O).

Again, computational intensity is the most important measurement in this framework. Supposing a computation-intensive ITS application needs to be completed in real time, it can be parallelized to execute on CI. The parallelization work first requires the application to be divided into multiple computing tasks. Since the efficiency of parallel computing is determined by the agreement between tasks loads and CI computing capabilities, the computational intensity is regarded as the right measurement that can quantify tasks loads during the task division. The details about the computational intensity will be specified in a case study later in this paper.

3.2. Techniques

3.2.1. Data Representation. Before addressing computational intensity, the explicit data representation which takes into account the characteristics of data and operations needs to be investigated. The Cyber-ITS framework adopts an ITS computational domain theory to formally represent heterogeneous data collected from multiple types of traffic sensors. ITS computational domain, which is derived from the idea of spatial computational domain [23], can project different types of traffic data from a high-dimensional data space to a three-dimensional spatiotemporal domain $D = (c_{i,j,k})$ consisting of a large amount of cells. For example, as shown in Figure 2, to represent traffic data from Sydney Coordinated Adaptive Traffic System (SCATS) detector loops and GPS probe vehicles, the cell $c_{i,j,k}$ can be defined as a vector $< s, v, f >$ at position (i, j, k). s denotes the sensor type which has two values: 0 and 1, 0 standing for SCATS and 1 standing for GPS. v and f denote the speed and flow of a road segment, respectively. The coordinates (i, j, k) indicate the discretized time and location indices of a road segment in the respective x_t, y_{lx}, and z_{ly} axes.

3.2.2. Domain Decomposition. When an application using data in the ITS computational domain requires CI resources for parallel computing, the domain first needs to be decomposed into subdomains to create multiple computing tasks. To maximize the efficiency of CI recourses, it is necessary to assure that the work loads are balanced among subdomains. The load balance of these subdomains can be achieved by using a technique called octree [24]. The octree would recursively divide a domain or subdomain into eight smaller subdomains until certain criterion on computational intensity achieving a threshold is met. In the octree-based ITS computational domain decomposition, computing time, memory, I/O, or their combination are the candidate criteria. The threshold is determined by dividing the computational

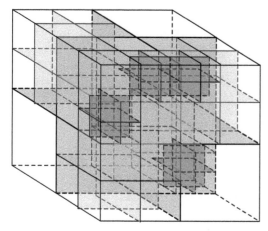

FIGURE 3: ITS computational domain is decomposed by octree.

FIGURE 4: A common portal system serves for Cyber-ITS-based traffic state estimation and traffic flow forecasting.

intensity of the whole computational domain by the maximum number of CI computing nodes. A demonstration of octree-based domain decomposition is shown in Figure 3.

3.2.3. Resource Allocation and Parallel Processing.

The subdomains generated from octree-based domain decomposition enable multiple computing tasks to be created from one single data-driven ITS application. These subdomains are then assigned to CI resources. As one of the most popular CI resources, a cluster computer consisting of a set of loosely connected computing nodes is commonly designed as a homogeneous architecture. Therefore, in the cluster computer the parallel processing on ITS computational domain can be implemented by simply allocating computing nodes to computing tasks on subdomains one by one. If the number of tasks is greater than the number of nodes, some algorithms are required to make the computing tasks scheduled to each node as load balanced as possible. For example, the max-min scheduling algorithm [25] combines a high-loaded task with a low-loaded task as one task package scheduled to one cluster node. This algorithm can avoid generating the weakest link in a chain of computational intensity assigned to each computing node and improve the efficiency of parallel processing in the Cyber-ITS framework.

3.3. Models

3.3.1. Data-Driven and Application-Oriented Models.

The aforementioned techniques of the Cyber-ITS framework are used in data-driven and application-oriented models. Diverse data-driven ITS applications share the same formally represented traffic data and utilize the corresponding methodology to process the data. For example, traffic state estimation [2] and real-time traffic flow forecasting [26] are two Cyber-ITS-based applications on ITS computational domain utilizing SCATS and GPS data. For traffic state estimation, the fusion of heterogeneous traffic data is adopted to combine the strength of different traffic sensors and compensates for their corresponding deficiencies. The fusion process consists of four steps: data smoothing, traffic state features estimation, features fusion, and decision making [3]. All four steps are

involved with the data processing on the ITS computational domain. For real-time traffic flow forecasting, SCATS and GPS data are first transformed to estimate the flow as the historical data. These data construct the covariance data matrix, which is used in the modal functions of spectral analysis. This method can predict the traffic flow of 1 hour and 15 minutes in the future within 15 minutes. The process of traffic flow forecasting consists of three steps: traffic flow estimation, covariance matrix construction, and online prediction by spectral analysis [26]. Similar to the previous traffic state estimation, all these three steps relate to the data processing on ITS computational domain. A common portal system of these two Cyber-ITS-based applications is shown in Figure 4. The portal system can provide basic input and output interfaces for the applications.

3.3.2. Component-and-Workflow-Based Model.

Diverse data-driven ITS applications not only share common formally represented data but also reuse several processing modules, for example, the features estimation in both traffic state estimation and traffic flow forecasting. The Cyber-ITS framework adopts a component-based model to encapsulate all processing modules as components. Some commonly used components are categorized as: (i) high-performance computing components encompassing CI-based parallel computing for ITS and data analysis; (ii) data-related components interacting with high-performance computing components to evaluate the computational intensity and process massive traffic data; (iii) collaboration components provide collaborative support for interactions management among different applications. These components can guide the implementation of data-driven ITS applications based on the Cyber-ITS framework.

The interoperable and reusable components can compose workflow to develop Cyber-ITS-based applications [27]. The workflow is based on flexible and scalable composition of individual components following common interfaces and standards [28]. For the example of traffic state estimation, the workflow is composed of high-performance computing components and data-related components to realize the capabilities of high-performance computing, traffic data processing, and features fusion. These components also need to be configured and managed in the specific contexts of ITS applications.

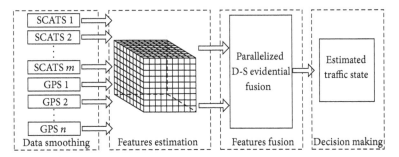

FIGURE 5: Flowchart of traffic state estimation consists of data smoothing, features estimation, features fusion, and decision making.

4. Case Study in Traffic State Estimation

4.1. Introduction. One typical data-driven ITS application, traffic state estimation by fusing SCATS and GPS data, is chosen as a case to study the implementation of the Cyber-ITS framework. The aforementioned four steps of traffic state estimation are flowcharted in Figure 5.

The data smoothing is first performed using Kalman filters to reduce the impact of noise on the collected data [9]. Then, the estimation algorithms are adopted to transform the filtered SCATS and GPS source data into traffic state features [14], such as speed and flow rate. These features are used to construct the ITS computational domain. Afterwards, the features from different kinds of sensors on one road segment are fused by Dempster-Shafer (D-S) evidence theory [29], which can overcome the conflict of estimated traffic states from different sensors. D-S evidence theory is a mathematical theory mostly used when combining evidence from different sources. The theory uses the belief function to express the probabilities of various combinations of evidence as degrees of belief. In traffic state estimation, the evidence is just the discretized values of traffic state estimated by different sensors, such as "congested," "medium," and "smooth." The algorithm of D-S evidential fusion on the discretized traffic state of a cell in the computational domain is shown as follows:

$$m\left(s_t\right) = m_1\left(s_{1,t}\right) \oplus m_2\left(s_{2,t}\right) \cdots \oplus m_X\left(s_{X,t}\right)$$

$$= \frac{\sum_{\cap_{i=1}^{X} s_{i,t}=s_t}\left(\prod_{i=1}^{X} m_i\left(s_{i,t}\right)\right)}{1 - \sum_{\cap_{i=1}^{X} s_{i,t}=\Phi}\left(\prod_{i=1}^{X} m_i\left(s_{i,t}\right)\right)}, \quad (1)$$

$$m_i\left(s_{i,t}\right) = \frac{n_{i,t}\left(s,d\right)}{n_{i,t}\left(d\right)}, \quad (2)$$

where $m(s_t)$ denotes basic probability assignment (BPA) of the specified traffic state s as the fusion result at time t, and $m_i(s_{i,t})$, $i = 1, 2, \ldots, X$ represents the BPA of this state from ith sensor at time t. The $m_i(s_{i,t})$ of one cell can be estimated by calculating the proportion which divides the number of its neighboring cells $n_{i,t}(s,d)$ within a specified distance d and having that state s by the number of all neighboring cells within d. Traffic state is determined following a typical decision rule in D-S evidence theory, maximum degree of belief [30].

4.2. Parallelized Fusion. As the amount of SCATS and GPS data is relatively high in the context of ITS applications, it is a great challenge to complete the data fusion on a real-time basis. In this study, data are collected from downtown Shanghai, where 2077 road segments are included. The GPS data are gathered from 8172 taxis belonging to Jinjiang and Bashi taxi companies, and the SCATS data are from 1836 loop detectors deployed on around 200 road intersections. All the collected data are uploaded to the server once every 2 minutes. The total number of SCATS and GPS data records during 10 minutes exceeds 50000; hence, it would take more than one hour to execute the aforementioned four steps of fusing traffic features by sequential computing. However, the real-time nature of the computation requires the calculation to take less than 10 minutes. Therefore, as a solution, data-centric parallelization of D-S evidential fusion is proposed to improve computing performance.

The parallelization process consists of (i) evaluating the computational intensity of data fusion by calculating CPU cycles; (ii) octree-based decomposition of the computational domain into subdomains according to the CPU cycle threshold; and (iii) scheduling subdomains to the computing nodes of a cluster computer for parallelized D-S evidential fusion. Specifically, as the computational intensity evaluation, the CPU cycles of data fusion on one road segment are counted as follows:

$$N_{CPU_{Cycles}} = BPA_{number} \times N_{neighbors} + BPA_{number} \\ \times \left(2 \times BPA_{number^2} + 2 \times BPA_{number^2}\right), \quad (3)$$

where $BPA_{number} \times N_{neighbors}$ indicates the number of CPU cycles for calculating the BPA values for all traffic states in (2), and two $2 \times BPA_{number^2}$, respectively, indicate the number of CPU cycles of $\sum_{\cap_{i=1}^{X} s_{i,t}=s_t}(\prod_{i=1}^{X} m_i(s_{i,t}))$ and $\sum_{\cap_{i=1}^{X} s_{i,t}=\Phi}(\prod_{i=1}^{X} m_i(s_{i,t}))$ in (1). The threshold is determined by dividing the number of CPU cycles of the whole computational domain by the number of cluster nodes [31], and the tasks scheduling is conducted using the max-min scheduling algorithm if the number of subdomains is greater than the number of computing nodes. In the above example, the CPU cycles of data fusion on one road segment are counted as follows:

$$N_{CPU_{Cycles}} = BPA_{number} \times N_{neighbors} + BPA_{number}$$
$$\times \left(2 \times BPA_{number^2} + 2 \times BPA_{number^2}\right) \quad (4)$$
$$= 3 \times N_{neighbors} + 108,$$

where BPA_{number} is equal to 3 standing for three values of discretized traffic states. Supposing that the number of neighboring cells $N_{neighbors}$ is set as 100, for all 2077 road segments, $N_{CPU_{Cycles}}$ is calculated as 847416. The corresponding threshold thr is determined by

$$thr = \frac{847416}{N_{nodes}}, \quad (5)$$

where N_{nodes} denotes the maximum number of computing nodes. The threshold is further used to conduct the domain decomposition.

4.3. Cyber-ITS-Based Implementation. The traffic state estimation is implemented fully based on the Cyber-ITS framework. Massive SCATS and GPS data are fused using the techniques including ITS computational domain, octree-based domain decomposition, max-min-based subdomains scheduling, and parallelized fusion, which, respectively, correspond to data representation, domain decomposition, resources allocation, and parallel processing in the technique level of Cyber ITS. In the model level, this implementation also follows the SCATS-and-GPS-data-driven and traffic-state-estimation-oriented model. The computational domain, domain decomposition, and task scheduling are all reusable components, which can be shared among diverse data-driven ITS applications. These reusable components are combined with other specialized data processing components to construct workflow for parallelized fusion.

5. Experimental Results and Analysis

5.1. Experiment Setup. The experiments on the Cyber-ITS-based traffic state estimation are conducted on a Dawning TC4000L cluster which includes 64 computing nodes equipped with Intel Xeon Dual Core 2.4 GHz CPU and 2G memory. The SCATS and GPS data are uploaded by loop detectors and taxis, respectively, every 2 minutes from 8:00 to 17:00 on the chosen 393 road segments in downtown Shanghai. The data gathered per 10 minutes are calculated as one unit. The speeds of road segments estimated from SCATS and GPS data are formally represented as a computational domain. The computational intensity of data fusion on the whole ITS computational domain is evaluated as 160344 CPU cycles. The threshold is calculated as 160344/64 = 2505.4. Therefore, the computational domain is decomposed into 71 subdomains by octree. Both accuracy and efficiency tests of speed estimation by parallelized fusion are carried out on 1, 2, 4, 8, 16, and 32 computing nodes respectively. The speed

can be discretized into "congested" (<5 km/h), "medium" (5 km/h–25 km/h), and "smooth" (>25 km/h). The accuracy of the fused traffic state is compared with a ground truth developed by manually analyzing available traffic video streams. From the captured snapshots of road intersections in the video, if all the vehicles waiting in the queue of a road segment cannot pass the intersection during one period of green light, we regard the traffic state of the road segment as "congested." If all the vehicles can pass the road intersection during a half period of green light, we regard the traffic state as "smooth." Otherwise, we regard it as "medium". This level of comparison is analogous to red/yellow/green traffic condition maps commonly provided on internet traveler information websites by transportation agencies.

5.2. Results and Analysis

5.2.1. Accuracy Test. The accuracy test uses a metric defined as follows:

$$A = \frac{n_c}{n_{all}}, \quad (6)$$

where A denotes the accuracy rate of traffic state estimation, n_c is the number of correctly estimated states, and n_{all} is the number of states of all road segments in the whole time range. n_c is counted by comparing the discretized speed estimated from the sensors with the ground truth traffic state estimated from videos. The test cases include the traffic state estimation using SCATS data, GPS data, and their fusion. In the case that the traffic state of a road segment cannot be estimated due to sensor malfunctions or missing data, we regard the result as incorrect estimation. The experimental results on A of three test cases are shown in Figure 6.

As shown in Figure 6, the estimated traffic state using SCATS data is more accurate than that using GPS data. This is mainly caused by the smaller number of available GPS taxi probes in the sampling, which causes gaps in the network monitored by the probe vehicles. The average A of data fusion is around 0.95, which is higher than that of either SCATS or GPS. This is because of the synergistic effect of different types of traffic sensors, which can mutually compensate the loss of accuracy or data availability for each sensor. This accuracy test shows that the Cyber ITS framework can keep data availability and accuracy of the original application algorithms.

5.2.2. Efficiency Test. The efficiency test uses speedup as the metric to evaluate the acceleration performance of Cyber ITS. This metric is defined as a ratio of sequential execution time over parallel execution time in the following equation:

$$S = \frac{T_1}{T_n}, \quad (7)$$

where S denotes the speedup, T_1 is the sequential execution time using one computing node, and T_n is the parallel execution time using n computing nodes. The experiment evaluates the computing performance of 10-minute data processing, which consists of domain decomposition, tasks scheduling, and parallelized fusion. Average execution time

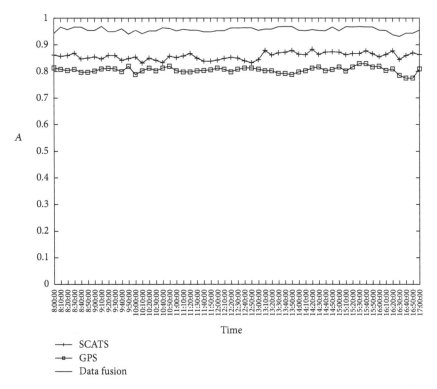

FIGURE 6: Accuracy rate of traffic state estimation is tested using SCATS data, GPS data, and their fusion.

TABLE 1: Average execution time and speedup using 1, 2, 4, 8, 16, and 32 computing nodes.

Number of computing nodes	Average execution time/seconds	Speedup
1	927.6	1
2	492.9	1.88
4	277.3	3.34
8	170.6	5.44
16	119.2	7.78
32	100.9	9.19

is calculated by running the whole process on different number of computing nodes, as listed in Table 1. The results of speedup are also listed in Table 1, and illustrated in Figure 7.

As shown in Figure 7, as the number of computing nodes increases from 1 to 32, the speedup increases significantly. Clearly, the parallelized process allows data fusion to occur to support real-time traffic state estimation. When only one computing node is used, the average execution time exceeds 15 minutes, which is too long to support real-time applications. When 32 computing nodes are used, the average execution time decreases to less than 2 minutes. However, it is also found that the speedup increases slower than the increment of computing nodes. For example, when the number of computing nodes increases to 32, the speedup only reaches 9.19. This nonlinear trend is caused by the sequential execution components, such as domain decomposition and tasks scheduling. These components are also regarded as the overhead part in the parallelization. In addition, assuming fixed overhead time, as more computing nodes are used, the sequential

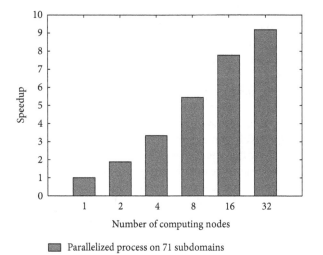

FIGURE 7: Speedup of parallelized process is tested on 1, 2, 4, 8, 16, and 32 computing nodes.

execution components bring more impact on speedup of the whole process. Nevertheless, this efficiency test clearly shows that the Cyber-ITS-based implementation can perform significant speedup by parallel computing.

6. Conclusions and Future Work

The general goal of this paper is to propose a Cyber-ITS framework for the synthesis of CI, ITS, and data analysis. The development of the framework is motivated by the challenge of solving computation-intensive problems on processing massive and heterogeneous traffic data in real time. The Cyber-ITS framework presents a way to transfer the data-driven ITS applications from single-CPU architectures to parallel computing architectures. This transfer requires the transformation of applications, which are based on a common design for processing massive traffic data on CI.

As the core component of Cyber-ITS, the computational intensity is used to efficiently decompose the data represented by ITS computational domain into load-balanced subdomains. Besides the computational domain and domain decomposition, the Cyber-ITS framework adopts two other techniques, CI resources allocation and parallel processing, to complete the efficient parallelization on traffic data processing. All four techniques are synergistically integrated to follow both data-driven and application-oriented models and can build a component-and-workflow-based model to interoperate and reuse functional components among diverse data-driven ITS applications.

An example of traffic state estimation by fusing SCATS and GPS data was presented to test the effectiveness of the proposed Cyber-ITS framework. The example was implemented by using parallelized D-S evidential fusion, which consists of evaluating the computational intensity in CPU cycles, octree-based domain decomposition based on the computational intensity, and max-min-based tasks scheduling for parallelized fusion. The fusion work used the discretized traffic state estimated from different sensors and calculated the probabilities of their combination for final determination. This implementation fully followed the SCATS-and-GPS-data-driven and traffic-state-estimation-oriented models.

Traffic state estimation was also examined to test the performance of the Cyber-ITS framework. Two performance metrics, accuracy rate and speedup, were defined to conduct the respective accuracy and efficiency tests. The experimental results show that the Cyber-ITS-based data fusion achieved higher accuracy rate in estimating traffic state than using any single type of traffic sensor. In addition, as more computing nodes are employed, the experiment demonstrated that the Cyber-ITS framework can facilitate significant computational speedup by parallel computing.

In future work, the research team will design a piece of scheduling middleware for the purpose of dynamically adapting to different types of CI resources employed in the Cyber-ITS framework. Further research will also focus on expanding the implementation of data-driven ITS applications based on the Cyber-ITS framework. Moreover, the common framework portal system could be improved to gain more interoperability and reusability among diverse applications.

Conflict of Interests

The authors do not have a direct financial relation with the commercial identities mentioned in this paper and have no conflict of interests to declare.

Acknowledgments

This paper draws on work supported in part by the following funds: National High Technology Research and Development Program of China (863 Program) under Grant no. 2011AA010101, National Natural Science Foundation of China under Grant no. 61002009, Key Science and Technology Program of Zhejiang Province of China under Grant no. 2012C01035-1, and Zhejiang Provincial Natural Science Foundation of China under Grant no. Z13F020026.

References

[1] J. Zhang, F. Y. Wang, K. Wang, W. Lin, X. Xu, and C. Chen, "Data-driven intelligent transportation systems: a survey," *IEEE Transactions on Intelligent Transportation Systems*, vol. 12, no. 4, pp. 1624–1639, 2011.

[2] Y. Xia, C. Wu, Q. Kong, Z. Shan, and L. Kuang, "A parallel fusion method for heterogeneous multi-sensor transportation data," in *Proceedings of the 8th International Conference on Modeling Decision for Artificial Intelligence*, pp. 31–42, Springer, Changsha, China.

[3] Y. Xia, Z. Shan, L. Kuang, and X. Shi, "A theoretical approach for ITS data analyses using cyberinfrastructure," in *Proceedings of the 1st International Conference on Transportation Information and Safety*, pp. 53–59, ASCE, Wuhan, China, 2011.

[4] F. Gross, K. Eccles, and D. Nabors, "Estimation of frequency and length of pedestrian stride in urban environments with video sensors," *Transportation Research Record*, vol. 2264, pp. 138–147, 2011.

[5] S. Hasan, C. F. Choudhury, M. E. Ben-Akiva, and A. Emmonds, "Modeling of travel time variations on urban links in London," *Transportation Research Record*, vol. 2260, pp. 1–7, 2011.

[6] T. H. Chang, C. S. Hsu, C. Wang, and L. K. Yang, "Onboard measurement and warning module for irregular vehicle behavior," *IEEE Transactions on Intelligent Transportation Systems*, vol. 9, no. 3, pp. 501–513, 2008.

[7] A. Kesting and M. Treiber, "Calibrating car-following models by using trajectory data methodological study," *Transportation Research Record*, no. 2088, pp. 148–156, 2008.

[8] N. E. El Faouzi and E. Lefevre, "Classifiers and distance-based evidential fusion for road travel time estimation," in *Proceedings of the 4th International Conference on Multisensor, Multisource Information Fusion: Architectures, Algorithms, and Applications*, pp. 1–16, SPIE, Orlando, Fla, USA, 2006.

[9] Q. J. Kong, Z. Li, Y. Chen, and Y. Liu, "An approach to Urban traffic state estimation by fusing multisource information," *IEEE Transactions on Intelligent Transportation Systems*, vol. 10, no. 3, pp. 499–511, 2009.

[10] T. Z. Qiu, X. Y. Lu, A. H. F. Chow, and S. E. Shladover, "Estimation of freeway traffic density with loop detector and probe vehicle data," *Transportation Research Record*, no. 2178, pp. 21–29, 2010.

[11] K. Kim, P. Pant, and E. Y. Yamashita, "Hit-and-run crashes: use of rough set analysis with logistic regression to capture critical attributes and determinants," *Transportation Research Record*, no. 2083, pp. 114–121, 2008.

[12] J. W. C. Van Lint, "Online learning solutions for freeway travel time prediction," *IEEE Transactions on Intelligent Transportation Systems*, vol. 9, no. 1, pp. 38–47, 2008.

[13] J. Niittymaki and S. Kikuchi, "Application of fuzzy logic to the control of a pedestrian crossing signal," *Transportation Research Record*, no. 1651, pp. 30–38, 1998.

[14] Y. Xia, Z. Ye, Y. Fang, and T. Zhang, "Parallelized extraction of traffic state estimation rules based on bootstrapping rough set," in *Ninth International Conference on Fuzzy Systems and Knowledge Discovery*, pp. 1548–1552, Chongqing, China, 2012.

[15] S. Wang and M. P. Armstrong, "A theoretical approach to the use of cyberinfrastructure in geographical analysis," *International Journal of Geographical Information Science*, vol. 23, no. 2, pp. 169–193, 2009.

[16] Y. Xia, L. Kuang, and X. Li, "Accelerating geospatial analysis on GPUs using CUDA," *Journal of Zhejiang University C*, vol. 12, no. 12, pp. 990–999, 2011.

[17] R. Aiken, M. Carey, B. Carpenter et al., "Network Policy and Services," A Report of a Workshop on Middleware RFC, 2768, The Internet Tasking Force, 2000.

[18] E. A. O'Cearbhaill and M. O'Mahony, "Parallel implementation of a transportation network model," *Journal of Parallel and Distributed Computing*, vol. 65, no. 1, pp. 1–14, 2005.

[19] R. Krishnan, V. Hodge, J. Austin, and J. W. Polak, "A computationally efficient method for online identification of traffic control intervention measures," in *Proceedings of the 42nd Annual Meeting of the Universities Transport Study Group*, pp. 1–11, Plymouth, UK, 2010.

[20] F.-Y. Wang, "Parallel control and management for intelligent transportation systems: concepts, architectures, and applications," *IEEE Transactions on Intelligent Transportation Systems*, vol. 11, no. 3, pp. 630–638, 2010.

[21] Y. Xia, Y. Fang, and Z. Ye, "MPI-based twi-extraction of traffic state evaluation rules," in *Proceedings of the 4th International Conference on Cyber-Enabled Distributed Computing and Knowledge Discovery*, pp. 1–4, IEEE, Sanya, China, 2012.

[22] O. Goldreich, *Computational Complexity: A Conceptual Perspective*, Cambridge University Press, Cambridge, U.K, 2008.

[23] S. Wang and M. P. Armstrong, "A Theory of the Spatial Computational Domain," GeoComputation, Ann Arbor, Mich, USA, 2005.

[24] C. L. Jackins and S. L. Tanimoto, "Oct-trees and their use in representing three-dimensional objects," *Computer Graphics and Image Processing*, vol. 14, no. 3, pp. 249–270, 1980.

[25] T. D. Braun, H. J. Siegel, N. Beck et al., "A comparison of eleven static heuristics for mapping a class of independent tasks onto heterogeneous distributed computing systems," *Journal of Parallel and Distributed Computing*, vol. 61, no. 6, pp. 810–837, 2001.

[26] T. Tchrakian, B. Basu, and M. O'Mahony, "Real-time traffic flow forecasting using spectral analysis," *IEEE Transactions on Intelligent Transportation Systems*, vol. 13, no. 2, pp. 519–526, 2012.

[27] G. C. Fox and D. Gannon, "Special issue: workflow in grid systems," *Concurrency Computation Practice and Experience*, vol. 18, no. 10, pp. 1009–1019, 2006.

[28] M. Giacobbe, A. Puliafito, and M. Villari, "A service oriented system for fleet management and traffic monitoring," in *Proceedings of the 15th IEEE Symposium on Computers and Communications, (ISCC '10)*, pp. 784–786, ita, June 2010.

[29] G. Shafer, *A Mathematical Theory of Evidence*, Princeton University Press, Princeton, NJ, USA, 1976.

[30] P. Smets and R. Kennes, "The transferable belief model," *Artificial Intelligence*, vol. 66, no. 2, pp. 191–234, 1994.

[31] Y. Xia, Y. Liu, Z. Ye, W. Wu, and M. Zhu, "Quadtree-based domain decomposition for parallel map-matching on GPS data," in *Proceedings of the 15th International Conference on Intelligent Transportation Systems Conference*, pp. 808–813, IEEE, Anchorage, Alaska, USA, 2012.

14

Bounds of the Spectral Radius and the Nordhaus-Gaddum Type of the Graphs

Tianfei Wang, Liping Jia, and Feng Sun

School of Mathematics and Information Science, Leshan Normal University, Leshan 614004, China

Correspondence should be addressed to Tianfei Wang; wangtf818@sina.com

Academic Editors: H.-L. Liu and Y. Wang

The Laplacian spectra are the eigenvalues of Laplacian matrix $L(G) = D(G) - A(G)$, where $D(G)$ and $A(G)$ are the diagonal matrix of vertex degrees and the adjacency matrix of a graph G, respectively, and the spectral radius of a graph G is the largest eigenvalue of $A(G)$. The spectra of the graph and corresponding eigenvalues are closely linked to the molecular stability and related chemical properties. In quantum chemistry, spectral radius of a graph is the maximum energy level of molecules. Therefore, good upper bounds for the spectral radius are conducive to evaluate the energy of molecules. In this paper, we first give several sharp upper bounds on the adjacency spectral radius in terms of some invariants of graphs, such as the vertex degree, the average 2-degree, and the number of the triangles. Then, we give some numerical examples which indicate that the results are better than the mentioned upper bounds in some sense. Finally, an upper bound of the Nordhaus-Gaddum type is obtained for the sum of Laplacian spectral radius of a connected graph and its complement. Moreover, some examples are applied to illustrate that our result is valuable.

1. Introduction

The graphs in this paper are simple and undirected. Let G be a simple graph with n vertices and m edges. For $v \in V$, denote by d_v, m_v, and N_v the degree of v, the average 2-degree of v, and the set of neighbors of v, respectively. Then $d_v m_v$ is the 2-degree of v. Let Δ, Δ', δ, and δ' denote the maximum degree, second largest degree, minimum degree, and second smallest degree of vertices of G, respectively. Obviously, we have $\Delta' < \Delta$ and $\delta' > \delta$. A graph is d-regular if $\Delta = \delta = d$.

The complement graph G^c of G is the graph with the same set of vertices as G, where two distinct vertices are adjacent if and only if they are independent in G. The line graph L_G of G is defined by $V(L_G) = E(G)$, where any two vertices in L_G are adjacent if and only if they are adjacent as edges of G.

Let X be a nonnegative square matrix. The spectral radius $\rho(X)$ of X is the maximum eigenvalue of X. Denote by B the adjacency matrix of L_G, then $\rho(B)$ is the spectral radius of B. Let $D(G)$ and $A(G)$ denote the diagonal matrix of vertex degrees and the adjacency matrix of G, respectively. Then the matrix $L(G) = D(G) - A(G)$ is called the Laplacian matrix of a graph G. Obviously, it is symmetric and positive semidefinite.

Similarly, the quasi-Laplacian matrix is defined as $Q(G) = D(G) + A(G)$, which is a nonnegative irreducible matrix. The largest eigenvalue of the Laplacian matrix, denoted by $\mu(G)$, is called the Laplacian spectral radius. The Laplacian eigenvalues of a graph are important in graph theory, because they have close relations to many graph invariants, including connectivity, isoperimetric number, diameter, and maximum cut. Particularly, good upper bounds for $\mu(G)$ are applied in many fields. For instance, it is used in theoretical chemistry, within the Heilbronner model, to determine the first ionization potential of alkanes, in combinatorial optimization to provide an upper bound on the size of the maximum cut in graph, in communication networks to provide a lower bound on the edge-forwarding index, and so forth. To learn more information on the applications of Laplacian spectral radius and other Laplacian eigenvalues of a graph, see references [1–4].

In the recent thirty years, the researchers obtained many good upper bounds for $\mu(G)$ [5–8]. These upper bounds improved the previous results constantly. In this paper, we focus on the bounds for the spectral radius of a graph, and the bound of Nordhaus-Gaddum type is also considered, which is the sum of Laplacian spectral radius of a connected graph G and its complement G^c.

At the end of this section, we introduce some lemmas which will be used later on.

Lemma 1 (see [9]). *Let $M = (m_{ij})_{n \times n}$ be an irreducible nonnegative matrix with spectral radius $\rho(M)$, and let $R_i(M)$ be the ith row sum of M; that is, $R_i(M) = \sum_j m_{ij}$. Then*

$$\min_{1 \leq i \leq n} R_i(M) \leq \rho(M) \leq \max_{1 \leq i \leq n} R_i(M). \tag{1}$$

Moreover, if the row sums of M are not all equal, then both inequalities are strict.

Lemma 2 (see [10]). *Let $G = [V, E]$ be a connected graph with n vertices; then*

$$\rho(G) \leq \frac{1}{2}\rho(L_G) + 1. \tag{2}$$

The equality holds if and only if G is a regular graph.

This lemma gives a relation between the spectral radius of a graph and its line graph. Therefore, we can estimate the spectral radius of the adjacency matrix of graph by estimating that of its line graph.

Lemma 3 (see [11]). *Let B be a real symmetric n×n matrix, and let $\rho(B)$ be the largest eigenvalue of B. If $P(\lambda)$ is a polynomial on λ, then*

$$\min_{v \in V} R_v(P(B)) \leq P(\rho(B)) \leq \max_{v \in V} R_v(P(B)). \tag{3}$$

Here $R_v(P(B))$ is the vth row sum of matrix P(B). Moreover, if the row sums of P(B) are not all equal, then both inequalities are strict.

Lemma 4 (see [11]). *Let G be a simple connected graph with n vertices and let $\rho(Q)$ be the largest eigenvalue of the quasi-Laplacian matrix of graph G. Then*

$$\mu(G) \leq \rho(Q), \tag{4}$$

with equality holds if and only if G is a bipartite graph.

By these lemmas, we will give some improved upper bounds for the spectral radius and determine the corresponding extremal graphs.

This paper is organized as follows. In Section 2, we will give several sharp upper and lower bounds for the spectral radius of graphs and determine the extremal graphs which achieve these bounds. In Section 3, some bounds of Nordhaus-Gaddum type will be given. Furthermore, in Sections 2 and 3, we present some examples to illustrate that our results are better than all of the mentioned upper bounds in this paper, in some sense.

2. Bounds on the Spectral Radius

2.1. Previous Results. The eigenvalues of adjacency matrix of the graph have wide applications in many fields. For instance, it can be used to present the energy level of specific electrons. Specially, the spectral radius of a graph is the maximum energy level of molecules. Hence, good upper bound for the spectral radius helps to estimate the energy level of molecules [12–15]. Recently, there are some classic upper bounds for the spectral radius of graphs.

In the early time Cao [16] gave a bound as follows:

$$\rho(G) \leq \sqrt{2m - \delta(n-1) + \Delta(\delta-1)}. \tag{5}$$

The equality holds if and only if G is regular graph or a star plus of K_2, or a complete graph plus a regular graph with smaller degree of vertices.

Hu [17] obtained an upper bound with simple form as follows:

$$\rho(G) \leq \sqrt{2m - n - \delta + 2}. \tag{6}$$

The equality holds if and only if G is $n-2$ regular graph. In 2005, Xu [18] proved that

$$\rho(G) \leq \sqrt{2m - n + 1 - (\delta - 1)(n - 1 - \Delta)}. \tag{7}$$

The equality holds if and only if G is regular graph or a star graph.

Using the average 2-degree of the vertices, the researchers got more upper bounds.

Cao's [16] another upper bound:

$$\rho(G) \leq \max_{u \in V(G)} \sqrt{d_u m_u}. \tag{8}$$

The equality holds if and only if G is a regular graph or a semiregular bipartite graph.

Similarly, Abrham and Zhang [19] proved that

$$\rho(G) \leq \max_{uv \in E(G)} \sqrt{d_u d_v}. \tag{9}$$

The equality holds if and only if G is a regular graph or a semiregular bipartite graph.

In recent years, Feng et al. [10] give some upper bounds for the spectral radius as follows:

$$\rho(G) \leq \max_{u \in V(G)} \sqrt{\frac{d_u^2 + d_u m_u}{2}}. \tag{10}$$

The equality holds if and only if G is regular graph.

$$\rho(G) \leq \max_{uv \in E(G)} \sqrt{\frac{d_u(d_u + m_u) + d_v(d_v + m_v)}{2}}. \tag{11}$$

The equality holds if and only if G is regular graph.

$$\rho(G) \leq \max_{u \in V(G)} \frac{d_u + \sqrt{d_u m_u}}{2}. \tag{12}$$

The equality holds if and only if G is regular graph.

$$\rho(G) \leq \max_{uv \in E(G)} \frac{d_u + d_v + \sqrt{(d_u - d_v)^2 + 4m_u m_v}}{4}. \tag{13}$$

The equality holds if and only if G is regular graph.

2.2. Main Results. All of these upper bounds mentioned in Section 2.1 are characterized by the degree and the average 2-degree of the vertices. Actually, we can also use other invariants of the graph to estimate the spectral radius. In the following, such an invariant will be introduced.

In a graph, a circle with length 3 is called a triangle. If u is a triangle's vertex in a graph, then u is incident with this triangle. Denote by T_u the number of the triangles associated with the vertex u. For example, in Figure 1, we have $T_u = 3$ and $T_v = T_w = 0$.

Let $N_u \cap N_v$ be the set of the common adjacent points of vertex u and v; then $|N_u \cap N_v|$ present the cardinality of $N_u \cap N_v$.

Now, some new and sharp upper and lower bounds for the spectral radius will be given.

Theorem 5. *Let G be a simple connected graph with n vertices. Then*

$$\rho(G) \le \max_{uv \in E(G)} \frac{d_u^2 m_u + d_v^2 m_v - 2(T_u + T_v)}{2(d_u d_v - |N_u \cap N_v|)}; \quad (14)$$

the equality holds if and only if G is a regular graph.

Proof. Let $K = \mathrm{diag}(d_u d_v - |N_u \cap N_v| : uv \in E(G))$ is a diagonal matrix and B is the adjacency matrix of the line graph. Denote $N = K^{-1}BK$, then N and B have the same eigenvalues. Since G is a simple connected graph, it is easy to obtain that N is nonnegative and irreducible matrix. The (uv, pq)th entry of N is equal to

$$\begin{cases} \dfrac{d_p d_q - |N_p \cap N_q|}{d_u d_v - |N_u \cap N_v|}, & pq \sim uv, \\ 0, & \text{else,} \end{cases} \quad (15)$$

here $pq \sim uv$ implies that pq and uv are adjacent in graph. Hence, the uvth row sum $R_{uv}(N)$ of N is

$$\sum_{pq \sim uv} \frac{d_p d_q - |N_p \cap N_q|}{d_u d_v - |N_u \cap N_v|}$$

$$= \frac{\sum_{q \sim u} d_u d_q + \sum_{p \sim v} d_p d_v - 2 d_u d_v}{d_u d_v - |N_u \cap N_v|}$$

$$- \frac{\sum_{q \sim u} |N_u \cap N_q| + \sum_{p \sim v} |N_p \cap N_v| - 2|N_u \cap N_v|}{d_u d_v - |N_u \cap N_v|}$$

$$= \frac{d_u^2 m_u + d_v^2 m_v - 2 d_u d_v - 2(T_u + T_v) + 2|N_u \cap N_v|}{d_u d_v - |N_u \cap N_v|}$$

$$= \frac{d_u^2 m_u + d_v^2 m_v - 2(T_u + T_v)}{d_u d_v - |N_u \cap N_v|} - 2. \quad (16)$$

From Lemmas 1 and 2, we have

$$\rho(G) \le \frac{1}{2}\rho(B) + 1$$

$$\le \max \left\{ \frac{1}{2} R_{uv}(N) + 1 : uv \in V(H) \right\}. \quad (17)$$

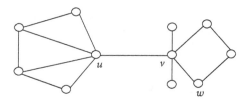

FIGURE 1: Graph with triangles.

It means that (14) holds and the equality in (14) holds if and only if G is a regular graph. □

In a graph, let α and β represent the number of vertices with the maximum degree and minimum degree, respectively. Then, we get the following results.

Theorem 6. *Let G be a simple connected graph with n vertices. If $\Delta \le \min\{n - 1 - \beta, n - 1 - \alpha\}$, then*

$$\rho(G) \le \sqrt{2m + \Delta(\delta' - 1) - \beta\delta - (n - 1 - \beta)\delta'}, \quad (18)$$

$$\rho(G) \ge \sqrt{2m + (\Delta' - 1)\delta - \alpha\Delta - (n - 1 - \alpha)\Delta'}; \quad (19)$$

the equality holds if and only if G is a regular graph.

Proof. Since $R_v(A^2)$ is exactly the number of walks of length 2 in G with a starting point v, thus

$$R_v(A^2) = \sum_{u \sim v} d_u = 2m - d_v - \sum_{u \nsim v} d_u. \quad (20)$$

Therefore, from Lemmas 1 and 3, if $\Delta \le n - 1 - \beta$, we have $d_v \le n - 1 - \beta$ for any $v \in V(G)$. Then

$$\rho(A^2) \le \max_{v \in V(G)} \left(2m - d_v - \sum_{u \nsim v} d_u \right)$$

$$\le \max_{v \in V(G)} \left(2m - d_v - (\beta\delta + (n - d_v - 1 - \beta)\delta') \right)$$

$$= \max_{v \in V(G)} \left(2m + (\delta' - 1)d_v - \beta\delta - (n - 1 - \beta)\delta' \right)$$

$$\le 2m + \Delta(\delta' - 1) - \beta\delta - (n - 1 - \beta)\delta'. \quad (21)$$

Hence, it is easy to obtain that (18) holds.

If equality in (18) holds, then all equalities in the above argument must hold. Thus, for all $v \in V(G)$

$$\sum_{u \nsim v} d_u = \beta\delta + (n - d_v - 1 - \beta)\delta'. \quad (22)$$

It means that $d_v = n - 1$ and $\delta' = \delta$, or $d_u = \delta = \delta'$; this shows that the graph G is regular. Conversely, if G is k-regular, it is not difficult to check that $\rho(G)$ attains the upper bound by direct calculation.

Similarly for the lower bound, if $\Delta \leq n - 1 - \alpha$, we have

$$\rho\left(A^2\right) \geq \min_{v \in V(G)} \left(2m - d_v - \sum_{u \neq v} d_u\right)$$

$$\geq \min_{v \in V(G)} \left(2m - d_v - \left(\alpha\Delta + (n - d_v - 1 - \alpha)\Delta'\right)\right)$$

$$= \min_{v \in V(G)} \left(2m + \left(\Delta' - 1\right)d_v - \alpha\Delta - (n - 1 - \alpha)\Delta'\right)$$

$$\geq 2m + \left(\Delta' - 1\right)\delta - \alpha\Delta - (n - 1 - \alpha)\Delta'.$$

$$(23)$$

It means that (19) holds and the equality in (19) holds if and only if G is a regular graph by similar discussion. $\square$

Theorem 7. *Let G be a simple connected graph with n vertices. If $\Delta \leq n - 1 - \beta$; then*

$$\rho(G) \leq \frac{\delta' - 1 + \sqrt{(\delta' + 1)^2 + 8m - 4\beta(\delta - \delta') - 4n\delta'}}{2};$$

$$(24)$$

the equality holds if and only if G is a regular graph.

Proof. According to the proof of Theorem 6, we have

$$R_v\left(A^2\right) = 2m - d_v - \sum_{u \neq v} d_u$$

$$\leq 2m + \left(\delta' - 1\right)d_v - \beta\delta - (n - 1 - \beta)\delta'.$$

$$(25)$$

Thus

$$R_v\left(A^2 - \left(\delta' - 1\right)A\right) \leq 2m - \beta\delta - (n - 1 - \beta)\delta'. \quad (26)$$

From Lemma 3, we have

$$\rho^2(A) - \left(\delta' - 1\right)\rho(A) - 2m + \beta\delta + (n - 1 - \beta)\delta' \leq 0.$$

$$(27)$$

Solving this quadratic inequality, we obtain that upper bound (24) holds.

If equality in (24) holds, then all equalities in the argument must hold. By the similar discussion of Theorem 6, the equality holds if and only if G is a regular graph. $\square$

2.3. Numerical Examples. In this section, we will present two graphs to illustrate that our some new bounds are better than other bounds in some sense. Let Figures 2 and 3 be graphs of orders 7 and 8.

The estimated value of each upper bound is listed in Table 1. Obviously, from Table 1, bound (24) is the best in all known upper bounds for Figure 2 and bound (14) is the best for Figure 3. Furthermore, bound (18) is the best except (13) and (24) for Figure 2. Hence, commonly, these upper bounds are incomparable.

3. Bounds of the Nordhaus-Gaddum Type

3.1. Previous Results. In this part, we mainly discuss the upper bounds on the sum of Laplacian spectral radius of a connected graph G and its complement G^c, which is called the upper bound of the Nordhaus-Gaddum type. For convenience, let

$$\sigma(G) = \mu(G) + \mu\left(G^c\right). \quad (28)$$

The following are some classic upper bounds of Nordhaus-Gaddum type. The coarse bound $\mu(G) \leq 2\Delta$ easily implies the simplest upper bound on $\sigma(G)$:

$$\sigma(G) \leq 2(n - 1) + 2(\Delta - \delta). \quad (29)$$

In particular, if both G and G^c are connected and irregular, Shi [20] gave a better upper bound as follows:

$$\sigma(G) \leq 2\left(n - 1 - \frac{2}{2n^2 - n}\right) + 2(\Delta - \delta). \quad (30)$$

Liu et al. [21] proved that

$$\sigma(G) \leq n - 2 + \left\{(\Delta - \omega)^2 + n^2 + 4(\Delta - \delta)(n - 1)\right\}^{1/2}, \quad (31)$$

where $\omega = n - \delta - 1$.

Shi [20] gives another upper bound

$$\sigma(G) \leq 2\left\{(n - 1)(2\omega - \delta) + (\Delta + \delta)^2 - \Delta + \delta\right\}^{1/2}. \quad (32)$$

To learn other bounds of the Nordhaus-Gaddum type, see references [22, 23]. In order to state the main result of this section, we first give an upper bound for the Laplacian spectral radius.

3.2. Laplacian Spectral Radius. Here we give a new upper bound for the Laplacian spectral radius. For convenience, let

$$f(m, \Delta, \delta) = \left(\left(\Delta - \frac{\delta}{2} - 1\right)^2 + 16m - 2\delta(4n - \delta - 2)\right)^{1/2}.$$

$$(33)$$

Theorem 8. *Let G be a simple connected graph of order n with Δ and δ; then*

$$\mu(G) \leq \frac{\Delta + (3/2)\delta - 1 + f(m, \Delta, \delta)}{2}, \quad (34)$$

with equality holds if and only if G is bipartite regular.

Proof. Let $K = Q - \delta E$; then $R_v(K) = 2d_v - \delta$, it means that $2d_v = R_v(K) + \delta$. Considering the vth row sum of matrix K^2, we have

$$R_v\left(K^2\right) = R_v\left(Q^2\right) - 2\delta R_v(Q) + \delta^2$$

$$= 2d_v^2 + 2\sum_{u\sim v} d_u - 4\delta d_v + \delta^2$$

$$= 2d_v^2 + 2\left(2m - d_v - \sum_{u\ne v, u\ne v} d_u\right) - 4\delta d_v + \delta^2$$

$$\le 2d_v^2 + 2\left(2m - d_v - (n - d_v - 1)\delta\right) - 4\delta d_v + \delta^2$$

$$= 2d_v^2 - 2d_v - 2\delta d_v + 4m - 2(n-1)\delta + \delta^2$$

$$= (2d_v - \delta)d_v - (2 + \delta)d_v$$
$$+ 4m - 2(n-1)\delta + \delta^2$$

$$\le \Delta R_v(K) - (2+\delta)\frac{R_v(K) + \delta}{2}$$
$$+ 4m - 2(n-1)\delta + \delta^2$$

$$= \left(\Delta - \frac{\delta}{2} - 1\right)R_v(K) + 4m - 2n\delta + \delta + \frac{\delta^2}{2}. \quad (35)$$

This is equivalent to the following inequality:

$$R_v\left(K^2 - \left(\Delta - \frac{\delta}{2} - 1\right)K\right) \le 4m - 2n\delta + \delta + \frac{\delta^2}{2}. \quad (36)$$

From Lemma 3, we obtain that

$$\rho^2(K) - \left(\Delta - \frac{\delta}{2} - 1\right)\rho(K) \le 4m - 2n\delta + \delta + \frac{\delta^2}{2}. \quad (37)$$

By simple calculation, we get the upper bound of the spectral radius of matrix K as follows:

$$\rho(K) \le \frac{\Delta - (\delta/2) - 1}{2}$$
$$+ \frac{\left((\Delta - (\delta/2) - 1)^2 + 16m - 2\delta(4n - \delta - 2)\right)^{1/2}}{2}. \quad (38)$$

Since $\rho(K) = \rho(Q) - \delta$, therefore from Lemma 4 we obtain that the result (34) holds.

If the spectral radius $\mu(G)$ achieves the upper bound in (34), then each inequality in the above proof must be equal. This implies that $\Delta = \delta$ for all $v \in V(G)$, thus G is regular graph. From Lemma 4 again, G is regular bipartite graph.

Conversely, it is easy to verify that equality in (34) holds for regular bipartite graphs. $\square$

3.3. Bound of the Nordhaus-Gaddum Type. In this part, based on Theorem 8, an upper bound of Nordhaus-Gaddum type of Laplacian matrix will be given.

Theorem 9. *Let G be a simple graph of order n with Δ and δ; then*

$$\sigma(G) \le \frac{5n - \Delta + \delta - 9 + \sqrt{2}\{2(2\Delta - \delta - 2)^2 + 8\delta(2 + \delta) + (\omega - \Delta)(n + 3\Delta - 3\delta - 5) + 32n\omega - 8\pi(3n + \Delta - 1)\}^{1/2}}{4} \quad (39)$$

here $\omega = n - \delta - 1$ and $\pi = n - \Delta - 1$. Moreover, if both G and G^c are connected, then the upper bound is strict.

Proof. According to the relation of a graph G and its complement, it is not difficult to obtain the invariants of G^c. Denote it by $\Delta(G^c) = n - \delta - 1$, $\delta(G^c) = n - \Delta - 1$, and $m(G^c) = C_n^2 - m$. From Theorem 8, we have

$$\mu(G^c) \le \frac{\Delta(G^c) + (3/2)\delta(G^c) - 1}{2}$$
$$+ \frac{f(m(G^c), \Delta(G^c), \delta(G^c))}{2}. \quad (40)$$

Let

$$g(m) = f(m, \Delta, \delta) + f(m(G^c), \Delta(G^c), \delta(G^c)). \quad (41)$$

Then the upper bound of the Nordhaus-Gaddum type of Laplacian matrix is

$$\sigma(G) = \mu(G) + \mu(G^c) \le \frac{5n - \Delta + \delta - 9 + 2g(m)}{4} \quad (42)$$

since

$$g'(m) = \frac{8}{f(m, \Delta, \delta)} - \frac{8}{f(m(G^c), \Delta(G^c), \delta(G^c))}. \quad (43)$$

Obviously, $g'(m) \ge 0$ holds if and only if the following inequality holds:

$$f(m, \Delta, \delta) \le f\left(C_n^2 - m, n - \delta - 1, n - \Delta - 1\right). \quad (44)$$

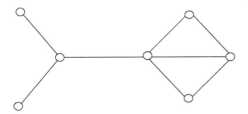

FIGURE 2: Graph of order 7.

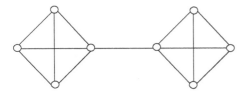

FIGURE 3: Graph of order 8.

Let m be a variable; then solving this inequality, we have

$$m \le \frac{(n - \delta - \Delta - 1)(n - 3\delta + 3\Delta - 5) + 32n(n + \delta - 1)}{128}$$

$$- \frac{8\delta(\delta + 2) - 8(n - \Delta - 1)(3n + \Delta - 1)}{128} = m^*.$$
(45)

Here, the symbol m^* represents the right hand of the above inequality. Then we can assert that $g(m)$ is an increasing function for $m \le m^*$, and it implies that $g(m) \le g(m^*)$. Therefore, we have

$$\sigma(G) \le \frac{5n - \Delta + \delta - 9 + 2g(m^*)}{4}$$

$$= \frac{5n - \Delta + \delta - 9 + 4f(m^*, \Delta, \delta)}{4}.$$
(46)

Simplifying this expression by direct calculation, we prove that the result (39) is correct.

If equality in (39) holds, then each inequality in the above proof must be equality. From Theorem 8, we obtain that both G and G^c are regular bipartite. But it is impossible for a connected graph, this implies that the Laplacian spectral radius of either G or G^c fails to achieve its upper bound and so does the sum. Hence the inequality in (39) is strict. □

3.4. Numerical Examples. In this section, we give some examples to illustrate that the new bound is better than other bounds for some graphs. Considering the graph of order 10 in Figure 4 and Figures 1–3, the estimated value of each upper bound of the Nordhaus-Gaddum type is given in Table 2.

Clearly, from Table 2, we can see that new bound (39) is the best in all known upper bounds for all figures mentioned in this paper.

4. Conclusion

From numerical examples of Sections 2 and 3, the estimated value of new upper bounds of the spectral radius and the

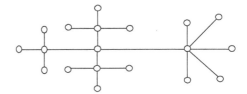

FIGURE 4: Graph of order 10.

TABLE 1: Estimated value of each upper bound.

Upper bounds	Figure 2	Figure 3
Bound (5)	3.1623	4.1231
Bound (6)	3.1623	3.6056
Bound (7)	3.1623	3.6056
Bound (8)	3.1623	4.0000
Bound (9)	3.4641	3.8079
Bound (10)	3.6056	3.8079
Bound (11)	3.2787	3.6056
Bound (12)	3.5811	3.8028
Bound (13)	3.0650	3.6250
Bound (14)	3.5000	3.5000
Bound (18)	3.1623	4.0000
Bound (24)	3.0000	4.0000
Actual value	2.7321	3.3028

TABLE 2: Estimated value of each upper bound.

Upper bound	Figure 1	Figure 2	Figure 3	Figure 4
Bound (29)	28	18	16	46
Bound (30)	27.98	17.96	15.96	45.99
Bound (31)	26.23	16.05	15.59	46.02
Bound (32)	28.43	17.44	18.22	50.52
Bound (39)	25.84	15.88	15.52	44.97

Nordhaus-Gaddum type of graphs are the smallest in all known upper bounds for the graphs considered in these examples. It means that our results are better than the existing upper bounds in some sense.

Acknowledgment

This work is supported by the Research Fund of Sichuan Provincial Education Department (Grant no. 11ZA159, 11ZZ020, 12ZB238, and 13ZB0108).

References

[1] R. Merris, "Laplacian matrices of graphs: a survey," *Linear Algebra and Its Applications*, vol. 197-198, pp. 143–176, 1994.

[2] B. Mohar, "Some applications of Laplace eigenvalues of graphs," in *Graph Symmetry*, G. Harn and G. Sabiussi, Eds., Kluwer Academic Publishers, Dordrecht, The Netherlands, 1997.

[3] I. Gutman, V. Gineityte, M. Lepović, and M. Petrović, "The high-energy band in the photoelectron spectrum of alkanes and its dependence on molecular structure," *Journal of the Serbian Chemical Society*, vol. 64, pp. 673–680, 1999.

[4] B. Mohar and S. Poljak, "Eigenvalues and the max-cut problem," *Czechoslovak Mathematical Journal*, vol. 40, pp. 343–352, 1990.

[5] T. F. Wang, "Several sharp upper bounds for the largest laplacian eigenvalue of a graph," *Science in China*, vol. 50, no. 12, pp. 1755–1764, 2007.

[6] X. D. Zhang, "Two sharp upper bounds for the Laplacian eigenvalues," *Linear Algebra and Its Applications*, vol. 376, no. 1-3, pp. 207–213, 2004.

[7] T. Wang, J. Yang, and B. Li, "Improved upper bounds for the Laplacian spectral radius of a graph," *Electronic Journal of Combinatorics*, vol. 18, no. 1, article P35, 2011.

[8] T. F. Wang and B. Li, "New upper bounds for the laplacian spectral radius of graphs," *Journal of Sichuan Normal University*, vol. 33, pp. 487–490, 2010.

[9] R. A. Horn and C. R. Johnson, *Matrix Analysis*, Cambridge University Press, New York, NY, USA, 1985.

[10] L. Feng, Q. Li, and X. D. Zhang, "Some sharp upper bounds on the spectral radius of graphs," *Taiwanese Journal of Mathematics*, vol. 11, no. 4, pp. 989–997, 2007.

[11] J. S. Li and Y. L. Pan, "Upper bounds for the laplacian graph eigenvalues," *Acta Mathematica Sinica*, vol. 20, pp. 803–806, 2004.

[12] J. L. Shu, Y. Hong, and R. K. Wen, "A Sharp upper bound on the largest eigenvalue of the Laplacian matrix of a graph," *Linear Algebra and Its Applications*, vol. 347, pp. 123–129, 2002.

[13] D. Cvetkovic, M. doob, and H. Sachs, *Spectral of Graphs: Theory and Applications*, Academic Press, New Work, NY, USA, 1997.

[14] D. M. Cvetkovic, M. Doob, I. Gutman, and A. Yorgasev, *Recent Results in the Theory of Graph Spectra*, North-Holland Publishing, Amsterdam, The Netherlands, 1988.

[15] N. L. Biggs, *Algebraic Graph Theory*, Cambridge University Press, Cambridge, 2nd edition, 1993.

[16] D. S. Cao, "Bounds on eigenvalues and chromatic number," *Linear Algebra and Its Applications*, vol. 270, pp. 1–13, 1998.

[17] S. B. Hu, "Upper bound on spectral Radius of graphs," *Journal of Hebei University*, vol. 20, pp. 232–234, 2000.

[18] H. J. Xu, "Upper bound on spectral radius of graphs," *Journal of Jiamusi University*, vol. 23, pp. 126–110, 2005.

[19] B. Abrham and X. D. Zhang, "on the spectral radius of graphs with cut vertices," *Journal of Combinatorial Thcory*, vol. 83, pp. 233–240, 2001.

[20] L. Shi, "Bounds on the (Laplacian) spectral radius of graphs," *Linear Algebra and Its Applications*, vol. 422, no. 2-3, pp. 755–770, 2007.

[21] H. Liu, M. Lu, and F. Tian, "On the Laplacian spectral radius of a graph," *Linear Algebra and Its Applications*, vol. 376, no. 1-3, pp. 135–141, 2004.

[22] Y. Hong and J. L. Shu, "A sharp upper bound for the spectral radius of the Nordhaus-Gaddum type," *Discrete Mathematics*, vol. 211, pp. 229–232, 2000.

[23] S. He and J. L. Shu, "Ordering of trees with respect to their spectral radius of Nordhaus-Gaddum type," *Journal of Applied Mathematics*, vol. 22, pp. 247–252, 2007.

15

An Integrated Fuzzy Approach for Strategic Alliance Partner Selection in Third-Party Logistics

Burak Erkayman, Emin Gundogar, and Aysegul Yılmaz

Department of Industrial Engineering, Sakarya University, 54187 Adapazarı, Sakarya, Turkey

Correspondence should be addressed to Burak Erkayman, erkayman@atauni.edu.tr

Academic Editors: G. Bordogna and P. Melin

Outsourcing some of the logistic activities is a useful strategy for companies in recent years. This makes it possible for firms to concentrate on their main issues and processes and presents facility to improve logistics performance, to reduce costs, and to improve quality. Therefore provider selection and evaluation in third-party logistics become important activities for companies. Making a strategic decision like this is significantly hard and crucial. In this study we proposed a fuzzy multicriteria decision making (MCDM) approach to effectively select the most appropriate provider. First we identify the provider selection criteria and build the hierarchical structure of decision model. After building the hierarchical structure we determined the selection criteria weights by using fuzzy analytical hierarchy process (AHP) technique. Then we applied fuzzy technique for order preference by similarity to ideal solution (TOPSIS) to obtain final rankings for providers. And finally an illustrative example is also given to demonstrate the effectiveness of the proposed model.

1. Introduction

Supply chain management involves the design and management of seamless, value-added processes across organizational boundaries to meet the real needs of the end customer [1–3]. Logistics play a significant role in integrating the supply chain of industries. However, as the market becomes more global, logistics are now seen as an important area where industries can cut costs and improve their customer service quality [4]. Logistics outsourcing and third-party logistics originated in the 1980s as important means of improving supply chain effectiveness [5].

Estimates indicate that the proportion of companies in the US implementing this approach has increased by 5–8% annually between 1996 and 2004 [6]. Moreover, in 2005 no less than 80% of the Fortune 500 Companies stated that they relied on TPL [7]. Current predictions indicate growth rates in the range of 15–20% between 2009 and 2011 in both Western Europe and the USA [8, 9].

Third it can be defined as a managed process of transferring activities to be performed by others. Logistics outsourcing or third party logistics (3PL) involves the use of external companies to perform logistics functions that have traditionally been performed within an organization [10]. Outsourcing can be a value-enhancing activity. However, the top benefits for companies outsourcing are often related to costs savings [11, 12]. Logistics outsourcing or third-party logistics (3PL) is an emerging trend in the global market. Basically, a 3PL provider (hereinafter referred to as provider) involves using external companies to perform logistics functions which have been conventionally operational within an organization [13].

Outsourcing involves the procurement of physical and/or service inputs from outside organizations either through cessation of an activity that was previously performed internally or abstention from an activity that is well within the capability of the firm [14]. The main benefits of logistics alliances are to allow the outsourcing company to concentrate on the core competence, increase the efficiency, improve the service, reduce the transportation cost, restructure the supply chains, and establish the marketplace legitimacy [15–17].

Finding the right partner requires careful screening and can be a time-consuming process. Developing an understanding of partners' expectations and objectives can also take time [18].

Multiple criteria decision-making (MCDM) is a powerful tool widely used for evaluating problems containing multiple, usually conflicting criteria [19]. In this study we defined the provider selection problem as MCDM problem, and proposed a fuzzy approach to solve it. Decision making problems subject to subjective evaluations must be considered in fuzzy environment. Because of this situation application of fuzzy MCDM approaches is preferred.

The proposed method integrates fuzzy AHP and fuzzy TOPSIS techniques for provider selection that satisfies the needs of Third-Party Logistics company. First, the weights of criteria have been calculated using fuzzy AHP, and fuzzy TOPSIS is used for the selection of providers.

The remainder of the study is arranged as follows: Section 2 briefly describes the proposed methods. Section 3 describes the proposed model. An illustrative example is given in Section 4. In Section 5, results and suggestions are discussed.

2. Methods

2.1. The Fuzzy AHP Method. AHP [20] is one of the most extensively used MCDM analysis tools for modeling the unstructured problems in different areas such as politics, economic, social, and management sciences. AHP assumes that evaluation criteria can be completely expressed in a hierarchical structure. The data acquired from the decision-makers are pairwise comparisons concerning the relative importance of each of the criteria, or the degree of preference of one factor to another with respect to each criterion. In the conventional AHP, the pairwise comparison is made by using a ratio scale. Even though the discrete scale has the advantages of simplicity and ease of use, it does not take into account the uncertainty associated with the mapping of one's perception (or judgment) to a number. In order to deal with the uncertainty and vagueness from the subjective perception and the experience of human in the decision-making process, many fuzzy AHP methods are proposed by various authors [18].

In this study we use the Chang's extent analysis method for fuzzy AHP. According to Chang [21], let $X = \{x_1, x_2, \ldots, x_n\}$ be an object set, and $U = \{u_1, u_2, \ldots, u_m\}$ be a goal set. According to the method of Chang's [21] extent analysis, each object is taken and extent analysis for each goal is performed, respectively. Therefore, m extent analysis values for each object can be obtained, with the following signs:

$$M_{g_i}^1, M_{g_i}^2, \ldots, M_{g_i}^m, \quad i = 1, 2, \ldots, n, \quad (1)$$

where all the $M_{g_i}^j$ ($j = 1, 2, \ldots, m$) are triangular fuzzy numbers.

The value of fuzzy synthetic extent with respect to the ith object is defined as

$$S_i = \sum_{j=1}^{m} M_{g_i}^j \otimes \left[\sum_{i=1}^{n} \sum_{j=1}^{m} M_{g_i}^j \right]^{-1}. \quad (2)$$

The degree of possibility of $M_1 \geq M_2$ is defined as

$$V(M_1 \geq M_2) = \sup_{x \geq y} \left[\min(\mu_{M_1}(x), \mu_{M_2}(y)) \right]. \quad (3)$$

When a pair (x, y) exists such that $x \geq y$ and $\mu_{M_1}(x) = \mu_{M_2}(y)$ then we have $V(M_1 \geq M_2) = 1$. Since M_1 and M_2 are convex fuzzy numbers we have

$$V(M_1 \geq M_2) = 1 \quad \text{if } m_1 \geq m_2,$$
$$V(M_1 \geq M_2) = \text{hgt}(M_1 \cap M_2) = \mu_{M_1}(d), \quad (4)$$

where d is the ordinate of the highest intersection point D between μ_{M_1} and μ_{M_2}.

When $M_1 = (l_1, m_1, u_1)$ and $M_2 = (l_2, m_2, u_2)$, the ordinate of D is given by

$$V(M_2 \geq M_1) = \text{hgt}(M_1 \cap M_2) = \mu_{M_2}(d)$$

$$= \begin{cases} 1 & m_2 \geq m_1, \\ 0 & l_1 \geq u_2, \\ \dfrac{l_1 - u_2}{(m_2 - u_2) - (m_1 - l_1)} & \text{otherwise.} \end{cases} \quad (5)$$

To compare M_1 and M_2, we need both the values of $V(M_1 \geq M_2)$ and $V(M_2 \geq M_1)$ and the intersection between M_1 and M_2.

The degree possibility for a convex fuzzy number to be greater than k convex fuzzy numbers M_i ($i = 1, 2, \ldots, k$) can be defined by

$$V(M \geq M_1, M_2, \ldots, M_k)$$
$$= V[(M \geq M_1), (M \geq M_2), \ldots, (M \geq M_k)] \quad (6)$$
$$= \min V(M \geq M_i), \quad i = 1, 2, \ldots, k.$$

Assume that

$$d'(A_i) = \min V(S_i \geq S_k). \quad (7)$$

For $k = 1, 2, \ldots, n; k \neq i$. Then the weight vector is given by

$$W' = (d'(A_1), d'(A_2), \ldots, d'(A_n))^T, \quad (8)$$

where A_i ($i = 1, 2, \ldots, n$) are n elements.

Via normalization, the normalized weight vectors are

$$W = (d(A_1), d(A_2), \ldots, d(A_n))^T, \quad (9)$$

where W is a nonfuzzy number.

2.2. The Fuzzy TOPSIS Method. The TOPSIS [22] is widely used for tackling ranking problems in real situations. Despite its popularity and simplicity in concept, this method is often criticized for its inability to adequately handle the inherent uncertainty and imprecision associated with the mapping of the decision-maker's perception to crisp values. In the traditional formulation of the TOPSIS, personal judgments are represented with crisp values. However, in many practical cases the human preference model is uncertain and decision-makers might be reluctant or unable to assign crisp values to the comparison judgments [23]. Having to use crisp values is one of the problematic points in the crisp evaluation process. One reason is that decision-makers usually feel more confident to give interval judgments rather than expressing their judgments in the form of single numeric values. As some criteria are difficult to measure by crisp values, they are usually neglected during the evaluation. Another reason is mathematical models that are based on crisp value. These methods cannot deal with decision-makers' ambiguities, uncertainties, and vagueness which cannot be handled by crisp values [24]. The use of fuzzy set theory [25] allows the decision-makers to incorporate unquantifiable information, incomplete information, non-obtainable information, and partially ignorant facts into decision model [26].

TFNs appear to be a valid tool, offering a well balanced compromise between computational costs and accuracy in the final ranking [27].

The steps of fuzzy TOPSIS are as follows [28, 29].

Step 1. Choose the appropriate linguistic variables for the alternatives with respect to criteria. The linguistic variables are described by TFNs, such as $\tilde{x}_{ij} = (a_{ij}, b_{ij}, c_{ij})$.

Step 2. Construct the fuzzy decision matrix and the normalized fuzzy decision matrix:

$$\tilde{R} = \left[\tilde{r}_{ij} \right]_{m \times n}. \tag{10}$$

Step 3. Calculate the weighted normalized fuzzy decision matrix. The weighted normalized value $\tilde{v}_{ij}$ is calculated as

$$\tilde{V} = \left[\tilde{v}_{ij} \right]_{n \times J}, \quad i = 1, 2, \ldots, n, \; j = 1, 2, \ldots, J. \tag{11}$$

Step 4. Identify positive-ideal (A^*) and negative ideal (A^-) solutions. The fuzzy positive-ideal solution (FPIS, A^*) and the fuzzy negative-ideal solution (FNIS, A^-) are shown in the following equations:

$$A^* = \{\tilde{v}_1^*, \tilde{v}_2^*, \ldots, \tilde{v}_i^*\},$$
$$A^- = \{\tilde{v}_1^-, \tilde{v}_2^-, \ldots, \tilde{v}_i^-\}, \tag{12}$$

where $\tilde{v}_{ij}^* = w_j \otimes (1,1,1)$, $\tilde{v}_{ij}^- = w_j \otimes (0,0,0)$ for all $j = 1, 2, \ldots, n$.

Step 5. Calculate the distance of each alternative from A^* and A^- using following equations:

$$D_j^* = \sum_{j=1}^{n} d\left(\tilde{v}_{ij}, \tilde{v}_i^*\right), \quad j = 1, 2, \ldots, J,$$
$$D_j^- = \sum_{j=1}^{n} d\left(\tilde{v}_{ij}, \tilde{v}_i^-\right), \quad j = 1, 2, \ldots, J. \tag{13}$$

Step 6. Determine the similarities to ideal solution

$$CC_j^* = \frac{D_j^-}{D_j^* + D_j^-}, \quad j = 1, 2, \ldots, J. \tag{14}$$

Step 7. Rank the preference order.

3. The Proposed Model

The model proposed for the provider selection problem consists of two different kinds of fuzzy MCDM approaches: fuzzy AHP, which we used for calculating weights of criteria, and fuzzy TOPSIS for the ranking of alternative providers.

At first step, a decision making group is organized from experts, managers, and academics. Decision makers determined the selection criteria and provider alternatives, then they built the hierarchical structure of decision model.

After building the hierarchical structure, pairwise comparison matrix is established to identify the weights of criteria. The weights have been calculated by Chang's [21] extent analysis on fuzzy AHP based on previously determined linguistic variables by decision makers.

Finally, provider ranks have been determined by fuzzy TOPSIS in accordance with the linguistic variable values of providers. The alternative having the maximum CC_j value is selected as the most appropriate provider.

4. Illustrative Example

Decision making group which is composed of experts, managers, and academics determined 6 important criteria out of 30 criteria. They eliminate the less important criteria in accordance with their experiments and knowledge. And the same group also determined 5 provider alternatives out of 15 firms. In order to take into account the uncertainty in judgements and vagueness in reasoning and by the help of membership functions we can exactly measure the perceptions. Therefore we used fuzzy linguistic variables applied. Figure 1 shows the linguistic scale of fuzzy triangular numbers.

4.1. Determination of Criteria Weights. Provider selection criteria in 3PL are decided as follows. Figure 2 shows the hierarchical structure of the model.

(1) Price (PR);

(2) General reputation (GR);

(3) Customer services (CS);

TABLE 1: Triangular fuzzy conversion scale.

Linguistic scale for importance degrees	Triangular fuzzy scale	Triangular fuzzy reciprocal scale
Equally important	(1/2, 1, 3/2)	(2/3, 1, 2)
Weakly important	(1, 3/2, 2)	(1/2, 2/3, 1)
Moderately important	(3/2, 2, 5/2)	(2/5, 1/2, 2/3)
Fairly important	(2, 5/2, 3)	(1/3, 2/5, 1/2)
Strongly important	(5/2, 3, 7/2)	(2/7, 1/3, 2/5)
Strongly more important	(3, 7/2, 4)	(1/4, 2/7, 1/3)
Very strongly important	(7/2, 4, 9/2)	(2/9, 1/4, 2/7)
Absolutely important	(4, 9/2, 5)	(1/5, 2/9, 1/4)

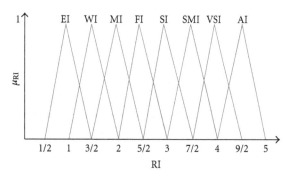

FIGURE 1: The linguistic scale of fuzzy triangular numbers.

(4) On-time delivery (OD);

(5) Information technologies (IT);

(6) Flexibility (FL).

Table 1 shows the Triangular fuzzy conversion scale of importance degrees and the pairwise comparison matrix of criteria is given in Table 2. After the calculations according to the pairwise comparison matrix in Table 3 through fuzzy AHP, the weights of criteria were determined.

4.2. Selection of the Provider. In this section we used the Chen's fuzzy linguistic scale as shown in Table 4 for calculations in fuzzy TOPSIS.

After the calculations according to Table 6 ranking of providers is determined. Fuzzy Evaluation Matrix for Providers is given on Table 5.

Same calculation steps are applied to all alternatives. Based on the CC_j values the maximum CC_j value is selected as the best provider (P3); after P3 the rank of alternatives in descending order is P5, P1, P4, and P2.

5. Conclusions

Due to the rapid growth of industries and increased global competition, firms must take care of all processes of business. In order to enrich competitive advantages in market, firms are considering different strategies. Logistic outsourcing is one of these strategies. An effective provider selection

TABLE 2: The pairwise comparison matrix of criteria.

	PR	GR	CS	OD	IT	FL
PR	—	MI	WI	EI	SI	VSI
GR		—	SMI			
CS		WI	—			
OD			SI	—	WI	SI
IT		SMI	MI		—	
FL		WI	EI		MI	—

TABLE 3: Weights of criteria.

W_{PR}	0.293
W_{GR}	0.101
W_{CS}	0.038
W_{OD}	0.299
W_{IT}	0.19
W_{FL}	0.079

TABLE 4: Chen's fuzzy scale.

Linguistic variable	Fuzzy scale
Very low (VL)	(0, 0, 0.1)
Low (L)	(0, 0.1, 0.3)
Medium low (ML)	(0.1, 0.3, 0.5)
Medium (M)	(0.3, 0.5, 0.7)
Medium high (MH)	(0.5, 0.7, 0.9)
High (H)	(0.7, 0.9, 1)
Very high (VH)	(0.9, 1, 1)

TABLE 5: Fuzzy evaluation matrix for providers.

	PR	GR	CS	OD	IT	FL
P1	M	ML	MH	MH	H	M
P2	H	MH	L	ML	MH	M
P3	VH	ML	ML	H	MH	H
P4	MH	ML	H	ML	MH	MH
P5	M	H	MH	H	ML	H

plays a vital role both for outsourcing company and the provider. In general the necessary data for MCDM problems are imprecise and uncertain. Solving problems through fuzzy techniques eliminates the limitation of crisp values. The importance of the model is the vagueness of the subjective decision making, taken into account by using fuzzy techniques in fuzzy environment. More dependable, more sensitive, and more flexible results can be obtained through fuzzy approaches. Weights of provider selection criteria are determined through FAHP and providers ranked through fuzzy TOPSIS. This model integrates different fuzzy MCDMs in order to take advantages of different approaches. Owing to the hybrid structure the disadvantages of dependency to only one method is eliminated. The hybrid model aims to integrate the strong aspects of different fuzzy methods.

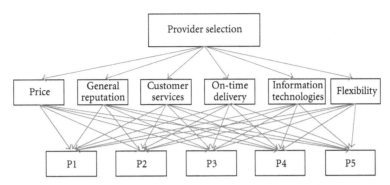

FIGURE 2: Hierarchical structure of the model.

TABLE 6: Fuzzy TOPSIS results.

Alternatives	D_j^*	D_j^-	CC_j	Ranking
P1	5.387	0.639	0.106	3
P2	5.411	0.616	0.102	5
P3	5.196	0.817	0.136	1
P4	5.398	0.629	0.104	4
P5	5.358	0.666	0.111	2

Future researches may try to extend this study as an integration of more fuzzy MCDM techniques to solve many other decision making problems in many other disciplines.

References

[1] M. L. Christopher, *Logistics and Supply Chain Management*, Pitman Publishing, London, UK, 1992.

[2] L. M. Ellram, "Supply chain management: the industrial organization perspective," *International Journal of Physical Distribution & Logistics Management*, vol. 21, no. 1, pp. 13–22, 1991.

[3] S. E. Fawcett, L. M. Ellram, and J. A. Ogden, *Supply Chain Management from Vision to Implementation*, Pearson Education, Upper Saddle River, NJ, USA, 2007.

[4] J. Yan, P. E. Chaudhry, and S. S. Chaudhry, "A model of a decision support system based on case-based reasoning for third-party logistics evaluation," *Expert Systems*, vol. 20, no. 4, pp. 196–207, 2003.

[5] M. J. Maloni and C. R. Carter, "Opportunities for research in third-party logistics," *Transportation Journal*, vol. 45, no. 2, pp. 23–38, 2006.

[6] B. Ashenbaum, A. Maltz, and E. Rabinovich, "Studies of trends in third-party logistics usage: what can we conclude?" *Transportation Journal*, vol. 44, no. 3, pp. 38–50, 2005.

[7] R. Lieb and B. A. Bentz, "The use of third-party logistics services by large American manufacturers: the 2004 survey," *Transportation Journal*, vol. 44, no. 2, pp. 5–15, 2005.

[8] J. Deepen, T. Goldsby, M. Knemeyer, and C. Wallenburg, "Beyond expectations: an examination of logistics outsourcing goal achievement and goal exceedance," *Journal of Business Logistics*, vol. 29, no. 2, pp. 75–106, 2008.

[9] L. E. Gadde and K. Hulthén, "Improving logistics outsourcing through increasing buyer-provider interaction," *Industrial Marketing Management*, vol. 38, no. 6, pp. 633–640, 2009.

[10] R. C. Lieb, R. A. Millen, and L. V. Wassenhove, "Third-party logistics services: a comparison of experienced American and European manufacturers," *International Journal of Physical Distribution & Logistics Management*, vol. 6, no. 23, pp. 35–44, 1993.

[11] Capgemini, "Third-partylogisticsstudy," 2005, http://www.scl.gatech.edu/research/supply-chain/20053PLReport.pdf.

[12] Capgemini, "Third-partylogistics," 2007, http://www.scl.gate-ch.edu/research/supply-chain/20073PLReport.pdf.

[13] G. Işiklar, E. Alptekin, and G. Büyüközkan, "Application of a hybrid intelligent decision support model in logistics outsourcing," *Computers and Operations Research*, vol. 34, no. 12, pp. 3701–3714, 2007.

[14] P. Barrar and R. Gervais, *Global Outsourcing Strategies: An International Reference on Effective Outsourcing Relationships*, Gower Publishing Company, Burlington, Vt, USA, 2006.

[15] R. Bhatnagar, A. S. Sohal, and R. Millen, "Third party logistics services: a Singapore perspective," *International Journal of Physical Distribution and Logistics Management*, vol. 29, no. 9, pp. 569–587, 1999.

[16] S. Hertz and M. Alfredsson, "Strategic development of third party logistics providers," *Industrial Marketing Management*, vol. 32, no. 2, pp. 139–149, 2003.

[17] T. Skjoett-Larsen, "Third party logistics-form an inter-organizational point of view," *International Journal of Physical Distribution and Logistics Management*, vol. 30, no. 2, pp. 112–127, 2000.

[18] G. Büyüközkan, O. Feyzioğlu, and E. Nebol, "Selection of the strategic alliance partner in logistics value chain," *International Journal of Production Economics*, vol. 113, no. 1, pp. 148–158, 2008.

[19] J. C. Pomerol and S. Barba Romero, *Multicriterion Decision in Management: Principles and Practice*, Kluwer Academic, Norwell, Mass, USA, 2000.

[20] T. L. Saaty, *The Analytic Hierarchy Process*, McGraw-Hill, New York, NY, USA, 1980.

[21] D. Y. Chang, "Applications of the extent analysis method on fuzzy AHP," *European Journal of Operational Research*, vol. 95, no. 3, pp. 649–655, 1996.

[22] C. L. Hwang and K. Yoon, *Multiple Attribute Decision Making: Methods and Applications: A State of the Art Survey*, Springer, New York, NY, USA, 1981.

[23] F. T. S. Chan, N. Kumar, M. K. Tiwari, H. C. W. Lau, and K. L. Choy, "Global supplier selection: a fuzzy-AHP approach," *International Journal of Production Research*, vol. 46, no. 14, pp. 3825–3857, 2008.

[24] M. Dağdeviren, S. Yavuz, and N. Kilinç, "Weapon selection using the AHP and TOPSIS methods under fuzzy environment," *Expert Systems with Applications*, vol. 36, no. 4, pp. 8143–8151, 2009.

[25] L. A. Zadeh, "Fuzzy sets," *Information and Control*, vol. 8, no. 3, pp. 338–353, 1965.

[26] O. Kulak, M. B. Durmuşoğlu, and C. Kahraman, "Fuzzy multi-attribute equipment selection based on information axiom," *Journal of Materials Processing Technology*, vol. 169, no. 3, pp. 337–345, 2005.

[27] E. Triantaphyllou and L. Chi-Tun, "Development and evaluation of five fuzzy multiattribute decision-making methods," *International Journal of Approximate Reasoning*, vol. 14, no. 4, pp. 281–310, 1996.

[28] C. T. Chen, "Extensions of the TOPSIS for group decision-making under fuzzy environment," *Fuzzy Sets and Systems*, vol. 114, no. 1, pp. 1–9, 2000.

[29] C. T. Chen, C. T. Lin, and S. F. Huang, "A fuzzy approach for supplier evaluation and selection in supply chain management," *International Journal of Production Economics*, vol. 102, no. 2, pp. 289–301, 2006.

16

Improving Vector Evaluated Particle Swarm Optimisation by Incorporating Nondominated Solutions

Kian Sheng Lim,[1] **Zuwairie Ibrahim,**[2] **Salinda Buyamin,**[1] **Anita Ahmad,**[1] **Faradila Naim,**[2] **Kamarul Hawari Ghazali,**[2] **and Norrima Mokhtar**[3]

[1] *Faculty of Electrical Engineering, Universiti Teknologi Malaysia, 81310 Johor Bahru, Malaysia*
[2] *Faculty of Electrical and Electronic Engineering, Universiti Malaysia Pahang, 26600 Pekan, Malaysia*
[3] *Department of Electrical Engineering, Faculty of Engineering, University of Malaya, 50603 Kuala Lumpur, Malaysia*

Correspondence should be addressed to Zuwairie Ibrahim; zuwairie@ump.edu.my

Academic Editors: P. Agarwal, V. Bhatnagar, and Y. Zhang

The Vector Evaluated Particle Swarm Optimisation algorithm is widely used to solve multiobjective optimisation problems. This algorithm optimises one objective using a swarm of particles where their movements are guided by the best solution found by another swarm. However, the best solution of a swarm is only updated when a newly generated solution has better fitness than the best solution at the objective function optimised by that swarm, yielding poor solutions for the multiobjective optimisation problems. Thus, an improved Vector Evaluated Particle Swarm Optimisation algorithm is introduced by incorporating the nondominated solutions as the guidance for a swarm rather than using the best solution from another swarm. In this paper, the performance of improved Vector Evaluated Particle Swarm Optimisation algorithm is investigated using performance measures such as the number of nondominated solutions found, the generational distance, the spread, and the hypervolume. The results suggest that the improved Vector Evaluated Particle Swarm Optimisation algorithm has impressive performance compared with the conventional Vector Evaluated Particle Swarm Optimisation algorithm.

1. Introduction

In multiobjective optimisation (MOO) problems, multiple objective functions are solved simultaneously by either minimising or maximising the fitness of the functions. These multiple objective functions usually conflict with each other. Therefore, the solution to an MOO problem is a set of multiple tradeoffs, or nondominated solutions, rather than a single solution.

The Vector Evaluated Particle Swarm Optimisation (VEPSO) [1] algorithm introduced by Parsopoulos and Vrahatis has been used to solve various MOO problems, such as the design of radiometer array antennas [2], the design of supersonic ejectors for hydrogen fuel cells [3], the design of composite structures [4], the design of steady-state performance for power systems [5], and the design of multiple machine-scheduling systems [6]. In the VEPSO algorithm, one swarm of particles optimises an objective function using guidance from the best solution found by another swarm.

The nondominated solutions found during the optimisation are usually preferred for effective guidance [7]. As an example, the multiobjective PSO (MOPSO) algorithm [8, 9] divides all nondominated solutions into several groups based on their locations in the objective space. Then, one of the nondominated solutions is randomly selected from the group that has the fewest solutions to be used as the particle guide. Furthermore, the nondominated sorting PSO (NSPSO) algorithm [10] uses the primary mechanism of nondominated sorting genetic algorithm-II [11], in which one nondominated solution is randomly selected to be used as the guide for the particles based on the niche count and nearest-neighbour density estimator. In addition, the optimised MOPSO (OMOPSO) algorithm [12] by Margarita Reyes-Sierra and Carlos Coello Coello uses the crowding distance mechanism for binary tournaments to select one of the nondominated solutions as the guide for each particle. Abido [13] uses two nondominated solutions, a local set and a global set, to optimise the problem. Each particle is guided by the nondominated solution that has smallest distance between the particle and both nondominated solution sets.

The conventional VEPSO algorithm solves an MOO problem by improving the solutions in a swarm under the guidance of the best solution with respect to a single objective, found by another swarm. However, the nondominated solution which has better fitness with respect to the other objectives may exist, but it was not used to guide the particles in other swarm. The nondominated solutions are always equal or better solutions compared with the best solution used in conventional VEPSO. The superiority of the nondominated solutions motivates the use of nondominated solutions as particle guides for each swarm in improving the VEPSO algorithm. Thus, in this study, the guidance of a swarm is selected by the nondominated solution which has best fitness with respect to a single objective function, optimised by the other swarm.

The paper is organized as follows. In Section 2, we explain some information on MOO problem. Then, in Section 3, we explain the particle swarm optimisation (PSO), the conventional VEPSO, and the improved VEPSO algorithms. In the next section, we demonstrate the simulation experiment which includes several performance measures and benchmark test problem, before we discuss the results. Lastly, we present the conclusion and include some suggestion for future work.

2. Multiobjective Optimisation

Consider a minimisation of a multiobjective problem:

minimise the fitness function,

$$\vec{F}(\vec{x}) = \left\{ f_m(\vec{x}) \in \mathfrak{R}^M, \ m = 1, 2, \ldots, M \right\}$$

subject to $g_j(\vec{x}) \leq 0, \quad j = 1, 2, \ldots, J,$

$$h_k(\vec{x}) = 0, \quad k = 1, 2, \ldots, K,$$

$$(1)$$

where $\vec{x} = \{x_n \in \mathfrak{R}^N, \ n = 1, 2, \ldots, N\}$ is the N-dimensional vector of decision variables that represent the possible solutions, M is the number of objectives, $f_m \in \mathfrak{R}^M$ is the objective function, and $\{g_j, h_k\} \in \mathfrak{R}$ are the inequality and equality constraint functions, respectively.

In explaining the concept of Pareto optimality, consider two vectors $\{\vec{F^a}, \vec{F^b}\} \in \mathfrak{R}^M$. $\vec{F^a}$ *dominates* $\vec{F^b}$ (denote as $\vec{F^a} \prec \vec{F^b}$) if and only if $f_m^a \leq f_m^b$ for $m = 1, 2, \ldots, M$ and $f_m^a < f_m^b$ at least once. The dominance relations $\vec{F^a} \prec \vec{F^b}$ and $\vec{F^a} \prec \vec{F^c}$ for a two-objective problem are indicated by the labelled circles in Figure 1. Hence, a vector of decision variables $\vec{x^a}$ is a *nondominated solution* if and only if there is no other solution $\vec{x^b}$ such that $\vec{F}(\vec{x^a}) \prec \vec{F}(\vec{x^b})$. The nondominated

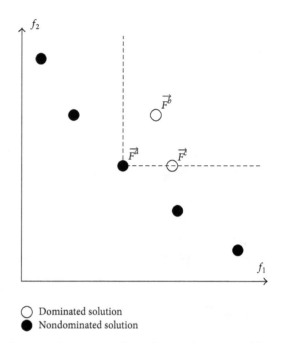

FIGURE 1: Dominance relation for two objectives problem.

○ Dominated solution
● Nondominated solution

solution is also known as the Pareto optimal solution. The set of nondominated solutions of an MOO problem is known as the *Pareto Optimal set*, $\mathscr{P}$. The set of objective vectors with respect to $\mathscr{P}$ is known as the *Pareto Front*, $\mathscr{PF} = \{\vec{F}(\vec{x}) \in \mathfrak{R}^M \mid \vec{x} \in \mathscr{P}\}$. The $\mathscr{PF}$ for a two-objective problem is illustrated by the black circles in Figure 1.

The goal of an MOO algorithm is to find as many nondominated solutions as possible according to the objective functions and constraints. The Pareto front corresponding to the nondominated set should be as close to and well distributed over the true Pareto front as possible. However, it is possible to have different solutions that map to the same fitness value in objective space.

3. Particle Swarm Optimisation

3.1. Original Particle Swarm Optimisation Algorithm. Based on the social behaviour of birds flocking and fish schooling, a population-based stochastic optimisation algorithm named Particle Swarm Optimisation (PSO) was introduced by Kennedy et al. [14, 15]. The PSO algorithm contains individuals referred to as particles that encode the possible solutions to the optimisation problem using their positions. These particles explore the defined search space to look for solutions that better satisfy the objective function of the optimised problem. Each particle collaborates with the others during the search process by comparing its current position with the best position that it and the other particles in the swarm have found [16].

Figure 2 shows the flow chart of the PSO algorithm. For the PSO algorithm, consider the following minimisation problem: there are I-particles flying around in an N-dimensional search space, where their positions, p_n^i ($i =$

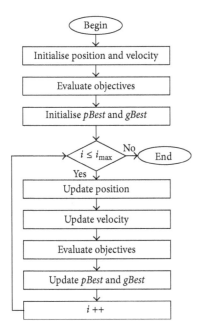

FIGURE 2: The PSO algorithm.

1, 2, ..., I; n = 1, 2, ..., N), represent the possible solutions. Initially, all particles are randomly positioned in the search space and assigned random velocities, $v_n^i(t)$. Then, the objective fitness, $\overrightarrow{F^i}(t)$, for each particle is evaluated by calculating the objective functions with respect to $p^i(t)$. Next, each particle's best position, $pBest^i(t)$, is initialised to its current position. Meanwhile, the best among all $pBest^i(t)$ is set as the swarm's best position, $gBest(t)$, as specified in (2), where S is the swarm of particles:

$$gBest = \left\{ pBest^i \in S \mid f\left(pBest^i\right) = \min f\left(\forall pBest^i \in S\right) \right\}. \tag{2}$$

Next, the algorithm iterates until the stopping condition is met; that is, either the maximum number of iterations is exceeded or the minimum error is attained. In each iteration, each particle's velocity and position are updated using (3) and (4), respectively,

$$v_n^i(t+1) = \chi \left[\omega v_n^i(t) + c_1 r_1 \left(pBest_n^i - p_n^i(t)\right) \right.$$
$$\left. + c_2 r_2 \left(gBest_n - p_n^i(t)\right) \right], \tag{3}$$

$$p_n^i(t+1) = p_n^i(t) + v_n^i(t+1), \tag{4}$$

where χ is the constriction factor and ω is the inertia weight. c_1 and c_2 are the cognitive and social coefficients, respectively. Meanwhile, r_1 and r_2 are both random values between zero and one. After the velocity and position are updated, the $\overrightarrow{F^i}(t)$ for each particle is evaluated again. Later, $pBest^i(t)$ is updated with the more optimal between the new position of the ith particle or $pBest^i(t)$. Then, the $gBest(t)$ is updated with the most optimal $pBest^i(t)$ among all the particles, as given in (2). Finally, when the stopping condition is met, $gBest(t)$

represents the optimum solution found for the problem optimised using this algorithm.

3.2. Vector Evaluated Particle Swarm Optimisation Algorithm. Parsopóulos and Vrahatis [1] introduced the VEPSO algorithm, which was inspired by the multiswarm concept of the VEGA algorithm [17]. In this multiswarm concept, each objective function is optimised by a swarm of particles using the $gBest(t)$ from another swarm. The $gBest(t)$ for the mth swarm is the $pBest^i(t)$ that has most optimal fitness with respect to the mth objective, among all $pBest^i(t)$ from the mth swarm, as given below:

$$gBest^m = \left\{ pBest^i \in S^m \mid f_m\left(pBest^i\right) \right.$$
$$= \min f_m\left(\forall pBest^i \in S^m\right) \right\}. \tag{5}$$

Generally, the PSO and VEPSO algorithms have similar process flows, except that all processes are repeated for M swarms when optimising problems with M objective functions. Because each swarm optimises using $gBest(t)$ from another swarm, in VEPSO, the velocity is updated using (6). The velocity equation for particles in the mth swarm updates $gBest^k(t)$, where k is given in (7):

$$v_n^m i(t+1) = \chi \left[\omega v_n^{mi}(t) + c_1 r_1 \left(pBest_n^{mi} - p_n^{mi}(t)\right) \right.$$
$$\left. + c_2 r_2 \left(gBest_n^k - p_n^{mi}(t)\right) \right], \tag{6}$$

$$k = \begin{cases} M, & m = 1, \\ m - 1, & \text{otherwise.} \end{cases} \tag{7}$$

In addition to the difference in the velocity equation, all nondominated solutions found during the optimisation are stored in an archive each time after the objective functions are evaluated. To ensure that the archive contains nondominated solutions only, the fitness $\overrightarrow{F^i}(t)$ of each particle is compared, based on the Pareto optimality criterion, to those of all particles before it is compared to the nondominated solutions in the archive. All nondominated solutions in the archive represent possible solutions to the MOO problem.

3.3. The Improved VEPSO Algorithm. In conventional VEPSO, each particle of a swarm is updated by the $gBest(t)$ from the other swarm that is optimal with respect to the objective function optimised by the other swarm. Consider a two-objective optimisation problem as an example; the $gBest(t)$ of the first swarm is only updated when a newly generated solution has better fitness with respect to the first objective, as specified in (5). Thus, $gBest(t)$ is not updated even if the new solution, nondominated solution, has equal fitness with respect to the first objective and better fitness with respect to the second objective. Hence, as in Figure 3(a), each particle from the second swarm moves under the guidance of the $gBest^1(t)$ but not the better, nondominated solutions.

However, this limitation can be overcome by updating $gBest(t)$ with a new solution, nondominated solution, that

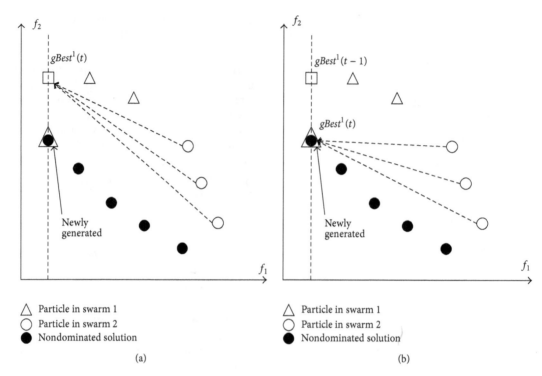

FIGURE 3: Particles guided by (a) the best solution from the other swarm and (b) a nondominated solution.

has equal fitness with respect to the optimised objective function and better fitness with respect to the other objective. This improved VEPSO algorithm is represented in Figure 3(b), where $gBest^1(t)$ is now a nondominated solution that is best with respect to the first objective function. Thus, each particle from the second swarm will be guided by its own $pBest^2i(t)$ and $gBest^1(t)$, which is a nondominated solution, with the hope that the particle will converge toward the Pareto front faster.

In the improved VEPSO algorithm, the generality of conventional VEPSO is not lost; so the $gBest(t)$ of a swarm is the best nondominated solution with respect to the objective function optimised by the swarm. Therefore, the $gBest(t)$ of the mth swarm is given as following:

$$gBest^m = \{X \in \mathscr{P} \mid f_m(X) = \min f_m \ (\forall X \in \mathscr{P})\}, \quad (8)$$

where X is a nondominated solution and $\mathscr{P}$ is the set of nondominated solutions in the archive. For a two-objective-function problem, the particles from the second swarm are guided by the nondominated solution that is best with respect to the first objective function. Meanwhile, the particles of the first swarm are guided by the nondominated solution that is optimal with respect to the second objective function. Thus, this improved algorithm is called Vector Evaluated Particle Swarm Optimisation incorporate nondominated solutions (VEPSOnds).

In addition, the PSO algorithm has the natural limitation that particles tend to become stuck in locally optimal solutions [18, 19]. Therefore, this improved VEPSO algorithm also includes the polynomial mutation mechanism from nondominated sorting genetic algorithm-II [11]. The polynomial mutation mechanism modifies the particle position with a certain probability such that the particle can mutate out from the locally optimal solution and continue the search for a globally optimal solution. In this work, one of every ten particles is mutated in the improved VEPSO algorithm.

4. Experiment

4.1. Performance Measure. In order to analyse the performance of the VEPSOml algorithm, several quantitative performance mesasures are used. Since MOO problems have different features, for example multilocal optima solution, which could trap the particles from obtaining more nondominated solutions; hence, the number of solution (NS) measure is used to quantify the total number of nondominated solutions found at the end of the computation. Besides, for example when the particles one trapped in a local optima solution, the obtained Pareto front will not be converged close to the true Pareto front which means that the best possible solutions were not found yet. Thus, the generational distance (GD) [20] is used and defined as the average Euclidean distance between the obtained Pareto front, $\mathscr{PF}_o$, and the true Pareto front, $\mathscr{PF}_t$, using (9). A smaller GD value indicates better performance:

$$GD = \frac{\left(\sum_{q=1}^{\|\mathscr{PF}_o\|} d_q^M\right)^{1/M}}{\|\mathscr{PF}_o\|},$$

$$d_q = \min_{1 \leq k \leq \|\mathscr{PF}_t\|} \sqrt{\sum_{j=1}^{M} \left(f_j^q - f_j^k\right)^2}. \quad (9)$$

A well-converged Pareto front does not guarantee to have good diversity of nondominated solutions along the Pareto front. Therefore, the third performance metric used is the spread (SP) [11], which is used to measure the extent of the distribution of the $\mathscr{PF}_o$ along the $\mathscr{PF}_t$. Equations (10), are used to measure SP, and smaller values indicate better performance:

$$SP = \frac{d_f + d_l + \sum_{q=1}^{\|\mathscr{PF}_o\|-1} |d_q - \overline{d}|}{d_f + d_l + (\|\mathscr{PF}_o\| - 1)\overline{d}},$$

$$\overline{d} = \frac{\sum_{q=1}^{\|\mathscr{PF}_o\|-1} d_q}{\|\mathscr{PF}_o\| - 1}, \qquad (10)$$

$$d_q = \sqrt{\left(f_1^q - f_1^{q+1}\right)^2 + \left(f_2^q - f_2^{q+1}\right)^2},$$

where d_f is the Euclidean distance between the first extreme members in $\mathscr{PF}_o$ and $\mathscr{PF}_t$ and d_l is the Euclidean distance between the last extreme members in $\mathscr{PF}_o$ and $\mathscr{PF}_t$. In some cases, the obtained Pareto fronts could be converged well to the true Pareto front but it has poor diversity performance. Hence, it is not fair by comparing different algorithms with the GD and SP measures only. Finally, the hypervolume (HV) [21] is used to measure the total space or area enclosed by the $\mathscr{PF}_o$ and a reference point, R, which is a vector constructed from the worst objective value from the $\mathscr{PF}_t$. Equation (11) is used to evaluate the HV value. The total area for HV is the enclosed area in Figure 4 and is calculated using (11). Larger HV values represent better performance:

$$HV = \sum_{q=1}^{\|\mathscr{PF}_o\|} v_q, \qquad (11)$$

where v_q is the space or area between R and the diagonal corner of qth solution of $\mathscr{PF}_o$.

4.2. Test Problems. Five of the benchmark test problems from ZDT [22] are used to evaluate the performance of the algorithm. Because this study focused on continuous search space problems, the ZDT5 problem is not used as it is for the evaluation of binary problems. All benchmark problems are set up using the parameter values recommended in the paper [22]. For evaluating the performance measure, the true Pareto front for each problem is obtained from the standard database generated by the jMetal (http://jmetal.sourceforge.net/problems.html).

4.3. Evaluation of VEPSO Algorithms. Because the VEPSOnds algorithm includes polynomial mutation, the experiment in this work should analyse a version of VEPSOnds that does not include polynomial mutation. This implementation exists because the polynomial mutation affects the algorithm's performance, and it is necessary to determine whether the change in performance is due to the use of multiple nondominated solutions or the polynomial mutation. Thus, in this work, the VEPSOnds algorithm without mutation is denoted as VEPSOnds1 and the VEPSOnds algorithm with mutation is denoted as VEPSOnds2.

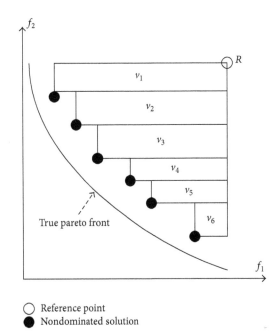

FIGURE 4: Hypervolume measure with area covered by the nondominated solutions and a reference point.

In this experiment, the total number of particles is fixed to 100 and divided equally among all swarms. The archive size is controlled by removing the nondominated solutions with the smallest crowding distance [11]. In addition, the maximum iteration and archive size are set to 250 and 100, respectively. During the computation, the inertia weight is linearly degraded from 1.0 to 0.4. The cognitive and social constants are both random values between 1.5 and 2.5. Moreover, the distribution index is set to 0.5 for the mutation operation. Each test problem is simulated for 100 runs to enable statistical analysis.

The performance of each algorithm tested on the ZDT1 problem is presented in Table 1. For the average NS measure, the number of nondominated solutions found by both improved VEPSO algorithms was significantly greater for conventional VEPSO. For the GD measure, VEPSOnds1 demonstrated significant improvement compared with the conventional VEPSO algorithm. Meanwhile, the VEPSOnds2 algorithm exhibited an extremely large improvement compared with both conventional VEPSO and VEPSOnds1. Similarly, the SP measures for both improved VEPSO algorithms also indicated significant improvement compared with conventional VEPSO. As expected, the HV performance also improved dramatically when the problem was optimised using multiple nondominated solutions as particle guides.

For better visual comparison, the Pareto fronts with the best GD value returned for each test problem are shown in Figure 5 through Figure 9. Figure 5 shows the plot of nondominated solutions with the best GD measure returned for the ZDT1 problem. The nondominated solutions obtained by VEPSO are clearly located very far away from the true Pareto front, which leads to a large GD value. Moreover, the obtained solutions are unevenly distributed around the

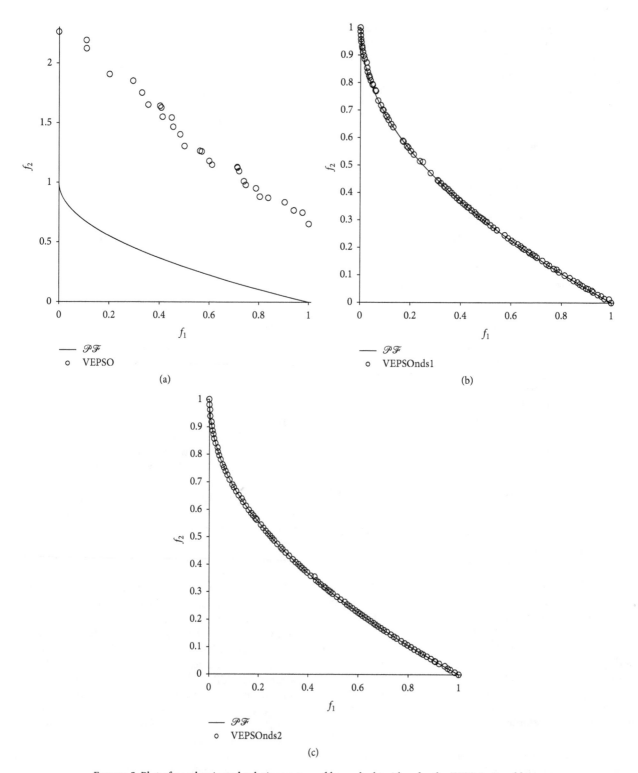

FIGURE 5: Plot of nondominated solutions returned by each algorithm for the ZDT1 test problem.

objective space, which yields a large SP value. In contrast, the VEPSOnds1 and VEPSOnds2 algorithms generated nondominated solutions close to and evenly distributed over the true the Pareto front. Therefore, the GD and SP values for both improved VEPSO algorithms are significantly smaller than those for conventional VEPSO. However, the VEPSOnds2 has better distribution of nondominated solutions than the VEPSOnds1.

Table 2 presents the performance measures for all algorithms tested on the ZDT2 problem. Again, both the

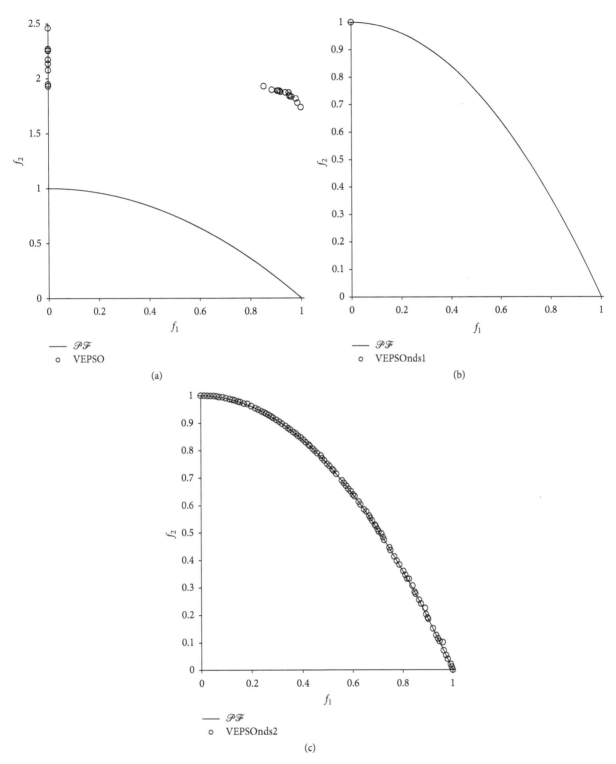

FIGURE 6: Plot of nondominated solutions returned by each algorithm for the ZDT2 test problem.

improved VEPSO algorithms dramatically improved the ability to obtain a large number of solutions compared with VEPSO, especially VPESOnds2. In addition to the NS performance, the GD and SP performances were also dramatically improved because the nondominated solutions used in the improved VEPSO algorithms are better guides compared with the best solution among each particle, which is used in conventional VEPSO. However, in SP measure, the VEPSOnds1 shows negligible improvement, whereas the VEPSOnds2 shows distinguished improvement over the conventional VEPSO. The conventional VEPSO algorithm was unable to yield a meaningful HV because the obtained

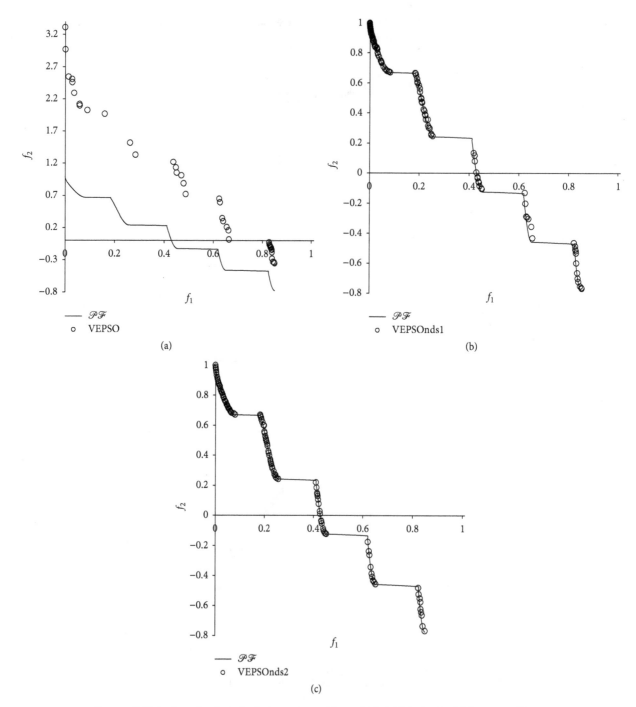

FIGURE 7: Plot of nondominated solutions returned by each algorithm for the ZDT3 test problem.

nondominated solutions were far worse than the true Pareto front. However, the VEPSOnds1 and VEPSOnds2 algorithms yielded good HV values.

Figure 6 shows the nondominated solutions with the best GD measure returned for the ZDT2 problem. The poor performance of conventional VEPSO is visible because the nondominated solutions found are very distant from the true Pareto front and distributed unevenly in the objective space.

Conversely, the VEPSOnds1 algorithm was able to obtain a nondominated solution that is located on the true Pareto front. However, there is only one nondominated solution, which increases the SP value of this algorithm. In contrast, the VEPSOnds2 algorithm successfully found nondominated solutions very close to the true Pareto front, and the non-dominated solutions found are distributed evenly over the true Pareto front. Thus, the polynomial mutation preventing

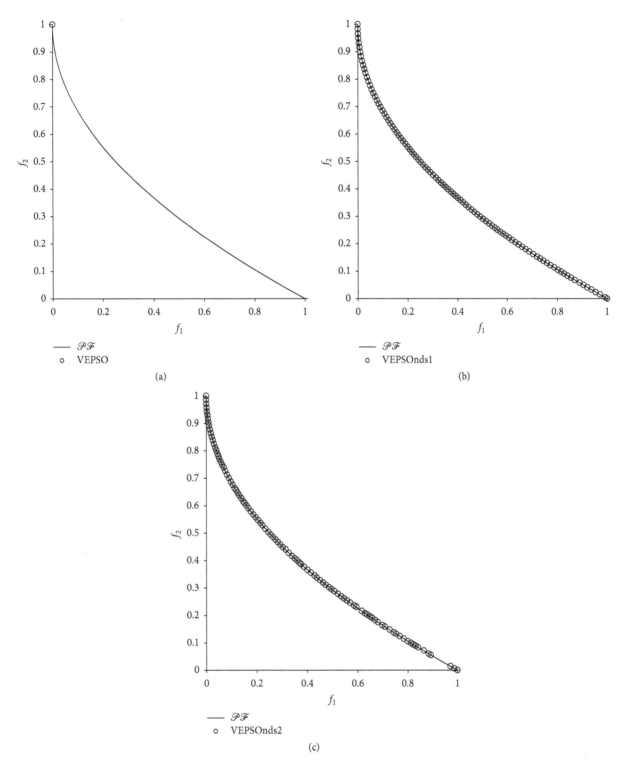

FIGURE 8: Plot of nondominated solutions returned by each algorithm for the ZDT4 test problem.

the particles from converging too early is an important mechanism in improving the diversity performance of the algorithm.

Table 3 presents the performance measures of all algorithms tested for the ZDT3 problem. Regarding the NS measure, both the improved VEPSO algorithms successfully obtained a large number of nondominated solutions. Moreover, both improved VEPSO algorithms yielded great improvement compared with the conventional VEPSO in terms of convergence. However, the SP value of the solutions

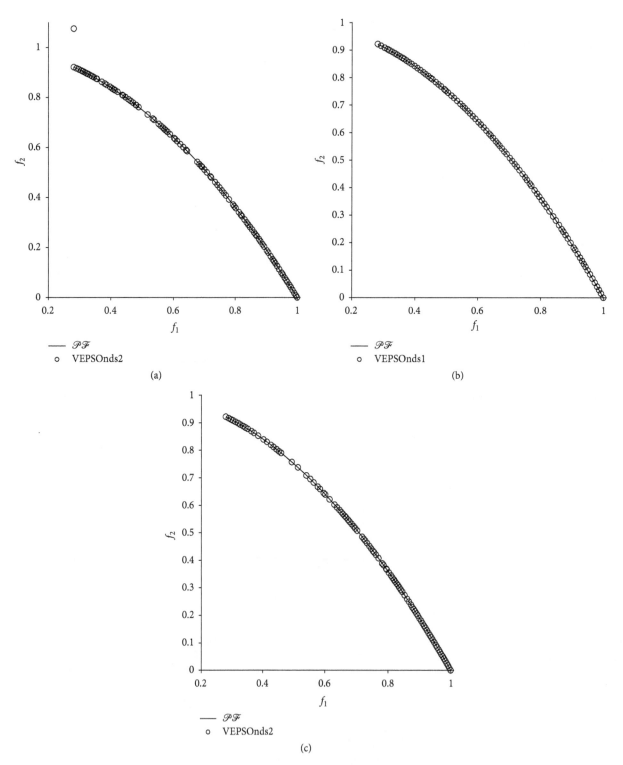

FIGURE 9: Plot of nondominated solutions returned by each algorithm for the ZDT6 test problem.

obtained by both improved VEPSO was degraded in this test. Even with the degradation in the diversity performance of both improved VEPSO, they still hold the performance advantages with their superior convergence improvement. Besides, both improved VEPSO performances are better as

their HV value was also improved when the particles in the algorithm used additional guides during the optimisation.

Figure 7 shows the nondominated solutions with the best GD measure returned for ZDT3 problem. Unavoidably, the nondominated solutions obtained by the conventional

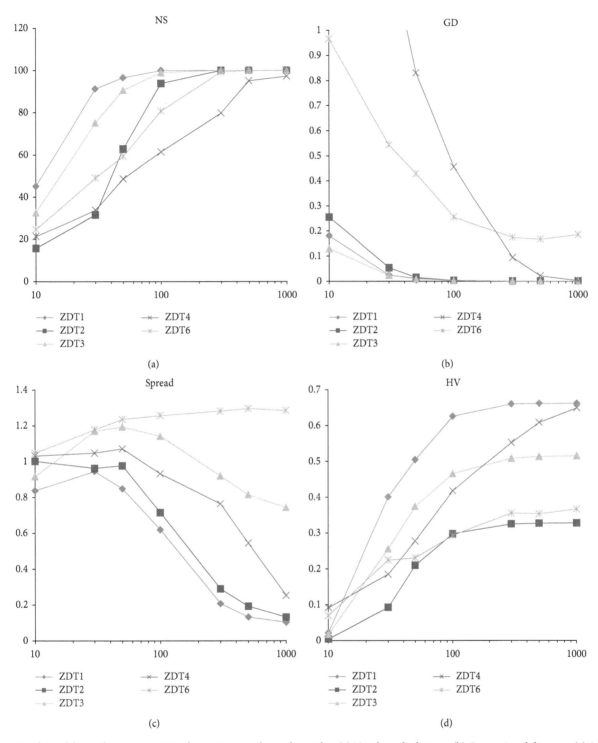

FIGURE 10: Plots of the performance metrics for various numbers of particles. (a) Number of solutions. (b) Generational distance. (c) Spread. (d) Hypervolume.

VEPSO algorithm are scattered far from the true Pareto front, which leads to poor performance. Conversely, both the improved VEPSO algorithms were able to obtain nondominated solutions that cover the true Pareto front almost perfectly. Hence, both the improved VEPSO algorithms exhibited almost equal improvement, but VEPSOnds1 has weaker diversity performance as there are lesser solutions at the middle of the Pareto front.

Table 4 presents the performance measures for all algorithms tested for the ZDT4 problem. The average number of nondominated solutions found by the conventional VEPSO algorithm is relatively low compared with VEPSOnds1, which found most of the solutions. The conventional VEPSO algorithm had great difficulty escaping from the multiple local optima, which resulted in a very large GD value. However, the improved VEPSO algorithms, in which particles are guided

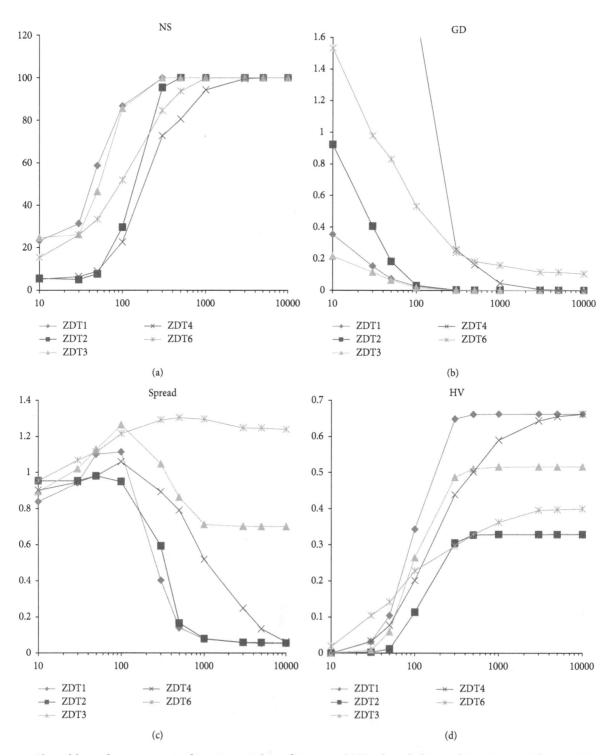

FIGURE 11: Plots of the performance metrics for various numbers of iterations. (a) Number of solution. (b) Generational distance. (c) Spread. (d) Hypervolume.

by the nondominated solutions, had less chance of being stuck in local optima. Meanwhile, the HV value yielded by the conventional VEPSO algorithm is relatively small compared with that of the improved VEPSO algorithms. Thus, the smaller SP value for conventional VEPSO does not mean it has better performance, as both improved VEPSO still

maintain performance advantages with their better GD and HV values.

Figure 8 shows the nondominated solutions with the best GD measure returned for the ZDT4 problem. The conventional VEPSO algorithm, in which particles follow only one guide, was easily stuck in local optima, as shown

TABLE 1: Algorithm performance tested on ZDT1 problem.

Measure	VEPSO	VEPSOnds1	VEPSOnds2
NS			
Ave.	30.220000	100.000000	99.790000
SD	5.697031	0.000000	1.458483
Min.	16.000000	100.000000	86.000000
Max.	44.000000	100.000000	100.000000
GD			
Ave.	0.295865	0.022637	0.002194
SD	0.051645	0.014201	0.003505
Min.	0.139491	0.000283	0.000169
Max.	0.432478	0.073477	0.019113
SP			
Ave.	0.834481	0.729350	0.571807
SD	0.039111	0.160298	0.248304
Min.	0.705367	0.322322	0.168144
Max.	0.917087	1.219625	1.127141
HV			
Ave.	0.001886	0.428153	0.631216
SD	0.010058	0.113432	0.046091
Min.	—	0.185313	0.438793
Max.	0.087426	0.659603	0.661363

TABLE 3: Algorithm performance tested on ZDT3 problem.

Measure	VEPSO	VEPSOnds1	VEPSOnds2
NS			
Ave.	35.150000	99.600000	99.400000
SD	6.853997	3.405284	6.000000
Min.	21.000000	66.000000	40.000000
Max.	53.000000	100.000000	100.000000
GD			
Ave.	0.173060	0.009607	0.002040
SD	0.031253	0.008293	0.002268
Min.	0.079595	0.000433	0.000223
Max.	0.276801	0.039481	0.013231
SP			
Ave.	0.871146	1.109448	1.121149
SD	0.043319	0.086041	0.099980
Min.	0.701884	0.902861	0.858725
Max.	1.001428	1.322024	1.362217
HV			
Ave.	0.004722	0.373133	0.471686
SD	0.021699	0.083015	0.038568
Min.	—	0.112859	0.332399
Max.	0.167359	0.506222	0.514600

TABLE 2: Algorithm performance tested on ZDT2 problem.

Measure	VEPSO	VEPSOnds1	VEPSOnds2
NS			
Ave.	8.070000	38.120000	97.490000
SD	6.356822	25.747131	7.832198
Min.	1.000000	1.000000	49.000000
Max.	24.000000	100.000000	100.000000
GD			
Ave.	0.766956	0.039653	0.002003
SD	0.324444	0.063791	0.003483
Min.	0.240509	0.000000	0.000198
Max.	1.679803	0.310345	0.017750
SP			
Ave.	0.944524	0.947356	0.687560
SD	0.065266	0.111963	0.278814
Min.	0.797757	0.695715	0.242474
Max.	1.080351	1.278655	1.460767
HV			
Ave.	—	0.137784	0.296372
SD	—	0.117596	0.053300
Min.	—	—	0.043514
Max.	—	0.311075	0.327309

TABLE 4: Algorithm performance tested on ZDT4 problem.

Measure	VEPSO	VEPSOnds1	VEPSOnds2
NS			
Ave.	6.610000	95.250000	64.220000
SD	3.920665	16.518967	38.860949
Min.	1.000000	15.000000	4.000000
Max.	21.000000	100.000000	100.000000
GD			
Ave.	5.062543	0.383646	0.349438
SD	3.167428	0.478535	0.431632
Min.	0.000000	0.000155	0.000165
Max.	13.350278	2.049212	1.923652
SP			
Ave.	0.858655	1.035510	0.962023
SD	0.147255	0.347336	0.367664
Min.	0.483073	0.077112	0.144160
Max.	1.236461	1.419225	1.435101
HV			
Ave.	0.228824	0.399914	0.437755
SD	0.188151	0.159971	0.155761
Min.	—	—	—
Max.	0.573978	0.661941	0.660821

TABLE 5: Algorithm performance tested on ZDT6 problem.

Measure	VEPSO	VEPSOnds1	VEPSOnds2
NS			
Ave.	76.590000	78.040000	81.030000
SD	32.884891	26.684055	25.075021
Min.	11.000000	22.000000	24.000000
Max.	100.000000	100.000000	100.000000
GD			
Ave.	0.338537	0.260666	0.266259
SD	0.370336	0.158592	0.168404
Min.	0.001746	0.044137	0.035520
Max.	1.552521	0.709692	0.735990
SP			
Ave.	1.201796	1.276529	1.286909
SD	0.146782	0.083293	0.075052
Min.	0.492064	0.987981	1.067748
Max.	1.435395	1.437289	1.410091
HV			
Ave.	0.304584	0.303381	0.281256
SD	0.134813	0.102216	0.119017
Min.	—	0.038143	0.026496
Max.	0.400964	0.400780	0.401005

in the first plot. Thus, the algorithm was able to find only one nondominated solution. However, both the improved VEPSO algorithms, in which additional guides are used, had less difficulty in obtaining a greater number of diverse nondominated solutions.

Table 5 presents the performance measures for all algorithms tested on the ZDT6 problem. Interestingly, all algorithms found approximately the same number of nondominated solutions. Moreover, the SP and HV values for all algorithms are also similar. However, noticeably, both improved VEPSO have outperformed the conventional VEPSO in terms of convergence performance.

Figure 9 shows the nondominated solutions with the best GD measure returned for the ZDT6 problem. As predicted, the plots of nondominated solutions are similar because all algorithms exhibit similar results in terms of convergence and diversity. However, the nondominated solutions for the VEPSOnds2 algorithm were not well distributed over the true Pareto front, middle of the Pareto front in this case, which caused the algorithm to have the largest SP value, as shown in Table 5.

For all test problems, the improved VEPSO algorithms exhibited significant improvement compared with the conventional VEPSO algorithm for most of the performance measures. The performance improvements occurred because the nondominated solutions always provide a better solution than a solution that optimises only a single-objective function. Using a better solution as the leader increases the quality of the result.

4.4. Analysis of the Number of Particles. The performance of the VEPSOnds2 algorithm with various numbers of particles is analysed in this experiment. Most of the parameters are the same as in the previous experiment, except that the particles are equally divided between swarms for a total of 10, 30, 50, 100, 300, 500, and 1000 particles. The performance measurements, taken for each total number of particles and for each benchmark problem, are plotted in Figure 10.

In short, the performance of VEPSOnds2 improves when the number of particles is increased. When VEPSOnds2 is computed with 250 iterations, the algorithm performs well at 300 particles, which is equivalent to 75 000 function evaluations. With a higher number of particles, the algorithm exhibits even better results, but the computational time increases dramatically.

4.5. Analysis of the Number of Iterations. The effect of various numbers of iterations on VEPSOnds2 performance is investigated in this experiment. In this experiment, the number of iterations becomes 10, 30, 50, 100, 300, 500, 1000, 3000, 5000, or 10 000. All parameters are set as in the previous experiments, and the number of particles is set to 100, which is divided equally between swarms. The plot of performance metrics for the various numbers of iterations for each benchmark problem is displayed in Figure 11.

When the number of iterations is increased, the performance of VEPSOnds2 improves. The VEPSOnds2 algorithm performs consistently and acceptably with 100 particles when there are 300 iterations or 30 000 function evaluations. Computation of the algorithm with a higher number of iterations, such as 3000 particles or 300 000 function evaluations, could result in a better performance but is only recommended if a powerful computing platform is used.

4.6. Benchmarking with the State-of-the-Art Multiobjective Optimisation Algorithms. The VEPSOnds2 algorithm performed better than the other algorithms in most test cases. Thus, the performance of this algorithm is compared to four other MOO algorithms which are nondominated sorting genetic algorithm-II (NSGA-II) [11], strength pareto evolutionary algorithm 2 (SPEA2) [23], archive-based hYbrid scatter search (AbYSS) [24], and speed-constrained multiobjective PSO (SMPSO) [25]. For a fair comparison, all algorithms compute 25 000 function evaluations with the archive size set to 100. The NSGA-II, commonly used for performing comparisons, was set to use a population size of 100 for optimisation. This algorithm was set to use the Simulated Binary Crossover (SBX) operator with the crossover probability $p_c = 0.9$ and polynomial mutation [26] operators with the mutation probability $p_m = 1/N$. The distribution index for both operators was set to $\mu_n = \mu_m = 20$. The SPEA2 was set to use the same parameters as in NSGA-II. The AbYSS was set to use a population size of 20. The pairwise combination parameters in AbYSS were set to $RefSet_1 = 10$ and $RefSet_2 = 10$. The polynomial mutation parameters were set to similar values as those in NSGA-II and SPEA2. In SMPSO, the population size and maximum iteration were set to 100 and 250, respectively. The

TABLE 6: Performance comparison based on ZDT1 test problem.

Measure	AbYSS	NSGA-II	SPEA2	SMPSO	VEPSOnds2
NS					
Ave.	100.000000	100.000000	100.000000	100.000000	99.790000
SD	0.000000	0.000000	0.000000	0.000000	1.458483
Min.	100.000000	100.000000	100.000000	100.000000	86.000000
Max.	100.000000	100.000000	100.000000	100.000000	100.000000
GD					
Ave.	0.000185	0.000223	0.000220	0.000117	0.002194
SD	0.000035	0.000038	0.000028	0.000031	0.003505
Min.	0.000125	0.000146	0.000154	0.000053	0.000169
Max.	0.000343	0.000374	0.000400	0.000172	0.019113
SP					
Ave.	0.105387	0.379129	0.148572	0.076608	0.571807
SD	0.012509	0.028973	0.012461	0.009200	0.248304
Min.	0.080690	0.282485	0.116765	0.056009	0.168144
Max.	0.136747	0.441002	0.174986	0.099653	1.127141
HV					
Ave.	0.661366	0.659333	0.659999	0.661801	0.631216
SD	0.000269	0.000301	0.000301	0.000100	0.046091
Min.	0.660267	0.658486	0.659347	0.661372	0.438793
Max.	0.661724	0.659909	0.660629	0.661991	0.661363

TABLE 7: Performance comparison based on ZDT2 test problem.

Measure	AbYSS	NSGA-II	SPEA2	SMPSO	VEPSOnds2
NS					
Ave.	100.000000	100.000000	100.000000	100.000000	97.490000
SD	0.000000	0.000000	0.000000	0.000000	7.832198
Min.	100.000000	100.000000	100.000000	100.000000	49.000000
Max.	100.000000	100.000000	100.000000	100.000000	100.000000
GD					
Ave.	0.000131	0.000176	0.000182	0.000051	0.002003
SD	0.000067	0.000066	0.000039	0.000003	0.003483
Min.	0.000056	0.000093	0.000090	0.000044	0.000198
Max.	0.000433	0.000707	0.000304	0.000060	0.017750
SP					
Ave.	0.130425	0.378029	0.158187	0.071698	0.687560
SD	0.090712	0.028949	0.027529	0.013981	0.278814
Min.	0.080831	0.311225	0.118114	0.035786	0.242474
Max.	0.833933	0.430516	0.365650	0.106749	1.460767
HV					
Ave.	0.325483	0.326117	0.326252	0.328576	0.296372
SD	0.023209	0.000297	0.000908	0.000077	0.053300
Min.	0.096409	0.325278	0.318785	0.328349	0.043514
Max.	0.328505	0.326696	0.327559	0.328736	0.327309

TABLE 8: Performance comparison based on ZDT3 test problem.

Measure	AbYSS	NSGA-II	SPEA2	SMPSO	VEPSOnds2
NS					
Ave.	100.000000	100.000000	100.000000	99.900000	99.400000
SD	0.000000	0.000000	0.000000	0.904534	6.000000
Min.	100.000000	100.000000	100.000000	91.000000	40.000000
Max.	100.000000	100.000000	100.000000	100.00000	100.000000
GD					
Ave.	0.000193	0.000211	0.000230	0.000203	0.002040
SD	0.000019	0.000013	0.000019	0.000061	0.002268
Min.	0.000144	0.000180	0.000184	0.000155	0.000223
Max.	0.000264	0.000268	0.000327	0.000717	0.013231
SP					
Ave.	0.707651	0.747853	0.711165	0.717493	1.121149
SD	0.013739	0.015736	0.008840	0.032822	0.099980
Min.	0.696859	0.715199	0.698590	0.697943	0.858725
Max.	0.796404	0.793183	0.775317	0.950901	1.362217
HV					
Ave.	0.512386	0.514813	0.513996	0.514996	0.471686
SD	0.011314	0.000159	0.000675	0.001737	0.038568
Min.	0.463776	0.514449	0.510764	0.500484	0.332399
Max.	0.515960	0.515185	0.514668	0.515818	0.514600

TABLE 9: Performance comparison based on ZDT4 test problem.

Measure	AbYSS	NSGA-II	SPEA2	SMPSO	VEPSOnds2
NS					
Ave.	99.680000	100.000000	100.000000	100.000000	64.220000
SD	3.100603	0.000000	0.000000	0.000000	38.860949
Min.	69.000000	100.000000	100.000000	100.000000	4.000000
Max.	100.000000	100.000000	100.000000	100.000000	100.000000
GD					
Ave.	0.001231	0.000486	0.000923	0.0001347	0.349438
SD	0.002632	0.000235	0.001428	0.000027	0.431632
Min.	0.000148	0.000163	0.000176	0.000070	0.000165
Max.	0.014472	0.001374	0.012292	0.000187	1.923652
SP					
Ave.	0.159842	0.392885	0.298269	0.092281	0.962023
SD	0.120180	0.037083	0.125809	0.011777	0.367664
Min.	0.078244	0.324860	0.137934	0.067379	0.144160
Max.	1.073669	0.473358	0.884091	0.124253	1.435101
HV					
Ave.	0.646058	0.654655	0.645336	0.661401	0.437755
SD	0.034449	0.003406	0.018773	0.000162	0.155761
Min.	0.472299	0.642177	0.505799	0.660934	0.000000
Max.	0.661594	0.659710	0.658784	0.661726	0.660821

TABLE 10: Performance comparison based on ZDT6 test problem.

Measure	AbYSS	NSGA-II	SPEA2	SMPSO	VEPSOnds2
NS					
Ave.	100.000000	100.000000	100.000000	100.000000	81.030000
SD	0.000000	0.000000	0.000000	0.000000	25.075021
Min.	100.000000	100.000000	100.000000	100.000000	24.000000
Max.	100.000000	100.000000	100.000000	100.000000	100.000000
GD					
Ave.	0.000549	0.001034	0.001761	0.012853	0.266259
SD	0.000015	0.000102	0.000192	0.024813	0.168404
Min.	0.000510	0.000804	0.001267	0.000502	0.035520
Max.	0.000596	0.001360	0.002207	0.092434	0.735990
SP					
Ave.	0.097740	0.357160	0.226433	0.390481	1.286909
SD	0.013129	0.031711	0.020658	0.497140	0.075052
Min.	0.070455	0.282201	0.179482	0.042666	1.067748
Max.	0.130389	0.441311	0.292897	1.377582	1.410091
HV					
Ave.	0.400346	0.388304	0.378377	0.401280	0.281256
SD	0.000172	0.001604	0.002714	0.000076	0.119017
Min.	0.399821	0.383637	0.371907	0.401081	0.026496
Max.	0.400842	0.392123	0.385626	0.401402	0.401005

terms $r_1 = r_2 = \text{random}[0.1, 0.5]$, and the terms $c_1 = c_2 = \text{random}[1.5, 2.0]$. This algorithm was also set to use polynomial mutation [27] with $p_m = 1/N$ and $\mu_m = 20$.

Table 6 lists the performance of the algorithms on the ZDT1 test problem. The number of solutions found by the VEPSOnds2 is comparable to the other algorithms. However, the average GD value of the VEPSOnds2 is at least 10 times greater than that of the others even though its minimum GD value is close to that of the other algorithms. VEPSOnds2 also has the highest average SP value, but its minimum SP is better than that of NSGA-II. The HV value for VEPSOnds2 is similar to that of the other algorithms.

Table 7 lists the performance of the algorithms on the ZDT2 test problem. VEPSOnds2 was able to obtain a reasonable number of solutions compared to the other algorithms. However, the GD value for VEPSOnds2 is the highest among all algorithms. Additionally, VEPSOnds2 has the greatest average SP value, even though its minimum SP value is better than that of NSGA-II. In the HV measure, the average value returned by VEPSOnds2 is relatively close to the other algorithms and even outperforms the NSGA-II with its maximum value.

Table 8 lists the performance of the algorithms on the ZDT3 test problem. SMPSO and VEPSOnds2 both show poor performance with respect to the maximum number of solutions for all runs. Again, VEPSOnds2 has a 10 times greater GD value compared to the other algorithms. Interestingly, the diversity performance of VEPSOnds2 is very poor, as the average SP value is higher than 1.0. However, the maximum

HV value of VEPSOnds2 was not the smallest, and its average is almost as large as the rest.

Table 9 lists the performance of the algorithms on the ZDT4 test problem. The multiple local optima featured in this problem challenged VEPSOnds2 greatly, as the number of solutions obtained is very low. In addition, the convergence and diversity performances were very poor, as the GD and SP values are both very large compared to the other algorithms. The HV value was also poor, as the multiple local optima feature is well known as a natural weakness in PSO-based algorithms [18, 19].

Finally, Table 10 lists the performances of the algorithms on the ZDT6 test problem. On average, VEPSOnds2 does not obtain the highest number of nondominated solutions, but the number is still in an acceptable range. However, the GD value for VEPSOnds2 was too far from the other algorithms. In addition, the SP value for VEPSOnds2 is extremely large compared to the other algorithms, and the average HV value for VEPSOnds2 is smaller than that for the other algorithms. On a positive note, the maximum HV value for VEPSOnds2 improves upon that for AbYSS, NSGA-II, and SPEA2.

The main purpose of this experiment is to present the overall performance of the improved VEPSO algorithm in comparison to state-of-the art algorithms, not to show how it outperforms them. Indeed, the overall performance of the VEPSOnds2 is not better than all the compared algorithms. However, relatively speaking, its performance is still within the acceptable range and is better than some of the other algorithms in certain cases.

5. Conclusions

The conventional VEPSO algorithm uses one swarm to optimise one objective function. The optimisation is guided using only one best solution found by another swarm with respect to the objective function optimised by that swarm. In contrast, recent PSO-based MOO algorithms prefer to use the nondominated solutions as the particle guides. Thus, it is possible to modify the VEPSO algorithm such that the particles are guided by nondominated solutions that are optimal at specific objective function. Five ZDT test problems were used to investigate the performance of the improved VEPSO algorithm based on the measures of the number of nondominated solutions found, the Generational Distance, the Spread, and the Hypervolume.

The experimental results show that the improved algorithms were able to obtain better quality Pareto fronts than conventional VEPSO, especially VEPSOnds2, which consistently returned the best convergence and diversity performance. On the other hand, the introduction of polynomial mutation should reduce the chance for a particle to get stuck in local optima, which features greatly in the ZDT4 test problem. However, VEPSOnds2 did not show much improvement compared to VEPSOnds1. This could possibly be due to the choice of the number of particles that are subject to mutation. Hence, the analysis for proper number of particles subject to mutation should be considered in future work. Even so, VEPSOnds2 is relatively better than VEPSOnds1, as confirmed by most of the performance measurements.

In addition, in VEPSOnds2, the particles of a swarm are guided by the same $gBest(t)$. Thus, there is a greater chance for them to converge prematurely around the $gBest(t)$ that might represent a locally optimal solution. On the other hand, in SMPSO, each particle will select one of the nondominated solutions by binary tournament, using the crowding distance as its guide. This means that in SMPSO, each particle has a different $gBest(t)$ as a guide during optimisation. Thus, the future VEPSOnds2 algorithm should reduce the chances for all particles to follow the same $gBest(t)$, in order to prevent premature convergence.

Acknowledgments

This work is supported by the Research University Grant (VOT 04J99) from Universiti Teknologi Malaysia, High Impact Research—UM.C/HIR/MOHE/ENG/16(D000016-16001), Research Acculturation Grant Scheme (RDU 121403), and MyPhD Scholarship from Ministry of Higher Education of Malaysia.

References

[1] K. E. Parsopóulos and M. N. Vrahatis, "Particle swarm optimization method in multiobjective problems," in *Proceeedings of the ACM Symposium on Applied Computing*, pp. 603–607, ACM, March 2002.

[2] D. Gies and Y. Rahmat-Samii, "Vector evaluated particle swarm optimization (VEPSO): optimization of a radiometer array antenna," in *IEEE Antennas and Propagation Society Symposium*, pp. 2297–2300, June 2004.

[3] S. M. V. Rao and G. Jagadeesh, "Vector evaluated particle swarm optimization (VEPSO) of supersonic ejector for hydrogen fuel cells," *Journal of Fuel Cell Science and Technology*, vol. 7, no. 4, Article ID 0410141, 2010.

[4] S. N. Omkar, D. Mudigere, G. N. Naik, and S. Gopalakrishnan, "Vector evaluated particle swarm optimization (VEPSO) for multi-objective design optimization of composite structures," *Computers and Structures*, vol. 86, no. 1-2, pp. 1–14, 2008.

[5] J. G. Vlachogiannis and K. Y. Lee, "Multi-objective based on parallel vector evaluated particle swarm optimization for optimal steady-state performance of power systems," *Expert Systems with Applications*, vol. 36, no. 8, pp. 10802–10808, 2009.

[6] J. Grobler, *Particle Swarm Optimization and Differential Evolution for Multi Objective Multiple Machine Scheduling [M.S. thesis]*, University of Pretoria, 2009.

[7] M. Reyes-Sierra and C. A. C. Coello, "Multi-objective particle swarm optimizers: a survey of the state-of-the-art," *International Journal of Computational Intelligence Research*, vol. 2, no. 3, 2006.

[8] C. A. Coello Coello and M. S. Lechuga, "MOPSO: a proposal for multiple objective particle swarm optimization," in *Proceedings of the Congress on Evolutionary Computation (CEC '02)*, vol. 2, pp. 1051–1056, 2002.

[9] C. A. Coello Coello, G. T. Pulido, and M. S. Lechuga, "Handling multiple objectives with particle swarm optimization," *IEEE Transactions on Evolutionary Computation*, vol. 8, no. 3, pp. 256–279, 2004.

[10] X. Li, "A non-dominated sorting particle swarm optimizer for multiobjective optimization," in *Genetic and Evolutionary Computation*, E. CantÃž-Paz, J. Foster, K. Deb et al., Eds., vol. 2723 of *Lecture Notes in Computer Science*, pp. 198–198, Springer, Berlin, Germany, 2003.

[11] K. Deb, A. Pratap, S. Agarwal, and T. Meyarivan, "A fast and elitist multiobjective genetic algorithm: NSGA-II," *IEEE Transactions on Evolutionary Computation*, vol. 6, no. 2, pp. 182–197, 2002.

[12] M. Reyes-Sierra and C. A. Coello Coello, "Improving PSO-based Multi-Objective optimization using crowding, mutation and ε,-dominance," in *Evolutionary Multi-Criterion Optimization*, C. A. Coello Coello, A. HernÃądez Aguirre, and E. Zitzler, Eds., vol. 3410 of *Lecture Notes in Computer Science*, pp. 505–519, Springer, Berlin, Berlin, 2005.

[13] M. A. Abido, "Multiobjective particle swarm optimization with nondominated local and global sets," *Natural Computing*, vol. 9, no. 3, pp. 747–766, 2010.

[14] J. Kennedy and R. Eberhart, "Particle swarm optimization," in *Proceedings of the IEEE International Conference on Neural Networks*, pp. 1942–1948, December 1995.

[15] J. Kennedy, R. C. Eberhart, and Y. Shi, *Swarm Intelligence*, The Morgan Kaufmann Series in Evolutionary Computation, Morgan Kaufmann Publishers, San Francisco, Calif, USA, 2001.

[16] H. El-Sayed, M. Belal, A. Almojel, and J. Gaber, "Swarm intelligence," in *Handbook of Bioinspired Algorithms and Applications*, S. Olariu and A. Y. Zomaya, Eds., Chapman AND Hall/CRC computer and information science series, pp. 55–63, Taylor & Francis, Boca Raton, Fla, USA, 1st edition, 2006.

[17] J. D. Schaffer, *Some Experiments in Machine Learning Using Vector Evaluated Genetic Algorithms (Artificial Intelligence, Optimization, Adaptation, Pattern Recognition) [Ph.D. thesis]*, Vanderbilt University, 1984.

[18] E. Ãűzcan and M. Yäślmaz, "Particle swarms for multimodal optimization," in *Adaptive and Natural Computing Algorithms*, B. Beliczynski, A. Dzielinski, M. Iwanowski, and B. Ribeiro, Eds., vol. 4431 of *Lecture Notes in Computer Science*, pp. 366–375, Springer, Berlin, Germany, 2007.

[19] I. Schoeman and A. Engelbrecht, "A parallel vector-based particle swarm optimizer," in *Adaptive and Natural Computing Algorithms*, B. Ribeiro, R. F. Albrecht, A. Dobnikar, D. W. Pearson, and N. C. Steele, Eds., pp. 268–271, Springer, Vienna, Austria, 2005.

[20] D. A. Van Veldhuizen, *Multiobjective Evolutionary Algorithms: Classiffications, Analyses, and New Innovations [Ph.D. thesis]*, Air Force Institute of Technology, Air University, 1999.

[21] E. Zitzler and L. Thiele, "Multiobjective evolutionary algorithms: a comparative case study and the strength Pareto approach," *IEEE Transactions on Evolutionary Computation*, vol. 3, no. 4, pp. 257–271, 1999.

[22] E. Zitzler, K. Deb, and L. Thiele, "Comparison of multiobjective evolutionary algorithms: empirical results," *Evolutionary Computation*, vol. 8, no. 2, pp. 173–195, 2000.

[23] E. Zitzler, M. Laumanns, and L. Thiele, "SPEA2: improving the strength pareto evolutionary algorithm for multiobjective optimization," in *Evolutionary Methods for Design, Optimisation and Control with Application To Industrial Problems*, E. ZitlLer, M. Laumanns, and L. Thiele, Eds., pp. 95–100, International Center for Numerical Methods in Engineering (CIMNE), 2002.

[24] A. J. Nebro, F. Luna, E. Alba, B. Dorronsoro, J. J. Durillo, and A. Beham, "AbYSS: adapting scatter search to multiobjective optimization," *IEEE Transactions on Evolutionary Computation*, vol. 12, no. 4, pp. 439–457, 2008.

[25] J. Durillo, J. GarcÃna-Nieto, A. Nebro, C. A. Coello Coello, F. Luna, and E. Alba, "Multi-objective particle swarm optimizers: An experimental comparison," in *Evolutionary Multi-Criterion Optimization*, M. Ehrgott, C. Fonseca, X. Gandibleux, J. K. Hao, and M. Sevaux, Eds., vol. 5467 of *Lecture Notes in Computer Science*, pp. 495–509, Springer, Berlin, Germany, 2009.

[26] K. Deb, *Multi-Objective Optimization Using Evolutionary Algorithms*, vol. 16 of *Systems and Optimization Series*, John Wiley and Sons, Chichester, UK, 2001.

[27] A. J. Nebro, J. J. Durillo, G. Nieto, C. A. C. Coello, F. Luna, and E. Alba, "SMPSO: a new pso-based metaheuristic for multi-objective optimization," in *Proceedings of the IEEE Symposium on Computational Intelligence in Multi-Criteria Decision-Making (MCDM '09)*, pp. 66–73, usa, April 2009.

17

A Multiuser Detector Based on Artificial Bee Colony Algorithm for DS-UWB Systems

Zhendong Yin, Xiaohui Liu, and Zhilu Wu

School of Electronics and Information Engineering, Harbin Institute of Technology, Harbin 150001, China

Correspondence should be addressed to Zhendong Yin; zgczr2005@yahoo.com.cn

Academic Editors: P. Agarwal, V. Bhatnagar, J. Yan, and Y. Zhang

Artificial Bee Colony (ABC) algorithm is an optimization algorithm based on the intelligent behavior of honey bee swarm. The ABC algorithm was developed to solve optimizing numerical problems and revealed premising results in processing time and solution quality. In ABC, a colony of artificial bees search for rich artificial food sources; the optimizing numerical problems are converted to the problem of finding the best parameter which minimizes an objective function. Then, the artificial bees randomly discover a population of initial solutions and then iteratively improve them by employing the behavior: moving towards better solutions by means of a neighbor search mechanism while abandoning poor solutions. In this paper, an efficient multiuser detector based on a suboptimal code mapping multiuser detector and artificial bee colony algorithm (SCM-ABC-MUD) is proposed and implemented in direct-sequence ultra-wideband (DS-UWB) systems under the additive white Gaussian noise (AWGN) channel. The simulation results demonstrate that the BER and the near-far effect resistance performances of this proposed algorithm are quite close to those of the optimum multiuser detector (OMD) while its computational complexity is much lower than that of OMD. Furthermore, the BER performance of SCM-ABC-MUD is not sensitive to the number of active users and can obtain a large system capacity.

1. Introduction

Since the concept of ultra-wideband (UWB) technology was put forward by FCC in the 1990s, UWB technique has drawn a lot of attention in the theoretic research, industrial application, and many other areas because of its attractive features such as high data transmission rate, low power density, high interference resistance, and strong multipath resolution [1–3].

Multiuser detection (MUD) is a method to eliminate the effect of multiple access interference (MAI). The multiple accesses are commonly divided into two paths: time hopping (TH-UWB) and direct sequence (DS-UWB) [4]. In recent years, the increase in demand for multiple access applications with high data transmission rates has prompted the development of multiuser detection (MUD) techniques in such systems to suppress the MAI and improve the system performance. Optimum multiuser detection (OMD) was provided by Verdu in 1986 [5]; OMD makes the BER performance of multiple access system approximate to single-user system. But it has a high computational complexity, so it has poor

real-time characteristic confines in engineering. Therefore, suboptimal detectors which may approximate OMD's BER performance with an acceptable computational complexity have become a focus of research. A code-aided interference suppression method was introduced for NBI restriction in DS-UWB systems [6]. A multiuser frequency-domain (FD) turbo detector was employed which combines FD turbo equalization schemes with soft interference cancellation [7]. Adaptive MUD methods using the recursive least square (RLS) principles were proposed in [8, 9]. However, the trade-off problem between BER performance and computational complexity still exists.

Swarm intelligence is a research branch that models the population of interacting agents or swarms that are able to self-organize. Several modern heuristic algorithms have been developed for solving combinatorial and numeric optimization problems [10]. Artificial Bee Colony (ABC) algorithm is an optimization algorithm based on the intelligent behavior of honey bee swarm [11, 12], and some extended and efficient

ABC algorithms are presented to improve the performance of ABC [13, 14].

It has been demonstrated that ABC algorithm for numerical optimization problems has more superior performance than those based on heuristics algorithm [15]. ABC algorithm has been widely used in neural network training practice [16], path optimization [17], and back analysis [18]. However, no literatures have been reported that ABC was used in the multiuser detection (MUD) fields. In order to possess a good BER performance and a low time complexity, we investigate an efficient multiuser detector by selection of initial states based on code mapping for the Artificial Bee Colony algorithm (SCM-ABC-MUD) in DS-UWB systems. As a kind of swarm intelligence methods, ABC is selected here for its significant ability to search for the global optimal value and to adapt its searching space automatically [19, 20]. And its basic motivation is to find the global optimum by simulating the bees' behaviors [21]. This proposed algorithm makes use of the thought of ABC's iterative optimization and the result of the suboptimal detectors based on code mapping. Simulation results show that the BER performance and near-far effect (NFE) resistance capability of this algorithm are better than those of matched filter (MF), DEC, and MMSE detectors and even close to OMD.

The paper is organized as follows. In Section 2, the MUD model is introduced and a suboptimal detector based on code mapping is proposed. Then in Section 3, the basic principles of the Artificial Bee Colony (ABC) algorithm and the proposed SCM-ABC-MUD algorithm are illustrated. In Section 4, simulation experiments that compare the performance of different MUD algorithms are analyzed, followed by conclusions given in Section 5.

2. MUD Models and Methods

2.1. Multiuser DS-UWB System Model. In theory, a K-user synchronous DS-UWB system under the additive white Gaussian noise (AWGN) channel is considered which is not subjected to the frequency selective multipath. And assume each user employs the binary phase-shift key (BPSK) modulation. Then the kth user's transmit signal can be written as

$$x_k(t)$$

$$= \sum_{i=1}^{M} \sum_{j=0}^{N_c-1} d_k(i) c_k \left(t - (i-1) T_s\right) p\left(t - (i-1) T_s - jT_c\right),$$

(1)

where M is the length of bits per packet and BPSK symbols $d_k(i) \in \{-1, 1\}_{i=1}^{M}$ are spread with the specific PN codes $c_k(t)$, which are the binary bit stream valued only by -1 or 1. T_s is the symbol duration, T_c is the pulse repetition period, N_c equals to T_s/T_c, and $p(t)$ represents the transmitted pulse waveform generally characterized as the second derivative of Gaussian pulse

$$p(t) = \left[1 - 4\pi\left(\frac{t - t_d}{\tau_m}\right)^2\right] \exp\left[-2\pi\left(\frac{t - t_d}{\tau_m}\right)^2\right],$$

(2)

where t_d and τ_m are the pulse center and the pulse shape parameter.

The total received signal composed by different signals of all users is

$$r(t) = v(t) + n(t) = \sum_{k=1}^{K} A_k x_k(t) + n(t),$$

(3)

where A_k is the amplitude of the kth received signal and $n(t)$ is zero-mean additive white Gaussian noise with the unilateral power spectral density of N_0.

2.2. Classical Multiuser Detectors

2.2.1. Matched Filters (MFs). The traditional receiver of a DS-UWB system consists of a pulse demodulator and a set of matched filters (MFs) corresponding to each user. Let the output of a bank of single-user MFs be a K-dimensional vector $\mathbf{y} = [y_1, y_2, \ldots, y_K]^T$, the vector $\mathbf{b} = [b_1, b_2, \ldots, b_K]^T$ represent the output of sign detectors, the vector $\mathbf{d} = [d_1, d_2, \ldots, d_K]^T$ denotes the correct bits of each user, and the vector $\mathbf{n} = [n_1, n_2, \ldots, n_K]^T$ denotes the output of noise from matched filters which is a zero mean Gaussian random. So, the output of the MFs can be represented as follows:

$$\mathbf{y} = \mathbf{RAb} + \mathbf{n},$$

(4)

$$\mathbf{b} = \text{sgn}(\mathbf{y}),$$

(5)

where $R = (r_{ij})_{K \times K}$ denotes the cross-correlation matrix, in which $r_{ij} = \sum_{l=0}^{N_c-1} c_i(l) c_j(l)$, and $\mathbf{A} = \text{diag}(A_1, A_2, \ldots, A_K)$ in which the diagonal element A_k ($k \in [1, K], k \in N$) represents the signal amplitude of the kth user.

2.2.2. Optimum Multiuser Detection (OMD). According to the theory of OMD, the optimum detection result satisfies the following expression:

$$\mathbf{b}_{\text{OMD}} = \arg\left\{\max_{b \in \{-1,1\}} \left(2\mathbf{b}^T \mathbf{Ay} - \mathbf{b}^T \mathbf{ARAb}\right)\right\}.$$

(6)

It is known that the selection of this optimal solution $\mathbf{b}_{\text{OMD}}$ in the K-dimensional Euclidean solution space is generally a nondeterministic polynomial hard problem, but the computational complexity of the OMD method is $O(K^2)$, and K is the number of active users.

2.2.3. Suboptimal Multiuser Detection Based on Code Mapping (SCM). In order to get a suboptimal solution, the candidate bits set output from the matched filters mapped to a one-dimensional feature space using a mapping function.

Let

$$F(\mathbf{b}) = \frac{1}{2}\mathbf{b}^T \mathbf{ARAb} - \mathbf{b}^T \mathbf{Ay}.$$

(7)

According to (6), if the elements in $\mathbf{b}$ are all right, the value of $F(\mathbf{b})$ will achieve the minimum. Making a partial derivation of (7), we get

$$\frac{\partial F}{\partial \mathbf{b}} = \mathbf{Hb} - \mathbf{Ay}.$$

(8)

By expanding (8), we get a Kth-order linear equations given as follows:

$$\frac{\partial F}{\partial b_1} = \sum_{j=1}^{K} A_1 A_j r_{1j} b_j - A_1 y_1,$$

$$\frac{\partial F}{\partial b_2} = \sum_{j=1}^{K} A_2 A_j r_{2j} b_j - A_2 y_2,$$

$$\vdots$$

$$\frac{\partial F}{\partial b_K} = \sum_{j=1}^{K} A_K A_j r_{Kj} b_j - A_K y_K. \qquad (9)$$

Now, we take into account that MAI is the main interference resource which largely affects the performance of the system. Let $L(b_i) = \sum_{j=1}^{K} A_i A_j r_{ij} b_j - A_i y_i$, $i = 1, 2, \ldots, K$. Bringing the candidate codes set $\mathbf{b}$ into (9), there are two situations illustrated as follows.

(1) No wrong code in $\mathbf{b}$. Based on the theory of extreme value, if MAI is the only interference resource without AWGN and the elements in $\mathbf{b}$ are all correct, the result of (9) strictly equals $\mathbf{0}$. And, in the condition of high SNR, bringing (4) to $L(b_k)$, we can see that $L(b_k) = -A_i n_i \sim N(0, A_i^2 N_c N_0/2)$ $(k = 1, 2, \ldots, K)$ when there is no error bit in the candidate codes set $\mathbf{b}$.

(2) Wrong codes exist in $\mathbf{b}$. Supposing b_i $(i \in [1, K]$, $i \in N)$ is the wrong code (in other words, $-b_i$ is the correct code), the other codes are correct. Substituting it to the ith equation of (9), we get

$$L(b_i) = \sum_{\substack{j=1 \\ j \neq i}}^{K} A_i A_j r_{ij} b_j - A_i y_i + A_i^2 r_{ii} b_i$$

$$= \sum_{\substack{j=1 \\ j \neq i}}^{K} A_i A_j r_{ij} b_j - A_i y_i + A_i^2 r_{ii} (-b_i) + 2A_i^2 r_{ii} b_i \qquad (10)$$

$$= 2A_i^2 N_c b_i - A_i n_i.$$

As for k which does not equal i, we get

$$L(b_k) = 2A_i A_k r_{ik} b_i - A_k n_k, \quad k = 1, 2, \ldots, K, \ k \neq i. \qquad (11)$$

According to (10) and (11), it can be seen when the ith user's code is wrong, $|L(b_i)| \gg |L(b_k)|$, $k = 1, 2, \ldots, K$, $k \neq i$. Therefore, the function $L(\mathbf{b})$ can obviously differentiate the wrong codes and the right codes through the absolute value of it. In addition, $L(\mathbf{b})$ is a Kth-order linear equation which can get the result of $L(\mathbf{b})$ without complex computations.

It is accessible to map b into a one-dimensional feature space $|L(\mathbf{b})|$ to identify the wrong codes in the candidate set. Figure 1 shows an example of the feature space mapping in the scenario of 10 users, with 6 dB signal-to-noise ratio (SNR).

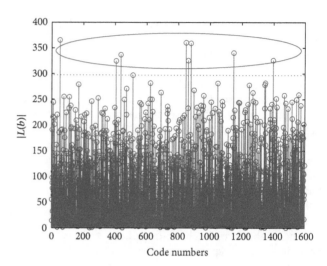

FIGURE 1: Relationship between code numbers and mapping function $|L(\mathbf{b})|$.

In Figure 1, it is clear that the wrong codes and the right ones have a significant difference in the feature space mapped by $|L(\mathbf{b})|$. Almost all the values of $|L(\mathbf{b})|$ corresponding to the wrong codes are greater than 280; in contrast the values of the right ones are smaller than 280. C-means clustering approach [22] is used to classify the candidate codes into right bits and wrong ones. The C-means clustering is a popular unsupervised clustering algorithm based on the partition of data, which can finish the classification without training samples.

In conclusion, the whole proposed approach can perform the multiuser detection with 3 steps. First, map the candidate bits set $\mathbf{b}$ into a one-dimensional feature space by mapping function $|L(\mathbf{b})|$. Second, aggregate and pick out the wrong bits among the candidate bits set by code clustering. And finally, correct the wrong bits to obtain a suboptimal solution.

3. The Proposed SCM-ABC-MUD Algorithm

3.1. The Basic Principle of ABC Algorithm. In the ABC algorithm, the colony of artificial bees consists of three kinds of bees: employed bees, onlookers, and scouts. In the algorithm, the number of employed bees is equal to the number of food sources around the hive. The employed bee whose food source is exhausted by the employed and onlooker bees becomes a scout. The position of a food source represents a possible solution of the optimization problem, and the nectar amount of a food source corresponds to the quality (fitness) of the associated solution. The number of the onlooker bees or the employed bees is equal to the number of food sources in the population.

The general scheme of the ABC algorithm is as follows.

Step 1. The first step is initialization. In this step, a set of food source positions is generated and distributed randomly. After initializing the solution population, the fitness value of each food source position is evaluated. In ABC algorithm, the fitness of each solution is the value of objective function. The ABC has some control parameters: food sources number (the number of food sources equal to the employed bees); limit, the value of predetermined number of cycles; and MCN, the maximum cycle number. Initially, the values of these control parameters are assigned.

Step 2. After initialization, the population is evaluated and is subjected to repeated cycles of the search processes of the employed bees, the onlooker bees, and scout bees. Employed bees search for new food sources (V_m) having more nectar within the neighborhood of the food source (X_m) in their memory. They find a neighbor food source and then evaluate its profitability (fitness). They can determine a neighbor food source V_m using the formula given by

$$v_{mi} = x_{mi} + \theta_{mi} (x_{mi} - x_{ki}), \qquad (12)$$

where x_k is a randomly selected food source, i is a randomly chosen parameter index, and θ_{mi} is random number between $[-1, 1]$.

Step 3. After producing the new food source V_m, its fitness is calculated and a greedy selection is applied between V_m and X_m. If the fitness of the new food source position is better than the old food source position, the employed bee moves from the old food source position to the new food source position, and the new food source takes place of old one in the population and becomes a new member.

The fitness value of the solution, $\text{fit}_m(X_m)$, might be calculated for minimization problems using the following formula:

$$\text{fit}_m (X_m) = \begin{cases} \dfrac{1}{1 + f_m (X_m)}, & \text{if } f_m (X_m) \geq 0, \\ 1 + \text{abs} (f_m (X_m)), & \text{if } f_m (X_m) \leq 0, \end{cases} \qquad (13)$$

where $f_m(X_m)$ is the objective function value of solution X_m.

Step 4. Unemployed bees consist of two groups of bees: onlooker bees and scouts. Employed bees share their food source information with onlooker bees waiting in the hive, and then onlooker bees probabilistically choose their food sources depending on the probability values calculated using the fitness values provided by employed bees.

Calculate the probability values P_i for the solutions using fitness of the solutions by

$$P_i = \frac{\text{fit}_m (X_m)}{\sum_{m=1}^{\text{SN}} \text{fit}_m (X_m)}, \qquad (14)$$

where SN represents the number of the food sources position.

After a food source X_m for an onlooker bee is probabilistically chosen, a neighborhood source V_m is determined by Step 2, and its fitness value is computed. As in Step 3, a greedy selection is applied between V_m and X_m. Hence, more onlookers are recruited to richer sources, and positive feedback behavior appears.

Step 5. If a predetermined number of trials cannot further improve a candidate solution represented by a food source then that food source, is considered abandoned and the employed bee associated with that food source becomes a scout. The new solution discovered by the scout can be defined by

$$x_{mi} = l_i + \text{rand}(0, 1) * (u_i - l_i), \qquad (15)$$

where l_i and u_i are the lower and upper bounds of the parameters x_{mi}. The abandoned food source is replaced by the randomly new food source.

Step 6. If a termination condition is reached, the process is stopped and memorizes the best solution achieved so far. Otherwise the algorithm returns to Step 2.

The general algorithmic structure of ABC optimization approach can be summarized as follows [23]:

(i) *Initialization Phase*

(ii) *Repeat*

      Employed Bees Phase

      Onlooker Bees Phase

      Scout Bees Phase

      Memorize the best solution achieved so far

(iii) *Until* (Cycle = Maximum Cycle Number).

3.2. The Discretization of Behavior Models. The mathematical model of OMD is considered as a combinatorial optimization problem, and ABC has a strong global searching capability to solve this problem. The optimization function for OMD is shown as (6), which is a discrete optimization function; for this reason, the behavior models of ABC should be discretized.

The discretization is defined as follows.

(1) The expression of artificial bee's state. In this solution space, the state of each artificial bee is encoded by −1 or +1. If there are K active users in this DS-UWB MA system, thus the state is a K-dimensional vector, like $X_0 = (x_1, x_2, \ldots, x_K)^T$, where $x_i \in \{-1, +1\}$ and $i = 1, 2, \ldots, K$.

(2) The food quality or the fitness function for artificial bees is the criterion of OMD in (6).

(3) X_c is the new food sources for each step; if the element of X_c is $x_{ci} > 0$, then assign $x_{ci} = +1$; otherwise, $x_{ci} = -1$.

(4) Initialization. The initial state of each artificial bee is selected randomly in the discrete space with 2^K likely solutions. But the ABC is an iterative optimization algorithm, which means that the selection of initial states has a great effect on the iteration times and the convergence rate. In this paper, we choose a suboptimal multiuser detection based on code mapping (SCM) and its variations as initial state values of artificial bees, which can ensure the artificial bees gather near the optimal value of the optimization problem because the suboptimal solution is quite close to the optimal value in the solution space. Besides, this selection method of initial states can speed up the convergence rate and reduce the iteration times for optimization.

3.3. The Specific Steps of the Initial Value Selection. The specific steps of the initial value selection are given as follows.

Step 1. Execute matched filter detection and code mapping to get a suboptimal solution first. Assign the result $b_{1 \times K} = (b_1, b_2, \ldots, b_K)$ to the first artificial bee as its initial state value, where $b_i \in \{-1, +1\}$ and $i = 1, 2, \ldots, K$.

Step 2. Change an element b_i of the result $b_{1 \times K}$ randomly, $b_i^* = -b_i$, and then assign this new result $b_{1 \times K}^*$ which changes from $b_{1 \times K}$ to the second artificial bee as its initial state value.

Step 3. Repeat Step 2 and assign these new results to other artificial bees.

Step 4. If all artificial bees have been assigned initial state values, the procedure of initial value selection comes to the end. And we can start the ABC to research the optimal value for MUD. In consideration of the previous statements, the overall structure of this proposed SCM-ABC-MUD detector is shown in Figure 2.

Figure 2 shows the block diagram of the algorithm. The implementation of this detector can be summarized as follows: firstly, the output of a bank of matched filter receivers is fed to suboptimal detectors based code mapping and clustering; secondly, the detection results of these suboptimal detectors are used to construct an initial solution space; finally, the ABC is executed in this space.

4. Simulation and Discussion

In order to analyze the proposed SCM-ABC-MUD algorithm, Monte Carlo simulations are utilized and the values of these majority parameters are assigned as Table 1.

4.1. The BER Performance versus SNR. The BER versus SNR curves with perfect power control in the AWNG are depicted in Figure 3. And there are 10 users in the system. As for ABC, we fix the number of initializing food sources (equal to employed bees) that is 3; limit, the value of predetermined number of cycles, that is 3; and MCN, the maximum cycle number, that is 20.

The performances of matched filter (MF), decor relating (DEC) [24], minimum mean square error (MMSE) [25], SCM-ABC-MUD, and OMD detectors are compared and depicted in Figure 3.

Figure 3 shows that the BER performance of SCM-ABC-MUD is superior to those of other suboptimal detectors including MF, DEC, and MMSE, and it even coincides with that of OMD. The reason is that this proposed SCM-ABC-MUD algorithm can make a search within a simplified solution space constructed by the solutions of these suboptimal detectors rather than a random search.

4.2. The BER Performance versus User Numbers K. The BER performances of these detectors with different number of active users K are analyzed in this experiment. The SNR of the AWGN channel is 5 dB. And the control parameters of ABC

TABLE 1: Simulation parameters.

System	DS-UWB
Modulation mode	BPSK
Spreading codes (SC)	m sequences
The length of SC	255
Communication channel	AWGN
The number of testing information bits	3200000
The width of UWB pulse	0.8 ns
The pulse repetition period	≈ 2 ns
Limit	3
Initializing food source number	3

are same as the BER performance versus SNR. Figure 4 shows the result of this experiment. According to Figure 4, the performance of SCM-ABC-MUD is the best of the suboptimum MUD except OMD. While the number of users increases, ABC needs a new group of control parameters. However, in this experiment, they are unchanged, resulting in the performance difference between SCM-ABC-MUD and OMD.

4.3. The NFE Resistant Capability Comparison. In this experiment, the SNR of the first user's received signal is assigned at 5 dB all the time, while the SNR of other users changs from 0 dB to 10 dB with per step of 1 dB. Besides, other parameters are set as same as those in the BER performance versus SNR. Figure 5 shows the first user's BER performances of different MUD detectors. It can be seen from Figure 5 that OMD has the best near-far effect resistant ability, and the SCM-ABC-MUD is very close to OMD.

4.4. BER Performance versus Different Initial States. As an iterative optimization algorithm, the convergence rate is as important as the optimization capability. And the selection of initial states has a great effect on the iteration times and the convergence rate. In this experiment two initial state values of artificial bees are employed as a comparison. One has random initial state values which is named as ABC-MUD; the other is SCM-ABC-MUD which is assigned a group of initial state values using the suboptimal solution of the code mapping-based multiuser detection. The BER performance is studied for both algorithms with the maximum cycle number (MCN) of 5, 15, and 20, respectively. Figures 6 and 7 are the convergence rates of ABC-MUD and SCM-ABC-MUD separately.

From Figures 6 and 7, the BER performance of SCM-ABC-MUD is much better than ABC-MUD with the same iteration times, and the former can achieve OMD's BER performance with 20 times iteration which is the global optimal solution. It can be concluded that the convergence rate of SCM-ABC-MUD is much quicker than that of ABC-MUD. Meanwhile, ABC-MUD only improves its BER performance a little than matched filter (shown in Figure 3). It is because that SCM-ABC-MUD makes full use of the suboptimal solution, the initial value of SCM-ABC-MUD is more close to OMD

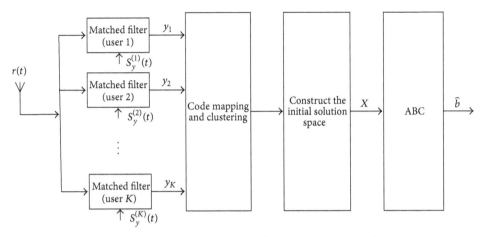

FIGURE 2: General schematic diagram of the SCM-ABC-MUD detector.

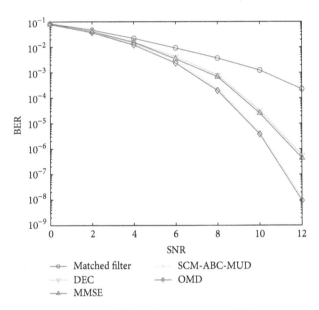

FIGURE 3: BER performance versus SNR.

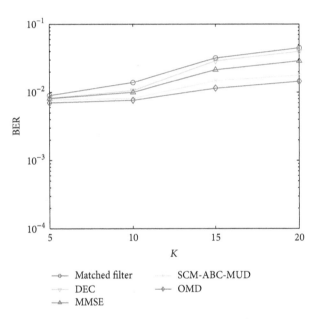

FIGURE 4: BER performance versus user numbers K.

than ABC-MUD, and so it can achieve the optimal value of OMD much quicker than ABC-MUD.

4.5. The Computational Complexity of the Proposed SCM-ABC-MUD. OMD can obtain the best BER performance while the computational complexity performance is too expensive to be implemented in practice. However, the computational complexity of SCM-ABC- MUD is much less than that of the OMD. In a K-user DS-UWB system, to detect the K-user vector **b**, the computational complexity of iterations of the OMD is 2^K. The computational complexity of the proposed method includes three parts. The first part is the computational complexity of the code mapping; according to Section 2.2.3, the mapping method is just a calculation of $L(\mathbf{b})$, so the computational complexity of the first part can be neglected. The second part is the computational complexity of C-means clustering; the complexity of iterations of the code

clustering is K. The third part is the complexity of the ABC algorithm. It depends on the convergence rate of SCM-ABC-MUD. In Section 4.4, we have obtained a conclusion that the SCM-ABC-MUD can achieve convergence with a much fewer iterations than OMD. Let the normalized operation time of per vector **b** using matched filter detector equal to 1 in the condition of 10 users. The simulation parameters are the same as Section 4.1. Table 2 lists the relative operation time using OMD, SCM-ABC-MUD, and matched filter.

From Table 2 we can see that the computational complexity of the SCM-ABC-MUD is in the same order of magnitude to the MMSE and DEC and far lower than OMD. This is because the iteration of SCM-ABC-MUD will be converged very soon and costs little quantity of computation. Hence, we can get a conclusion that the SCM-ABC-MUD can get good BER performance with low computational complexity.

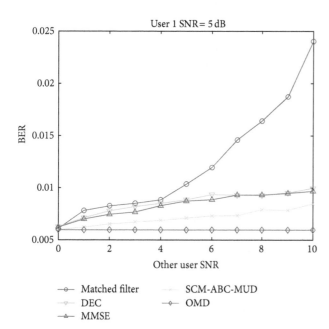

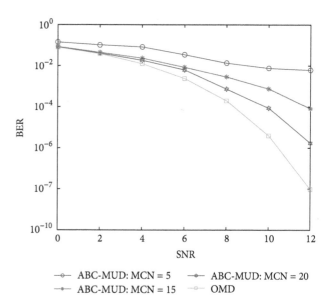

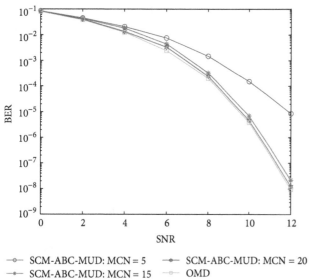

FIGURE 5: Near-far effect resistant of different MUD algorithms.

FIGURE 7: The BER performance with different iteration times of ABC-MUD.

TABLE 2: The comparison of computational complexity using different MUD algorithms.

OMD	MMSE	DEC	SCM-ABC-MUD	MF
58.9	1.38	1.30	1.21	1

of the suboptimal solution and advantages of ABC to study the optimal value in the solution space. Simulation results have indicated that the BER performance, user capacity, and the NFE resistant ability of this novel algorithm are quite close to those of OMD, and they are also superior to those of MF, DEC, and MMSE. Furthermore, the convergence rate of SCM-ABC-MUD is better than that of ABC-MUD. And the computational complexity of the SCM-ABC-MUD is much lower than that of OMD.

Acknowledgments

The research in this paper is supported by the National Natural Science Foundation of China (Grant no. 61102084), Foundation of China Academy of Space Technology (CAST), and the China Postdoctoral Science Foundation (Grant no. 2011M500665).

FIGURE 6: The BER performance with different iteration times of SCM-ABC-MUD.

5. Conclusions

In this paper, we firstly employed the Artificial Bee Colony algorithm in the DS-UWB MUD. In consideration of the high computational complexity of OMD, the proposed MUD is a hybrid method which combines ABC algorithm and a suboptimal solution of the code mapping-based MUD. First, the bits set output from the matched filters is mapped into a one-dimensional feature space to obtain a suboptimal solution; then the initial solution space is constructed based on the suboptimal solution; finally, the optimal solution is found by operating the different behaviors of artificial bees in solution space. The proposed multiuser detector can make full use

References

[1] M. Z. Win and R. A. Scholtz, "Impulse radio: how it works," *IEEE Communications Letters*, vol. 2, no. 2, pp. 36–38, 1998.

[2] X. Shen, M. Guizani, H. H. Chen et al., "Guest editorial ultra-wideband wireless communications-theory and applications," *IEEE Journal on Selected Areas in Communications*, vol. 24, no. 4, pp. 713–716, 2006.

[3] J. Ahmadi-Shokouh and R. C. Qiu, "Ultra-wideband (UWB) communications channel measurements—a tutorial review," *International Journal of Ultra Wideband Communications and Systems*, vol. 1, no. 1, pp. 11–31, 2009.

[4] I. Oppermann, M. Hämäläinen, and J. Iinatti, Eds., *UWB: Theory and Applications*, Wiley, 2005.

[5] S. Verdu, "Minimum probability of error for asynchronous Gaussian multiple-access channels," *IEEE Transactions on Information Theory*, vol. 32, no. 1, pp. 85–96, 1986.

[6] C. Wang, M. Ma, R. Ying et al., "Narrowband interference mitigation in DS-UWB systems," *IEEE Signal Processing Letters*, vol. 17, no. 5, pp. 429–432, 2010.

[7] P. Kaligineedi and V. K. Bhargava, "Frequency-domain turbo equalization and multiuser detection for DS-UWB systems," *IEEE Transactions on Wireless Communications*, vol. 7, no. 9, pp. 3280–3284, 2008.

[8] G. S. Biradar, S. N. Merchant, and U. B. Desai, "Performance of constrained blind adaptive DS-CDMA UWB multiuser detector in multipath channel with narrowband interference," in *Proceedings of IEEE Global Telecommunications Conference (GLOBECOM '08)*, pp. 1–5, November-December 2008.

[9] Q. Z. Ahmed and L. L. Yang, "Reduced-rank adaptive multiuser detection in hybrid direct-sequence time-hopping ultrawide bandwidth systems," *IEEE Transactions on Wireless Communications*, vol. 9, no. 1, pp. 156–167, 2010.

[10] M. Woodside-Oriakhi, C. Lucas, and J. E. Beasley, "Heuristic algorithms for the cardinality constrained efficient frontier," *European Journal of Operational Research*, vol. 213, no. 3, pp. 538–550, 2011.

[11] B. Basturk and D. Karaboga, "An artificial bee colony (ABC) algorithm for numeric function optimization," in *Proceedings of IEEE Swarm Intelligence Symposium*, pp. 12–14, May 2006.

[12] D. Karaboga and B. Basturk, "A powerful and efficient algorithm for numerical function optimization: artificial bee colony (ABC) algorithm," *Journal of Global Optimization*, vol. 39, no. 3, pp. 459–471, 2007.

[13] W. Zou, Y. Zhu, H. Chen et al., "A clustering approach using cooperative artificial bee colony algorithm," *Discrete Dynamics in Nature and Society*, vol. 2010, Article ID 459796, 16 pages, 2010.

[14] Y. Xu, P. Fan, and L. Yuan, "A simple and efficient artificial bee colony algorithm," *Mathematical Problems in Engineering*, vol. 2013, Article ID 526315, 9 pages, 2013.

[15] D. Karaboga and B. Akay, "A comparative study of artificial bee colony algorithm," *Applied Mathematics and Computation*, vol. 214, no. 1, pp. 108–132, 2009.

[16] D. Karaboga, B. Akay, and C. Ozturk, "Artificial bee colony (ABC) optimization algorithm for training feed-forward neural networks," in *Modeling Decisions for Artificial Intelligence*, pp. 318–329, Springer, Berlin, Germany, 2007.

[17] L. P. Wong, M. Y. H. Low, and C. S. Chong, "A bee colony optimization algorithm for traveling salesman problem," in *Proceedings of the 2nd Asia International Conference on Modelling and Simulation (AICMS '08)*, pp. 818–823, IEEE, May 2008.

[18] F. Kang, J. Li, and Q. Xu, "Structural inverse analysis by hybrid simplex artificial bee colony algorithms," *Computers and Structures*, vol. 87, no. 13-14, pp. 861–870, 2009.

[19] D. Karaboga and B. Akay, "A modified artificial bee colony (ABC) algorithm for constrained optimization problems," *Applied Soft Computing Journal*, vol. 11, no. 3, pp. 3021–3031, 2011.

[20] B. Akay and D. Karaboga, "A modified artificial bee colony algorithm for real-parameter optimization," *Information Sciences*, vol. 192, pp. 120–142, 2012.

[21] B. Alatas, "Chaotic bee colony algorithms for global numerical optimization," *Expert Systems with Applications*, vol. 37, no. 8, pp. 5682–5687, 2010.

[22] C. Xu, P. Zhang, B. Li et al., "Vague C-means clustering algorithm," *Pattern Recognition Letters*, vol. 34, no. 5, pp. 505–510, 2012.

[23] D. Karaboga, "Artificial bee colony algorithm," *Scholarpedia*, vol. 5, no. 3, p. 6915, 2010.

[24] S. Im and E. J. Powers, "An iterative decorrelating receiver for DS-UWB multiple access systems using biphase modulation," in *Proceedings of IEEE Workshop on Signal Processing Systems Design and Implementation*, pp. 59–64, October 2004.

[25] G. C. Chung, "Multi-user access interference suppression for UWB system," in *Proceedings of the International Conference on Computer & Information Science (ICCIS '12)*, vol. 2, pp. 670–675, June 2012.

18

Combined Simulated Annealing Algorithm for the Discrete Facility Location Problem

Jin Qin,[1] Ling-lin Ni,[1,2] and Feng Shi[1]

[1] School of Traffic and Transportation Engineering, Central South University, Changsha 410075, China
[2] Business Administration College, Zhejiang University of Finance & Economics, Hangzhou 310018, China

Correspondence should be addressed to Jin Qin, csu_qinjin@hotmail.com

Academic Editors: C. W. Ahn, B. Alatas, P. Bala, P.-A. Hsiung, and Y. Jiang

The combined simulated annealing (CSA) algorithm was developed for the discrete facility location problem (DFLP) in the paper. The method is a two-layer algorithm, in which the external subalgorithm optimizes the decision of the facility location decision while the internal subalgorithm optimizes the decision of the allocation of customer's demand under the determined location decision. The performance of the CSA is tested by 30 instances with different sizes. The computational results show that CSA works much better than the previous algorithm on DFLP and offers a new reasonable alternative solution method to it.

1. Introduction

The classical facility location problem (FLP) is one of the most important models in combinatorial optimization, which is to determine the number and locations of the facilities and allocate customers to these facilities in such a way that the total cost is minimized. The FLP may be the most critical and most difficult decision in the designing of an efficient supply chain for the facilities are costly and difficult to reverse after being located. The problem is also encountered in other areas such as material distribution, transportation network, and telecommunication network.

The FLP can be classified in two categories as discrete problem and continuous problem according to whether the sets of demand points and facility locations are finite. The discrete facility location problem (DFLP) assumes that the solution space is discrete and generally the facilities are located on the nodes of the network, which brings a lot of complexities to the problem. And many practical problems without facilities to locate, such as cluster analysis, machine scheduling, economic lot sizing, portfolio management, and computer network design, can also be modeled as DFLP [1]. Due to its strategic nature, DFLP has been widely studied by researchers over many years, especially developing solution methods for the DFLP has been a hot topic of research for the last 30 years. Many successful contributions of the DFLP have

been reported both in theory and in practice. The Daskin [2] and Melo et al. [1] provided thorough reviews of the DFLP.

The DFLP is a NP-hard problem, and this nature makes the exact algorithms only for small problems and heuristics the natural choice for larger instances. Therefore much attention has been focused on designing heuristics algorithms with good performance. Following the first heuristics algorithm presented by Shmoys et al. [3], there was a long list of work on designing heuristics algorithms for this problem over the years. As a result, four basic algorithms with different features have been emerged, namely, LP-rounding [3–8], primal-dual [9–11], dual-fitting [12–14], and local search [15–18]. Although LP-rounding could be used to design algorithm with better results than other three, it is noncombinatorial in nature and needs more CPU time. Primal-dual and dual-fitting method could be adapted to solve variants of the FLP but are less robust. Recently some applications have proved that local search is more powerful on the hard DFLP [16]. And along with the development of the computation method, more and more researchers use the heuristic algorithms based on the local search to solve the problem, such as simulated annealing [19–21] and genetic algorithm [20, 22].

In this paper, a general algorithmic framework of combined simulated annealing (CSA) is developed for the DFLP, and its performance is compared with other existed solution methods.

The rest of this paper is organized as follows. In Section 2, we describe the general model of DFLP. The basic procedures of the SA and CSA are presented in Sections 3 and 4 respectively. Section 5 shows the computational results on test instances, and Section 6 concludes the paper.

2. The Formulation of DFLP Model

We start by giving the mathematical formulation of a general model for DFLP with a minimized objective function. In the model, $I = \{1, 2, \ldots, n\}$ is used to represent the set of the customers and $J = \{1, 2, \ldots, m\}$ is used to represent the set of the potential location sites. f_j is used to represent the fixed cost of opening a facility at site $j \in J$, v_j is the service capacity of facility at site j, d_i is the demand of customer $i \in I$, and c_{ij} is the cost of serving one unit of demand at customer i from site j, in other word, the unit variable shipping cost between customer i from site j. We reasonably assume that $c_{ij} \geq 0$, $f_j \geq 0$, and $v_j \geq 0$ for all $i \in I$, for all $j \in J$.

And two binary variables are set as:

$$X_j = \begin{cases} 1 & \text{if a facility setup on site } i; \\ 0 & \text{otherwise}; \end{cases}$$

$$Y_{ij} = \begin{cases} 1 & \text{if facility } j \text{ serves customer } i; \\ 0 & \text{otherwise}. \end{cases} \tag{1}$$

Then the general model of DFLP could be stated as the following linear mixed-integer program:

$$\min \quad \Phi = \sum_{j=1}^{m} f_j X_j + \sum_{i=1}^{n} \sum_{j=1}^{m} d_i c_{ij} Y_{ij} \tag{2}$$

$$\text{Subject to} \quad \sum_{j=1}^{m} Y_{ij} = 1 \quad \forall i \in I \tag{3}$$

$$\sum_{i=1}^{n} d_i Y_{ij} \leq v_j X_j \quad \forall j \in J \tag{4}$$

$$Y_{ij} - X_j \leq 0 \quad \forall i \in I, \forall j \in J \tag{5}$$

$$X_j \in \{0, 1\} \quad \forall j \in J \tag{6}$$

$$Y_{ij} \in \{0, 1\} \quad \forall i \in I, \forall j \in J. \tag{7}$$

The objective function (2) is to minimize the total system cost, including the location cost and the shipment cost. Constraint (3) is the demand constraint, which makes the demand of each customer be met; (4) is the variable upper bound constraint; (5) is the capacity constraint of facility; (6) and (7) are standard binary integrality constraints.

3. Simulated Annealing Algorithm for DFLP

Kirkpatrick et al. [23] introduced the concept of simulated annealing (SA) algorithmin 1983, which is a stochastic optimization technique. To be specific, SA is a probabilistic heuristic for the global optimization problems of finding a good approximation to the global optimum of a given objective function in the search space. It is often used when the solution space is discrete. In the searching process, the SA accepts not only better but also worse neighboring solutions with a certain probability. This means that the SA has the ability to escape from the local minima. Therefore, it can find high-quality solutions that do not strongly depend upon the choice of the initial solution compared to other local search algorithms. And its another advantage over the other heuristic algorithms is the ease of implementation. So we adopted SA as the basic solution method to solve the DFLP.

In last 30 years, SA has been studied widely and used extensively in many optimization problems [24–29], which have proved that SA is an effective tool for approximating globally optimal solutions to many NP-hard optimization problems.

In order to describe the procedure of the SA, **S**, **S′**, **S″**, and **S̄** are used to represent the different feasible solutions of the model; $D(T_i)$ is the cooling function of temperature, in which T_i is the current temperature value. T_f is the stop temperature value. N is the maximum iteration number at each temperature value. $\Phi(\mathbf{S})$ is used to represent the objective function value of the solution **S**. According to Jayaraman and Ross [19], the SA for DFLP could be given as follows.

Step 1 (initialization). Set iteration counter $i = 1$. Generate an initial feasible solution **S** and regard **S** as the optimal solution. Set the initial temperature T_i and the stop temperature T_f are specified. Define the cooling function $D(T_i)$.

Step 2 (generate a feasible neighboring solution). Perform the neighboring function on current solution **S** and get the new neighboring solution **S′**.

Step 3 (evaluate current solution with neighboring solution). If the objective function value of the new solution **S′** is no less than that of the current solution **S**, namely, $\Phi(\mathbf{S'}) \geq \Phi(\mathbf{S})$, then proceed to Step 4; otherwise, if $\Phi(\mathbf{S'}) < \Phi(\mathbf{S})$, then **S** = **S′**, proceed to Step 5.

Step 4 (examine metropolis condition). Determine the difference ΔC between the incumbent solution **S** and the neighboring solution **S′**, as $\Delta \Phi = \Phi(\mathbf{S'}) - \Phi(\mathbf{S})$. Generate a random number ρ from the interval $(0,1)$, if $\rho < \exp(-\Delta\Phi/T_i)$, then **S** = **S′**. Proceed to Step 5.

Step 5 (check increment counters). Set $i \leftarrow i + 1$. If $i \leq N$, then return to Step 2. Otherwise proceed to Step 6.

Step 6 (adjust temperature). Adjust temperature by the cooling function, Mathematically this is $T_i \leftarrow D(T_i)$.

Step 7 (convergence check). If $T_i \geq T_f$, then reset $i = 1$ and return to Step 2. Otherwise, stop and output the optimal solution **S**.

4. Combined Simulated Annealing (CSA)

The solution of DFLP includes two parts: X_js and Y_{ij}s. X_j denotes whether or not open the facility at site j, while Y_{ij} denotes the service demand allocation. The two variables are interdependent and interactional. As each demand must allocate to an opening facility, we could can conclude that the variable Y_{ij} is subject to the variable X_j. This relation also can be seen from the constrain (4) in the model in Section 1.

CSA works in two layers as internal layer and external layer to solve the problem. The internal layer subalgorithm (ILSA) would optimize the facility location decision variable X_j. The external layer subalgorithm (ELSA) would perform the allocation optimization under fixed X_js which determined in the internal layer. In each layer the SA is used and they make up of the CSA. The method that divides the problem into two layers could make the search in the procedure explores in smaller solution space each time, so it increases the probability of obtaining the global optimal solution.

Some parameters should be initialized before the performance of CSA, including the initial temperature and stop temperature, cooling ruler of the temperature, iteration maximum in each temperature. The initialization of the parameters could be determined in similar ways to these in the SA. And the **S**, **S′**, **S″**, **S̄** are also used to represent the different feasible solutions here.

In addition, CSA must start with an initial solution or with a solution produced using a heuristic. In this work, we use the randomly generated initial solution, which proposed in Qin et al. [30].

4.1. Neighboring Functions. Similar to the SA, the CSA algorithm is an iterative search procedure based on the neighboring function. The quality of the optimal solution is very sensitive to the way that the candidate solutions are selected. Thus, the neighboring function is crucial to the good performance of the CSA algorithm.

The ELSA would optimize the facility location decision. So the neighboring function of the ELSA to modify the configuration of the current solution and generate a neighboring solution could perform three different operations:

(1) If the number of the located facilities is less than the allowed maximum M ($\sum_{j=1}^{m} X_j < M$), then select a candidate site i which satisfies $X_j = 0$ in current solution S randomly and set $X_j = 1$, namely, there would locate a new facility.

(2) If the number of the locate facility no less than 1 ($\sum_{j=1}^{m} X_j \geq 1$), then select a site j randomly which satisfies $X_j = 1$ in solution S and set $X_j = 0$, namely, there would close a open facility.

(3) Select a site j which satisfies $X_j = 0$ and another site j' which satisfies $X_{j'} = 1$ in current solution S, then set $X_j = 1$ and $X_{j'} = 0$.

In the implementation of the ELSA, we could select only one operation from the above three operations to perform the neighboring function each time. And after implementing the operation, it should allocate the customers' demand to the opened facilities again, as generate an initial solution again.

ILSA is to determine the demand allocation decision. According to the features of the allocation decision, there are two operations to generate the neighboring solutions in the ILSA.

(1) Select two allocation variables Y_{ij} and $Y_{ij'}$ that satisfy $Y_{ij} = 1$ and $Y_{ij'} = 0$; then set $Y_{ij'} = 1$, $Y_{ij} = 0$, namely, it allocates the demand of customer i from facility j to facility j'.

(2) Exchange the facilities which serve two customers respectively with each other. To be specific, select four allocation variables as $y_{i_1 j_1} = 1$, $y_{i_2 j_2} = 1$, $y_{i_1 j_2} = 0$, $y_{i_2 j_1} = 0$, then set $y_{i_1 j_2} = 1$, $y_{i_2 j_1} = 1$, $y_{i_1 j_1} = 0$, $y_{i_2 j_2} = 0$.

Similarly, the neighboring function of the ILSA could select only one operation to perform each time. In addition, it must ensure that demands of all customers must be satisfied and the facilities have no capacity violations exist. Otherwise, it should return to the old solution and reselect an operation to perform.

4.2. The Procedure of CSA. The following is a step-by-step description of the procedure of CSA.

Step 1 (initialization). Set iteration counter $i = 1$, $k = 1$. Set the initial temperature T_i, and stop temperature T_f, the initial feasible solution is **S**, and let **S** be the optimal solution at the same time. Define the cooling function $D(T_i)$. Generate a feasible solution by randomly allocation with capacity restricted.

Step 2 (check feasibilities). The method now checks the demand allocations to ensure that no capacity violations exist. The demands of the customers are also checked. If the solution **S** is not feasible, we should return to Step 1.

Step 3 (generate a neighboring solution). Perform the external layer neighboring function on solution **S**, and generate a neighboring feasible solution **S′**.

Step 4 (perform ILSA). *Step 4.1.* Set $k = 1$. Regard solution **S′** as the initial solution and the current optimal solution.

Step 4.2. Perform the internal layer neighboring function on solution **S′**, and generate a neighboring feasible solution **S″**.

Step 4.3. If $\Phi(\mathbf{S''}) < \Phi(\mathbf{S'})$, then set **S′** = **S″**; otherwise, generate a random number ρ from (0,1), if $\rho < \exp(-(\Phi(\mathbf{S''}) < \Phi(\mathbf{S'}))/T_i)$, then set **S′** = **S″**.

Step 4.4. Consider $k \leftarrow k + 1$. If $k \leq N_2$, then return to Step 2. Otherwise proceed to Step 5.

Step 4.5. Stop and output the optimal solution **S′**, return to the ELSA.

Step 5 (save the global optimal solution). If $\Phi(\mathbf{S'}) < \Phi(\mathbf{\overline{S}})$, then **S̄** = **S′**.

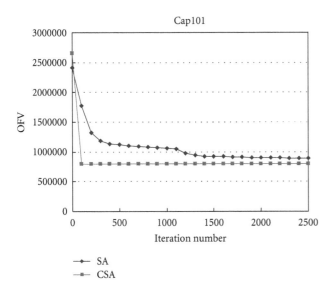

FIGURE 1: OFV versus iteration number in Cap101.

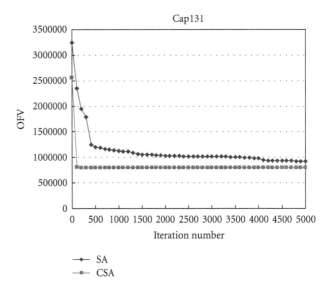

FIGURE 2: OFV versus iteration number in Cap131.

Step 6 (evaluate current solution). Evaluate current solution with neighboring solution. If $\Phi(\mathbf{S}') < \Phi(\mathbf{S})$, then let $\mathbf{S} = \mathbf{S}'$ proceed to Step 7; otherwise, proceed to Step 7.

Step 7 (examine metropolis condition). A random number ρ is generated from $(0,1)$, if $\rho < \exp(-(\Phi(\mathbf{S}') - \Phi(\mathbf{S}))/T_i)$ then $\mathbf{S} = \mathbf{S}'$. Proceed to Step 8.

Step 8 (increment counters). Set $i \leftarrow i + 1$. If $i \leq N_1$, then return to Step 3; otherwise, proceed to Step 9.

Step 9 (adjust temperature). Adjust temperature by the cooling function: $T_i \leftarrow D(T_i)$.

Step 10 (convergence check). If $T_i \geq T_f$, then reset $i = 1$ and return to Step 3. Otherwise, stop and output the optimal solution $\overline{\mathbf{S}}$.

N_1, N_2 are the given maximum iteration number in ELSA and ILSA respectively. The Step 5 is to save the global optimal solution that has been found so far in the CSA. This operation does not take the acceptance probability of worse solution into consideration. So it could help the algorithm avoid losing the global optimal solution.

5. Computational Experiments

To assess the practical effectiveness of the proposed CSA algorithm, we use 30 instances with different sizes as benchmark problems. Twelve "Capacitated warehouse location" instances were given by Beasley [31], which are publicly available from the OR-Library and could be downloaded directly from the website: http://people.brunel.ac.uk/~mastjjb/jeb/orlib/capinfo.html. The other 18 instances were proposed by Ghosh [32].

To perform the CSA, the initial temperature T_1 could be set equal to the objective function value of the initial solution. The cooling ruler is equal-ratio cooling, and the cooling ratio $\alpha = 0.95$. The iteration maximum $N_1 = m$,

$N_2 = 5n$, the stop temperature value $t_f = 0.001$. The SA is used to solve the instances too, and its iteration maximum under the same temperature is $5mn$; other parameters are same as CSA. So the total iteration numbers in the SA and CSA are equal. We also use the randomly generated method to find an initial feasible solution.

The model and CSA were implemented in Visual C# 2010. A personal computer with Intel E5800 CPU, 2G RAM and Windows XP Profession operating system was used for all tests.

Example 1 (OR-Library Instances). The instances in OR-Library are more than 150, and we selected 12 instances with different size to be solved by the CSA and compared with theirs optimal solution (all instances have been exactly solved by the Lindo software and provide their optimal solutions by the author).

Computational results of these OR-Library instances are reported in Table 1. Each row of the table gives the results of one individual instance. The instance names are originally used in the OR-Library. The gap in the table represented the relative error between the result and the optimal solution.

It can be observed from Table 1 that the CSA found optimal solutions for all these instances without any exception, while the SA didn't find anyone. The CPU time used by SA for each instance is from 3 to 8 times of that used by CSA.

The computation process of instances Cap101 and Cap131 with CSA and SA are depicted in Figures 1 and 2. The OFV is the objective function value. As shown in the figures, we can find that the convergence speed of CSA is more quickly than that of SA. The iteration time for converging to the optimal solution used by SA for each instance is from 10 to 25 times of that used by CSA.

Example 2 (The Ghosh Instances). The Ghosh instances are 90 instances in total, and with $n = m$ on all cases. These instances of the same size are divided into two categories,

TABLE 1: Comparison for OR-Library instances.

	Instances			SA			CSA	
Name	Size ($m \times n$)	Optimal solution	Result	Gap (%)	CPU time[S]	Result	Gap (%)	CPU time[S]
Cap71	16×50	932615.750	1192413.575	6.995	4.233	932615.750	0	0.921
Cap72	16×50	977799.400	1012970.190	5.970	4.690	977799.400	0	1.599
Cap73	16×50	1010641.450	1100470.190	8.179	4.435	1010641.450	0	0.732
Cap74	16×50	1034976.975	1212970.191	12.276	6.438	1034976.975	0	1.499
Cap101	25×50	796648.440	886494.475	9.250	12.552	796648.440	0	2.192
Cap102	25×50	854704.200	998953.625	15.698	13.652	854704.200	0	2.612
Cap103	25×50	893782.1125	1002291.150	11.412	12.002	893782.1125	0	1.798
Cap104	25×50	928941.750	1177291.150	24.333	18.263	928941.750	0	5.048
Cap131	50×50	793439.5620	856571.455	6.607	54.688	793439.562	0	24.723
Cap132	50×50	851495.3250	1011571.450	16.732	45.563	851495.325	0	19.803
Cap133	50×50	893076.7120	1219071.450	32.485	56.549	893076.712	0	8.842
Cap134	50×50	928941.7500	1374071.452	41.690	49.156	928941.750	0	14.972

TABLE 2: Comparison for the Ghosh instances.

Size ($m \times n$)	Instances		Hybrid		CLM		GTS		TS		CSA	
	Class	Range	Result	CPU time[1]	Result	CPU time[1]	Result	CPU time[1]	Result	CPU time[1]	Result	CPU time
250×250	Symmetry	A	257806.8	4.328	257895.2	86.482	257832.6	2.828	257805.0	3.687	**257293.0**	66.652
250×250	Symmetry	B	276035.2	7.774	276352.2	34.634	276185.2	5.628	276035.2	5.347	**275560.0**	69.339
250×250	Symmetry	C	*333671.6*	8.702	*333671.6*	69.458	333820.0	9.878	*333671.6*	10.384	334127.0	70.588
250×250	Asymmetry	A	257923.4	4.636	258032.6	86.506	257978.4	2.618	257917.8	3.487	**257179.0**	81.706
250×250	Asymmetry	B	276053.2	8.082	276184.2	33.688	276467.2	5.790	276053.2	5.501	**275111.0**	75.473
250×250	Asymmetry	C	332897.2	7.776	333058.4	89.990	333237.6	9.196	*332897.2*	9.736	343270.0	70.329
500×500	Symmetry	A	511196.4	27.644	511487.2	946.028	511383.6	15.616	511180.4	14.835	**511113.0**	541.772
500×500	Symmetry	B	*537912.0*	34.196	538685.8	294.656	538480.4	31.432	*537912.0*	29.860	*537912.0*	579.244
500×500	Symmetry	C	621059.2	40.376	621172.8	437.462	621107.2	71.106	621059.2	67.551	**620112.0**	663.167
500×500	Asymmetry	A	511145.0	20.232	511393.4	921.208	511251.6	13.760	511140.0	13.072	**511097.0**	543.235
500×500	Asymmetry	B	537863.4	31.300	538421.0	311.344	538144.0	34.748	537847.6	33.011	**535665.0**	358.807
500×500	Asymmetry	C	621463.8	47.790	621990.8	388.210	621811.8	72.064	*621463.8*	68.461	630861.0	509.046
750×750	Symmetry	A	763706.6	49.214	763978.0	3650.662	763830.8	39.812	763693.4	37.821	**763417.0**	1250.775
750×750	Symmetry	B	796632.2	92.886	797173.4	1583.170	796919.0	93.352	796571.8	88.684	**794970.0**	1517.086
750×750	Symmetry	C	900272.0	113.640	900785.2	1194.534	901158.4	229.914	*900158.6*	218.418	926358.0	1387.104
750×750	Asymmetry	A	763731.2	59.130	764019.2	3658.588	763836.6	39.650	763717.0	34.667	**763498.0**	1548.608
750×750	Asymmetry	B	796396.8	73.322	796754.2	1606.778	796859.0	95.430	796374.4	90.660	**793668.0**	1598.631
750×750	Asymmetry	C	*900193.2*	112.994	900349.8	1325.812	900514.2	236.902	*900193.2*	205.060	919453.0	1337.671

Note: CPU time[1] is on Sun Enterprise 3000 Server ($4 \times$ CPU, 6 G memory).

symmetric, where the transportation cost $c_{ij} = c_{ji}$ holds, and asymmetric, where $c_{ij} = c_{ji}$ does not necessarily hold. Each group contains three values of $m \times n$: 250×250, 500×500, and 750×750. The instances in each category are further divided into three instance classes, and they differ in the range of values from which opening costs f_j are drawn, which could be chosen from the $[100, 200]$ (Range A), $[1000, 2000]$ (Range B), and $[10000, 20000]$ (Range C) randomly.

The optimal solutions of the Ghosh instances were not presented, but there used to be several methods to solve the instances and compared the results with each other in the literature [33]. And we compare the results of the CSA with them as reported in Table 2, in which we reported the results of the instances obtained by hybrid, CLM, GTS, TS, and CSA.

As shown in Table 2, for all instances, CSA found solutions better than those of other methods with only five exceptions, and found solutions with the same result for symmetric instance with $m \times n = 500 \times 500$ in type C. Even in the five exceptions, the gaps between the solutions were found by CSA and the best solutions found by other methods are very small, and the maximal relative gap is only 3.1% in asymmetric instance with $m \times n = 250 \times 250$ in type C.

6. Conclusions

The DFLP is to determinate the facility location and demand allocation so as to minimize the total cost, based on the demands of customers satisfied without violating the capacity restriction of any facility. The CSA was proposed for the DFLP, which is a two-layer algorithm. Its external layer subalgorithm optimizes the facility location decision, while the internal layer subalgorithm optimizes the demand allocation under the fixed facility location which is determined by the external layer. The each local search process in CSA focuses on the smaller solution space, which could not only increase the probability of obtaining the global optimal solution, but also save computational time.

The performance of CSA is evaluated with 30 instances with different sizes. Those instances are solved by CSA in a very reasonable amount of time, and the solutions are compared with that of previous studies in the literature. It is showed that the new algorithm could give better results (or at least same) than the others for nearly all instances. Hence, the CSA works much better than the previous work and offers a reasonable alternative solution method to the DFLP.

Acknowledgment

This research was supported by the National Natural Science Foundation of China (Grant no. 71101155).

References

[1] M. T. Melo, S. Nickel, and F. Saldanha-da-Gama, "Facility location and supply chain management—a review," *European Journal of Operational Research*, vol. 196, no. 2, pp. 401–412, 2009.

[2] M. S. Daskin, "What you should know about location modeling," *Naval Research Logistics*, vol. 55, no. 4, pp. 283–294, 2008.

[3] D. B. Shmoys, E. Tardos, and K. Aardal, "Approximation algorithms for facility location problems," in *Proceedings of the 29th Annual ACM Symposium on Theory of Computing*, pp. 265–274, ACM Press, May 1997.

[4] A. F. Gabor and J. K. C. W. van Ommeren, "A new approximation algorithm for the multilevel facility location problem," *Discrete Applied Mathematics*, vol. 158, no. 5, pp. 453–460, 2010.

[5] Z. Wang, D. Du, A. F. Gabor, and D. Xu, "An approximation algorithm for the κ-level stochastic facility location problem," *Operations Research Letters*, vol. 38, no. 5, pp. 386–389, 2010.

[6] L. Yan and M. Chrobak, "Approximation algorithms for the Fault-Tolerant Facility Placement problem," *Information Processing Letters*, vol. 111, no. 11, pp. 545–549, 2011.

[7] A. Marín, "The discrete facility location problem with balanced allocation of customers," *European Journal of Operational Research*, vol. 210, no. 1, pp. 27–38, 2011.

[8] Y. Li, D. Xub, and D. Du, "Improved approximation algorithms for the robust fault-tolerant facility location problem," *Information Processing Letters*, vol. 112, no. 10, pp. 361–364, 2012.

[9] D. Fotakis, "A primal-dual algorithm for online non-uniform facility location," *Journal of Discrete Algorithms*, vol. 5, no. 1, pp. 141–148, 2007.

[10] J. Dias, M. Eugénia Captivo, and J. Clímaco, "Efficient primal-dual heuristic for a dynamic location problem," *Computers and Operations Research*, vol. 34, no. 6, pp. 1800–1823, 2007.

[11] D. Du, R. Lu, and D. Xu, "A primal-dual approximation algorithm for the facility location problem with submodular penalties," *Algorithmica*, vol. 63, no. 1-2, pp. 191–200, 2012.

[12] K. Jain, M. Mahdian, and A. Saberi, "A new greedy approach for facility location problems," in *Proceedings of the 34th Annual ACM Symposium on Theory of Computing (STOC '02)*, pp. 731–740, May 2002.

[13] K. Jain, M. Mahdian, E. Markakis, A. Saberi, and V. V. Vazirani, "Greedy facility location algorithms analyzed using dual fitting with factor-revealing LP," *Journal of the ACM*, vol. 50, no. 6, pp. 795–824, 2003.

[14] M. Mahdian, Y. Ye, and J. Zhang, "Approximation algorithms for metric facility location problems," *SIAM Journal on Computing*, vol. 36, no. 2, pp. 411–432, 2006.

[15] S. Guha and S. Khuller, "Greedy strikes back: improved facility location algorithms," *Journal of Algorithms*, vol. 31, no. 1, pp. 228–248, 1999.

[16] J. Zhang, B. Chen, and Y. Ye, "A multiexchange local search algorithm for the capacitated facility location problem," *Mathematics of Operations Research*, vol. 30, no. 2, pp. 389–403, 2005.

[17] J. K. Sankaran, "On solving large instances of the capacitated facility location problem," *European Journal of Operational Research*, vol. 178, no. 3, pp. 663–676, 2007.

[18] V. P. Nguyen, C. Prins, and C. Prodhon, "A multi-start evolutionary local search for the two-echelon location routing problem," *Engineering Applications of Artificial Intelligence*, vol. 25, no. 1, pp. 56–71, 2012.

[19] V. Jayaraman and A. Ross, "A simulated annealing methodology to distribution network design and management," *European Journal of Operational Research*, vol. 144, no. 3, pp. 629–645, 2003.

[20] M. A. Arostegui Jr., S. N. Kadipasaoglu, and B. M. Khumawala, "An empirical comparison of Tabu Search, Simulated Annealing, and Genetic Algorithms for facilities location problems," *International Journal of Production Economics*, vol. 103, no. 2, pp. 742–754, 2006.

[21] R. Şahin, "A simulated annealing algorithm for solving the bi-objective facility layout problem," *Expert Systems with Applications*, vol. 38, no. 4, pp. 4460–4465, 2011.

[22] M. Solimanpur and M. A. Kamran, "Solving facilities location problem in the presence of alternative processing routes using a genetic algorithm," *Computers & Industrial Engineering*, vol. 59, no. 4, pp. 830–839, 2010.

[23] S. Kirkpatrick, C. D. Gelett, and M. P. Vecchi, "Optimization by simulated annealing," *Science*, vol. 220, no. 4598, pp. 671–680, 1983.

[24] D. Bertsimas and J. Tsitsiklis, "Simulated annealing," *Statistical Science*, vol. 8, no. 1, pp. 10–15, 1993.

[25] N. Boissin and J. L. Lutton, "A parallel simulated annealing algorithm," *Parallel Computing*, vol. 19, no. 8, pp. 859–872, 1993.

[26] P. Tian, J. Ma, and D. M. Zhang, "Application of the simulated annealing algorithm to the combinatorial optimization problem with permutation property: an investigation of generation mechanism," *European Journal of Operational Research*, vol. 118, no. 1, pp. 81–94, 1999.

[27] B. Suman, N. Hoda, and S. Jha, "Orthogonal simulated annealing for multiobjective optimization," *Computers & Chemical Engineering*, vol. 34, no. 10, pp. 1618–1631, 2010.

[28] Z. Xinchao, "Simulated annealing algorithm with adaptive neighborhood," *Applied Soft Computing Journal*, vol. 11, no. 2, pp. 1827–1836, 2011.

[29] R. S. Tavares, T. C. Martins, and M. S. G. Tsuzuki, "Simulated annealing with adaptive neighborhood: a case study in off-line robot path planning," *Expert Systems with Applications*, vol. 38, no. 4, pp. 2951–2965, 2011.

[30] J. Qin, F. Shi, L. X. Miao, and G. J. Tan, "Optimal model and algorithm for multi-commodity logistics network design considering stochastic demand and inventory control," *System Engineering*, vol. 29, no. 4, pp. 176–183, 2009.

[31] J. E. Beasley, "Lagrangean heuristics for location problems," *European Journal of Operational Research*, vol. 65, no. 3, pp. 383–399, 1993.

[32] D. Ghosh, 2001, http://www.mpi-inf.mpg.de/departments/d1/projects/benchmarks/UflLib/ORLIB.html.

[33] D. Ghosh, "Neighborhood search heuristics for the uncapacitated facility location problem," *European Journal of Operational Research*, vol. 150, no. 1, pp. 150–162, 2003.

19

Reinforcement Learning Based Artificial Immune Classifier

Mehmet Karakose

Computer Engineering Department, Firat University, Elazig, Turkey

Correspondence should be addressed to Mehmet Karakose; mkarakose@firat.edu.tr

Academic Editors: P. Agarwal, S. Balochian, and Y. Zhang

One of the widely used methods for classification that is a decision-making process is artificial immune systems. Artificial immune systems based on natural immunity system can be successfully applied for classification, optimization, recognition, and learning in real-world problems. In this study, a reinforcement learning based artificial immune classifier is proposed as a new approach. This approach uses reinforcement learning to find better antibody with immune operators. The proposed new approach has many contributions according to other methods in the literature such as effectiveness, less memory cell, high accuracy, speed, and data adaptability. The performance of the proposed approach is demonstrated by simulation and experimental results using real data in Matlab and FPGA. Some benchmark data and remote image data are used for experimental results. The comparative results with supervised/unsupervised based artificial immune system, negative selection classifier, and resource limited artificial immune classifier are given to demonstrate the effectiveness of the proposed new method.

1. Introduction

Artificial immune systems are one of the algorithms that forms the basis of classification methods and they can be used in many areas of daily life. The basis of these algorithms is based on the human immune system, and they have been usually used in popular areas such as the classification, anomaly detection, and the computer virus detection. Human immune system known as the natural immune system is an effective mechanism for protecting the human body against foreign cells. By utilizing these features of natural immune systems, artificial immune systems have been developed for solving the scientific and engineering problems. Artificial immune systems are used in many applications such as optimization, classification, and pattern recognition. In classification algorithms, there are various algorithms that are different from artificial immune systems. These algorithms are based on maximum likelihood and minimum distance. They are used on parallel and piped images [1]. These type algorithms used in the classification of images generally need the preclassified data. In classification methods, there are two basic learning method such as supervised and unsupervised learning algorithms. Block diagrams of some artificial immune classifiers in the literature are given in Figure 1.

Supervised and unsupervised learning algorithms are widely used methods in classification problems [2–13]. Some algorithms such as K-Means [4], ISODATA, Fuzzy C-Means, and AIS (Artificial Immune System) [2] are known as unsupervised classification methods, and they cluster data without the need for the training data. Zhong et al. [2] proposed unsupervised artificial immune classification method for multi-hyperspectral remote sensing images. Four different structures such as water, plants, roads, and buildings are classified by using unsupervised artificial immune system. Afterwards, the obtained results with the results of other methods such as K-Means, ISODATA, Fuzzy C-Means, and SOM methods were compared. In another study, Zhong et al. [3] proposed supervised artificial immune classification for remote sensing images. The effectiveness of the proposed algorithm is verified via simulation results. Another study of Zhong and Zhang [5] supervised adaptive artificial immune network was proposed for multi/hyperspectral remote sensing images. Aydin et al. [7] proposed an adaptive artificial immune algorithm for fault diagnosis of induction motors faults. The classification was made by using three-phase current signals taken from a real induction motor. Stator and broken rotor bar faults are detected by using this classification method.

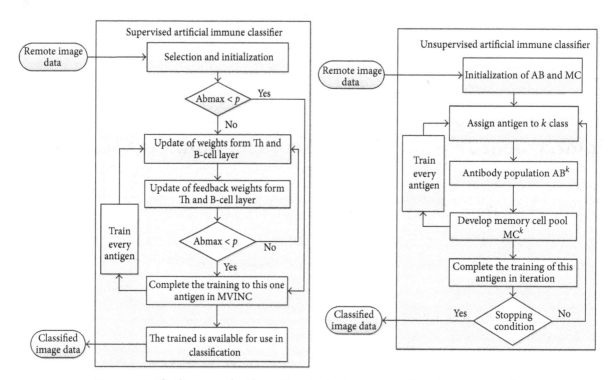

FIGURE 1: Artificial immune classifiers with supervised-unsupervised learning models [2, 3].

Supervised and unsupervised learning methods have some advantages over one another, though they have some disadvantages according to reinforcement learning. Reinforcement learning presents a wide solution framework in planning and control. This learning method aims to obtain most suitable results with award values for each action of an agent. The purpose of the training process continues until agent reaches the awards. Q learning algorithm is a reinforcement learning algorithm. Q learning algorithm is based on status and action value of Q and converges according to award value of action and Q values of next status. The reinforcement learning has been used for many applications such as fuzzy systems, neural networks, and classification applications [8–11].

This paper presents a new artificial immune classifier based on reinforcement learning. The proposed approach has a self-learning structure using clonal selection and memory cells. Especially this algorithm is trained by reinforcement learning with feedback of mutation rate. Thus best antibodies are obtained to recognize antigens. In this paper, Section 2 presents algorithms for artificial immune systems. Section 3 provides details of the proposed new approach. Section 4 presents the validation of the proposed approach using experimental results and Section 5 gives the conclusions.

2. Artificial Immune Systems

Artificial immune system was exposed by inspiring the human immune system. The method is used in many fields, especially engineering [12]. Artificial immune systems have

been developed to detect and destroy viruses with the emergence of computer viruses and used in the antivirus detection process. Immune systems are effective protection mechanisms that protect the human body from foreign antigens or pathogens [13]. The artificial immune algorithm has been uncovered by considering the importance of the artificial immune system in human life. The base of the artificial immune algorithm is the same with artificial immune system. Furthermore, the method has become indispensable for optimization and classification problems. Different types of methods have emerged with creation of the artificial immune algorithm. Some of these methods have become important algorithms which form the basis of the artificial immune algorithm. Artificial immune systems basically consist of two sections. These important algorithms are clonal selection algorithm and negative selection algorithm.

The clonal selection algorithm is based on the cloning of immune cells in type B antigen recognition. The structures that will be used as a set of data structures for the algorithm have been applied in the clonal selection structure. The pseudocode of the clonal selection algorithm is given in Pseudocode 1. The algorithm that used in pattern recognition is shown in Pseudocode 1. The similarities between antibodies and antigens are found and the clones are formed from antibodies with high similarity.

The negative selection algorithm is often used in determination of the undesirable situations. Particularly, this method is use in the operating of virus detection software. The implementation and the operation of the algorithm are quite easy. First, a set of is produced with this method and this candidate detector set is matched with the self-set. If there is a matching, these candidates are transferred to the

```
Start
(1)    Ag determination antigen set
(2)    k the number of steps, N population size
(3)    ab_b the number of antibody for cloning
(4)    ab_k the number of low similarity elements for end of iteration
(5)    P, randomly production of n sized population
(6)    j = 0;
(7)    While j < g do
(8)            similarity (P, Ag) ← computation between antibody and antigen
(9)            P_1 ← Selection(P, ab_b) //selection of best n1 antibody for cloning
(10)           C ← Cloning(P_1, Similarity(P_1)) //clones from P_1
(11)           C_1 ← Mutation(C, Similarity(C)) //Mutation for C by similarity
(12)           Similarity(C_1, Aj) ← similarity between clone set(C_1) and antigen
(13)           M ← Selection(C_1)
(14)           P ← Displacement(P, at_k)
(15)           j ← j + 1
       End while
```

PSEUDOCODE 1: The pseudocode of clonal selection algorithm.

```
Start
(1)    Creation of self sample set (K)
(2)    While (for end of training)
(3)        Production of random detectors (P)
(4)        If(match detector with self sample set)
(5)            Remove detector from set
(6)        Else
(7)            Add detector to set
(8)        End else
(9)    End while
(10)   Creation of test sample set (K)
(11)   While (for end of testing)
(12)       If(match detector with test sample set)
(13)           Anomaly detection according to active detectors
(14)       End if
(15)   End while
```

PSEUDOCODE 2: The pseudocode of negative selection algorithm.

main detector set. Afterwards, the detector set compared by entering the test data. If this test data is recognized by any detector, the desired operation is performed. The training and the test phase of the negative selection algorithm are expressed with pseudocode given in Pseudocode 2.

3. The Proposed Approach

The reinforcement based artificial immune classifier is proposed for classification in this study. Reinforced artificial immune classifier method can be easily used in all areas in which using the computational intelligence is convenient and can produce the best results in used areas. This method is welded from reinforcement learning algorithm which is a machine learning method. Successful results were obtained by using reinforcement learning algorithm in machine learning. The difference of reinforcement learning algorithm from other algorithms is to calculate all probabilities of current states to identify the next state. So, each step that algorithm operates is used as reinforcement for the next operation. The reinforced artificial immune classifier is composed by using this algorithm in combination with an artificial immune system. The flow chart of proposed method is given in Figure 2.

Q learning algorithm is a reinforcement learning algorithm. According to the Q learning algorithm, the existing situation and the Q value of its action converge with a certain coefficient to the award value of the action and Q values of the arriving situations. In the Q learning algorithm, the situation of the algorithm for step and the best possible step for next

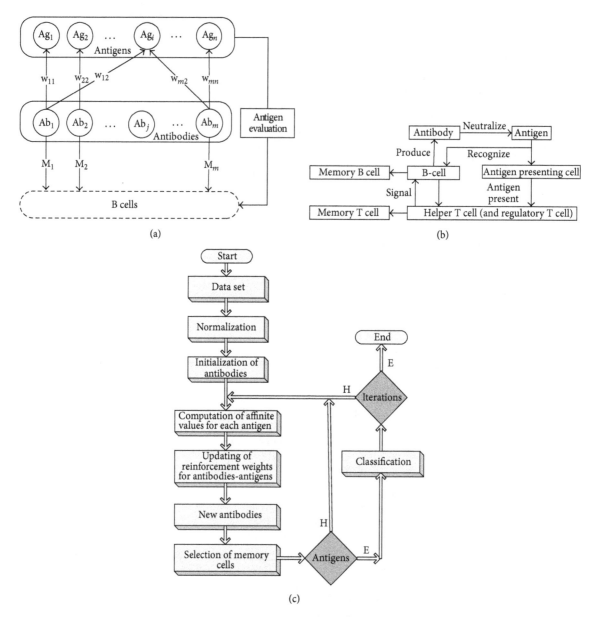

FIGURE 2: Block diagram and flow chart of the proposed approach.

situations are determined by considering this situation. The Q value of the next situation in algorithm is calculated by (1)

$$Q\,(\text{status, action})$$
$$= R\,(\text{status, action})$$
$$+ \sigma \max\,(Q\,(\text{next status, all mutation actions}))\,. \tag{1}$$

The R value given in (1) indicates the current status of the algorithm. σ max value is the most high affinity value of the steps for the next situation. The pseudocode of Q learning algorithm is given in Pseudocode 3.

Q learning is a commonly used algorithm in reinforcement learning methods. A new reinforced artificial immune

```
Start
(1)     Import of R award status
(2)     Initizialiton of Q values
(3)         For all Q status
(4)         While (arrive to goal status)
(5)             Random start value
(6)             All actions and computation of next status
(7)             Next maximum Q value status
(8)             From current status to next status
(9)         End while
(10)        Update Q status
(11)    End of algorithm
```

PSEUDOCODE 3: The pseudocode of Q learning algorithm.

```
Start
(1)    Loading of training data
(2)    Random starting of antibody set
(3)        While (maximum iteration step)
(4)            Computation of affinity value for each antigen
(5)            Update of reinforcement weights between each antibody and antigen
(6)            Creation of clones of antibodies
(7)            Selection of memory cells
(8)        End while
(9)        Classification of Q memory cells
(10)   End of algorithm
```

PSEUDOCODE 4: The pseudocode of reinforcement learning based artificial immune classifier.

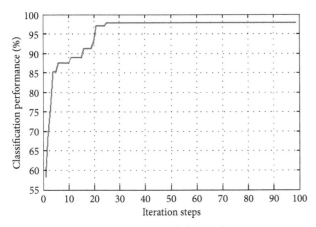

FIGURE 3: A test result for iris data.

classifier was proposed by applying the algorithm given the steps in Figure 2 to artificial immune system. Each antigen is recognized by an antibody (Ab). The connection between antigens and antibodies is updated according to Q learning algorithm in reinforced learning. Antibodies turn to the antigens is achieved through the clonal selection and mutation operators in immune selection. Antibodies that recognize the antigens are formed B-cell cells as memory cell. The pseudo code of proposed algorithm is given in Pseudocode 4.

In this study, the set of antigens have been identified as training data. Each antigen is represented by Ag, and the set of each antigen is expressed by AG. The set of antibodies is started in solution space at random locations. Each antibody is represented by Ab, and the set of antibodes is expressed by AB. The affinity of any i. Antibody is calculated by two factors given in (2) and (3):

$$D_s = \sum_{j \in \{d\}} \frac{1}{d_{ij} + 1}, \qquad (2)$$

$$Y_s = \sum_{j \in \{y\}} \frac{1}{d_{ij} + 1}. \qquad (3)$$

The set of d indicates the number of antigens that are correctly classified by i antibody in the previous equations. The set of misclassified samples with the same antibody is expressed

with y in the second equation. According to these two equations, the affinity account is maintained as (4)

$$
ab \cdot af = \begin{cases}
\dfrac{D_s}{N} + 2.0, & \text{If } \{d\} \neq 0 \text{ ve } \{y\} = 0, \\[2mm]
\dfrac{D_s - Y_s}{D_s + Y_s} + 1.0, & \text{If } \{d\} \neq 0 \text{ ve } \{y\} \neq 0, \\[2mm]
0, & \text{If } \{d\} = 0 \text{ ve } \{y\} = 0.
\end{cases} \qquad (4)
$$

Each antigen is recognized by an antibody. Each connection of an antibody with antigens is updated as (5)

$$w_{ij}(t+1) = w_{ij}(t) + \alpha \left(r_{ij}(t+1) - w_{ij}(t) \right). \qquad (5)$$

In (5), α indicates learning constant and $r_{ij}(t)$ indicates the award obtained in step t. The affinity value is used as an award here. Learning constant α is determined in $[0, 1]$. If an antibody recognizes an antigen, the antibody memory cell turns into (B cell). The weight value between the antibody turned into the cell and B cell, M_k is 1. This value determines the excitation level of related B cell. The antibodies transformed memory cell before is updated according to (6)

$$M_k = \beta M_k. \qquad (6)$$

β is the reduction factor used in (6) and gets value in $[0, 1]$. The clones of antibodies are generated proportional with their affinity. The clone are not created for antibodies whose affinities are over 2.0. The clones are formed as (7) for antibodies whose affinities are under 2.0

$$N_c = \sum_{k=1}^{n} \text{round} \left(c_{\text{rate}} * ab_k \cdot aff \right). \qquad (7)$$

The mutation is applied on the clones obtained in (7) according to affinity values. The mutation process is maintained as claimed in (8)

$$Ab_c(i) = Ab_c(i) + \text{rand}(-s, s), \qquad (8)$$
$$\text{if } d < \text{mutate}_{\text{rate}}.$$

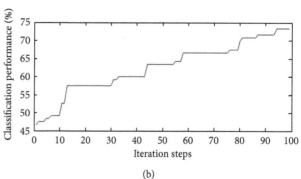

(a)   (b)

FIGURE 4: (a) Example remote image (400 × 400 pixel). (b) Performance graphic.

(*d*) number is a random number generated in $[0, 1]$. If this number is lower than mutation possibility, the mutation is applied to this antibody gene. The best mutated clone of an antibody is selected as a memory cell. According to the obtained memory cells, the performed classification process depending on the nearest neighbor algorithm is given in (9):

$$\text{Classification performance}$$
$$= \frac{\text{Successful classification samples}}{\text{Total samples}} * 100. \quad (9)$$

4. Experimental Results

The proposed reinforcement learning based artificial immune classifier has been implemented using software written in Matlab m-file and hardware in FPGA. The Iris data and remote image data were used to evaluate performances of the proposed approach and other artificial immune classifiers.

Iteration steps: firstly, performance of the proposed approach has been tested using the iris data. The iris controled the diameter and size of the pupil is a thin and circular structure in the eye. 768 × 4 matrix obtained by processing of iris images is used for classification and results is compared other artificial immune classification methods. In this process, data is divided into 10 parts, 9 parts are used for training, and one part is also used for testing of algorithm. Performance of algorithm is obtained by average of results computed with 10 test processes. The classification performance of the proposed approach for iris data is shown in Figure 3. The comparative results between the proposed approach and other artificial immune classifiers have been given in Table 1. Conventional artificial immune classifiers have large classification time for large data size. In addition, they use many memory cells for classification process. As shown in Table 1, the proposed approach has more effective classification performance and less memory cells according to other methods.

Secondly, performance of the proposed approach has been tested using the remote image data. 400 × 400 pixel color image has been used for this purpose. If image has

TABLE 1: Comparative results for the proposed approach.

Classification methods	Iris	Wine	Sonar
	Classification performances		
Proposed classifier	**97.33 ± 3.06**	**97.6 ± 3.98**	**92.17 ± 2.92**
[5]	96.3 ± 4.7	96.1 ± 4.7	—
[3]	94.8	—	89.1
[2]	95.7	—	84.9
	Number of memory cells		
Proposed classifier	**21**	**30**	**60**
[5]	100	100	—
[3]	28	—	71
[2]	32	—	177

plant, water, building, and ways areas, performance and effectiveness of the proposed approach can be well presented. Figure 4 and Table 2 show an image used for experiments and comparative classification performance of the proposed approach.

5. Conclusions

Artificial immune systems have an important role for classification methods that are commonly used in real-world applications. However, there are many approaches to improve the performance of artificial immune systems in the literature. For this purpose, supervised and unsupervised learning algorithms are used in many studies. But artificial immune systems that used supervised or unsupervised learning algorithms have many disadvantages in terms of today's data features. Therefore, a new artificial immune classifier based on reinforcement learning has been proposed for classification applications in this study. The proposed approach that used reinforcement learning algorithm for computation of memory cells of artificial immune system aimed to obtain a new classifier that is faster in real time, has less memory cells, has higher accuracy in results, and more effectively. Performance and effectiveness of the proposed approach has been shown using some benchmark data and

TABLE 2: Comparison of results for the proposed approach.

Class	Samples	Award function values	[5]	[1]	Proposed approach
Water	950	00111100, 0010111, 00011000	97%	96%	**99%**
Plant	350	00110000, 00111000, 010110	82%	78%	**84%**
Road	250	00000011, 00010110, 00000110	85%	—	**88%**
Building	300	10100110, 0110011, 0101111	80%	82%	**85%**

remote image data. Comparative results between proposed approach and some methods in the literature have been given with experimental results. The reinforcement learning based artificial immune classifier provides higher accuracy with less memory cells as seen in the experimental results.

References

[1] D. Landgrebe, "Hyperspectral image data analysis," *IEEE Signal Processing Magazine*, vol. 19, no. 1, pp. 17–28, 2002.

[2] Y. Zhong, L. Zhang, B. Huang, and P. Li, "An unsupervised artificial immune classifier for multi/hyperspectral remote sensing imagery," *IEEE Transactions on Geoscience and Remote Sensing*, vol. 44, no. 2, pp. 420–431, 2006.

[3] Y. Zhong, L. Zhang, J. Gong, and P. Li, "A supervised artificial immune classifier for remote-sensing imagery," *IEEE Transactions on Geoscience and Remote Sensing*, vol. 45, no. 12, pp. 3957–3966, 2007.

[4] S. Arunprasath, S. Chandrasekar, K. Venkatalakshmi, and S. M. Shalinie, "Classification of remote sensed image using rapid genetic k-means algorithm," in *Proceedings of the IEEE International Conference on Communication Control and Computing Technologies (ICCCCT '10)*, pp. 677–682, October 2010.

[5] Y. Zhong and L. Zhang, "An adaptive artificial immune network for supervised classification of multi-/hyperspectral remote sensing imagery," *IEEE Transactions on Geoscience and Remote Sensing*, vol. 50, no. 3, pp. 894–909, 2012.

[6] X. H. Quah, C. Quek, and G. Leedham, "Pattern classification using fuzzy adaptive learning control network and reinforcement learning," *International Conference on Neural Information Processing*, vol. 3, pp. 1439–1443, 2002.

[7] I. Aydin, M. Karakose, and E. Akin, "An adaptive artificial immune system for fault classification," *Journal of Intelligent Manufacturing*, vol. 23, pp. 1489–1499, 2012.

[8] J. Shen, G. Gu, and H. Liu, "Automatic option generation in hierarchical reinforcement learning via immune clustering," in *Proceedings of the 1st International Symposium on Systems and Control in Aerospace and Astronautics*, pp. 497–500, January 2006.

[9] W.-C. Wong, S.-Y. Cho, and C. Quek, "R-POPTVR: a novel reinforcement-based POPTVR fuzzy neural network for pattern classification," *IEEE Transactions on Neural Networks*, vol. 20, no. 11, pp. 1740–1755, 2009.

[10] R. Ramos Da Silva and R. A. F. Romero, "Relational reinforcement learning and recurrent neural network with state classification to solve joint attention," in *Proceedings of the International Joint Conference on Neural Network (IJCNN '11)*, pp. 1222–1229, August 2011.

[11] M. A. Wiering, H. van Hasselt, A.-D. Pietersma, and L. Schomaker, "Reinforcement learning algorithms for solving classification problems," in *Proceedings of the IEEE Symposium on Adaptive Dynamic Programming and Reinforcement Learning (ADPRL '11)*, pp. 91–96, April 2011.

[12] I. Aydin, M. Karakose, and E. Akin, "Artificial immune classifier with swarm learning," *Engineering Applications of Artificial Intelligence*, vol. 23, no. 8, pp. 1291–1302, 2010.

[13] R. Zhang, T. Li, X. Xiao, and Y. Shi, "A danger-theory-based immune network optimization algorithm," *The Scientific World Journal*, vol. 2013, Article ID 810320, 13 pages, 2013.

20

Unsupervised User Similarity Mining in GSM Sensor Networks

Shafqat Ali Shad and Enhong Chen

Department of Computer Science and Technology, University of Science and Technology of China, Huangshan Road, Hefei, Anhui 230027, China

Correspondence should be addressed to Shafqat Ali Shad; shafqat@mail.ustc.edu.cn

Academic Editors: Y.-P. Huang and M.-A. Sicilia

Mobility data has attracted the researchers for the past few years because of its rich context and spatiotemporal nature, where this information can be used for potential applications like early warning system, route prediction, traffic management, advertisement, social networking, and community finding. All the mentioned applications are based on mobility profile building and user trend analysis, where mobility profile building is done through significant places extraction, user's actual movement prediction, and context awareness. However, significant places extraction and user's actual movement prediction for mobility profile building are a trivial task. In this paper, we present the user similarity mining-based methodology through user mobility profile building by using the semantic tagging information provided by user and basic GSM network architecture properties based on unsupervised clustering approach. As the mobility information is in low-level raw form, our proposed methodology successfully converts it to a high-level meaningful information by using the cell-Id location information rather than previously used location capturing methods like GPS, Infrared, and Wifi for profile mining and user similarity mining.

1. Introduction

Successful mobility profile building is the basis of a wide range of applications which includes viral advertisement systems [1, 2], potential warning systems [3], city-wide mapping and sensing [4], pollution detection and exposure [5], social networking, and community finding [6]. All of the mentioned applications are based on mobility profile building where a low-level raw mobility information is interpreted into a high-level meaningful information which can be utilized for useful purposes. As the mobility profile building is based on two potential parameters, that is, dwell time extraction and significant location finding, spatial data-based applications use the discrete location and continuous time information over mixed model.

As location extraction is a trivial task in mobility profile building, there are two broad classifications of location extraction methods: Active badge [7] and Active bat [8], where Active badge mainly represents the indoor technologies like Bluetooth, RFID, and Infrared, while Active bat represents the outdoor technologies like GPS, assisted faux GPS, and GSM. As Active badge is limited in terms of

its usage and implementations, Active bat is popular for location extraction in mobility. In case of Active bat, GPS and assisted GPS are not so encouraging because of high power consumption and extra equipment installation in the network. So, the only available and suitable method is GSM [9], where cell global identity (CGI) can be used for readily extraction of location. Cell global identity is a four-set header, that is, mobile country code (MCC) varies with country of the operator, mobile network code (MNC) binds with every network operator, location area code (LAC) assigned and arranged by the network operator for cells arrangement, cell ID given to every user connected to the network. MCC, MNC, LAC, and cell ID as a whole identify the user over its unique location in the network anytime.

CGI represents the approximate location of user through its four-set header which can be converted into latitude and longitude coordinates using public cell ID databases. This location information can be used for the determination for significant places for mobility profile building of the user. However, extraction of significant locations is a trivial task due to many reasons like missing values, cell oscillation, and exact coordinate mapping for location. Additionally, the

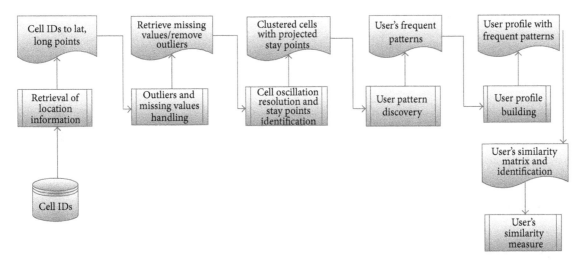

FIGURE 1: The proposed framework for user's similarity measure.

semantic information about the locations visited by the user can also be used for the mobility extraction through its mapping with physical location coordinates.

As the low-level mobility data cannot be used for the high-level potential mobility applications, we introduced a complete framework in this paper to describe how this information can be used to develop a mobility profile using the unsupervised clustering approach. So, the paper presents the extraction of spatiotemporal mobility trends and mobility profile building approach using the cellphone low-level log data. The contributions of the paper are (1) missing values extraction and removal of outliers using public cell ID and semantic information, (2) cell oscillation resolution and extraction of significant locations, (3) extraction of significant locations using overlapped area over time span, and (4) semantic information usage for final mobility profile building and user's similarity finding.

2. Related Work

Over recent years, mobility data has become a rich source of human life trends, and a lot of work has been done in the area of spatial information extraction. This motive is the main basis for many applications like city-wide sensing [10–14], where the privately held sensors were used through a developed model, while personal sensors like mobile phones and cameras are used for traffic monitoring system [15] through capturing the location information, while social behavior is studied in their work [16–18] where information is exploited through identification of significant places where users are active and later similarity analysis between them. While route prediction and recommendation is studied by Hull et al. [19] through GPS installed sensors in a taxi using the technique of opportunistic message forwarding. On the other hand, their work [20–22] is a cell-based location awareness for user mobility analysis.

In their work, Zonoozi and Dassanayake [23] proposed time optimization technique over cell residence for human mobility analysis, while Markoulidakis et al. [24] proposed

prediction model through cell handover residence based on Markov model by introducing Kalman filter for future visit prediction. Akyildiz et al. [25, 26] proposed a prediction model that is based on motion, speed, position, and history. Musolesi and Mascolo [27] categorized the mobility models into traces and synthetics, where they suggested that trace-based mobility models are more easy to implement as compared to synthetic based due to its public data gathering. González et al. [28] studied the spatiotemporal nature of user mobility based on pattern analysis through extraction of top K locations from mobility data of 100 K. Nurmi and Koolwaaij [29] proposed a clustering technique for the extraction of significant places using a graph-based transitional model over cell tower location data.

All of the above-mentioned work is related to the mobility analysis done over complete information about location without consideration of missing values and change in network structure fall under data preprocessing and focused on location extraction either all dependent on semantic awareness or otherwise ignoring the semantic information all together. In our work, we have tackled with data preprocessing, where outliers have been eliminated and data is made consolidated for analysis, and further cell oscillation issue is resolved for complete mobility profile building, then all this clustered information has been used for the mobility profile building through a proposed clustering technique which is a mixture of semantic information and GSM network property usage. Our work is mainly focused on successful mobility profile building based on a naive approach that is a mixture of both semantic information and raw location information, where prior to profile building outlier, extraction of location information from GSM cell global identity (CGI) and cell oscillation phenomenon are well dealt by experimenting them on MIT reality mining mobility dataset.

3. Methodology

Figure 1 shows the overall process of proposed methodology.

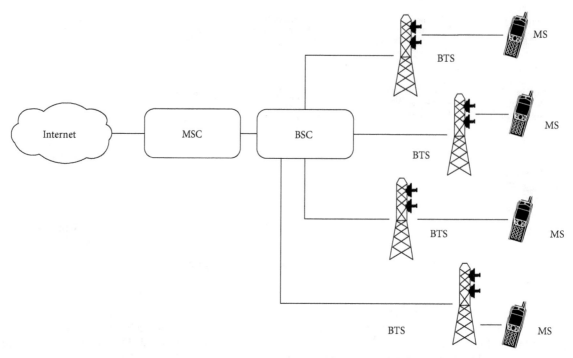

FIGURE 2: Architecture of functional GSM network.

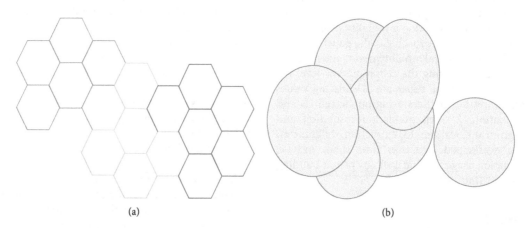

(a)   (b)

FIGURE 3: (a) Network topology: hexagonal view. (b) Cells overlapped view.

3.1. Location Information Retrieval and Outlier Removal.
The basic GSM structure is shown in Figure 2. As shown, the base transceiver station (BTS) is a basic unit being a representative of the location area where multiple cells fall in. This distribution is dependent on mobile operator and is hidden from users or public use.

Mobile station (MS) moves in the network and gets its connection through base station controller (BSC). While BSC is connected to mobile services switching center (MSC), which connects different BSCs and MSCs over network. One important identity is the location area which all BSCs share connected to common MSC.

Each cell conceptually has polygon shape (Figure 3(a)), but actually it has overlapping bubble shape as shown in Figure 3(b).

Now there are two main concerns regarding the extraction of information from dataset; firstly as mentioned earlier the dataset is taken from MIT reality mining, which has partial information of cell global identity (CGI) about user location, that is, LAC and Cell ID, so it is apparently hard to determine whether this partial set of information is enough for location extraction; secondly the GSM network is changing over time, so LAC is reorganized or thrown away by the operator, so it is obvious that there will be missing values and outlier issues in dataset beside shift of GSM to 3G technologies nowadays which disable us from determining most of the location information using MIT dataset collected in 2008.

We proposed the methodology to deal with all these problems in our work [30], where we used the basic network information to solve the missing values issue and the outlier resolution along with precise clustering of cells for future location extraction and mobility profiling. We proposed and used the clustering methodology where LAC and cell ID provide all set of information for mobility profiling basic building using the open source Google location API reverse engineering. And for missing values, we utilized the semantic information provided by the user in the dataset for precise location extraction and mobility profile building.

3.2. Cell Oscillation Resolution and Role of Semantic Information. As stated earlier in the problem statement, cell oscillation is a common phenomenon in GSM network, where a user can be assigned multiple cell IDs while static, which leads to a fake mobility during mobility profile building due to change in cell IDs over time. We presented a methodology in our work [31] for cell oscillation resolution using the semantic tagging information and introducing the time stay phenomenon, where overlapping cells represent the location of interest rather than mobility. In our mentioned work, we not only resolved the oscillation phenomenon successfully but also we clustered the cells on the basis of semantic information provided by user, for example, home, lab, airport, club, and so forth and overlapping time stay area, so that later during mobility profiling, this clustered information can be utilized for stay location identification. We used the overlapped location information for identification of significant places which can later be utilized for mobility profiling.

3.3. Mobility Profile Building. Mobility profile building is one of the trivial tasks in any of the location base service (LBS), where the mobility profiling is done through extraction of significant places. The significant places can be defined as the places which are important for a user over geocoordinates, and most of the time the user stays on these locations. User usually semantically tags these locations or spends significant amount of time on these location or visits them frequently over the period of observation. So, it is clear that a significant place can be a place where user spends most of time (home, work, etc.) or user visits it frequently over a period of time (super market, club) or user spends time significantly without frequent visit (conference, seminar, travel). So, it makes the discovery of significant places valuable for LBS, where user behavior is the main source of stimulation. As described in previous sections, the cell ID is the only viable solution for user profile building, where the coverage is wide, low in energy consumption, no data plan is required, and available in all kinds of mobile phones, so user movement is available in data as set of different cell IDs are distributed over a network. By observing the precise transition over these cells and using the effective technique, this information can be used for mobility profile building. But construction of mobility profile building is a complex process, as it must deal with some of the following questions like when user moves over thousands of cell IDs during period of time many of them cannot be available to extract their location information through cell ID databases, for example, Google, Open Cell ID, so these

cells will lead to misinterpreted profiling; there are dark places where user lost the connection or user switched off the cell, which seems to be significant places due to time spent by the user, and there is a lot of cell oscillations during user movement, which seems to be mobility even when user is static. We have divided it into three parts (1) clustering of the cells for path finding and their fingerprinting, (2) grouping of similar patterns for projection of trends, (3) profile building, and (4) similarity measure between different users through sharing property as adopted from [32]. The whole process of mobility profiling can be elaborated as follows.

Let $T = \{t_1, t_2, \ldots, t_n\}$ is set of towers/locations visited by the user during the mobility, we are interested in identification of pattern group PG $= \{pg_1, pg_2, \ldots, pg_n\}$, which satisfies the $TH_{groupcount}$ which is group threshold, where PG is extracted from frequent mobility user history (FUH) defined over transition threshold $TH_{transition}$, location area threshold $TH_{loctaion\ area}$, and semantic tag information SEM. FUH is retrieved through the visiting history VH retrieved through oscillation removal method [31] and time-stamping methods.

Algorithm 1. Frequent pattern discovery from user's mobility history.

(1) Select complete list of user mobility in terms of cell towers visited T.

(2) Apply cell oscillation technique on it and retrieved clustered cells C.

(3) Apply proper time stamping on the clustered cells retrieved after oscillation removal as visit history of user VH with complete spatiotemporal information.

(4) Identify the frequent user mobility patterns FUH defined over $TH_{loctain\ area}$ and $TH_{transition}$. Group the identified patterns G on the basis of their spatiotemporal nature and semantic tags information using prefix-span algorithm.

(5) Repeat step (i) to (ii) until only supported group of patterns PG is identified

    (i) if size of group g satisfies the group support threshold $TH_{Gorupcount}$,

    (ii) assign the group to supported group pattern set.

Let the set of users $U = \{u_1, u_2, \ldots, u_n\}$ with the complete information of pattern groups PGs, we are interested to build an $M[i][j]$ on the basis of each set of patterns p_i and q_j, where two patterns belong to two potentially similar users. The similarity between two patters is calculated over LnCSS (longest common subsequence) and CoL (colocation probability measure).

Algorithm 2. User's similarity measurement.

(1) Select the users.

(2) Select the pattern group of two users.

(3) Repeat step (i) to (ii) for each p and q belongs to two different users

(i) calculate the LnCSS and CoL property of two given patterns,

(ii) if two patterns satisfy the minimum support of similarity than compute $M(p, q)$ as 1 otherwise compute it as 0.

(4) Calculate the user's similarity based on similarity matrix.

3.3.1. Clustering of Subsequences in Mobility History Data. As mentioned earlier, we retrieved the clustered cells by implementing the cell oscillation algorithm where it is guaranteed that the data has no oscillation problem. We adopted naïve clustering approach, which clusters the cells on the basis of circular subsequences. The baseline algorithm works on the fact that common cell IDs can be merged together to make a circular subsequence which can represent user behavior [31]. We implemented two proposed algorithms successfully [31] for the resolution of cell oscillation and retrieval of common clustered cells to represent the significant place for the user using the overlapped area; however, details of the algorithm are given in our previous work. It is also of due importance that as mentioned earlier the proposed algorithm also resolved the problem of missing values which can occur due to network change or nonavailability of cell-ID information in open cell-ID databases. For example, the mobility sequence C_1, C_2, C_3, C_4, C_5 has C_3 and C_4 no retrievable through cell-ID database which obliviously will lead to a mislead mobility of the user; our algorithm will replace these two cells using the majority voting mechanism with the most likely cell in the cluster, so that mobility remains traceable with the most likely authentication. The retrieved clusters carry the information about significant places as a semantic tag like home, lab, club, and so forth, as the derived algorithm can infer the significant place based on time spent over an overlapped area between different cells; we tagged such location with a convention of *"stay point"*. After the retrieval of the clustered cells, we implemented the fingerprinting on them to represent the percentage of time spent by the user on particular cells and as a whole on one cluster, that is, stay points. Each cluster is being represented as a sequence of cell IDs, that is,

$$\text{Cluster}_1 [C_1, C_2, C_{15}],$$

$$\text{Cluster}_2 [C_3, C_5, C_7, \ldots, C_{19}]$$

$$\vdots \tag{1}$$

$$\text{Cluster}_n [C_7, C_{18}, \ldots, C_{24}].$$

Each cluster represents the stay point which may or may not have user defined semantic tag associated with it.

3.3.2. Time Stamping of Clustered Cells. We bound the time percentage with each of the cells in the cluster along with total time spends on that particular cluster with time stamp. The time stamping is the most important part of fingerprinting,

where user behavior can be determined easily over time/date slicing. The structure of fingerprint is as

$$[\{\{C_1, \%T_1\}, \{C_2, \%T_2\}, \ldots, \{C_n, \%T_n\}\},$$

$$\text{Total.time, Time stamp, Semantic tag}], \tag{2}$$

where each cluster represents the stay point of the user along with percentage time on it as $\%T$, date, and semantic tag information if available. After this process, we have a set of all the stay points or significant places user had visited over time, so we converted the given history of user distributed over cell IDs to stay points in form of clusters as follows:

$$\text{VH} = \{\text{Cluster}_1, \text{Cluster}_2, \ldots, \text{Cluster}_n\}, \tag{3}$$

where VH represents the complete mobility history of the user in terms of stay points in form of spatiotemporal clusters, that is, $\text{Cluster}_1, \text{Cluster}_2, \ldots, \text{Cluster}_n$. This information can be used to identify the Trajectory patterns against a particular user to build up the mobility profile by grouping them distributed over time. After the extraction of patterns, we need to group the patterns and discard infrequent pattern through usage of minimum support count otherwise the resultant pattern will be in millions for such a huge amount of data, which will be a burden in the memory. So, we are interested in only frequent pattern through usage of spatiotemporal information and support count. So, we can define group G as subset of VH such that it satisfies the following two rules:

(i) $P_1, P_2, \ldots, P_n \in g$ if $g \cdot \text{Distance} \leq \text{TH}_{\text{location area}}$ and $g \cdot \text{Time} \leq g \cdot \text{TH}_{\text{stay time}}$

(ii) $|g| \geq \text{TH}_{\text{group support}}$.

3.3.3. Extraction of Mobility Patterns from Clustered Stay Points. After the retrieval of all the stay points in the given spatiotemporal history of mobile user, we can transform it into trajectory pattern which the user follows over time. We can define a pattern P as a trip over two or more consecutive stay points SPs in ordered set of VH or trip between stay point SP and first/last point of user mobility history VH. We can define the pattern P as

$$P = \{\text{SP}_m, \ldots, \text{SP}_n\}, \quad \text{where } 0 < m \leq n,$$

$$P_i (\text{VH}_i \{\ldots, \text{SP}_m\} \cap \text{VH}_{i+1} \{\text{SP}_n, \ldots\}) \quad \text{Or}$$

$$P = \{\text{SP}_1, \ldots, \text{SP}_m\}, \quad \text{where } 0 < m \leq o,$$

$$P_i (\text{VH}_i \{\text{SP}_m, \ldots\}) \quad \text{Or} \tag{4}$$

$$P = \{\text{SP}_n, \ldots, \text{SP}_o\}, \quad \text{where } 0 < n \leq o,$$

$$P_i (\text{VH}_i \{\ldots, \text{SP}_n\}).$$

Further for the extraction of the true patterns from user mobility, we introduced the transition time threshold to ensures the continuity of the trip, where this transition threshold ensure the smooth transition of user from one stay point to another and differentiates one visiting pattern from another. For the extraction of mobility pattern from the semantically arranged stay points, we used prefix-span algorithm [33] on user mobility history. The result of algorithm gave semantic pattern of the user over time, for example, $\langle\{\text{Home}\}, \{\text{Lab, Google}\}, \{\text{Grand parents}\}\rangle$ along with all of its subsequences. As the result of the algorithm gave redundant patterns, we adopted maximal trajectory pattern [34] technique for the representation of user mobility pattern. So, the resultant extracted patterns are true representatives of frequent mobility of user (FUM) called over time as

$$
\begin{aligned}
\text{FUM} = \{\text{Ptn}_1 &: \langle\{\text{Home}\}, \{\text{Stay point}\}, \{\text{Office, Google}\}, \\
&\quad \{\text{Stay point }\}\rangle, \\
\text{Ptn}_2 &: \langle\{\text{Home}\}, \{\text{Super market, Topo hub}\}, \\
&\quad \{\text{Grand parents, Club}\}\rangle, \dots, \\
\text{Ptn}_n &: \langle\{\text{Office, Bank}\}, \{\text{Stay Point, Park}\}\rangle\}.
\end{aligned}
\tag{5}
$$

3.3.4. Projection of Similarity between Different Users Through Pattern Matching. After the successful extraction of user pattern, we determine if two patterns are similar through the longest common subsequence (LnCSS) measure. For example, if there is pattern $P = \langle\{\text{Home}\}, \{\text{Stay point}\}, \{\text{Office, Google}\}, \{\text{Stay point}\}\rangle$ and $Q = \langle\{\text{Home}\}, \{\text{Office, Bank}\}, \{\text{Stay point}\}\rangle$, their LnCSS will be $= \langle\{\text{Home}\}, \{\text{Office}\}, \{\text{Stay point}\}\rangle$, which we can define as

$$
\begin{aligned}
&\text{Ratio}\left(\text{LnCSS}\left(p, q\right), p\right) \\
&= \frac{\sum_{i=1}^{|p|} \sum_{j=1}^{|\text{LnCSS}(p,q)|} \text{M}\left(p_i, \text{LnCSS}_j\right)}{|p|} \\
&\text{M}\left(p_i, \text{LnCSS}_j\right) = \frac{p_i \in \text{LnCSS}_j}{|p|}
\end{aligned}
\tag{6}
$$

if LnCSS_j is matching to p_i otherwise $= 0$.

But the longest common subsequence (LnCSS) measurement is not only based on merely semantic tag based as same place is tagged with different names against different users, for example, Media Lab is tagged as Lab, Media Lab, Work lab, and so forth, so we introduced the time threshold for the transition, that is, TH_{trans} between two stay points (as every semantically tagged location consists of cell towers); further we introduced the spatial property threshold using location $\text{TH}_{\text{location area}}$ area, so it together joins the spatiotemporal property of user mobility.

So, we can define the similarity between two users; given two frequent user mobility (FUH) $\text{FUH}_1 = \{\text{Pattern}_{1,1}, \text{Pattern}_{1,2}, \dots, \text{Pattern}_{1,n}\}$ and $\text{FUH}_2 = \{\text{Pattern}_{2,1}, \text{Pattern}_{2,2}, \dots, \text{Pattern}_{2,n}\}$ and defined time threshold

$\text{TH}_{\text{time cover}}$ and location area threshold $\text{TH}_{\text{location area}}$, we can define similarity between users as

$$
\begin{aligned}
&\text{Similarity}\left(\text{FUH}_1, \text{FUH}_2, \text{TH}_{\text{time cover}}, \text{TH}_{\text{location area}}\right) \\
&= \text{Location area}\left(\text{Ptn}_{1.1}, \text{Ptn}_{2.i}\right) \\
&\quad + \text{Distance}\left(\text{Ptn}_{1.n}, \text{Ptn}_{2.j} \leq \text{TH}_{\text{location area}}\right), \\
&\quad \text{CoL}\left(\text{Ptn}_{1.1}, \text{Ptn}_{2.i}\right) \leq 1, \quad \text{where} \\
&\quad i, j \text{ belongs to } N \mid 0 < i \leq j \leq m,
\end{aligned}
\tag{7}
$$

where CoL is colocation property of that find is user x and y visit location l at the same time to exploit their spatiotemporal property beside semantic tags; as mentioned, semantic tags cannot assure the true accuracy of similarity measure due to different conventions used by different users for the same place. Colocation rate idea is adopted from their work [35], where the most likely location of the user x is defined as

$$
L(x) = \text{arg}_{l \in \text{Loc}} P(x, l),
\tag{8}
$$

where L is the most likely location of user x, and Loc represents the cell towers or locations set user traversed over time during mobility, while P is the probability of the user x to visit location l and can be defined as

$$
P(x, l) = \sum_{i=1}^{n(x)} \frac{\delta\left(l, L_i(x)\right)}{n(x)},
\tag{9}
$$

where $\delta(x, y) = 1$ if $x = y$ otherwise it is 0. Further distance between user x and y can be defined as $d(x, y) = \text{dist}(L(x), L(y))$ to represent physical distance between their frequent locations. So, on the basis of it colocation rate can be defined as follows:

$$
\text{CoL} =
$$

$$
\frac{\sum_{i=1}^{n(x)} \sum_{j=1}^{n(y)} \Theta\left(\Delta T - \left|T_i(x) - T_j(y)\right|\right) \delta\left(L_i(x) - L_j(y)\right)}{\sum_{i=1}^{n(x)} \sum_{j=1}^{n(y)} \Theta\left(\Delta T - \left|T_i(x) - T_j(y)\right|\right)}.
\tag{10}
$$

As (10) shows that colocation rate counts both time and location simultaneously for two users, that is, x and y. So, it binds both spatiotemporal trends together normalized over the number of times the users visited the location, where Θ is Heaviside function and ΔT is equal to $T_{\text{stay time}}$.

On the basis of the above similarity measuring value, we can calculate the similarity between the given user pairs through comparing their patterns over three basic units: semantic tag, spatial value, and temporal value. For this we construct a similarity matrix which gives a clear picture of similarity measure against every frequent pattern pair of two different users. After calculating the similarity between patterns of two users, these values are used to calculate the overall similarity measure between two users to infer if they are related to each other or not. For example, we have two user's $\text{FUH}_1 = \{P_{1.1}, P_{1.2}\}$ and $\text{FUH}_2 = \{P_{2.1}, P_{2.2}\}$ to find their similarity with a given pair of

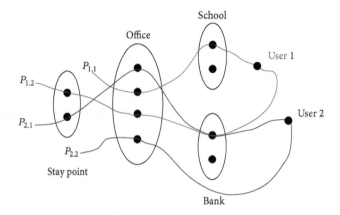

FIGURE 4: User mobility pattern.

patterns, where $P_{1.1}$ = {⟨Home⟩⟨Bank, Office⟩⟨Stay point⟩} and $P_{1.2}$ = {⟨Home⟩, ⟨School⟩, ⟨Office⟩}, while $P_{2.1}$ = {⟨Home⟩⟨Bank, Office⟩⟨Stay point⟩} and $P_{2.2}$ = {⟨Home⟩, ⟨Office⟩}. Figure 4 shows the spatial incidence of these patterns. We can construct a similarity matrix through it as shown in Table 1.

So, the similarity measure can be concluded as = Sum of all extracted similarity weights/Total number of patterns, where the high value represents the most similarity among two users, while the lower value represents the dissimilarity between the two users.

So, on the basis of the above similarity measure, we can define the profile sharing measurement of the given users as

$$\text{Sharing value} \left(\text{FUH}_1, \text{FUH}_2, \text{TH}_{\text{location area}}, \text{TH}_{\text{transition}} \right)$$

$$= \frac{\left| \{ p \in \text{FUH}_1 \mid \exists q \in \text{FUH}_2 \cdot \text{similarity}\,(p, q, \text{CoL}) \} \right|}{\left| \text{FUH}_1 \right|}. \tag{11}$$

4. Dataset

As mentioned earlier, the selected dataset is taken from mining project group of MIT Media labs [36]. This dataset is collected from 100 people who are students for a period of 9 month with total activity span of 350 K hours. The collected data is logged on Symbian mobile, that is, Nokia 6600 which has no GPS in it, so all of the information related to user location is identified by cell ID only. While in this dataset, cell global identity header has partial information, where only LAC and cell ID are available for location tracking of the user. However, users have provided semantic tagging information to the most important locations over mobility history in data logs. But overall, this semantic tag information varies a lot in terms of annotations and usage from user to user. And among these users only, 94 gave their full information regarding similarity measure through online survey for social interactions. From these 94 users, 7 of the users do not have cell logs and 10 have no cell annotation logs. So, for our analysis there are only 77 users available for analysis and evaluation.

TABLE 1: Similarity matrix.

	$P_{1.1}$	$P_{1.2}$	$P_{2.1}$	$P_{2.2}$
$P_{1.1}$	—	—	1	0
$P_{1.2}$	—	—	0	1
$P_{2.1}$	1	0	—	—
$P_{2.2}$	0	1	—	—

5. Experiments and Results

As mentioned, we have chosen the reality mining dataset for our experimental purposes. The results are as follows.

5.1. Retrieval of Location Information and Removal of Outliers Using Raw Cell ID. As the data is quite old in its nature and there are frequent changes in mobile network, so presences of outliers and missing values are obvious in the dataset, so we applied our clustering approach [30] on the raw data to remove spatial outliers from the data and extract their location information through Google APIs [30]. The result of applied technique is shown in Table 2.

Figure 5(a) shows the cells retrieved from the Google API, and Figure 5(b) shows the consolidated data without outliers, while Figure 5(c) shows the complete effect of spatial clustering over the data.

5.2. Observation of Semantic Tags in Dataset. After the extraction of outlier free data points, we applied our spatial clustering techniques [30, 31] on the clean data to cluster them in terms of stay points which may or may not have semantic tags in them. As Table 2 shows that each semantic location observed can carry multiple cell IDs, so these cells can be clustered together to define a common location. As most of the time stays at known places are usually tagged, so these semantic locations are of more importance than untagged stay points [31], as shown in Table 3.

5.3. Cell Oscillation Resolution and Discovery of Stay Points. As defined previously cell, oscillation is a phenomenon obvious in GSM dataset, where user is assigned multiple

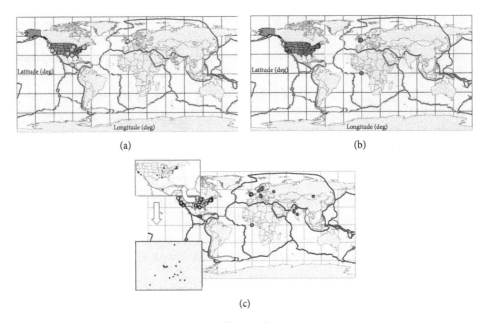

(a)   (b)

(c)

FIGURE 5

TABLE 2: Locations retrieved with respect to user mobility.

	# of cells	%
Total number of unique cells against subject X	1744	100%
# of cell's location retrieved through Google API	680	39%
# of cell's location retrieved through semantic tagged algorithm	88	3%
Total # of cell's location retrieved	768	42%

TABLE 3: Semantic location with # of representative cells.

Semantic location	Number of cells incidence
Mgh	5
Office	4
Airport	4
Home	4
Greg's apt	4
Grand parents	3
Google	3
Redhat	3
Chicago O'Hare	2
Topo hub	2

TABLE 4: Overlapping of locations.

Cells (LAC. Cell ID)	# of locations represented
C_{30}	7
C_{40}	6
C_{23}	6
C_{14}	5
C_{56}	4
C_{44}	4
C_{25}	3
C_{47}	2
C_{27}	2
C_{39}	2

user otherwise. And as per our previous assumption, GSM cells are distributed in bubble form that they overlap with each other; this assumption is evident from resultant Table 4.

As result we retrieved all the locations as a clustered cells which are representative of user mobility history rather the raw cells. In Figure 6 of the tagged locations are plotted over geographical map which shows the vicinity of tagged places, further Figure 6 shows our assumption is correct as Chicago O'Hare airport is tagged twice with overlapped cells by the user which shows overlapping of cells and oscillation over same place.

5.4. Discovery of Mobility Patterns. After the extraction of mobility history in form of clustered cells where each cluster represents the stay point with or without user defined semantic tag, we applied time-stamping methodology on it defined in Section 3.3.2. On this time-stamped clustered history, we applied the mobility pattern extraction technique proposed in Section 3.3.3. We used the $TH_{stay\ time}$ of 20 minutes along with $TH_{transition}$ of 10 minutes which are

cell IDs while being stationary for load balancing. Table 2 shows that semantic location can be identified with multiple cell IDs which make it clear that beside the semantic tag information, we are bound to use spatiotemporal analysis with location for pattern building and finding similar users, as this semantic tag is limited in the data. We have applied our spatial clustering technique [31] on the dataset for the removal of cell oscillation, and using the overlapping area analysis, we identified stay points which are not semantically tagged by the

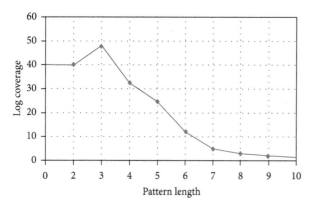

FIGURE 6: Semantic location plotted over geographical map.

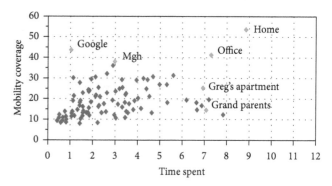

FIGURE 8: Locations visit over log.

FIGURE 7: Mobility pattern length over log.

We plotted user mobility ratio in term of exploration with time for further analysis in Figure 9, which shows that user visit average is of 2–5 places daily, while in exception cases user visited more than 7 locations at a single day. We plotted the location visiting frequency over a data of 30 consecutive days.

5.5. Similarity Measure between Users. For the calculation of similarity measure, we constructed the similarity matrix on the basis of two main parameters, that is, semantic pattern and spatiotemporal similarity. For this we use LnCSS and set the $TH_{location\ area}$ to 10 being a Euclidean distance between the two points of location that belong to two different users to ensure if they fall in same area or not; further we set the $TH_{timecover}$ as 20 minutes as described in Section 3.3.4.

After formulating the similarity matrix, we plotted similarity measure between user x and other users along with other user similarity measurement models, that is, spatial cosine similarity (SCS) and extra-role colocation rate (ERCR) [37] for evaluation. Spatial cosine similarity can be defined as similarity of visitation frequencies of user x and y assigned by cosine of angle between the two vectors with respect to number of visit at each location. And extra-role colocation is based on probability of two users x and y to colocate in the same hour at night or on weekends. This relationship serves as a great indicator to determine the friendship between two users.

We plotted the similarity measure between users using our proposed methodology named HA (Hybrid approach), SCS, and ERCR using the two metrics, that is, mean average precision (MAP) and normalized discounted cumulative gain (NDCG).

In Figure 10, we plotted the user similarity based on MAP matrices where MAP can be defined as

$$MAP = \frac{1}{N} \sum_{i=1}^{N} \frac{\sum_{T=1}^{K} \left(P_i(r) \times rel_i(r) \right)}{|R_i|}, \quad (12)$$

where N is number of test users and $|R_i|$ indicates number of similar users for test user x, r donates cut-off rank and $P_i(r)$ represents precision of U_i over binary function $rel_i(r)$.

We plotted the similarity measure between users using the NDCG matrices as defined by [38] in Figure 11.

adopted form our work [31]. After extraction of these mobility patterns, we implemented the maximal trajectory pattern technique proposed in Section 3.3.3 for the representation of the most frequent mobility pattern. We plotted graph in Figure 7 representing the log time coverage of the user mobility with respect to the length of pattern to analyze the most frequent pattern length.

The figure clearly shows that most of the patterns which cover the log of user mobility are of length 3, after which the coverage is declined tremendously. This result gives information about the transition phase, length set for LnCSS, and trend of user over time, which we will be using later during similarity measure.

As the explored patterns carry all the basic information like location, semantic tag, and time stamping, we can plot the user trend quite easily. As shown in Figure 8, we plotted the user location visit history against log history period, and we have selected top locations only due to of space limitation. We selected only two-month user history for this plotting. The figure clearly shows that user spent most of his time at known places and rarely explored new places, and this also shows one important fact about mobility data that user spent most of his time on the location which he tagged semantically, that is, home, MGH, office, and so forth. This satisfies our assumption in Section 3 about trend of the use mobility. This trend also shows some facts like that the user visits some locations like home everyday regardless of weekdays and weekend and some locations like office every weekday only, whereas some locations like Greg's home and grandparents user usually visit once in a week and on weekends.

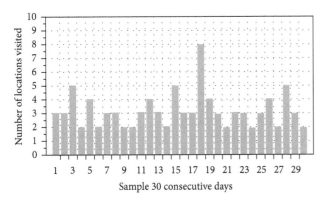

FIGURE 9: User's locations visit over days.

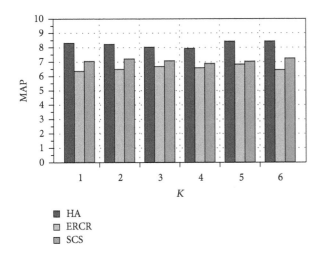

FIGURE 10: MAP with respect to proposed methodology performance.

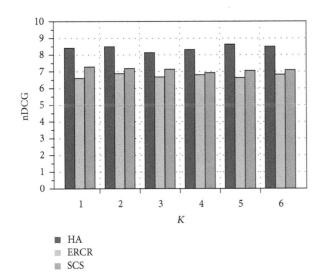

FIGURE 11: nDCG with respect to proposed methodology performance.

Figures 10 and 11 clearly show that our proposed methodology outperforms with respect to spatial cosine similarity (SCS) and extra-role colocation rate (ERCR) over the indicated matrices. The experiments show that our proposed methodology outperforms on real dataset of MIT as compared to other mentioned methodologies.

6. Conclusion and Future Work

In this paper, we presented the two phases methodology of building mobility profile and finding user similarity, which is unsupervised approach based on the semantic tag information along with the spatiotemporal trends. As our methodology uses both semantic and spatiotemporal trends, this makes it outperform over the mere use of tag, spatial- or spatiotemporal-based methodologies defined earlier. As discovering the similar user can play a vital role in many potential applications related to location-based services (LBS), so our approach is quite efficient where semantic tag along with spatiotemporal trends can serve as a precise approach towards similarity measurement between different users. Further, this methodology is complete framework which resolves all mobility profiling issues, that is, outlier detection, missing values retrieval, cell oscillation, user trajectory profiling, and similarity measure.

Future studies can be carried out on the behavior of users depending on transient reactions like civil work on road, and a special event together with their trajectories to determine the exact behavior of user for its application in real scenarios for location-based services.

Acknowledgments

The work described in this paper was supported by grants from Natural Science Foundation of China (Grant no. 60775037), The National Major Special Science and Technology Projects (Grant no. 2011ZX04016-071), The HeGaoJi National Major Special Science and Technology Projects (Grant no. 2012ZX01029001-002), and Research Fund for the Doctoral Program of Higher Education of China (20093402110017, 20113402110024).

References

[1] M. Couceiro, D. Suarez, D. Manzano, and L. Lafuente, "Data stream processing on real-time mobile advertisement," in *Proceedings of the 12th IEEE International Conference on Mobile Data Management*, pp. 313–320, June 2011.

[2] Ad Orchestrator, http://prodcat.ericsson.se/frontend/category.action?code=FGD%20101%20008.

[3] C. Yang, J. Yang, X. Luo, and P. Gong, "Use of mobile phones in an emergency reporting system for infectious disease surveillance after the Sichuan earthquake in China," *Bulletin of the World Health Organization*, vol. 87, no. 8, pp. 619–623, 2009.

[4] S. S. Kanhere, "Participatory sensing: crowdsourcing data from mobile smartphones in urban spaces," in *Proceedings of the 12th IEEE International Conference on Mobile Data Management (MDM '11)*, pp. 3–6, June 2011.

[5] L. Chen, M. Lv, Q. Ye, G. Chen, and J. Woodward, "A personal route prediction system based on trajectory data mining," *Information Sciences*, vol. 181, no. 7, pp. 1264–1284, 2011.

[6] http://thenextweb.com/mobile/2011/07/03/the-rise-of-the-mobile-social-network/.

[7] A. Harter and A. Hopper, "Distributed location system for the active office," *IEEE Network*, vol. 8, no. 1, pp. 62–70, 1994.

[8] A. Harter, A. Hopper, P. Steggles, A. Ward, and P. Webster, "The anatomy of a context-aware application," *Wireless Networks*, vol. 8, no. 2-3, pp. 187–197, 2002.

[9] "Location technologies for GSM, GPRS and WCDMA networks," White Paper, SnapTrack, A QUALCOMM, November 2001.

[10] M. Garetto and E. Leonardi, "Analysis of random mobility models with pde's," in *Proceedings of the 7th ACM International Symposium on Mobile Ad Hoc Networking and Computing (MobiHoc '06)*, pp. 73–84, Florence, Italy, May 2006.

[11] T. Abdelzaher, Y. Anokwa, P. Boda et al., "Mobiscopes for human spaces," *IEEE Pervasive Computing*, vol. 6, no. 2, pp. 20–29, 2007.

[12] M. Demirbas et al., "iMAP: indirect measurement of air pollution with cellphones," *CSE Technical Reports*, 2008.

[13] A. Pentland, "Automatic mapping and modeling of human networks," *Physica A: Statistical Mechanics and Its Applications*, vol. 378, no. 1, pp. 59–67, 2007.

[14] A. Krause, E. Horvitz, A. Kansal, and F. Zhao, "Toward community sensing," in *Proceedings of the International Conference on Information Processing in Sensor Networks (IPSN '08)*, pp. 481–492, April 2008.

[15] K. Laasonen, "Clustering and prediction of mobile user routes from cellular data," in *Proceedings of the 9th European Conference on Principles and Practice of Knowledge Discovery in Databases (PKDD '05)*, pp. 569–576, 2005.

[16] A. Lindgren, C. Diot, and J. Scott, "Impact of communication infrastructure on forwarding in pocket switched networks," in *Proceedings of the SIGCOMM Workshop on Challenged Networks (SIGCOMM '06)*, pp. 261–268, 2006.

[17] L. Wang, Y. Jia, and W. Han, "Instant message clustering based on extended vector space model," in *Proceedings of the 2nd International Conference on Advances in Computation and Intelligence (ISICA '07)*, pp. 435–443, 2007.

[18] N. D. Ziv and B. Mulloth, "An exploration on mobile social networking: dodgeball as a case in point," in *Proceedings of the International Conference on Mobile Business (ICMB '06)*, Copenhagen, Denmark, June 2006.

[19] V. Bychkovsky, K. Chen, M. Goraczko et al., "Cartel: a distributed mobile sensor computing system," in *Proceedings of the 4th International Conference on Embedded Networked Sensor Systems (SenSys '06)*, pp. 125–138, November 2006.

[20] J. Burke, D. Estrin, M. Hansen et al., "Participatory sensing," in *Proceedings of ACM Sensys World Sensor Web Workshop*, 2006.

[21] D. Kirovski, N. Oliver, M. Sinclair, and D. Tan, "Health-OS: a position paper," in *Proceedings of the ACM SIGMOBILE International Workshop on Systems and Networking Support for Healthcare and Assisted Living Environments*, pp. 76–78, June 2007.

[22] E. M. Daly and M. Haahr, "Social network analysis for routing in disconnected delay-tolerant MANETs," in *Proceedings of the 8th ACM International Symposium on Mobile Ad Hoc Networking and Computing (MobiHoc '07)*, pp. 32–40, September 2007.

[23] M. M. Zonoozi and P. Dassanayake, "User mobility modeling and characterization of mobility patterns," *IEEE Journal on Selected Areas in Communications*, vol. 15, no. 7, pp. 1239–1252, 1997.

[24] J. G. Markoulidakis, G. L. Lyberopoulos, D. F. Tsirkas, and E. D. Sykas, "Mobility modeling in third-generation mobile telecommunications systems," *IEEE Personal Communications*, vol. 4, no. 4, pp. 41–51, 1997.

[25] I. F. Akyildiz and W. Wang, "The predictive usermobility profile framework for wireless multimedia networks," *IEEE/ACM Transactions on Networking*, vol. 12, no. 6, pp. 1021–1035, 2004.

[26] A. Chaintreau, P. Hui, J. Crowcroft, C. Diot, R. Gass, and J. Scott, "Impact of human mobility on opportunistic forwarding algorithms," *IEEE Transactions on Mobile Computing*, vol. 6, no. 6, pp. 606–620, 2007.

[27] M. Musolesi and C. Mascolo, "Mobility models for systems evaluation. A survey," in *Middleware for Network Eccentric and Mobile Applications*, Springer, Berlin, Germany, 2009.

[28] M. C. González, C. A. Hidalgo, and A. L. Barabási, "Understanding individual human mobility patterns," *Nature*, vol. 453, no. 7196, pp. 779–782, 2008.

[29] P. Nurmi and J. Koolwaaij, "Identifying meaningful locations," in *Proceedings of the 3rd Annual International Conference on Mobile and Ubiquitous Systems: Networking and Services (MobiQuitous '06)*, IEEE Computer Society, Sun Jose, Calif, USA, July 2006.

[30] S. A. Shad and E. Chen, "Precise location acquisition of mobility data using cell-id," *International Journal of Computer Science Issues*, vol. 9, no. 3, pp. 222–231, 2012.

[31] S. A. Shad, E. Chen, and T. Bao, "Cell oscillation resolution in mobility profile building," *International Journal of Computer Science Issues*, vol. 9, no. 3, pp. 205–213, 2012.

[32] R. Trasarti, F. Pinelli, M. Nanni, and F. Giannotti, "Mining mobility user profiles for car pooling," in *Proceedings of the 17th ACM SIGKDD International Conference on Knowledge Discovery and Data Mining*, pp. 1190–1198, ACM, 2011.

[33] J. Pei, J. Han, B. Mortazavi-Asl et al., "PrefixSpan: mining sequential patterns efficiently by prefix-projected pattern growth," in *Proceedings of the 17th International Conference on Data Engineering (ICDE '01)*, pp. 215–224, April 2001.

[34] C. Luo and S. Chung, "Efficient mining of maximal sequential patterns using multiple samples," in *Proceeding of the SIAM International Conference on Data Mining (SDM '05)*, pp. 415–426, Newport Beach, Calif, USA, 2005.

[35] D. Wang, D. Pedreschi, C. Song, F. Giannotti, and A. -L. Barabasi, "Human mobility, social ties, and link prediction," in *Proceedings of the 17th ACM SIGKDD International Conference on Knowledge Discovery and Data Mining*, San Diego, Calif, USA, August 2011.

[36] 2012, http://reality.media.mit.edu/download.php.

[37] N. Eagle, A. Pentland, and D. Lazer, "Inferring friendship network structure by using mobile phone data," *Proceedings of the National Academy of Sciences of the United States of America*, vol. 106, no. 36, pp. 15274–15278, 2009.

[38] K. Järvelin and J. Kekäläinen, "IR evaluation methods for retrieving highly relevant documents," in *Proceedings of the 23rd Annual International ACM SIGIR Conference on Research and Development in Information Retrieval (SIGIR '00)*, pp. 41–48, ACM, New York, NY, USA, 2000.

Permissions

The contributors of this book come from diverse backgrounds, making this book a truly international effort. This book will bring forth new frontiers with its revolutionizing research information and detailed analysis of the nascent developments around the world.

We would like to thank all the contributing authors for lending their expertise to make the book truly unique. They have played a crucial role in the development of this book. Without their invaluable contributions this book wouldn't have been possible. They have made vital efforts to compile up to date information on the varied aspects of this subject to make this book a valuable addition to the collection of many professionals and students.

This book was conceptualized with the vision of imparting up-to-date information and advanced data in this field. To ensure the same, a matchless editorial board was set up. Every individual on the board went through rigorous rounds of assessment to prove their worth. After which they invested a large part of their time researching and compiling the most relevant data for our readers. Conferences and sessions were held from time to time between the editorial board and the contributing authors to present the data in the most comprehensible form. The editorial team has worked tirelessly to provide valuable and valid information to help people across the globe.

Every chapter published in this book has been scrutinized by our experts. Their significance has been extensively debated. The topics covered herein carry significant findings which will fuel the growth of the discipline. They may even be implemented as practical applications or may be referred to as a beginning point for another development. Chapters in this book were first published by Hindawi Publishing Corporation; hereby published with permission under the Creative Commons Attribution License or equivalent.

The editorial board has been involved in producing this book since its inception. They have spent rigorous hours researching and exploring the diverse topics which have resulted in the successful publishing of this book. They have passed on their knowledge of decades through this book. To expedite this challenging task, the publisher supported the team at every step. A small team of assistant editors was also appointed to further simplify the editing procedure and attain best results for the readers.

Our editorial team has been hand-picked from every corner of the world. Their multi-ethnicity adds dynamic inputs to the discussions which result in innovative outcomes. These outcomes are then further discussed with the researchers and contributors who give their valuable feedback and opinion regarding the same. The feedback is then collaborated with the researches and they are edited in a comprehensive manner to aid the understanding of the subject.

Apart from the editorial board, the designing team has also invested a significant amount of their time in understanding the subject and creating the most relevant covers. They scrutinized every image to scout for the most suitable representation of the subject and create an appropriate cover for the book.

The publishing team has been involved in this book since its early stages. They were actively engaged in every process, be it collecting the data, connecting with the contributors or procuring relevant information. The team has been an ardent support to the editorial, designing and production team. Their endless efforts to recruit the best for this project, has resulted in the accomplishment of this book. They are a veteran in the field of academics and their pool of knowledge is as vast as their experience in printing. Their expertise and guidance has proved useful at every step. Their uncompromising quality standards have made this book an exceptional effort. Their encouragement from time to time has been an inspiration for everyone.

The publisher and the editorial board hope that this book will prove to be a valuable piece of knowledge for researchers, students, practitioners and scholars across the globe.

List of Contributors

Mehmet Karakose
Computer Engineering Department, Firat University, Elazig, Turkey

Ugur Cigdem
Computer Programming Department, Gaziosmanpasa University, Tokat, Turkey

Santiago-Omar Caballero-Morales
Technological University of the Mixteca, Road to Acatlima K.m. 2.5, 69000 Huajuapan de Leon, OAX, Mexico

Ziying Dai, Xiaoguang Mao, Yan Lei, Yuhua Qi and Rui Wang
School of Computer, National University of Defense Technology, Changsha 410073, China

Bin Gu
Beijing Institute of Control Engineering, Beijing 100190, China

Mingsheng Tang
College of Computer, National University of Defense Technology, Changsha 410073, China
LIP 6, Universite Pierre et Marie Curie, 75006 Paris, France

Xinjun Mao
College of Computer, National University of Defense Technology, Changsha 410073, China

Zahia Guessoum
LIP 6, Universite Pierre et Marie Curie, 75006 Paris, France

Zhenwen Wang, Fengjing Yin, Wentang Tan and Weidong Xiao
College of Information System and Management, National University of Defense Technology, Changsha 410073, China

Amir Hossein Azadnia, Muhamad Zameri Mat Saman and Kuan Yew Wong
Department of Manufacturing and Industrial Engineering, Faculty of Mechanical Engineering, Universiti Teknologi Malaysia, Johor Bahru, 81310 UTM Skudai, Malaysia

Shahrooz Taheri
Department of Computer Science, Faculty of Computer Science, Universiti Teknologi Malaysia, Johor Bahru, 81310 UTM Skudai, Malaysia

Pezhman Ghadimi
Enterprise Research Centre, University of Limerick, Limerick, Ireland

Jie Zhang
School of Computer Science and Technology, Xidian University, Xian 710071, China
Department of Computer Science and Technology, Guangzhou University Sontan College, Zengcheng, Guangzhou 511370, China

Yuping Wang
School of Computer Science and Technology, Xidian University, Xian 710071, China

Junhong Feng
Department of Computer Science and Technology, Guangzhou University Sontan College, Zengcheng, Guangzhou 511370, China

Yuksel Celik
Department of Computer Programming, Karamanoglu Mehmetbey University, Karaman, Turkey

Erkan Ulker
Computer Engineering Department, Selcuk University, Konya, Turkey

Kaikuo Xu
College of Computer Science & Technology, Chengdu University of Information Technology, Chengdu 610225, China

Yexi Jiang
School of Computing and Information Sciences, Florida International University, Miami, IN 33199, USA

Mingjie Tang
Department of Computer Science, Purdue University, West Lafayette, FL 47996, USA

Changan Yuan
Guangxi Teachers Education University, Nanning 530001, China

Changjie Tang
School of Computer Science, Sichuan University, Chengdu 610065, China

Qingjian Ni
School of Computer Science and Engineering, Southeast University, Nanjing 211189, China
Provincial Key Laboratory for Computer Information Processing Technology, Soochow University, Suzhou 215006, China

Jianming Deng
School of Computer Science and Engineering, Southeast University, Nanjing 211189, China

Mustafa Serter Uzerb and Nihat Yilmaz
Electrical-Electronics Engineering, Faculty of Engineering, Selcuk University, Konya, Turkey

Onur Inan
Computer Engineering, Faculty of Engineering, Selcuk University, Konya, Turkey

Peng Jiang, Qiaoyan Wen, Wenmin Li, Zhengping Jin and Hua Zhang
State Key Laboratory of Networking and Switching Technology, Beijing University of Posts and Telecommunications, Beijing 100876, China

Yingjie Xia
Hangzhou Institute of Service Engineering, Hangzhou Normal University, 222Wenyi Road, Hangzhou 310012, China
Department of Civil and Environmental Engineering, University of Virginia, 351 McCormick Road, Charlottesville, VA 22903, USA

Jia Hu and Michael D. Fontaine
Department of Civil and Environmental Engineering, University of Virginia, 351 McCormick Road, Charlottesville, VA 22903, USA

Tianfei Wang, Liping Jia and Feng Sun
School of Mathematics and Information Science, Leshan Normal University, Leshan 614004, China

Burak Erkayman, Emin Gundogar and Aysegul Yılmaz
Department of Industrial Engineering, Sakarya University, 54187 Adapazarı, Sakarya, Turkey

Kian Sheng Lim, Salinda Buyamin and Anita Ahmad
Faculty of Electrical Engineering, Universiti Teknologi Malaysia, 81310 Johor Bahru, Malaysia

Faradila Naim, Zuwairie Ibrahim and Kamarul Hawari Ghazali
Faculty of Electrical and Electronic Engineering, Universiti Malaysia Pahang, 26600 Pekan, Malaysia

Norrima Mokhtar
Department of Electrical Engineering, Faculty of Engineering, University of Malaya, 50603 Kuala Lumpur, Malaysia

Zhendong Yin, Xiaohui Liu, and Zhilu Wu
School of Electronics and Information Engineering, Harbin Institute of Technology, Harbin 150001, China

Ling-lin Ni
School of Traffic and Transportation Engineering, Central South University, Changsha 410075, China
Business Administration College, Zhejiang University of Finance & Economics, Hangzhou 310018, China

Jin Qin and Feng Shi
School of Traffic and Transportation Engineering, Central South University, Changsha 410075, China

Mehmet Karakose
Computer Engineering Department, Firat University, Elazig, Turkey

Shafqat Ali Shad and Enhong Chen
Department of Computer Science and Technology, University of Science and Technology of China, Huangshan Road, Hefei, Anhui 230027, China

Printed in the USA
CPSIA information can be obtained
at www.ICGtesting.com
JSHW051438221024
72173JS00006B/1509